Rinehart Radio Series

THEATRE GUILD ON THE AIR

THEATRE
GUILD
ON THE AIR

Edited by

H. WILLIAM FITELSON

RINEHART & COMPANY
INCORPORATED
New York   Toronto

ACKNOWLEDGMENTS

ALL THE RADIO adaptations of the plays in this collection have been reprinted with the permission of the following authors, publishers, adapters, and holders of copyright of the original versions of the plays from which the adaptations have been made, to whom especial thanks are due:

STRANGE INTERLUDE. By Eugene O'Neill. Original printed text, copyright, 1932, by Eugene O'Neill, published by Random House, Inc. Radio adaptation by Arthur Arent.

THE GUARDSMAN. By Ferenc Molnar, published by Liveright Publishing Corporation. Translated by Grace I. Colbron and Hans Bartsch; original play copyright, 1924, by Hans Bartsch. All rights reserved therein, particularly all broadcasting and television rights. Radio adaptation by Arthur Miller. Publication by permission of Ferenc Molnar and Hans Bartsch.

THE SILVER CORD. Adapted from the play by Sidney Howard. Copyright, 1927, by Sidney Howard, published by Charles Scribner's Sons. Radio adaptation by Erik Barnouw.

ON BORROWED TIME. By Paul Osborn, based on the novel by Lawrence Edward Watkin. Copyright, 1942, by Paul Osborn (revised). From the novel *On Borrowed Time*, copyright, 1937, by Lawrence Edward Watkin. Dramatized version copyright, 1937, by Paul Osborn. Published by Alfred A. Knopf, Inc. Radio adaptation by Paul Peters.

AH, WILDERNESS! By Eugene O'Neill. Original printed text, copyright, 1933, by Eugene O'Neill, published by Random House, Inc. Radio adaptation by Arthur Arent.

THREE MEN ON A HORSE. By John Cecil Holm and George Abbott. Copyright, 1934–1935, by John Cecil Holm. Radio adaptation by Arthur Miller. Used by arrangement with the authors and Samuel French.

PAYMENT DEFERRED. By Jeffrey Dell, based on the novel by C. S. Forester. Copyright, 1934, by Samuel French, Ltd. Radio adaptation by Gerald Holland. Used by arrangement with the authors and Samuel French, Ltd.

DEAD END. By Sidney Kingsley. Original printed text, copyright, 1936, by Sidney Kingsley, published by Random House, Inc. Radio adaptation by Paul Peters.

THEY KNEW WHAT THEY WANTED. By Sidney Howard. Copyright, 1925, by Sidney Howard, published by Doubleday & Company, Inc. Radio adaptation by Kenyon Nicholson.

I REMEMBER MAMA. By John Van Druten. Copyright, 1944, 1945, by John Van Druten. Adapted from Kathryn Forbes' book, *Mama's Bank Account*. Both published by Harcourt, Brace and Company, Inc. Radio adaptation by Erik Barnouw.

THE SHOW-OFF. By George Kelly. Copyright, 1924, by George Kelly, published by Little, Brown & Company. Radio adaptation by Arthur Arent.

FOREWORD

THE PURPOSE of this anthology of Theatre Guild plays is not merely to provide pleasant and interesting reading, but also to give that portion of the public which is interested an opportunity to study the actual technique employed in transposing a dramatic play from stage form into radio form. Probably few members of the radio audience realize how much original work is done by the author of a radio play in translating the story from one medium to another. In all forms of writing, it is hard to know where craftsmanship ends and where creation begins, but it may be said that the writing of the best radio dramas calls for both creative writing and craftsmanship of a substantial order.

The Theatre Guild was formed originally by a group of theatre-lovers who wished to bring better plays to the attention of the American public. In the succeeding quarter of a century its belief that there is a large audience for fine plays in this country has been fully justified. But fine stage plays are usually available only to the residents of our larger cities where adequate theatres exist. Realizing this, the Guild turned to radio as a means of bringing such drama to the whole of the American public.

The Theatre Guild was fortunate in finding a sponsor in the United States Steel Corporation, which for decades had maintained high standards of quality in its own products, and was looking for a radio program in which the same high standards would be present. For the United States Steel Corporation, the Guild has undertaken the presentation of a program of plays which constitute a cross section of the American theatre during the past thirty years.

We undertook this program with considerable trepidation: radio was a new medium to us, and since the program was not to be limited to our own plays, it also called for a complete study of the successful productions of others during this period. As it turned out, this enhanced our own creative interest in the program. It was not merely enjoyable to transfer our own plays to the air; there was the added pleasure of working creatively on other productions which we had not presented in the theatre, and to which we could give a new and fresh attack.

We made a faltering beginning. We learned that a knowledge of theatre technique was not enough. We also learned that a knowledge of radio technique was not enough. In order to produce radio plays of the kind which would measure up artistically to the stage productions these plays had received, we found it was necessary to combine both theatre and radio techniques. Practically all of the radio versions of plays included in this volume result from a combination of both techniques.

As a result of experience—which now extends over nearly two years— in the production of radio plays, our Radio Department has been able to formulate some general ideas on the writing of radio scripts made from stage plays. Naturally, the writer is asked to use his own creative ideas, and whatever is suggested by us to the writer is not by way of limitation or to fetter his imagination. On the contrary, the more imagination shown in transferring from the stage medium to the radio medium, the better we like it. In all cases, the writer is asked to preserve the spirit of the stage play and to take every possible advantage of the radio medium in bringing out the meaning of the play.

Advantages of the radio medium include the possibility of moving from place to place, both in time and in space, instead of being confined to one or more sets, as is usual in the theatre. Another advantage is the use of sound and sound effects with great freedom to visualize and enhance the drama. Music is also used to intensify emotion, underline dramatic or comedic situations, or point to the locale. By the ingenious use of a narrator, or a character who appears in the first person, it is possible to bridge the gap between the actor and the audience and to create an intimacy not possible in the theatre itself.

In moving from one scene to another, in addition to the musical bridge, our writers are urged to present a visualization by the character or characters of the place where they are now located. We think we emphasize this more in our scripts than is done in other radio scripts. Moreover, where possible, we like to have one scene build out of the scene which went before it. Where this is not possible—and it often is not —we like to lead into each new scene with some indication of its relation to the story line. With regard to the story itself, with as limited a time as one hour, we try to hew to the line of the main characters with as few subsidiary characters and situations as are needed to enable one to follow the main story line. The characters, if possible, should be limited to ten in number. As a general rule, where there are one or more leading players, for the purpose of holding the radio audience we like to begin the play with a scene for the leading players. In radio drama, the old French

adage for the construction of a good play can almost always be followed:
"In Act I, get your characters up a tree. In Act II, throw stones at them.
In Act III, bring them down again."

In presenting the views of our Radio Department, we emphasize that
we do not claim to have any formulas for the preparation of scripts which
are better than formulas used by others. There is, indeed, no rule in art
which cannot be broken. What we do claim, however, is that good plays,
well produced, with the parts played by good actors, appeal to a large
part of the listening public of the United States, and that if the demand
of this public is supplied, its appetite will continue to grow, and it will
ask for more and more of the good things of the theatre on the air.
We hope that we may continue to do our share in satisfying this interest,
and that this little book of plays, which have been listened to by our
audience of millions, will testify to the fact that our faith in the American
listening public is justified.

LAWRENCE LANGNER
THERESA HELBURN
Directors
The Theatre Guild, Inc.

New York
August, 1947

PREFACE

THIS COLLECTION incorporates a dozen representative radio scripts selected from the Theatre Guild's first season on the air, together with introductions by the radio writers that describe their problems in adapting the original plays to radio. The number of requests from many individuals, schools, colleges, and universities for scripts of our radio programs has been increasing so rapidly that some way of making them permanently available had to be found.

The playwrights permit us to engage writers to adapt the original plays, without restrictions; hence the original plays should not be confused with the radio versions. The United States Steel Corporation, sponsor of the program, prepares the messages heard between the acts of each broadcast, and has selected those included in this volume. Actually, however, the messages which appear following Acts I and II of *They Knew What They Wanted* in this book were not broadcast with that play but with *Ned McCobb's Daughter*, December 9, 1945, and with *The Royal Family*, December 16, 1945, respectively.

However one regards radio, it cannot be denied that it is a mass medium which vitally affects the lives of nearly everyone of us. According to the survey made by Paul F. Lazarsfeld and Harry Field in their book, *The People Look at Radio*, the average man in the United States listens to the radio for three hours each day, and the average woman, four hours. Do we devote as much time to the theatre, movies, newspapers, books, schools, concerts, or the church? Yet radio, which in many ways combines all these media, is looked upon askance by many who can contribute so much to it. True it is an art which, generally speaking, has become a business. This distortion is unfortunate. For although radio in the United States cannot function without the support of business, there is no reason why the art itself should become mere business. If more capable craftsmen would recognize this and seriously devote themselves to this important medium, they could introduce both greater artistry and higher quality which would be welcomed by listeners, and also by sponsors. For there is a large potential audience for programs of quality, and there are many sponsors who are interested in quality as well as quantity. The air was never meant to be used exclusively as a sales agency. And it is cynicism to convert its use to the sole purpose of selling goods. The United States Steel Corporation's attitude is reflected in its messages, which tell the story of a growing American industry rather than attempt to sell steel.

The Theatre Guild, Inc., and its sponsor, embarked on this radio project not only to appeal to the largest number of people but to transfer to this important means of communication plays of distinction and performances of quality, such as the Guild has been presenting in the theatre for more than twenty-five years. The Guild believed that quality listening is as worth while as quantity listening, and it has been gaining listeners at such a rate that it is possible to say that quality and quantity are not inconsistent.

As to censorship, we have learned that most of it is self-imposed; we have found that a work which has quality need encounter no serious difficulty if the broadcaster has courage and exercises discretion.

The Theatre Guild, Inc., did not produce in the theatre all the plays it produced on the air. Of the twelve radio versions selected for inclusion in this volume, the Guild produced on the stage the following:

The Guardsman, by Ferenc Molnar (1924)
Strange Interlude, by Eugene O'Neill (1928)
They Knew What They Wanted, by Sidney Howard (1924)
Ah, Wilderness!, by Eugene O'Neill (1933)
The Silver Cord, by Sidney Howard (1926)

The other plays were produced in the theatre, as follows:

Dead End, by Sidney Kingsley, was produced on the stage by Norman Bel Geddes (1935).

I Remember Mama, by John Van Druten, adapted from Kathryn Forbes' *Mama's Bank Account*, was produced on the stage by Rodgers and Hammerstein (1944).

The Show-Off, by George Kelly, was produced on the stage by Stewart and French (1924).

On Borrowed Time, by Paul Osborn, based on the novel by Lawrence Edward Watkin, was produced on the stage by Dwight D. Wiman (1938).

Payment Deferred, by Jeffrey Dell, based on the novel by C. S. Forester, was produced on the stage by Gilbert Miller (1931).

Three Men on a Horse, by John Cecil Holm and George Abbott, was produced on the stage by George Abbott (1935).

No credit is due me for this book; it is the work of others. The radio writers were given carte blanche to write what they wished to precede their scripts. All the royalties which will be earned from the publication of the book will be paid to the authors of the original plays and the radio writers.

Special thanks go to Phyllis Anderson, an able member of the Guild's staff, for reading and correcting the scripts and proof, and to my assistant at the Theatre Guild, Martha Harris, who attended to the burdensome but necessary details of arranging contracts and clearances with the playwrights, radio writers, their agents and publishers, in her usual efficient way.

H. W. F.

New York
August, 1947

CONTENTS

STRANGE INTERLUDE

(Part One)

Original Play

by Eugene O'Neill

Radio Adaptation

by Arthur Arent

CAST

(for radio performance)

NINA	Lynn Fontanne
MARSDEN	Alfred Shirley
DARRELL	Walter Abel
EVANS	Donald MacDonald
LEEDS	Reginald Mason
MRS. EVANS	Jean Adair

STRANGE INTERLUDE

Part One

Radio adaptation by

ARTHUR ARENT

THERE WERE a number of problems in adapting to radio what is probably the most famous play ever written by an American. The question of network censorship was not the least of these since, through the years, certain conventions have come about regarding what is and what is not fit for the ears of children (of whatever ages). One of the first problems, then, was to prune judiciously whatever clarity became frankness. Surprisingly enough, the network, once it had accepted the whole, found little fault with any of its parts. I did, of course, use discretion before presenting the script for certification. All references to Nina's extracurricular activities in the hospital had been deleted. Also eliminated was the fifth and final scene (in the play) of Part One, in which Nina and Darrell rhapsodize over their love and certain amorous events of recent occurrence. This is the scene that ends with Darrell's renunciation and flight to Europe.

The use of Marsden—a writer and a very introverted one at that—as the Narrator appeared as a must before I had got very far in my reading of Part One. He was the only one who knew the complexities of the situation, who could be *of* it and still *outside* it. He could tell it, I decided, as though he were writing it—a blurting, long-delayed attempt to find peace for his soul by giving utterance to the truth. When I reached that speech in Part Two in which O'Neill has him say that some day he would write this story—of himself and Nina and the others—I knew I was on the right track.

The probings into the minds of the characters—the asides—presented less of a problem than had been anticipated. There were three possibilities: a filter mike, a musical underlining, a vocal adjustment. We tried the filter but it didn't work. There was something almost eerie about it

3

that detracted from the flesh and blood. The musical underscoring we jettisoned (without trying) as being too monotonous, producing a "Here we go again, boys!" feeling every time Hal Levey raised his baton. The only thing left was the adjustment of the voice—a kind of sotto voice effect that really gave the impression of a person talking to himself—which, after all, was what we wanted.

The direction [*Filter*] was left in the script as an aid to the actor. No filter was ever used.

STRANGE INTERLUDE

ANNOUNCER

INTRODUCTION FOR THE THEATRE GUILD

ACT I

MARSDEN. My name is Charles Marsden. Perhaps you've seen it on the
cover of a book. I write them, you know. Not best sellers, of course.
No. I couldn't write the trash that everybody reads. Historical pot-
boilers all sexed up to catch the matinee trade! No. My name on a
book is a guarantee of good taste served up in polished prose. I don't
go in for that realistic stuff, either. You know, where people suffer
and turn their insides out for all the world to see . . . I remember
many years ago Nina Leeds said to me . . .

NINA. Charlie, why don't you write about things that are going on all
around you—the big important things—with characters that live and
breath? Why don't you tell us what they're really thinking about
inside? Why must you always be so clever—and so *dishonest?*

MARSDEN. That's what Nina Leeds said to me. She was young then—a
dark-haired, brown-eyed girl with a low, cool voice. Of course I
laughed at her. And now, after all these years, I'm going to write that
story—the story of Nina herself, and all of us who knew her.

[Music: Short phrase]

MARSDEN. Yes, I've thought this all out. "Tell what they're really thinking
about inside!"—that's what Nina said. And that's what I'll do. When
one of my characters has something to say, he'll say it. Take Dr.
Darrell, for instance . . .

DARRELL. I'm glad to meet you, Mr. Marsden. Nina's mentioned you a lot.
I've been looking forward to seeing you.

MARSDEN. Sounds harmless enough, doesn't it? Just what everybody says

5

when they're being polite. But what was Dr. Darrell thinking? I'll tell you that, too.

DARRELL [*Filter*]. This Marsden. A strange case. Look how scared he is! He feels things—like a woman! If he senses that I'm trying to pump him about Nina's past he'll close up like a clam. Oh, lord, why did I ever decide to be a *doctor!*

[*Music: Chord*]

MARSDEN. Secrets! Everybody's secret thoughts! The things Nina would be thinking about when she said . . .

NINA. My, isn't it a lovely day! Look, Charlie, look at those tiny puffs of clouds away off in the distance! And that little church down there in the valley! You can hardly see it! [*Filter*] I don't have to see it! I know it's there! I was going to be married in that church—Oh, dearest God, why did he have to die? Why did he have to go off to war and leave me? Oh, Gordon, Gordon, how could you die when I loved you so?

[*Music: Up and under*]

MARSDEN. And now for the story of Nina Leeds. It properly begins in 1919, just after the First World War.

The day after I got back from France I hurried over to her home. As I expected, her father—he taught Greek at the University—was in the library seated in his ancient black leather chair poring over an old manuscript . . . [*Fades*]

LEEDS. Why, Charlie! What a surprise! We didn't expect you back so soon!

MARSDEN. Hello, Professor. How've you been? Where's Nina?

LEEDS. She'll be right down. You'll find Nina changed, Charlie, greatly changed.

MARSDEN. Does she still think about Gordon?

LEEDS. [*Resentfully*]. Think about him? She *dreams* about him!

MARSDEN. Of course she does. No girl could forget a man like Gordon in a hurry, Professor, especially after the shock of his tragic death! By the way, I located the spot in France where he was shot down. Nina asked me to, you know.

LEEDS [*Irritated*]. For heaven's sake, don't remind her! Give her a chance to forget if you want to see her well again. After all, Charlie, life must be lived and Nina can't live with a corpse forever!

MARSDEN. A corpse, Professor?

LEEDS. A memory, a ghost, if you like. Not only that, but—Charlie, it may sound incredible, but Nina has begun to act as if she hated me!

MARSDEN. Oh, come now! Why, Nina has always idolized you! What possible reason—?

LEEDS. She has a reason. Just before he sailed for the front, Gordon wanted to marry her. I, however, felt it was ill advised and I took Gordon aside and pointed out to him that such a precipitate marriage would be unfair to Nina, that he might be killed—

MARSDEN [Wonderingly]. You said that to Gordon?

LEEDS [Unheeding]. —leaving her a widow, perhaps with a baby.

MARSDEN. And now he's dead.

LEEDS. Yes.

MARSDEN. And Nina suspects it was you who prevented the marriage?

LEEDS. Yes. She knows in some queer way. And she acts toward me exactly as if she thought I had deliberately destroyed her happiness—

MARSDEN. You don't mean to tell me she has accused you—

LEEDS. Oh, no, Charles. Only by looks, hints, innuendoes. Ssssh! I hear her coming now.

MARSDEN [Filter]. She's coming! My heart is pounding! Why? Do I love her? No, of course not! Couldn't love any woman that way! Dear old Charlie! The friend of the family—that's me!

NINA [Fading on]. Hello, Charlie . . . Father, I have made up my mind.

LEEDS. Really, Nina, you're absolutely rude! Here is Charlie, just returned from Europe, and you treat him as though—

NINA [In a cool tone]. Did I seem rude, Charlie? I didn't mean to be. Welcome home! There, I've kissed you just over the left eyebrow!

MARSDEN. Rude, Nina? Not a bit. You couldn't be. [Filter] Cold lips . . . the kiss of contempt . . . for dear old Charlie!

NINA. I must finish what I started to say, father. I've thought it all out and decided that I simply must get away from here at once—or go crazy! So, I'm leaving tonight.

LEEDS. This is rather a sudden decision, isn't it? I really think, Nina, in justice to yourself, you ought to consider this step with great care before you definitely commit yourself. First and foremost . . . [Fading] [Slowly] There is your health to be taken into consideration. You have been very ill, Nina. How perilously so you are not completely aware—but I assure you, and Charlie can corroborate my statement, that six months ago the doctors thought it might be years

before—and yet, by staying home and resting and finding healthy
outdoor recreation among your old friends, and keeping your mind
occupied with the routine of managing the household . . .

NINA [*Over the fading*]. [*Filter*] My father, the professor of dead lan-
guages, is talking again . . . His words arising from the tomb of a
soul in puffs of ashes . . . [*Torturedly*] Ashes! Oh, Gordon, my dear
one! Oh, lips on my lips, oh, strong arms around me . . . oh spirit
so brave and generous and gay! Gone! Gone forever from me!

LEEDS [*His voice rising*]. No, Nina, frankly I can't see your going to
New York. You know I would gladly consent to anything in the
world to benefit you, but—surely, you can't have reflected.

NINA. Father, life doesn't mean anything to me without Gordon. I'm tired
of groping in darkness. I've got to try and find some light again. No,
darling. No, it's no use talking, father. I *have* reflected and I am going!

LEEDS [*With asperity*]. You cannot go to New York, Nina. It is quite
impossible! I don't like to bring up the money consideration—and
how will you support yourself, if I may ask?

NINA. Money! Support! Consideration! Those are just words, father!
[*Filter . . . Desperately*] I must keep calm . . . I mustn't let go or
I'll tell him everything . . . and I mustn't tell him . . . he's my
father!
Father, I have already had six months' training as a nurse. There
is a doctor I know at a Veterans' Hospital—a friend of Gordon's.
I can be useful there.

LEEDS. You seriously mean to tell me you, in your exhausted condition,
want to nurse in a soldiers' hospital! Absurd!

MARSDEN. Your father is right, Nina. You're sick—

NINA [*Slowly and strangely*]. I'm not sick. I'm too well. But those
soldiers are sick and I must give my health to help them to live on,
and to live on myself. [*With sudden intensity*] I must pray for my
cowardly treachery to Gordon! You should understand this, father,
you who—[*Filter . . . Desperately*] I am beginning to tell him! . . .
I mustn't . . . He's my father!

LEEDS [*With guilty fear*]. What do you mean, Nina?

NINA. I must pay! It's my plain duty! Gordon is dead! What use is my
life to me or anyone? But I must make it of use—by giving it! Don't
you see?

LEEDS [*Sharply*]. No, I can't see—nor anyone else! Can you, Charlie?

MARSDEN. What do you mean, you owe it to Gordon, Nina?

LEEDS [*Bitterly*]. Yes, how ridiculous! It seems to me when you gave him your love—

NINA [*With fierce self-contempt*]. I gave him? What did I give him? It's what I didn't give him! That last night before he sailed—knowing all that night—something in me knowing he would die, that he would never kiss me again—knowing this so surely, yet with my cowardly brain lying: "No, wait, he'll come back and marry you, you'll be happy ever after and have his children looking up at you with eyes so much like his—"

LEEDS. Nina! This is really going too far!

MARSDEN [*With a superior sneer*]. Oh come, now, Nina! You've been reading books. Those don't sound like your thoughts.

NINA [*Intensely*]. Gordon wanted me! I wanted Gordon! We should have had each other! We should have married! I knew he would die and I would have no children, that there would be no big Gordon or little Gordon left to me, that happiness was calling me, never to call again if I refused! And yet I did refuse! [*Fiercely*] Why did I refuse? What was that cowardly something in me that cried, "No, you mustn't, what would your father say?"

LEEDS. Nina! I really can't listen!

NINA [*Savagely*]. And that's exactly what my father did say! "Wait," he told Gordon! "Wait for Nina till the war's over, and you've got a good job and can afford a marriage license!"

LEEDS [*Crumbling pitifully*]. Nina! I—! [*Stops*]

NINA [*Coldly and deliberately*]. Don't lie any more, father! I know now why Gordon suddenly dropped all idea of marriage before he left, how unfair to me he suddenly decided it would be! Unfair to me! Oh, that's funny! To think I might have had happiness, Gordon, and now Gordon's child—[*Accusingly*] You told him it'd be unfair, you put him on his honor, didn't you, father?

LEEDS [*Woodenly*]. Yes. I did it for your sake, Nina.

NINA [*Coldly*]. It's too late for lies.

LEEDS [*Woodenly*]. Let us say then that I *persuaded* myself it was for your sake. That may be true. You are young. You think one can live with the truth. Very well. It is also true I was jealous of Gordon. I was alone and I wanted to keep your love . . . Forgive me, Nina.

NINA. Oh, I forgive you—and that's that! Come on upstairs, Charlie, and help me pack!

MARSDEN. Why must you go away? I don't understand this, Nina!

NINA. No? Some day I'll read it all in one of your books, Charlie, and it will be so diluted and easy and simple that I won't be able to recognize it, let alone understand it! [*Laughs teasingly*] Dear old Charlie!

[*Music*]

MARSDEN. Nina went to New York. In the year that followed, I drove down and saw her two or three times. She was still working as a nurse in the Veterans' Hospital. But it didn't help her forget Gordon. And then one winter night Professor Leeds died of a cerebral hemorrhage. I notified Nina and she came home immediately. As I stepped into the well-remembered library for the first time in many months, a strange young man greeted me. He said his name was Sam Evans . . . [*Fading*]

EVANS. That's right, Sam Evans. [*Awkwardly*] Guess you don't remember me, Mr. Marsden. Miss Leeds introduced us one day at the hospital.

MARSDEN. Oh, yes.

EVANS. I was there today when your wire came. Ned and I came along to see if we could help.

MARSDEN. And who is Ned?

EVANS. Dr. Darrell. He's an old friend of Nina's. Got her the job in the hospital. Let's sit down, shall we?

MARSDEN. By all means. [*Pause*] [*Filter*] This Evans is certainly no giant intellect. Overgrown boy . . . likable quality though . . .

EVANS [*Uneasy*]. [*Filter*] Hmmm—this Marsden . . . giving me the once-over . . . seems like a good egg . . . Nina says he is . . . suppose I ought to say something about his books, but I can't even remember a title of one . . .
[*Suddenly*] Mr. Marsden, you've known Nina—Miss Leeds—ever since she was a kid, haven't you?

MARSDEN. Yes. How long have you known her?

EVANS. Well, really only since she has been at the hospital, although I met her once years ago at a prom with Gordon Shaw.

MARSDEN [*Indifferently*]. Oh, you knew Gordon?

EVANS [*Proudly*]. Sure thing! I was in his class! He sure was a wonder, wasn't he?

MARSDEN. A fine boy!

EVANS. He sure was! Great athlete, too! Four-letter man!

MARSDEN [*Filter*]. Another Gordon worshipper! This Evans must be the apple of Nina's eye.

Is this Dr. Darrell a close friend of yours?

EVANS [*Hesitant*]. Well, sort of. I wouldn't say Ned was close to anyone, though. He's a dyed-in-the-wool doc. Only close to whatever ails you. [*Chuckles*] You know him, don't you?

MARSDEN [*Stiffly*]. Barely. Nina introduced us once. [*Filter*] What are this Darrell's relations with Nina? Only medical? . . . Darn these thoughts! Why should I care?

[*Indifferently*] Is Dr. Darrell a particular friend of Miss Leeds?

EVANS. Sure. He's always trying to bully her into taking better care of herself. She works too hard. But she only laughs at him. [*Filter*] What's this Marsden getting at? . . . Ned's my best friend. Doing all he can to help me with Nina . . . Lord, if she'd only marry me! I wouldn't expect her to love me at first . . . be happy just to take care of her . . . wait on her . . . just to kiss her hair!

[*Earnestly*] Mr. Marsden, I—there's something I think I ought to tell you, I think. You see, Nina has talked a lot about you. I know how much she thinks of you. And now her old man—I mean her father's dead—[*Stops*]

MARSDEN [*In a panic*]. [*Filter*] What's this . . . a proposal . . . for her hand . . . to me? No more good old Charlie! Father Charlie, now!

EVANS [*Blundering on*]. I know it's hardly the proper time—

MARSDEN [*Interrupting—Drily*]. Perhaps I can anticipate. You want to tell me you are in love with Nina?

EVANS. Yes, sir, and I've asked her to marry me.

MARSDEN [*Filter*]. Lord, he calls me *sir*. I'm an old man now! What did she say?

EVANS [*Sheepish*]. Nothing. She just smiled.

MARSDEN [*Relieved*]. Ah! . . . Well, what could you expect? Surely you must know she still loves Gordon.

EVANS. Sure I know it—and I admire her for it! Most girls forget too easily. I know I'm an awful washout compared to Gordon—but I love her as much as he did, or anyone could!—

MARSDEN [*Sharply*]. And just what do you expect me to do about all this?

EVANS [*Taken aback*]. Why—er—nothing, sir. I just thought you ought to know.

MARSDEN [*Filter*]. Hmmm, this Evans might be good for Nina . . . if she were married to this simpleton, would she be faithful? . . . if not, then I . . . what a vile thought! I don't mean that!

[*Forcing a kindly tone*] You see, Evans, old man, there's really nothing I can do about it. Except—wish you good luck.

EVANS [*Full of boyish gratitude*]. Thanks! That's darn fine of you, Mr. Marsden.

EVANS [*Footsteps approach*]. Hello, Ned.

DARRELL. Hello, Sam. You remember Mr. —

DARRELL. Sure. Here, Sam. Run along up the street and get this prescription filled.

EVANS. Sure thing.

DARRELL. It's for Nina. Hurry back . . . Hello, Marsden.

MARSDEN. Hello, Darrell.

EVANS [*Off mike*]. Be back in a jiffy. [*Door closes*]

DARRELL. Nice to see you again, Marsden.

MARSDEN. Nice to see you, doctor. [*Filter*] Hmmm. He's giving me the fishy, diagnosing eye they practice at medical school.

DARRELL. Guess I'll sit down. I'm tired. [*Filter*] This Marsden doesn't like me . . . but he interests me . . . Those novels of his . . . No depth, no digging underneath . . . why? Has the talent, but doesn't dare . . . I know, afraid he'll meet himself somewhere!

[*Brusquely*] Marsden, Nina's gone to pot again! Had to give her a sedative. She's upstairs now trying to goad herself into feeling grief for her father!

MARSDEN [*Resentfully*]. I think you are mistaken. She loved her father—

DARRELL. We can't waste time being sentimental, Marsden! I've got a lot to talk over with you.

MARSDEN. Just a minute—

DARRELL [*Unheeding*]. Nina has a real affection for you and I imagine you have for her. Then you'll want as much as I do to get her straightened out. She's a corking girl. She ought to have every chance for a happy life. [*Sharply*] But the way she is conditioned now, there's no chance!

MARSDEN [*Angry*]. Exactly what do you mean by that?

DARRELL. Nina has been giving way more and more to a morbid longing for martyrdom. The reason for it is obvious. Gordon went away without marrying her. The war killed him. She was left suspended. Unfortunately, working in the hospital hasn't helped any. If anything, it's made her worse.

MARSDEN [*With authority*]. Then she mustn't go back to the hospital!

DARRELL. You're quite right. And that brings me to what I want you to urge her to do.

MARSDEN [*Coldly*]. Perhaps you exaggerate my influence.

DARRELL [*Eagerly*]. Not a bit. You're the last link connecting her with the girl she used to be before Gordon's death. You're the only person she still respects—and really loves . . . Oh, you needn't look frightened. [*Laughs*] I mean the sort of love she feels for an uncle.

MARSDEN [*Frigidly*]. I am not frightened, Dr. Darrell! [*Filter*] Frightened? . . . Am I . . . only person she loves . . . like an uncle . . . Uncle Charlie now!

DARRELL. And that's why I have done all this talking. You've got to help her snap out of it.

MARSDEN. How?

DARRELL. Get her to marry Sam Evans.

MARSDEN [*Astonished*]. Evans? [*Filter*] So I was wrong again! . . . He isn't interested in Nina, himself! . . . But why does he want her married to . . . It's some trick!

DARRELL. Evans is in love with her and it's one of those unselfish loves you read about. And she is fond of him. In a maternal way, of course. And that's why this is important—it would give her a chance to have children. She's got to find normal outlets for her craving for sacrifice. Now, marrying Sam ought to do the trick. *Ought* to. Naturally no one can say for certain. Doesn't that seem good sense to you?

MARSDEN [*Still suspicious*]. I am sorry, but I am in no position to say. I don't know anything about Evans for one thing.

DARRELL. Well, I do. He's a fine, healthy boy, clean and unspoiled. Holding down a fair job, too, considering he's just started in the advertising business—

MARSDEN [*Snobbishly*]. Do you know his family—what sort of people?—

DARRELL [*Bitingly*]. I'm not acquainted with their social qualifications, if that's what you mean! They're upstate country folk—fruit growers, I believe.

MARSDEN [*Changing the subject*]. Have you suggested this match to Nina?

DARRELL. Yes, a good many times in a half-joking way. If I were serious she wouldn't listen. She'd say I was prescribing again.

MARSDEN [*Forcing a joking tone*]. Do you know what I'm inclined to suspect, doctor, that you may be in love with Nina yourself.

DARRELL [*Astonished*]. The deuce you do! What in the devil makes you think that? Not that any man mightn't fall in love with Nina! Most of them did at the hospital. But I didn't happen to. And what's more, I never could. In my mind she always belongs to Gordon. It's probably a reflection of her own silly fixed idea about him. [*Harshly*] And I couldn't share a woman—even with a ghost! Sssh! She's coming down. [*Whispers*] She should be sleeping. I gave her a sedative!

[*Footsteps approach . . . A pause*]

NINA [*In a queer flat voice*]. My father is dead. There is only his death living. It lives now to draw nearer me, to draw me nearer, to become my death! . . . How we poor monkeys hide ourselves behind the sounds called words!

MARSDEN [*Timidly*]. Nina!

NINA. You look frightened, Charlie. Do I seem queer? It's because I have suddenly seen the lies in the sounds called words. You know—grief, sorrow, love, father—those sounds our lips make and our hands write. You ought to know about words. You work with them. But now I think of it, you are just the one who couldn't know what I mean. With you the lies have become the only truthful things. And I suppose that's the logical conclusion to the whole evasive mass, isn't it?

DARRELL. Why not sit down, Nina? And let us two gentlemen sit down?

NINA [*Sarcastically*]. Prescribing for me again, Ned? This is my pet doctor, Charlie. Did you ever know a young scientist, Charlie? He believes if you pick a lie to pieces, the pieces are the truth! I like him because he is so inhuman. But once he kissed me—in a moment of carnal weakness! I was as startled as if a mummy had done it! And then he looked so disgusted with himself! I had to laugh.

DARRELL [*Good-naturedly*]. That's right! Rub it in! [*Filter*] I'd forgotten about that kiss . . . I was sore at myself afterwards . . . She was so darn indifferent!

If you don't mind I think I'll go out and stretch my legs.

MARSDEN [*In a panic*]. Wait a minute Darrell!—I am sure Nina would rather—[*Filter*] I don't want to be alone with her! I don't know her any more! . . . I am afraid!

NINA [*Dully*]. Let Darrell go. I have said everything I can ever say—to him. I want to talk to you, Charlie.

DARRELL. See you both later.

[*Footsteps recede . . . Door closes . . . Pause*]

NINA [*With pity and scorn*]. Why have you always been so timid, Charlie?

Why are you always afraid? What are you afraid of?

MARSDEN [*Filter*]. She sneaked into my soul to spy. [*Boldly*] Well then, a little truth for once!

[*Timidly*] I am afraid of life—of life, Nina.

NINA [*Slowly*]. I know. [*Queerly*] Oh, Charlie, I want to believe in something. I want to believe so I can feel! I want to feel that he is dead—my father! And I can't feel anything, Charlie. I can't feel anything at all! [*She begins to sob*]

MARSDEN. There—there—don't—Nina, please—don't cry—you'll make yourself sick—come, now, Nina—sit down.

NINA. Yes, Charlie, let me sit in your lap, Charlie—like when I was a little girl? May I?

MARSDEN [*Uncertain*]. Why—er—yes, Nina. If you'd like to.

NINA. Oh, Charlie! Dear old Charlie! Be kind to me! Tell me what to do!

MARSDEN. What to do, Nina?

NINA. Everything is mixed up. I still dream about Gordon! Last night I saw him diving down out of the sky in flames and he looked at me with such sad, burning eyes—You're my father, now. Father, tell me what to do!

MARSDEN [*Bitterly*]. [*Filter*] Father Charlie! . . . Ha! . . . that's how she loves me—very well, then . . .

[*Judiciousy*] Well, now, Nina, considering the circumstances—

NINA [*Repeating mechanically*]. Considering the circumstances, father . . .

MARSDEN [*In a tone like her father's*]. —having weighed the pros and cons, so to speak, I should say that decidedly the most desirable course—

NINA [*Drowsily*]. Yes, father?

MARSDEN. —is for you to marry that young Evans.

NINA [*Drowsily*]. Sam, he is a nice boy. But I don't love him, father.

MARSDEN. He loves you devotedly and it's time you are having children. When children come, love comes, you know.

NINA [*Drowsily*]. Yes, yes, I do want children. I must become a mother so I can give myself. I am sick of sickness.

MARSDEN [*Briskly*]. Then it's all settled?

NINA [*Drowsily*]. If you say so, father.

MARSDEN. I do say so.

NINA [*Same*]. Then it's all settled, father.

[*Music*]

END OF ACT I

ER

CIAL

STATION IDENTIFICATION

[*Music under*]

ANNOUNCER

ACT II

MARSDEN. Nina Leeds and Sam Evans were married the next week. They settled down in Nina's home in the small college town, and Sam became one of those commuters catching the eight-twenty to New York every morning . . . After they'd been married about six months, the summer rolled around, and they decided to spend Sam's vacation at his mother's farm in upstate New York . . . The morning after they arrived, Nina wrote a letter to Dr. Darrell . . . [*Fading*]

NINA [*Reading*]. Dear Ned . . . it's over six months since Sam and I were married and we haven't seen hide nor hair of you since the the ceremony. Do you think that is any nice way to act? We are up here paying our first visit to Sam's mother. You really must meet her sometime. She's a strange woman, with a curious tragic quality, from the bit I saw of her last night. She has been writing Sam regularly once a week ever since she's known we were married, the most urgent invitations to visit her. They were really more like commands, or prayers. I suspect she is terribly lonely all by herself in this big house . . .

[*Footsteps approach during above*]

[*Filter*] Sam and his mother are coming. She wants to talk to me . . . I can feel it . . . But first I want to finish this letter to Ned . . . I'd better go out on the porch!

[*Chair scraping, Door closes . . . A pause . . . Footsteps approach*]

EVANS [*Fading in*]. Mother, in a few years you won't have to worry one way or another about the darned old apple crop. Since I got married to Nina I'm making good, all right, all right.

MRS. EVANS [*Vaguely*]. That's fine, Sammy. Just fine.

EVANS. Only last week Cole—he's my boss—asked me if I was married— said he was glad to hear it because marriage was what put the right kind of ambition into a fellow—unselfish ambition. [*Embarrassed*] He even asked me if we were expecting an addition to the family.

MRS. EVANS [*Quickly*]. I've been meaning to ask you that myself, Sam [*Apprehensively*] She—Nina—she isn't going to have a baby, is she?

EVANS. Why—why—I don't think so, Mother. [*Filter*] If that'd only happen! . . . Gosh, it'd make me happy . . . If that'd happen . . . then I'd feel sure she loved me! . . . It'd be there . . . half Nina, half me . . . the living proof! . . . And I know she wants one! Why did you ask me that, Mother? Do you think—?

MRS. EVANS [*Quickly*]. No, indeed! I don't think so! I wouldn't say so at all!

MRS. EVANS. Look here, Sam! You drive into town or take a walk or something. Give me a chance to get to know my daughter-in-law, and call her to account for how she's taking care of you! [*Forced laugh*]

EVANS [*Happily*]. Better than I deserve! She's an angel, Mother. I know you'll love her!

MRS. EVANS [*Gently*]. I do already, Sammy! She's so pretty and so sweet! Now run along and I'll go out on the porch and sit with my daughter-in-law.

EVANS. All right, Mother, see you later.

[*Door closes . . . A pause*]

MRS. EVANS [*Filter*]. He loves her! He's happy! That's all that counts! Being happy! [*Apprehensively*] If only she doesn't care so much about having a child! . . . I've got to have it out with her . . . got to! This terrible thing has got to end with my boy . . . and he's got to live happy!

[*Footsteps . . . Screen door opens*]

MRS. EVANS. Good morning, Nina.

NINA. Good morning—[*Shyly*] Mother.

MRS. EVANS. My, the air is nice out here this morning! Notice my holly-hocks? I took a prize with 'em at the Fair last year. Best in the county. Had enough breakfast, dear?

NINA. I ate so much I am ashamed of myself.

MRS. EVANS. Good for you!

NINA. Sam said you wanted to talk to me.

MRS. EVANS. Yes, Nina.

NINA [*Filter*]. Why have I that sick, dead feeling? . . . like when something is going to happen! . . . I felt it before I got the cable from Gordon.

MRS. EVANS [*Dully*]. I want to talk to you. [*Pause*] You love my boy, don't you?

NINA [*Startled*]. Why, of course!

MRS. EVANS [*Blurting it out*]. Are you going to have a baby, Nina?

NINA. No, Mother. But I do want one, desperately.

MRS. EVANS [*Flatly, but with mechanical rapidity*]. Don't you think it's too soon? Don't you think you'd better wait until Sammy's making more money? Why don't you just go on being happy together, just the two of you?

NINA. But, why, Mother? Why? [*Filter*] What is behind what she's saying? . . . That bad feeling . . . I'm getting it again!

No, I don't think any of those things, Mrs. Evans. I want a child before everything! We both do!

MRS. EVANS [*Hopelessly*]. I know . . . [*Grimly*] But you can't! You've got to make up your mind you can't.

NINA [*Bewildered*]. What do you mean? How can you say a thing like that?

MRS. EVANS [*Tenderly*]. It's because I want Sammy—and you, too, child, to be happy.

NINA [*Violently*]. I don't believe you know what you are saying! It's too terrible for you—Sam's own mother—how would you have felt if someone came to you and said such a thing.

MRS. EVANS [*Tonelessly*]. They did say! Sam's own father did—my husband! And I said it to myself! But Sammy came just the same! And I prayed and prayed! And when he was born, healthy and smiling, we just had to love him and live in fear.

NINA. Fear?

MRS. EVANS. And that's what you'd be in for. And your baby, if you ever were to have one—you'd be bringing it into torment! [*Violently*] I

tell you it'd be a crime—a crime worse than murder! [*With pity*] So
you just can't, Nina!

NINA [*Slightly hysterical*]. What do you mean? Why don't you speak
plainly?

MRS. EVANS. I am, daughter. [*Filter*] I know what she's doing now . . .
just what I did . . . trying not to believe . . . [*Fiercely*] But I'll
make her! . . . She's got to help me save Sammy!
[*Relentlessly*] Nina, I thought I was plain, but I'll be plainer. Only
remember, it's a family secret and now you are one of the family.
It's a curse on the Evanses. My husband's mother—she was an only
child—died in an asylum—and her father before her. And my husband's sister, Sammy's aunt, she's out of her mind. My husband
didn't tell me about the family until after we were married. He asked
me to forgive him. Said he loved me so much he'd have gone mad
without me.

NINA [*In a dull moan*]. I don't believe you! I won't believe you!

MRS. EVANS [*Droning on*]. My husband began to go queer in his head
when Sammy was eight. Every time the child was sick, or had a
headache or bumped his head, or had a nightmare and screamed, or
said something queer—like children do naturally—my husband
thought the curse had got him! [*Harshly*] Living with that fear is
awful torment. It nearly drove me crazy, too!—but I didn't have it in
my blood! It only got Sammy's father!

NINA [*In a frenzy*]. I don't believe you! I don't believe Sam would ever
have married me if he knew!

MRS. EVANS [*Sharply*]. Who said he knew? Did I? *Did* I?

NINA. But—but—how could you?

MRS. EVANS. Sammy didn't know a single thing about it. That's been
the work of my life, keeping him from knowing. And, Nina, I am
certain sure my husband might have kept his mind, with the help
of my love, if there'd been just the two of us. He *worried* himself
into it.

NINA [*With wild mockery*]. And I thought Sam was so normal—so
healthy and sane—not like me! I'd thought he'd give me such
healthy, happy children and I'd forget myself in them and learn
to love him!

MRS. EVANS [*Horrified*]. Learn to? You told me you did love Sammy!

NINA. Maybe I was beginning to—but I hate him now! I hate you,
too. [*Begins to weep hysterically*] Take your hand away! Don't

touch me! I hate you, too! Why didn't you tell him he must never marry?

MRS. EVANS. What reason could I give, without telling him everything? And I never heard about you till after you were married. That's why I kept insisting in my letters that he bring you here! [*Pause*] I thought you'd love him like I did his father, and be satisfied with him alone.

NINA [*Wildly*]. No! I don't! I won't! I'll leave him!

MRS. EVANS [*Fiercely*]. You can't! Do you hear me! You can't!

NINA. Don't! Don't! Stop shaking me! Stop it!

MRS. EVANS. He'd go crazy sure, then! You'd be a devil! Don't you see how he loves you?

NINA [*Harshly*]. Well, I don't love him! I only married him because he needed me and I needed children!

MRS. EVANS [*Sadly and bitterly*]. Don't you think he needs you now— more'n ever?

NINA. Can you tell me not to leave him—if I don't love him?

MRS. EVANS. You oughtn't to have married him when you didn't love him. And it will be your fault, what'll happen.

NINA [*Torturedly*]. What do you mean?—Sam will be all right—just as he was before—and it's not my fault anyway!—It's not my fault! [*Filter*] Poor Sam! . . . She's right . . . not his fault . . . it's mine . . . I wanted to use him to save myself . . . I acted the coward again as I did with Gordon . . .

MRS. EVANS [*Grimly*]. You know what'll happen to him if you leave him—after all I've told you! [*Pleadingly*] Oh, I get down on my knees to you, don't make my boy run that risk! You've got to give one Evans, the last one, a chance to live in this world! And you'll learn to love him, if you give up enough for him! [*Pause*]

NINA. All right, Mother. I'll stay with Sam. There's nothing else I can do, is there, when it isn't his fault, poor boy! [*A despairing cry*] But I'll be so lonely! [*Piteously*] Oh, Mother, how can I keep on living?

MRS. EVANS. You will learn, dear. As I did! [*Filter*] Now. Now she knows my suffering. Now I've got to help her . . . she's giving her life to save my Sammy. I've got to save her! Maybe, Nina, maybe, if . . .

NINA [*Dully and resentfully*]. And how about Sam? You want him to be happy, don't you? It's just as important for him as it is for me that we should have a child some day! If you know anything at all about him, you ought to see that!

MRS. EVANS [*Sadly*]. I know that. I see that in him, Nina. [*Gropingly*] There must be a way—somehow. I remember when I was carrying Sam, sometimes I'd forget I was a wife, I'd only remember the child in me. And then I used to wish his father had been someone else—*anybody* else—so long as he was healthy!—*Anybody* else, Nina.

NINA. What are you trying to tell me, Mother?

MRS. EVANS [*Unheeding*]. He loved children so, my poor husband did, and the way they took to him you never saw anything like it. He was a natural born father. And Sammy's the same.

NINA [*Strangely*]. Yes, Sammy's the same. But I'm not the same as you.

MRS. EVANS. That's right. You have courage. It'd be easy for you.

NINA. Easy for me? *What* would be easy for me, Mother?

MRS. EVANS [*Unheeding*]. Being happy, that's the nearest we can ever come to knowing what's good! Being happy, that's good! The rest is just talk!

NINA. Yes, yes, I believe that, too, Mother.

MRS. EVANS. I love my boy Sammy. I could see how much he wants you to have a child. Sammy's got to feel sure you love him—to be happy. Whatever you can do to make him happy is good—is good, Nina! I, his mother, tell you that! You understand, daughter?

NINA [*Whisper*]. Yes, yes, I understand, Mother.

MRS. EVANS [*Gently*]. I know what you're suffering, Nina. And I wouldn't say what I just said now, only I know we two mustn't see each other ever again. You and Sammy have got to forget me.

NINA. No—No, No—

MRS. EVANS [*Inexorably*]. Oh, yes, you will—easy. People forget everything. They've got to, poor people! And I'm saying what I say about you two both needing a child so's you'll remember it when you need to, after you've forgotten all about me.

NINA [*Pitifully*]. Don't! Please, Mother!

MRS. EVANS [*Tenderly*]. Come here. Let me take you in my arms . . . There, *that* is good, too. [*Pause*] You poor child! You're like the daughter of my sorrow! You're closer to me now than ever Sammy could be! I want you to be happy!

NINA. Yes, Mother. [*She begins to sob . . . Hold, and music*]

END OF ACT II

ANNOUNCER

COMMERCIAL

ACT III

MARSDEN. When Nina returned from her visit with Sam's mother she was a changed woman. I didn't know at the time what had happened, of course—nor why. As for Nina, she hardly spoke . . . And so the months went by . . . One night Sam was seated at the professor's old desk in the library, sweating out a piece of advertising copy . . . [*Fades*]

> [*Typewriter pounding spasmodically . . . It starts and stops again*]

EVANS. Heck! I can't do this junk! [*Filter . . . Tormentedly*] Been going stale ever since we came back from that trip to mother's . . . no ideas . . . I'm sterile. [*With guilty terror*] Sterile—no—am I? [*Despondently*] Certainly been a big change in Nina . . . constantly ill . . . What happened between her and Mother? If we only had a kid . . . then I'd show them what I could do! Cole always thought I had the stuff and Ned certainly thought so. [*With sudden relieved excitement*] By gosh, I was forgetting! Ned's coming here tonight . . . Forgot to tell Nina. Mustn't let her get wise I got him to come to look her over. Oh, well, let's have another go at this tripe!

> [*Typewriter pounding again . . . And into it are heard footsteps approaching*]

NINA. Still at it, Sam?

EVANS. Nina, dear! I thought you were lying down! Did the noise of my typing bother you? I'm terribly sorry.

NINA. But there's nothing to be terribly sorry about. [*Filter*] Why is he always cringing . . . if he'd only fall in love with someone else . . . go away . . . leave me free . . . if he'd die! [*Remorsefully*] I must stop such thoughts. I don't mean it. Poor Sam! He's so weak . . . trying so hard . . . loving me so much. Look at him! He feels my scorn . . . Oh why did his mother have to . . . I must be nice to him! I must!

You didn't wake me, dear. And don't look so tragic about it.

EVANS [*Contritely*]. I wouldn't be working home nights if Cole hadn't given me a warning to buck up or get out.

NINA. Well, it isn't a job to worry much about losing, is it?

EVANS. Oh, I can get another one, I suppose, if I have to.

NINA [*Reassuringly*]. Certainly you can! And it isn't your fault, you big goose. It's mine. I know how hard it makes everything for you, being tied to a wife who's too sick to be a wife.

EVANS [*Passionately*]. No! Don't say that! It's you who ought to have married someone worth while, not a poor fish like me! But no one could love you more than I do, no matter what he was!

NINA [*Trying to be sincere*]. And I love you, Sam. Kiss me, dear. [*Filter*] I almost do . . . sometimes . . . as his mother loves him. I must try to make him feel secure.
[*Gently*] I want you to be happy, Sam.

EVANS [*Transported with happiness*]. I am—a hundred times more than I deserve!

NINA [*Gently*]. Sssh. Put your head on me . . . there!

EVANS [*Very softly*]. I'm happy now, Nina.

NINA. Sssh. [*Pause*] [*Filter*] Oh, what shall I do! Gordon, tell me! Shall I stick to him—

[*Knock on door*]

NINA [*Startled*]. Who's that?

EVANS [*Somewhat embarrassed*]. I—er—forgot to tell you. Ned's coming out tonight.

NINA [*Astonished*]. Ned Darrell!

[*Knock on door is repeated*]

EVANS. Sure. I happened to run into him in town and invited him out. I'd better go let him in.

NINA. No. Wait. It might be Charlie Marsden. He said he was coming over, too. I'm going upstairs. Come up and tell me if it's Ned. If it's Charlie, get rid of him.

[*Footsteps recede*]

EVANS. All right, Nina.

[*Knock is repeated*]

EVANS. I'm coming.

[*Door opens*]

EVANS. Hello, Charlie. Come on in. Nina is lying down upstairs.

MARSDEN. Then by all means don't disturb her. I just dropped in with my suggestions for her outline for Gordon's biography. I couldn't have stayed but a minute. My mother is a bit under the weather.

EVANS [*Perfunctorily*]. Too bad. I suppose you've got to be careful of every little thing when you get her age.

MARSDEN [*Bristling*]. Her age? Mother isn't so old!

EVANS. I didn't mean—I'll give these to Nina first thing in the morning.

MARSDEN [*Filter*]. Why is she writing Gordon's biography? Why am I helping her with it? To be near her? Why doesn't she have a child? She ought to . . . for her peace of mind . . . and mine. Yes, it would free me . . . It would free me from all thoughts of— [*Violently*] Shut up . . . what a low creature I'm becoming!—to have such thoughts when mother is sick.

[*Knock on door*]

EVANS. That must be Ned. You remember Darrell. He's coming out for a little visit.

[*Knock repeated*]

MARSDEN. Well, go ahead! Let him in.

[*Footsteps recede . . . Door opens*]

MARSDEN [*Filter*]. Darrell? What's he doing here? Have they been meeting, he and Nina? What a sordid mess!

[*Footsteps approach*]

EVANS. Ned, you remember Charlie Marsden.

MARSDEN [*Polite*]. How are you, doctor.

DARRELL. Hello.

EVANS. I'll go up and tell Nina you're here, Ned.

[*Footsteps recede*]
[*A pause*]

MARSDEN [*Awkwardly*]. I was just on the point of leaving, doctor.

DARRELL. Were you? [*Filter*] This Marsden! What kind of a man is he? I know! An old maid who has affairs in his novels . . . I'd like a chance to study him more closely.

MARSDEN. Darrell, before I go I'd like to ask a favor, a word of advice as to the best specialist, the very best, it would be possible to consult.

DARRELL [*Sharply*]. On what?

MARSDEN [*Almost naïvely*]. My mother has a pain in her stomach.

DARRELL [*Dryly*]. Possibly she eats too much.

MARSDEN. She doesn't eat enough to keep a canary alive! It's a dull constant pain, she says. She's terrified at the idea of cancer. But, of course, that's perfect rot, she's never been sick a day in her life.

DARRELL [*Sharply*]. She's showing more intelligence about her pain than you are.

MARSDEN [*Fearful*]. I don't understand—do you mean to say you think—?

DARRELL [*Brutally*]. It's possible.

MARSDEN [*Angrily*]. What—that's nonsense!

DARRELL. People who are afraid to face unpleasant possibilities until it's too late commit more murders and suicides than—Dr. Schultz is your man! Take her to see him—tomorrow!

MARSDEN [*Bursting out*]. Look here, Darrell, you're condemning her without—[*Chokingly*] You've no right—no right!

DARRELL [*Contritely*]. I beg your pardon, Marsden. [*Filter*] [*Astonished and contrite*] And I thought he was so ingrown he didn't give a hoot about anyone! His *mother*! Now I begin to understand him! [*Kindly*] I'm sorry, old man. I only wanted to drive it in that all delay is dangerous. Here's Dr. Schultz's address.

MARSDEN [*Gratefully*]. Thank you. I'll take her to see him tomorrow.

[*Footsteps approach*]

EVANS [*Fading on*]. Charlie, can you give me a lift? Nina wants some things at the store before it closes, and—

MARSDEN [*Dully*]. Sure, Sam. Come along . . . Goodnight, doctor—and thank you.

EVANS. Nina'll be right down, Ned. [*Whisper*] For Pete's sake, have a good heart-to-heart talk with her!

[*Door closes*]

[*Pause*]

DARRELL [*Filter*]. Sam's upset. What's happened to their marriage? Re-

member their wedding! In a way I envied him. Nina . . . strong
physical attraction for me . . . the time I kissed her . . . That's why
I've steered clear since! No emotional didos for me! Need all my
mind on my work . . . She's a strange case though . . . can't understand her not having a child.

[*Footsteps approach*]

NINA. Hello, Ned!

DARRELL. Hello, Nina.

NINA. I'm certainly glad to see you again—after all these years!

DARRELL. Not as long as all that, is it? [*Filter . . . Admiringly*] Wonderful looking as ever. Sam is a lucky devil!

NINA [*Teasingly*]. I ought to cut you dead after the shameful way
you've ignored us! [*Filter*] He has strong hands like Gordon's. They
take hold of your hand . . . not like Sam's . . . yielding fingers
that let you fall back on yourself . . .
Let's sit out in the garden, shall we, Ned? It's cooler.

[*Footsteps . . . Screen door closes . . . Crickets . . . Footsteps
continue*]

DARRELL. My goodness! Crickets! I haven't heard those in years! It must
be very pleasant, Nina, living out here. [*Filter*] Hmmm. She's been
through a lot since I saw her . . . face shows it . . . nervous tension
pronounced . . . hiding behind her smile.

[*Footsteps stop*]

NINA. Let's sit here . . . I've missed you, Ned. We've both missed you.
[*Filter . . . Uneasily*] I hate that professional look in his eyes . . .
watching symptoms . . . without seeing me.
[*Laughing nervously*] Ned, I suppose you can't help your diagnosing stare.

DARRELL [*Jokingly*]. Same old, unjust accusation! You were always
reading diagnosis into me, Nina, when what I was really thinking
was what fine eyes you had, or what a becoming gown, or—

NINA [*Lightly*]. Or what a becoming alibi you could cook up! Oh, I know
you! [*Laughs gaily and naturally*] But you're forgiven—that is, if
you can explain why you've never been to see us.

DARRELL. Honestly, Nina, I've been rushed with work. I haven't had a
chance to go anywhere.

NINA [*Teasingly*]. By the way, if it isn't too rude to inquire, aren't you getting yourself engaged to some fair lady or other?

DARRELL [*Emphatically*]. Not me. Not on your life!

NINA [*Sarcastically*] Then you don't believe in taking your own medicine? Why, doctor! Think of how much good it would do you! [*Excitedly with sarcasm*]—"if you had a nice girl to love"—or did you say "learn to love?"—and what else did you tell me, doctor? Oh, yes! You ought to have a baby, doctor! [*Bitterly sarcastic*] You will never know what life is, you'll never be really happy until you've had a baby, doctor— a fine, healthy baby! [*She laughs bitterly*]

DARRELL. I recognize my arguments, Nina. [*Filter*] She's bitter . . . Good! She's going to tell.
[*Meekly*] Was I really wrong on every point, Nina?

NINA [*Harshly*]. On every single point.

DARRELL. But how? You haven't given the baby end of it a chance yet, have you?

NINA [*Bitterly*]. How do you know I'm destined to bear babies, doctor?

DARRELL [*Startled*]. What? Why don't you begin at the beginning and tell me all about it? I feel responsible.

NINA [*Fiercely*]. You are! [*Then wearily*] And you're not. No one is. You didn't know. No one could know.

DARRELL. Know what? Tell me. I want to help you, Nina.

NINA [*Touched*]. It's too late, Ned. [*Then suddenly*] I've just thought— Sam said he happened to run into you. That isn't so, is it? He went to see you and told you how worried he was about me and asked you out here to see me, didn't he?

DARRELL. Yes.

NINA [*Mockingly*]. Well, since you are out here professionally, and my husband wants me to consult you, I might as well give you the whole case history! I hope it will teach you not to be so cocksure in the future. [*Bitterly*] I must say you proceeded very unscientifically, doctor.

DARRELL. How do you mean?

NINA [*Flat and lifeless*]. Sam's mother told me we couldn't have children.

DARRELL [*Astonished*]. What?

NINA. You see, doctor, Sam's great-grandfather was insane, and Sam's grandmother died in an asylum, and Sam's father had lost his mind for years before he died, and an aunt who is still alive is crazy. A pretty picture, isn't it, doctor?

DARRELL [*Tenderly*]. Good lord! I simply can't believe it! Poor Sam, of all people. There's only one possible thing to do now. You'll have to make Sam give you a divorce.

NINA [*Bitterly*]. Yes? Then what do you suppose would be his finish? No, I've enough guilt in my memory now, thank you! I've got to stick to Sam!

DARRELL. You've got to think of yourself, Nina.

NINA. No. I've got to make Sam happy.

DARRELL. But how? How can you—

NINA [*Flatly*]. There's only one way to make him happy. He must have a child—somehow—don't you agree, doctor? To make us both happy?

DARRELL [*Confused*]. Honestly, Nina, I don't know what to think.

NINA [*With monotonous insistence*]. You must know what to think. I can't think it out myself any more. I need your advice—your scientific advice this time, if you please, doctor. I've thought and thought about it. I've told myself it's what I ought to do. Sam's own mother urged me to do it.

DARRELL [*Astonished*]. Sam's mother!

NINA. Yes. It's sensible and kind and just and good. I've told myself this a thousand times and yet I can't quite convince something in me that's afraid of something. I need the courage of someone who can stand outside and reason it out as if Sam and I were no more than guinea pigs. You've got to help me, doctor!

DARRELL. Of course I want to help you, Nina! [*Filter . . . Confusedly*] What do I have to do? This was all my fault. I owe them something in return. [*Irritably*] What's this humming in my ears—like a fever! I've got to keep cool! Let me see . . .

DARRELL [*Coldly professional*]. A doctor must be in full possession of the facts if he is to advise. What is it precisely that Sam's wife has thought so much of doing?

NINA [*Insistently*]. Of picking out a healthy male, about whom she cared nothing, and having a child by him that Sam would believe was his child. Those were the instructions of Sam's mother. This child would give Sam confidence in his own living. It would be for him a living proof that his wife loved him. [*Confusedly and purposefully*] This doctor—what is his name? Oh, yes, Darrell! This Dr. Darrell is healthy.

DARRELL [*Still professional*]. I see. But this needs a lot of thinking over. It isn't easy to prescribe . . .

[*An ethereal music is heard, very soft and far away . . . It rises and then swirls and eddies under the next three soliloquies*]

DARRELL [*Filter*]. Now, let's see . . . I have a friend who has a wife. I was envious at his wedding . . . but what has that to do with it? Confound it, my mind won't work! It keeps running away to her . . . Why? In the interest of science? Don't lie to yourself!

NINA [*Filter*]. This doctor is nothing to me but a healthy male. When he was Ned he once kissed me . . . But I cared nothing about him . . . so that's all right, isn't it, Sam's mother?

DARRELL [*Filter*]. Hmmm . . . let me see . . . I am in the laboratory and they are guinea pigs. In fact, in the interest of science, I can be, for the purpose of this experiment, a healthy guinea pig myself and still remain an observer . . . For example, I observe my pulse is high and that's obviously because I am stricken with a recurrence of an old desire . . . Desire? What is that? Desire is a natural male reaction to the beauty of the female . . . Also her husband is my friend. I have always tried to help him.

[*Music out*]

DARRELL [*Coldly*]. Nina, I have been considering what Sam's wife told me and her reasoning is quite sound.

NINA. Then you agree with Sam's mother? She said, "Being happy is the nearest we can ever come to knowing what good is!"

DARRELL. I agree with her decidedly. Sam's wife should have a child. It is her duty to her husband. It would give him happiness.

NINA [*Timidly and guiltily*]. This will have to be hidden from Sam so he can never know! Oh, doctor, Sam's wife is afraid!

DARRELL [*Sharply professional*]. Nonsense! This is no time for timidity! Happiness hates the timid! So does science! Certainly Sam's wife must conceal her action! To let Sam know would be insanely cruel of her—and stupid—for then no one could be the happier for her act!

NINA [*Pleadingly*]. You must give his wife courage, doctor. You must free her from her feeling of guilt. She knows this thing is wrong.

DARRELL [*Coldly*]. Wrong! Would she rather see her husband go to pieces worrying about why he has no children—and wind up in an asylum— as his father did? Would she rather face the prospect of going to pot mentally, morally, physically, herself—through year after year of deviling herself and him? Really, Madam, if you can't throw overboard all such irrevelant moral ideas, I'll have to give up this case here and now! [*Filter . . . Frightened*] Who is talking? Is the doctor suggesting me . . . ? But you know very well I can't be the one.

NINA [*Pleading*]. Please, doctor, you must give the patient strength to do this right thing that seems to her so right and then so wrong! Please, take the patient's hand.

DARRELL [*Filter . . . Frightened*]. Whose hand is this? It burns me . . . I kissed her once . . . her lips were cold. Now they would burn with happiness for me!

NINA. That's it. Take her other hand, too . . . Now she feels your strength. It gives her courage—the courage to ask you, doctor, to suggest the father. She needs your courage to choose!

DARRELL [*Filter*]. My courage?

[*Judiciously calm*] Well, Madam, the man must be someone who is not unattractive to her, of course.

NINA. Ned Darrell always attracted her.

DARRELL [*Filter . . . Frightened*]. What's that she said . . . Ned? Attracts?

[*Evenly*] And the man should have a scientific mind that can truly understand . . .

NINA. She always thought Ned had a superior mind.

DARRELL [*Filter . . . Frightened*]. Did she say "Ned"?

The man should like and admire her. But he should not love her!

NINA. Ned does not love her—but he used to like her. Does he now, doctor?

DARRELL [*Filter*]. Does he? . . . Who is he? . . . He is Ned! . . . Ned is I!—

[*Trembling now, gently*] But, Madam, I must confess, the Ned you are speaking of is I, and I am Ned.

NINA [*Gently*]. And I am Nina, who wants a child—for myself, and for my husband, Sam. [*Softly*] I should be so grateful, Ned. [*Submissively*] I should be so humbly grateful.

[*Pause*]

DARRELL [*Suddenly, with a sob*]. Yes—yes, Nina . . . Yes—for your happiness—in that spirit!

NINA. In that spirit! Only in that spirit. [*She sobs—softly first—then brokenly*]

[*Music*]

ANNOUNCER

CREDITS

STRANGE INTERLUDE

(Part Two)

Original Play
by Eugene O'Neill

Radio Adaptation
by Arthur Arent

CAST

(for radio performance)

NINA	Lynn Fontanne
MARSDEN	Alfred Shirley
DARRELL	Walter Abel
EVANS	Donald MacDonald
GORDON (as a boy)	Michael Artist
GORDON (as a young man)	Donald Buka
MADELINE	Joan Thompkins

STRANGE INTERLUDE

Part Two

Radio Adaptation by
ARTHUR ARENT

SINCE BOTH PARTS were to be considered as entities, with a listener who had not heard Part One able to follow the events of Part Two without undue strain, a flash-back technique was used to "brief" him on events to date. This included, beside the Narrator's résumé, an explanatory repetition of the technique involved in the asides—Marsden introducing the characters, who spoke in a conversational tone and then dropped their voices to indicate what they were thinking. As one of these flash-backs I also had Darrell voice his decision to run away—all that was used of the eliminated Scene Five of Part One, and without which the ensuing events would be unclear.

The scene of the little Gordon discovering the boat was relocated (from the living room to the hall) and built up to achieve some suspense for what seemed one of the most dramatic situations in the play.

While it was mentioned earlier that music was not used to underline the asides, there are two exceptions to this, one in each part. These occurred at moments of great impact, when a kind of cosmic finger pointing was achieved as the thoughts of Nina and Darrell swirled and intertwined.

For those who did not hear the production, I might say that both direction and company were beyond praise, with Miss Fontanne magnificent in the part she had so memorably created, and Jean Adair heartbreaking as Sam's mother in Part One.

STRANGE INTERLUDE

ANNOUNCER

INTRODUCTION FOR THE THEATRE GUILD

ACT I

MARSDEN. My name is Charles Marsden. I am a writer . . . the author of a dozen lovingly created novels, all carefully manicured so as not to offend, or to give pain, or to cause you to think that life is anything but beautiful . . . And now, toward the end of my life, I find myself telling a story that does not meet these specifications—the story of Nina Evans, and Sam, her husband, and Dr. Darrell and myself!

   [*Music: Short phrase*]

MARSDEN. I've already told you about Nina, and how she had been engaged to Gordon Shaw who was shot down in the First World War. Grieving for Gordon almost killed Nina. She was in a dangerous neurotic state—when Sam Evans came along. Dr. Darrell and I advised her to marry Sam, to have children. We thought it would make her forget Gordon. She did marry him. But there were no children—because Sam's mother, meeting Nina for the first time, had told her —Well, let Nina tell it as she told it later to Dr. Darrell—

NINA. You see, Doctor, it's a great secret. Even Sam doesn't know. His great grandfather was insane, and his grandmother died in an asylum, and his father lost his mind for years before he died, and an aunt who is still alive is crazy. But *I* know—now! A pretty picture, isn't it?

   [*Music: Short phrase*]

MARSDEN. As the months went by, and Nina bore Sam Evans no child, Sam became more and more despondent—he was licked . . . And

37

then, after weeks of searching her soul, Nina spoke to Dr. Ned
Darrell . . .

NINA. There was something else Sam's mother said, Doctor. She said,
"Nina, when I was carrying Sam I used to wish his father had been
anybody else—*anybody else,* do you understand? You have courage.
It would be easy for you." [*Hysterically*] *"Easy,"* she said! It would
be *easy* for me!

DARRELL. Exactly what is it you want of me, Nina?

NINA. I want your advice, your *scientific* advice, doctor.

DARRELL. Sam's mother is right . . . Nina, I observe this as a scientific
experiment . . . Sam's wife should have a child! It is her duty to
her husband. Without a child he would go to pieces!

NINA. You must give Sam's wife courage, Doctor. You must free her from
her feeling of guilt . . . and shame . . . Please, Doctor, take the
patient's hand . . . Now she has the courage, the courage, Doctor,
to ask you to suggest the father—to suggest that you—[*Trembling*]
Oh, Ned, I should be so grateful! I should be so humbly grateful!

DARRELL. Yes, in that spirit, Nina. Only in that spirit!

[*Music: Chord*]

MARSDEN. And then, a few months before the child was born, Sam Evans,
Nina's husband, spoke to Dr. Ned Darrell . . . [*Fades*]

SAM. Nina wants you to stay to lunch, Ned. She said there's something
important you both want to tell me.

DARRELL. Of course, I'll stay to lunch, Sam.

MARSDEN [*Quoting*]. "Of course I'll stay to lunch, Sam" . . . that's what
Dr. Darrell said. But what was he really thinking? I've got to tell you
that because in this story I'm telling, you also hear what people think.
These were Dr. Darrell's thoughts.

DARRELL [*Filter*]. After lunch! She wants to tell Sam . . . tell her own
husband she loves me now . . . that I love her!—that the child is
mine . . . no! . . . I can't. It would kill him! . . . and my career?
. . . finished! love! . . . I'm caught in it! . . . she touches my hand,
her eyes get in mine, I lose my will! . . . I've *got* to find a way out!
. . . I've got to—Europe! . . . That's it! . . . I'll run away!
Look here, Sam. I can't stay to lunch. Got to pick up my passport.
I'm sailing for Europe, you know.

EVANS. But what—what's the big secret, Ned?

DARRELL. You're going to be a father, old man. Your wife's going to have a baby. And now I've got to run. See you again in a year or so! Give my love to Nina! So long!

[*Music: Up and under*]

MARSDEN. And that was that . . . the great revelation was postponed—for the time being . . . One Sunday afternoon about a year later, we were in the library of Nina's house in a New York suburb. Nina sat beside the open fire. She was sewing on something for the baby— Gordon, she called him, after the other Gordon who was killed. I glanced at her over the top of my newspaper, wondering what she was thinking . . .

[*Fades*]

NINA [*Filter*]. I wonder if there's a draught in the baby's room . . . maybe I'd better close the window . . . little Gordon . . . why hasn't Ned written? . . . it's better he hasn't . . . but I forgive him . . . I have my baby.

EVANS [*Calling, off*]. Nina! You downstairs?

NINA [*Calling*]. Yes, Sam! Here I am, dear! With Charlie! [*Filter*] Sam is a wonderful father . . . he's become a new man in the past year . . . I have a genuine respect for him now . . . and I am making him happy! How queerly things worked out! . . . And I don't feel wicked . . . I feel good!

[*Footsteps approach during the above*]

EVANS [*On mike*]. Hello, dear, how do you feel? . . . Hi, Charlie. How's the boy?

MARSDEN. Hello, Sam. I am as always. Good old Charlie! By the way, Nina, did I tell you I ran into Dr. Darrell in Munich?

NINA [*Stammering*]. You saw—Ned? [*Filter*] Ned! . . . he saw Ned! . . . why hasn't he told me before? . . . why did he look at me like that? . . . does he suspect?

MARSDEN [*Casually*]. Yes, I happened to run into him. [*Filter*] [*With savage satisfaction*] That struck home! look at her! . . . guilty! Nina and Darrell! . . . then I was right when I thought . . . When I saw him he was with a rather startling looking blonde— quite beautiful, if you like the type. I gathered they were very good friends.

NINA [*Airily*]. Why tell me, Charlie? It's nothing to me if he has fifty blondes— [*Filter*] [*Distractedly*] Nothing to me? Oh, Ned, why haven't you written? . . . stop it! . . . what a fool I am! . . . Ned's dead for me! . . . Oh, I hate Charlie! . . . why did he have to tell me?

EVANS. Did Ned say anything about coming back?

MARSDEN. No, but he did ask about you, Nina. Wanted to know about your baby.

EVANS [*Proudly*]. Too bad he couldn't see what a world-beater we've got! Eh, Nina?

NINA [*Mechanically*]. Yes, dear. [*Filter . . . Joyfully*] Ned asked about my baby! . . . Then he hasn't forgotten! . . . if he came back, he'd come to see his baby! . . .

EVANS. Hadn't you better go up and have a look at young Gordon?

NINA. Yes, dear, I'm going now . . . See you later, Charlie.

EVANS. Wait, Nina. I'll come with you. I want to say good-night to my son . . . Be right down, Charlie.

[*Footsteps recede*]

MARSDEN. All right.

[*Door closes*]

MARSDEN [*Filter . . . Excited*]. What happened then? . . . That look in her eyes . . . when I mentioned Darrell . . . does she still . . . [*Miserably*] What am I hoping for? What do I want? If Nina were free . . . what could I offer her? Myself? What a prize! [*Bitterly*]

[*Footsteps approach during the above*]

EVANS. That kid of mine is certainly a world-beater, Charlie! When he grows up, he'll be a crack athlete. I'm going to train him for that!

MARSDEN. How about training his mind, Sam?

EVANS. Oh, that'll take care of itself. He's got Nina for a mother, hasn't he?

MARSDEN [*Amused*]. You're the only genuinely modest person I know, Sam.

EVANS [*Embarrassed*]. Oh—me—I'm the boob of the family. [*Hastily*] Except when it comes to business. I'll make the money. And you can bet your sweet life on that!

MARSDEN. I'm quite sure of that.

EVANS [*Confidently*]. You know, Charlie, I couldn't have said that two years ago. But, since the baby was born, I've felt as if I had a shot of dynamite in each arm! Well, guess I'll go sit out on the back porch. Soak up some sun. Want to come along?

MARSDEN. No, thanks. I'll just stay here. I want to think out the plot for my new novel.

EVANS. Go to it, old man. See you later.

[*Footsteps recede . . . Door closes*]

MARSDEN [*Bitterly*]. [*Filter*] "Go to it, old man!" How that idiot patronizes me! Dear old Charlie! Nice doggie! We've had him for years!

[*Knock on door*]

NINA [*Calling, off*]. Open the door, Charlie, will you, please?

MARSDEN. All right.

[*Footsteps . . . Door opens*]

MARSDEN. Well, if it isn't—

NINA [*Off*]. Who is it, Charlie?

DARRELL [*Calling*]. It's I, Nina—Ned Darrell.

NINA [*Off—A glad cry*]. Ned! [*Frightened—trying to control herself*] I—make yourself at home. I'll be right down!

DARRELL [*Calling*]. All right, Nina! [*Filter*] Here again! . . . dreamed of this house . . . ran away from here once . . . now I've come back . . . my turn to be happy! . .

MARSDEN. You're looking fine, Doctor. [*Filter, savagely*] Now, I know! . . . absolutely! . . . his face! . . . her voice! . . . they did love each other!

[*Sharply*] When did you get back from Europe?

DARRELL [*Curtly*]. This morning on the "Aquitania." [*Filter . . . Cautiously*] Look out for this Marsden . . . always had it in for me . . . smells out love . . . like a woman . . . [*Suddenly, boldly*] Well, what do I care now! . . . all got to come out! . . . Nina wanted to tell Sam . . . now, I'll tell him myself! . . .

MARSDEN. What brought you back so soon? When I saw you in Munich—

DARRELL [*Shortly*]. My father died three weeks ago. I've had to come back about his estate. [*Filter*] That's a lie . . . I came back because I love her! . . . I'm licked! . . . No use fighting it . . . I've done my best!

[*Footsteps descending stairs*]

MARSDEN [*Insistently*]. That's Nina coming now, Darrell.

DARRELL [*Filter*]. [*Frightened*] She's coming! . . . In a second I'll see her! [*Terrified*] Does she still love me? . . . She may have forgotten . . . no, it's my child! . . . she can never forget that!

NINA. Ned!

DARRELL. Hello, Nina.

NINA. This is a wonderful surprise! [*Filter . . . Triumphantly*] He loves me! . . . I can tell! . . . He's mine! . . . now more than ever! . . . He'll never dare leave me again!

[*Calmly*] How are you, Ned? When did you get back?

DARRELL [*Taken aback—confusedly*]. I'm—all right, Nina.

MARSDEN [*Almost mockingly*]. Darrell's father died, Nina. He had to come back to see about the estate.

NINA. Your father, Ned. Oh, I'm sorry.

DARRELL. I was coming back anyway. [*Intensely*] I was coming back anyway, Nina!

NINA [*Matter-of-fact*]. Were you? [*Filter . . . Happily*] You darling you! . . . as if I didn't know that! . . . oh, my dearest! . . .

MARSDEN [*Suave*]. You're going to be amazed at the change in Sam, Darrell. If ever a man was bound for success, Sam is . . . You know, he's the proudest parent I've ever seen.

DARRELL. Really? [*Filter . . . Irritated*] What's he driving at? . . . Why doesn't he get the devil out of here and leave us alone? . . . But I'm glad Sam is on his feet . . . makes it easier to tell him the truth . . .

NINA. Yes, Sam makes a wonderful father, Ned. [*Filter . . . Worriedly*] What's Charlie talking about? . . . Oh, Ned, I do love you! . . . and I already know what you're hoping, darling, but I can't . . . I can't take Sam's baby away from him . . . I can't run away with you and leave my baby . . .

MARSDEN [*With driving insistence*]. If anything happened to that child, I actually believe Sam would lose his reason! Don't you think so, Nina?

NINA [*Emphatically*]. I know I'd lose mine! Little Gordon has become my whole life! You'll love him too, Ned.

DARRELL. I'm sure I will, Nina. [*Filter . . . With bitter irony*] "Little Gordon" . . . Nina called my son after Gordon who is dead! . . . Gordon, her first love, is still her lover! . . . Gordon, Sam, and Nina! . . . and my son! . . . closed corporation! . . . I'm forced out! . . . [*Furiously*] No! . . . not yet! . . . I'll smash it up! . . . I'll tell Sam the truth! . . .

MARSDEN. I'll tell Sam you're here. [*Pointedly*] You two probably have a lot to talk over.

[*Door closes . . . A pause*]

DARRELL. Nina!

NINA. Ned! Darling!

DARRELL [*Stammering*]. Nina—I—I've come back to you—do you—do you still care—Nina?

NINA [*Passionately*]. I love you, Ned! . . . come here, my darling, into my arms!

[*Pause*]

DARRELL [*Awkwardly*]. I—I didn't know—you seemed so cold today. Confound Marsden! he suspects, doesn't he?—but it makes no difference now, does it? [*Then in a flood of words*] Oh, it's been horrible, Nina! I couldn't forget you! Other women—they only made me love you more! Lord, how I've thought of you!—lying awake—recalling every word you said, every expression on your face, smelling your hair—Nina! I love you so!

NINA. And I've longed for you so much! Do you think I've forgotten! Do you? [*In anguish*] Oh, Ned, why did you run away?

DARRELL [*Violently*]. I was a fool! I thought of Sam! Oh, it wasn't all noble, I'll confess. I thought of myself and my career! My career! A lot of good it did that. But I know better now! The time for lying is past! You've got to come away with me!

NINA [*Passionately*]. Yes! Yes! Yes! [*Suddenly*] No! You're forgetting Sam—and Sam's baby!

DARRELL [*Wildly*]. Sam's baby? Are you joking? Why—we'll take him with us, of course!

NINA [*Sadly*]. And Sam?

DARRELL. He's got to give you a divorce! Let *him* be generous for a change!

NINA [*Sadly*]. He would be. You'll have to admit that, Ned.

DARRELL. All the better, then.

NINA [*With determination*]. Sam would give his life for my happiness. And that's what this would mean. His life. Could we be happy then? You know we couldn't—

DARRELL. We could.

NINA. And I've changed, Ned. You've got to realize that. I still love you.

I will always love you. But now I love my baby, too. His happiness comes first with me! And we mustn't forget Sam—

DARRELL [*Distracted*]. Sam! Sam! For the Lord's sake, Nina—you haven't come to love Sam, have you? Then—I'll go—I'll go away again—I'll never come back—I tried not to this time—but I had to, Nina!

NINA [*Softly*]. Put your arms around me, darling . . . kiss me . . . [*Pause, then very softly*] No, don't go away, darling—ever again. I don't love Sam. I love you!

DARRELL [*Miserably*]. But I don't understand! Sam gets everything—and I have nothing!

NINA. You have my love.

DARRELL [*With a harsh laugh*]. And that's what you call playing fair to Sam?

NINA [*With finality*]. That's the only possible solution, Ned, for all our sakes.

DARRELL [*Repulsed*]. Nina! How can you be so inhuman and calculating?

NINA [*Stunned—mockingly*]. It was you who taught me the scientific approach, wasn't it?

DARRELL [*In a queer, futile rage*]. You think I'll stay—come to this house —watch Sam with the woman I love and my child—you think that's what I came back to you for? You can go to the devil, Nina!

NINA [*Calmly*]. But what else can I—

[*Door opens, off*]

NINA [*Warningly*]. Ssh! They're coming, dear. Sam and Charlie.

DARRELL [*Angrily*]. What else can you do? Liar! But I can do something else! I can smash your whole calculating game for you! I can tell Sam—and I will—right now—

NINA [*Quietly*]. No, no. You won't. You can't do that to Sam.

DARRELL [*Savagely*]. The devil, I can't!

EVANS [*Fading on*]. Ned! You old son-of-a-gun! Why didn't you let a guy know you were coming?—Gee, you look thin! We'll fatten him up, won't we, Nina? Why, you old son-of-a—

NINA. Mercy, Sam, give Ned a chance to get a word in!

[*Taps nervously with thimble*]

MARSDEN [*Maliciously*]. Sure, Sam, give him a chance! Nina, why are you tapping with that thimble? You're not nervous, are you?

NINA. Nervous? Why should I be—

MARSDEN. Darrell, it couldn't be that you have something to tell Sam, could it?

EVANS. Tell me? I've got something to show you! My son! Ned, that kid is a world-beater. He is the most intelligent, best-looking, smartest kid that ever—

NINA [*Kindly*]. Yes, dear. Ned will see him later . . . Ned, do you want to tell Sam something?

DARRELL. Yes—I mean—No! Sam, I just want to say how darn glad I am—about everything . . . [*Filter . . . Miserably*] I can't tell him! . . . I can't tell him! I can't tell him!

EVANS. Gee thanks, Ned.

NINA. We both thank you, Ned. [*Filter . . . With triumphant calm*] There! . . . That's settled for all time . . . poor Ned! . . . How crushed he looks! I mustn't let them look at him! . . . If we're going to talk, we might as well sit down . . . you there, Charlie . . . and you over there, Sam . . . and you there, Ned . . . [*With possessive elation*] That's it! Make yourselves at home. You are my three men! This is your home with me! I should be the happiest woman in the world! . . . only I better knock on wood . . . [*Filter*] My three men! . . . I feel their desires converge in me! . . . to form one complete beautiful desire which I absorb! They dissolve in me . . . their life is my life . . . three! . . . and the fourth man . . . little Gordon! . . . he is mine, too! . . . That makes it perfect . . . [*With suppressed exultance*] Why, I should be the proudest woman on earth! . . . I'd better knock on wood.

[*Taps on table*]

[*Music*]

END OF ACT I

ANNOUNCER

COMMERCIAL

STATION IDENTIFICATION

ACT II

[*Music under*]

MARSDEN. The years went by . . . The advertising agency which Sam had acquired became one of the most successful in the city. And the lives of all of us took on the routine of a well-ordered existence. Nina and her three men! Only Darrell would escape for a time—to Paris or Antigua—but he always came back. The pull of Nina was too strong.

[*Music: Short phrase*]

MARSDEN. It is Gordon's eleventh birthday. He is stretched out on the floor of the living room in Sam Evans' Park Avenue apartment. Nina, thirty-five now, watches him lovingly. And Darrell? Darrell watches Nina . . . What are they thinking, these three? Let's find out. Young Gordon, first . . .

[*Ethereal music*]

GORDON [*Filter . . . Resentfully*]. I wish Darrell'd get out of here! . . . Why couldn't Mother let me run my own birthday? . . . I'd never have him here, you bet! . . . What's he always hanging around here for? . . . It's a good thing for him he didn't bring me any birthday present . . . I'd smash it first chance I got! . . .

MARSDEN. That was Gordon . . . age eleven . . . thinking of the father he didn't know was his father . . . And now Nina . . .

NINA [*Filter . . . Brooding with loving tenderness*]. No longer my baby . . . eleven years! . . . I can't believe it! . . . how handsome he is . . . Poor Ned, I've made him suffer a great deal! If he could only have been contented with what I was able to give him! . . . but he has always wanted more! . . . yet never had the courage to insist on all or nothing . . . he has shared me for his comfort! . . . with a little gratitude and a big bitterness.

MARSDEN. And now, I give you the thoughts of Dr. *Ned* Darrell . . .

[*Ethereal music*]

DARRELL [*Filter*]. What is she thinking? . . . We sit together in silence, thinking . . . thoughts that never know the other's thoughts . . . strangers . . . Well, whatever it is that binds us together, it's strong!

. . . Once, when she saw there was some chance I might break loose, she found some way to pull me back . . . and I forgot my longing for freedom . . . I came back wagging my tail . . . No, guinea pigs have no tails . . . well, I hope my experiment has proved something.

NINA. When are you going back to the West Indies, Ned?

DARRELL. Soon!

NINA. I don't see how you can afford to leave your work for such long periods.

DARRELL. My work?

NINA. Your experiments and things. Don't you grow rusty?

DARRELL. My life work is to rust—nicely and unobtrusively! [*Bitterly*] My real work was finished twelve years ago. As I believe you know, I ended it with an experiment which resulted so successfully that any further meddling with human lives would be superfluous!

NINA [*Low*]. How can you be so bitter, Ned—on Gordon's birthday?

DARRELL. Bitterness knows no holidays, Nina. [*Filter . . . Cynically*] She expects me to love the child she deliberately took from me and gave to another man! . . . No thank you, Nina! . . . I've been hurt enough! . . . I'll not leave myself open there! . . . [*Bitterly*] Every day he gets more like Sam, doesn't he?

GORDON [*Resentfully*]. Sure I do. I look just like my daddy. [*Filter*] He'd better look out! . . . he'd better look out what he says about my father! . . .

NINA. You know, Ned, he always reminds me of his namesake—Gordon Shaw.

DARRELL. Gordon? Not a bit. I'd much rather have him grow up to be an exact duplicate of the esteemed Samuel!

GORDON [*Filter . . . Resentfully*]. He's always making fun of my father! . . . He'd better look out! . . . [*Suddenly*] You—Darrell—you—shut up—making fun of my father!

NINA. Gordon!

DARRELL [*Mockingly*]. My dear boy, I wouldn't make fun of your father for the world.

GORDON [*Trembling*]. You—you did, too! [*Intensely*] I hate you!

NINA [*Shocked*]. Gordon! How dare you talk like that to your Uncle Ned!

GORDON. He's not my uncle! He's not my anything!

NINA. Not another word or you'll be punished, whether it's your birthday or not! [*Filter . . . Remorsefully*] Is this my fault? . . . I've done my best to get him to love Ned! . . . but it only makes him worse! . . .

GORDON [*Sullenly*]. I don't care! I'll tell Dad!

NINA. Leave the room! And don't come near me again, do you hear, until you've apologized to Uncle Ned.

DARRELL [*Bored*]. Oh, never mind, Nina!

GORDON. I'll leave the room—but I won't 'pologize—never!

[*Footsteps recede . . . Door slams*]

DARRELL [*Irritably*]. What if he does hate me? I don't blame him!

NINA. But he shouldn't say he hates you!

DARRELL. Nina, let me warn you about your son. If you would keep his love, hate me—hate me as he does!

NINA [*Sharply*]. No. I won't believe it. If Gordon doesn't love you, it's because you've never made the slightest attempt to be lovable to him! It's his birthday today, and you never even brought him a present, Ned!

DARRELL [*With bitter sadness*]. I did bring him a present. It's out in the hall. I bought him a costly, delicate one, so he can get full satisfaction and yet not strain himself when he smashes it, as he's smashed every present of mine in the past!

NINA. Ned! Don't! How can you torture us like that? . . . Oh, it's too dreadful—what I have done to you all these years . . . and why?

DARRELL. We did it for Sam, Nina. To keep him from losing his mind. Sam had to have a child. We gave him ours. Remember?

NINA. Forgive me, Ned.

DARRELL [*Tenderly*]. Nina, you've given me the only happiness I've ever known! And no matter what I may say or do, in bitterness, I'm proud—and grateful. I'm going away now on a trip. Good-bye, Nina.

NINA. Good-bye, Ned. Good-bye, my dear. [*Pause*]

DARRELL. Once more, Nina. Kiss me again.

NINA. Always and forever, darling. Always and— [*Door creaks*] what's that? [*Uneasily*] Ned, did you see—? I had the queerest feeling just then that someone was standing—

GORDON [*Calling off*]. Mother! Uncle Charlie's here. Shall he come right up?

NINA [*Straining to be casual*]. Yes, Gordon—of course! [*Worriedly*] His voice sounded funny. Did it to you? Do you suppose he saw . . . ?

DARRELL [*Wryly*]. It's possible. To be on the safe side, you'd better tell him you'd kissed me good-bye to get rid of me!

[*Footsteps approach*]

MARSDEN. Hello, Nina! Congratulations on your son's birthday! [*Coldly*] Hello, Darrell.

DARRELL. Hello, Marsden.

MARSDEN. Last time I saw you, you were leaving the next day for the West Indies. [*Maliciously*] Something here you couldn't tear yourself away from?

NINA. Ned is sailing this week, Charlie.

DARRELL. Yes. Expect to be gone at least two years this time—two years of hard work.

MARSDEN. Biology must be an interesting study. I wish I knew more about it.

DARRELL [*Ironically*]. Too bad you don't, Marsden. Then you might write more about life and less about dear old ladies and enchanting bachelors! Why don't you write a novel about life sometimes, Marsden?

MARSDEN. I will one day, Darrell. I promise you!

DARRELL. What will you call it? "My Barren Years"?

NINA [*Quickly*]. Charlie, I've got a job for you. Make the salad dressing for lunch. You know, the one I'm so crazy about.

MARSDEN. Righto, Nina. You bet!

NINA. And, Ned, wait here a moment while I see what Gordon is up to! I'm—er—worried about him!

[*Music: Short phrase*]

[*Footsteps accompanying*]

GORDON [*Singing—not very happily*].
> Happy birthday to me,
> Happy birthday to me,
> Happy birthday, dear Gordon,—

[*Footsteps stop*]

[*Filter*] What's this? . . . a package! . . . maybe it's a present, huh? . . . then what's it doing out here in the hall? [*Paper rustling as package is opened*] Holy smoke! . . . lookee! . . . a boat! . . . gosh, she's *beautiful*! . . . look at that mast! . . . and the rigging! . . . gee! . . . I wonder who—[*Reading*] "To Gordon, from his

Uncle Ned, with love and affection" . . . It's from him—Darrell! . . . [*Pause*] I don't want it! . . . I hate it! . . . but—it's so pretty! . . . why did it have to come from him? . . . [*With stubborn determination*] I've got to do it! . . . I got to! . . . he kissed Mother! . . . just a minute ago! . . . she kissed him! . . . I saw them! . . . *I've got to do it!* . . .

[*Running footsteps accompanying*]

GORDON [*Shrieking*]. Darrell! Darrell!

[*Footsteps stop . . . Door opens*]

GORDON [*Defiantly*] Hey—Darrell—did you—?
DARRELL [*With strained kindliness*]. Did I—?
GORDON [*Stammers angrily*]. I found this—out in the hall—your present!
DARRELL [*Steeling himself*]. I was hoping you'd like it.
GORDON [*Trembling with rage*]. No! And here's what—I think of you! [*He begins to cry—and over the crying we hear the sound of the boat being smashed to pieces and Gordon stamping on it*] There! There's your old boat! In a million pieces! You can keep it!

[*Pieces flung to floor*]

DARRELL [*His anger overcoming him*]. You—mean, little devil, you! You don't get that from me— [*Pulls himself up—then, trembling with deeply wounded affection*] You shouldn't have done that, son. What difference do I make? It was never my boat. But it was your boat. You should consider the boat, not me. Don't you like boats for themselves? I thought you did. That's why I brought it—
GORDON [*Sobbing miserably*]. It was awful pretty! I didn't want to do it! Honest I didn't! I love boats! [*Passionately*] But I hate you!
DARRELL [*Drily*]. So I've observed.
GORDON. More'n ever now! More'n ever! [*Blurting it out*] I saw you kissing Mother! I saw Mother, too!
DARRELL. But I was saying good-bye. We're old friends. You know that.
GORDON. You can't fool me. This was different! [*Explosively*] It would serve you good and right—and Mother, too—if I was to tell Dad on you!
DARRELL [*With great seriousness*]. Listen! There are things a man of honor doesn't tell anyone—not his mother or father. You want to be

a man of honor, don't you? [*Intensely*] Boy, there are things we **don't** tell, you and I! [*Filter*] This is my son! . . . I love him! . . .

GORDON. We?—Who do you mean?— [*Filter . . . Terribly torn*] Why do I like him now? . . . I like him awful!

[*Crying*] Listen, Darrell! I've got honor!—More'n you! . . . You don't have to tell me!—I wasn't going to tell Dad anyway, honest I wasn't!

[*Door opens*]

EVANS [*Heartily—off*]. Hello, everybody!

DARRELL [*Sotto voce*]. Buck up, son! Wipe those tears! Here's your dad! Hurry! Hide that broken boat under the sofa, or he'll ask questions!

[*Footsteps approach*]

EVANS [*Slightly off mike*]. How's the old son? How's the birthday coming along?

GORDON. Fine, Dad, fine.

EVANS [*On mike*]. Hello, Ned! Isn't this kid of mine a whopper for his age, though! Just a chip off the old block, eh?

DARRELL. Yes. [*Filter . . . in anguish*] Now it hurts! . . . to see my son his son! . . . I've had enough! . . . get out! . . . any excuse! . . . If I stay here one moment longer, I'll yell out the whole business! . . . I was just leaving, Sam.

EVANS [*Disappointed*]. Then you won't be here for lunch?

DARRELL. Sorry. [*Filter*] I'll yell the truth into your ears if I stay a second longer . . . you half-witted fool! . . .

Lots to do, Sam. [*Hurriedly*] Sailing in a few days! So long! So long—Gordon.

GORDON [*Moved*]. So long—Uncle Ned.

[*Music*]

END OF ACT II

ANNOUNCER

COMMERCIAL

ACT III

[*Music in full*]

MARSDEN. One, two, five, ten, eleven years went by. Nina, approaching fifty, still retained much of her lovely, youthful figure. Sam was a millionaire now. He took on weight, and his face reddened when he was excited. Ned Darrell seemed to come through the ordeal of time in the best shape. Somehow he seemed younger than the rest of us.

[*Music: Short phrase*]

MARSDEN. It was on a June day that we were all together again, the four of us. Also Gordon's fiancée, a girl named Madeline Arnold. We'd gone up the Hudson in Sam Evans' yacht to see the Poughkeepsie Regatta—and especially to watch Gordon, now a senior at college, who was rowing in his last race . . . [*Fades*]

[*Establish sound*]

EVANS [*Excited*]. Can't see a thing! Here, Madeline, take these binoculars. You've got young eyes.

MADELINE. Thank you, Mr. Evans.

EVANS. Soon be time for the race to start. Gosh, I'll bet Gordon's some keyed up right at this moment!

MADELINE. Poor kid! I'll bet he is! Don't you think so, Mrs. Evans?

NINA [*Flatly*]. Yes, my son must be quite nervous. [*Filter . . . Bitterly*] That tone in her voice! . . . her love already possesses him! . . . my son! . . . [*Vindictively*] But she won't! . . . she won't have him! . . . as long as I live, I'll keep my son! . . .

EVANS [*Yelling*]. Come on, Gordon!

NINA [*With nervous irritation*]. Sam! I told you I have a splitting head-ache!

EVANS [*Resentfully*]. I'm sorry. Why don't you take some aspirin?

NINA [*With malice*]. And don't get so excited. It's bad for your blood pressure.

[*Footsteps approach*]

DARRELL. Hello, everybody. Race start yet?

NINA. Not yet, Ned. Come here and tell Sam how bad all this yelling and excitement is for him.

DARRELL. Oh, I guess Sam's all right, Nina. [*Filter*] He does look as if he might have a bad blood pressure, though . . . what hope that would have given me at one time! . . . no more, thank the Lord! . . .

EVANS [*Jovially*]. Come on in the cabin, Ned, and shoot a drink. We can't see the start of the race from here. Maybe we can catch it on the radio.

NINA [*Quickly*]. No, Sam. Leave Ned with me. I want to talk to him. Charlie's in there and you can take Madeline.

EVANS. Okay. How about a drink, Madeline?

MADELINE. Thank you. I don't mind if I do! [*Filter . . . Resentfully*] She takes a fine do-this-do-that-little-girl tone toward me! . . . I'll give into her now . . . but once I'm married to Gordon things will be different! [*Fades*]

[*Door closes . . . A pause*]

NINA. Well, Ned?

DARRELL. Well, Nina?

[*Music: Of an ethereal quality, it swirls under the following two soliloquies*]

NINA [*Filter . . . Sadly*]. My old lover . . . how well and young he looks . . . now we no longer love each other at all . . . our account with the Creator is settled . . . happiness paid for with years of pain . . . love, passion, ecstasy . . . in what far-off life were they alive? . . . the only living life is in the past and future . . . the present is an interlude . . . strange interlude in which we call upon the past and future to bear witness we are living! . . . I must be careful with Ned . . . I must keep very cool and sensible, or he won't help me against Madeline . . . what is he thinking, I wonder? . . .

DARRELL [*Filter . . . With melancholy interest*]. And now? . . . what? what is she thinking? . . . I can look into her eyes . . . strange eyes that will never grow old . . . without desire or jealousy or bitterness . . . can she be the mother of my child? . . . is there such a person as my son? . . . I can't think of these things as real any more . . . they must have happened in another life . . .

[*Music: Out abruptly*]

NINA. Ned!

DARRELL. Yes, Nina?

NINA. Ned, I haven't seen you look so young and handsome since I first knew you. Tell me your secret.

DARRELL [*Proudly*]. That's easy. Work! I've become as interested in biology as I ever was in medicine, Nina. Our Experimental Station in Antigua is a big success. We've made some pretty important discoveries. I say "we." I really mean young Preston. [*With proud affection*] He's a fine boy, Nina. One who possesses the rare virtue of gratitude.

NINA. So you have found a son while I was losing mine—who is yours, too!

DARRELL. What do you mean, Nina, "while you were losing—"?

NINA [*Sadly*]. I've lost my son, Ned. Sam has made him all his. And it was done so gradually that, although I realized what was happening, there was never any way I could interfere. What Sam advised was always what Gordon himself wanted! What do I care whether he's an athlete or not! It's such nonsense, all this fuss! I'm not the slightest bit interested in whether Gordon's crew come in first or last!

[*Door opens*]

MADELINE [*Off . . . Excited*]. They're off! Mr. Evans is getting something on the radio! Navy and Washington are leading!—Gordon's third!

[*Door slams shut*]

DARRELL [*Drily*]. There's a young lady who seems to care a lot whether Gordon comes in last or not!

NINA [*Trying to be sorrowful and appealing*]. Yes. Gordon is hers now, Ned. [*Vindictively*] That is, they're engaged. But, of course, that doesn't necessarily mean—can you imagine him throwing himself away on a little fool like that? Why, she's hardly even pretty, and she's deadly stupid—

DARRELL. I can't agree with you, Nina. I find her quite charming.

NINA [*Unheeding*]. If he marries her, it means he'll forget me! She'll keep him away from me! Oh, I know what wives can do! He mustn't marry her, Ned! Our son mustn't marry her! . . . You'll have to give our son a good talking-to, Ned . . . You must keep him from ruining his life.

DARRELL [*Sternly*]. I swore I'd never again meddle with human lives, Nina! [*Harshly*] And I wouldn't help you in this anyway! You've

got to give up owning people, meddling in their lives as if you were
God and had created them.

NINA [*Forlorn*]. I don't know what you mean, Ned! Gordon is my son,
isn't he?

DARRELL [*Violently*]. And mine! Mine, too! Don't forget that, Nina!

[*Door opens and footsteps approach during the above*]

NINA. Ssh! Here's Sam!

EVANS [*Excited*]. Last I got on the radio, Gordon third, Navy and Washington leading. Gordon said they're the ones to fear—Navy, especially.
[*With amusement*] You ought to see old Charlie! He started throwing Scotch into him as if he was drinking against time! I had to take
the bottle away from him! . . . Madeline asked if you'd like to come
in and listen, Nina?

NINA. No thanks, you go ahead.

EVANS. All right. I don't want to miss anything! [*Fades*]

[*Door closes, off*]

NINA [*Filter . . . Bitterly*]. Madeline's Gordon! . . . Sam's Gordon! . . .
the thanks I get for saving Sam at the sacrifice of my own happiness!
. . . I won't have it! . . . What do I care what happens to Sam
now? . . . I hate him! . . . I'll tell him Gordon is not his child! . . .
and threaten to tell Gordon, too, unless he finds some excuse to break
their engagement! . . . but Ned must back me up or Sam won't
believe me! . . .
[*With fierce intensity*] Ned, isn't it time to tell Sam the truth? We've
suffered all our lives for his sake! We've made him rich and happy!
It's time he gave us back our son!

DARRELL. Gave us back—? [*Filter*] Aha . . . so that's it! . . . tell Sam the
truth? . . . at last! . . . so that's what she . . .
[*With a sneer*] Our son? You mean yours, my dear! Kindly count
me out of any further meddling with—

NINA. But Sam won't believe me if I'm the only one to tell him. You've
got to tell him too, Ned!

DARRELL [*Harshly*]. I've stopped meddling in Sam's life, I tell you!

NINA [*Insistently*]. Think of what Sam's made us go through, of how
he's made us suffer! You've got to tell him! You still love me a little,
don't you, Ned? [*Pause, then intensely*] Oh, if I'd only gone away
with you that time when you came back from Europe! How happy

we would have been, dear! How our boy would have loved you—if it hadn't been for Sam!

DARRELL. Would he? [*Filter*] Yes, if it hadn't been for Sam, I would have been happy! . . . I would have been the world's greatest neurologist! . . . my boy would have loved me, and I'd have loved him! . . .

NINA [*Striving to break down his last resistance*]. You must tell him, Ned! . . . For my sake! Because I love you! Because you remember us! You must tell Sam!

DARRELL [*Beaten—dazedly*]. Must I—Nina?

NINA [*Insistent*]. Yes, you must!

DARRELL [*Same*]. Must what? What must I do? Meddle again?

[*Door opens, off*]

MARSDEN [*Off, singing drunkenly*].

> Then he would row, row, row,
> Way up the river he would—

[*Calling*] How about a drink, Darrell?

DARRELL [*Filter*]. Marsden! Thank goodness!

[*Calling*] Come on over here, Charlie, and sit down! [*Filter*] He's drunk! Good old Charlie . . . he saved me . . . from her! . . . I must get this over quickly! . . .

[*Triumphantly*] No, Nina—sorry—but I can't help you. I told you I'd never meddle again with human lives! I mean that with all my heart.

NINA [*Dully*]. Very well, Ned. [*Filter . . . With dull fatalism*] I've lost him . . . he'll never tell Sam now . . . oh, dear God, help me to get back my son! . . . I must find some way . . .

[*Footsteps approach during the above*]

MARSDEN [*With drunken wisdom*]. Hello, you two! Why do you both look so guilty? Never mind! [*Singing*] "Then he would row, row, row,—"

DARRELL [*Excitedly*]. Look! There are oars flashing in the water way up there! They're coming! I'll tell Sam!

[*Running footsteps receding*]

NINA [*A cry*]. Ned, don't go—

[*Door slams shut, off*]

NINA [*Filter . . . Dully*]. What did he say? . . . he'll tell Sam! . . . he'll tell . . . no, he doesn't mean that . . . I must find some other way . . .

MARSDEN. Now, Nina, don't worry your pretty head! It will all come out all right! We'll only have a little while longer to wait, and then you and I'll be quietly married! [*Filter . . . Frightened*] The devil! . . . what am I saying! . . . I'm drunk! . . . all right, all the better! I've wanted all my life to tell her!

Of course, Nina, I realize you've got a husband at present, but, never mind, I can wait. I've waited a lifetime already . . .

[*Door opens—running footsteps approach*]

MADELINE [*Excited*]. They're coming! Over here, Mr. Evans, you can see them!

EVANS [*Excited*]. Give me those binoculars . . . yes, I see them! . . . [*Pounding on rail, yelling*] Come on, Gordon, boy!

MADELINE [*Shouting*]. Come on, Gordon! . . . Can you see from there, Mrs. Evans? Wouldn't you like to come up here and—

NINA. No, thank you. [*Filter*] How I hate her! . . . I must think of something! *Something*! [*With cold calculation*] Why not tell her? . . . as Sam's mother told me? . . . of the insanity? . . . after all, she does think Gordon is Sam's son! . . . [*Triumphantly*] That will be poetic justice! . . . that will solve everything! . . . she won't marry Gordon! . . . Gordon will turn to me for comfort! . . . but I must plan it out carefully! . . .

[*Intermittant boat whistles, voices shouting*]

EVANS [*Shouting*]. Who's ahead? Confound it, I can't tell! Can you see, Nina?

NINA. No, dear. [*Filter . . . Triumphantly*] I can tell Madeline . . . confidentially . . . I can pretend I am forced to tell her . . . as Sam's mother did with me . . . because I feel it's due to her happiness and Gordon's . . . it will explain my objection to the engagement . . . Oh, it can't help succeeding! . . . My son will come back! . . . I'll see he never gets away again! . . .

[*Calling*] Madeline!

EVANS [*Excited*]. Navy is ahead!—half a length!—Come on, Gordon!

NINA [*Over the receding footsteps*]. Madeline!

DARRELL. Mrs. Evans is calling you, Madeline. [*Filter*] Why is she calling

Madeline? . . . I've got to watch Nina . . . I've got to watch her carefully . . .

MADELINE [*Slightly off*]. Yes, Mrs. Evans?

NINA. Come here a moment, dear. I want to talk to you.

MADELINE [*Impatiently, off*]. But they're getting closer! Why don't you come over to the rail and watch?

NINA. There's something I must tell you.

MADELINE [*In hopeless irritation, off*]. But—oh, all right . . . Excuse me, Dr. Darrell . . .

DARRELL. Certainly, my dear.

MADELINE [*On mike*]. Yes, Mrs. Evans?

NINA [*Impressively*]. Madeline, you must first give me your word of honor that you'll never reveal a word of what I'm going to tell you to a living soul—above all, not to Gordon!

MADELINE. Couldn't you tell me later, Mrs. Evans—after the race?

NINA. No, now! Do you promise?

MADELINE. Yes, Mrs. Evans.

NINA [*Sternly*]. For the sake of your future happiness, and my son's, I've got to speak! Madeline, you can't·marry Gordon! I speak as your friend!

MADELINE [*Panic-stricken*]. But why—why?

NINA. Why? I'll tell you why! I'll tell you exactly—

DARRELL [*Calling*]. No, Nina—

NINA [*Implacably*]. Madeline, I've something to tell you that will make it clear to you why you and Gordon can never—

DARRELL [*Sharply, fading in*]. I said no, Nina . . . [*Calmly*] Madeline, as a doctor I feel it my duty to tell you that Mrs. Evans isn't herself. Pay no attention to anything she may say to you. She's very nervous and upset just now. She is also morbidly jealous of you and subject to queer delusions!

NINA. How dare you, Ned?

DARRELL [*Kindly*]. So, go ahead, get back to your post on the rail and watch the race!

MADELINE [*Gratefully*]. Thank you, Dr. Darrell. I understand, I think. Poor Mrs. Evans!

NINA [*Accusingly*]. Ned! Why did you—?

DARRELL [*Calmly*]. I'm sorry, Nina, but I warned you not to meddle. [*Affectionately*] And Gordon is, well—sort of my stepson, isn't he? And I want to see him happy.

EVANS [*Wildly*]. They're coming! Can you see them, Madeline? Can you tell which is—

MADELINE [*Excited*]. No—not yet—they all look even from here! Oh, dear, this is awful! Come on, Gordon!

DARRELL [*Excited*]. The one in the middle seems to be ahead. Sam, is that Gordon?

EVANS [*Wildly excited*]. No, it's Navy! Come on, Gordon! Put your back into it! Sprint! Look, Gordon's drawing up on Navy!

MADELINE. Here they come! Here they come! They're both sprinting! I can see Gordon!

[*Noise of crowd increases*]

EVANS [*Yelling*]. Come on, son! Lift her out of the water! Stroke! Stroke! He's gaining! Now! Stroke! You're near the finish! Stroke! Str-r- [*A loud moan and the sound of a body dropping to the floor . . . Madeline screams*]

NINA [*Screaming*]. Sam! Sam!

MADELINE. Oh! Oh! Mrs. Evans—he—he—fainted.

NINA. Ned! It's Sam! What happened—?

DARRELL [*Working over him*]. Just a minute . . . Look's like a bad stroke. . . . He's alive, though! Give me a hand with him, Charlie, we've got to get him into the—

[*Suddenly bedlam breaks loose as the race is over . . . We hear the sound of boat whistles, train whistles, horns, sirens, and the roar of thousands of voices . . . A pause as this registers, then*]

MARSDEN [*Soberly*]. The race is over. Gordon won.

[*Music*]

MARSDEN. Sam Evans died a few months later. After the funeral, we all returned to the Evans home on Long Island. As I wandered through the corridors of the silent, empty house, I noticed Gordon and Madeline out on the terrace, talking . . . [*Fades*]

MADELINE [*Tenderly*]. There, dear! I know how horribly hard it is for you. I loved him, too. Your father was always so wonderful and sweet to me!

GORDON [*His voice trembling*]. I didn't realize he was gone—until out there at the cemetery—[*His voice breaks*]

MADELINE. Gordon! Darling! Please don't!

GORDON [*Rebelliously*]. Why? I still don't see why he had to die! . . . It was that constant grind at the office! I couldn't watch him! [*Bitterly*] But I can't see why Mother didn't!

MADELINE [*Reprovingly*]. Now! You mustn't start feeling bitter toward her.

GORDON [*Contritely*]. I know I shouldn't—but—

MADELINE. Since he was taken sick, she's been with him every minute. I never saw such devotion.

GORDON [*Proudly*]. Yes, she sure was wonderful to him all right! . . . But—this may sound rotten of me—I always had a queer feeling she was doing it as a duty . . . [*As if from some inner compulsion*] . . . Madeline, I've never told you this, but I've always felt, ever since I was a little kid, that she didn't really love Dad. She liked him, and respected him. She was a wonderful wife. But, I'm sure she didn't love him. [*Blurting it out*] I'll tell you, Madeline! I've always felt she cared a lot for—Darrell! [*Hastily*] Of course, I might be wrong! [*Bursting out*] No, I'm not wrong! I felt it too strongly, ever since I was a kid. And then when I was eleven—something happened. I've been sure of it since then.

[*Footsteps approach*]

MARSDEN. Sorry to disturb you two young people.

GORDON. That's all right, Uncle Charlie.

MARSDEN. I've been picking some roses for your mother, Gordon . . . Here you are, Madeline, a rose for you. Hail, Love! We who have died, salute you!

MADELINE. Thank you, Uncle Charlie.

GORDON. Where's Mother—still in the house?

MARSDEN. Yes. I'm going in now. Shall I tell her you want to see her?

GORDON. Please. And ask Darrell to come out with her.

[*Footsteps recede*]

MADELINE [*Sotto voce—over the footsteps*]. I'll go down to the plane and wait for you, dear. You want to fly back before dark, don't you?

GORDON. Yes.

MADELINE. Good-bye for a while, darling. Don't be too long. [*Fading . . . Footsteps recede*]

GORDON. I won't . . . [*Filter*] Madeline's wonderful! . . . I surely don't deserve my luck! . . . [*Pause*] . . . It seems rotten and selfish to be happy ... when Dad ... it's funny how I got to care more for Dad than for Mother ... I suppose it was finding out she loved Darrell ... I can remember that day seeing her kiss him ...

[*Footsteps approach*]

GORDON [*Filter*]. Here they come—Mother and Darrell ... funny! ... I can't stand it even now! ... when I see him with Mother! ... I'd like to beat him up! ...

Mother, I asked you to come out here because there are certain things connected with Dad's will I thought I ought to—[*With satisfied superiority*] I don't believe Dad told you about his will, did he, Mother?

NINA [*Indifferently*]. No.

GORDON. Well, the whole estate goes to you and me, of course. [*Somewhat resentfully*] But there is one provision that is peculiar, to say the least. It concerns you, Dr. Darrell—a half-million for your Experimental Station to be used in biological research work.

DARRELL [*Angrily*]. What's that? You're not serious! ... I won't accept it—and that's final!

GORDON [*Coldly*]. It's not left to you, but to the Station. If you won't carry on, I suppose whoever is in *real* charge down there will be only too glad to accept it.

DARRELL [*Stupefied*]. That means my assistant—Preston! But Sam didn't even know him! ... No! Preston is none of his business! I'll advise him to refuse it! [*Filter ... Torturedly*] But it's for science! ... I have no right to refuse! ... blast Sam! ... wasn't it enough for him to own the woman I love and our son, in his lifetime? ... now in death, he reaches out to steal Preston! ... to steal my work! ...

NINA [*Sympathetically*]. It isn't for you, Ned—nor for Preston. It's for science. You must look at it that way.

GORDON [*Sneering*]. You'd better accept. Half millions aren't being thrown away for nothing every day!

NINA [*Sharply*]. All right, Gordon! I think you've said enough!

GORDON [*Trying to control himself*]. I haven't said all I'm going to say, Mother!

NINA. Gordon! Don't! [*Slight pause*].

DARRELL. Well, what have you got to say? Your Mother and I are waiting.

GORDON [*Furiously*]. Shut up, you! Don't take that tone with me, or I'll forget your age—and give you a spanking!

NINA. Gordon! [*Filter*] Spanking! . . . the son spanks the father! . . . [*Laughing hysterically*] Oh, Gordon, don't make me laugh! It's all so funny!

DARRELL [*Solicitously*]. Nina! Don't mind him! He doesn't realize—

GORDON [*Losing control*]. Don't I? I realize a lot! I realize you've acted like a cur! And here's something—I've been meaning to do since—the day I was eleven years old!

[*A slap is heard . . . Nina screams*]

NINA [*Piteously—hysterically*]. Stop! Gordon! What would your father say? You don't know what you're doing! You're hitting your father!

DARRELL [*Chokingly*]. No—it's all right, Son—all right—you didn't know—

GORDON [*Overcome by remorse*]. I'm sorry—sorry—You're right, Mother—Dad would feel as if I'd hit him—just as bad as if I'd hit him!

DARRELL. It's nothing, Son—nothing!

GORDON [*Brokenly*]. That's swell of you, Darrell. It was a rotten, dirty trick! Accept my apology, Darrell, won't you?

DARRELL. Sure . . . sure, Son. [*Filter . . . Stupidly*] Darrell? . . . he calls me Darrell! . . . but doesn't he know? . . . I thought she told him! . . .

NINA. Gordon, how could you— [*Filter . . . Laughing hysterically*] I told him he hit his father . . . but he can't understand me! . . . why, of course he can't! . . . how could he? . . . after all these years! . . .

GORDON [*Soothing*]. Mother! Stop laughing! Please! It's all right—all right between Darrell and me! I've apologized! [*Nina grows calmer*] I just want you to know how fine I think you've both acted. I've known ever since I was a kid that you and Darrell were in love with each other. I hated the idea on Father's account—that's only natural, isn't it?—but I knew it was unfair, that people can't help loving each other any more than . . . [*Breaking down*] I've got to say good-bye, Mother! Good-bye, Darrell! I hope you two will get married right away!

DARRELL. Wait, Gordon . . . [*Filter . . . Suffering*] Why does he keep on calling me Darrell? . . . he's my boy . . . I'm his father! . . . I've got to make him realize I'm his father! . . .

Listen, Gordon—Son . . . It's my turn now. I've got to tell you something—

NINA. Ned! [*Filter . . . Torturedly*] Oh, he mustn't! . . . I feel he mustn't! . . . he mustn't tell! . . . not now!

[*Sharply*] Ned! Please! First, let me ask Gordon a question!

GORDON. Yes, Mother, what is it?

NINA [*Slowly and impressively*]. Gordon, do you think Ned and I—that is, that we ever—

GORDON [*Shocked and horrified*]. Mother, what do you think I am! I know that you're the best woman that ever lived—the best of all! I don't even except Madeline!

NINA [*With a sobbing triumphant cry*]. My dear Gordon! You do love me, don't you?

GORDON [*Brokenly*]. Of course, Mother! I've always loved you.

NINA [*Tenderly*]. And now, go! Hurry! Madeline is waiting! Give her my love! And come to see me once in a while in the years to come! Good-bye, dear! . . . [*Imploringly*] Ned, do you still want to tell Gordon something?

DARRELL. No, Nina. Not for anything in the world. Good-bye, Son.

GORDON. Good-bye, Uncle Ned.

[*Footsteps recede . . . Door closes . . . A pause*]

NINA [*Gratefully*]. Poor, dear Ned, you've always had to give! How can I ever thank you?

DARRELL [*Ironically—Jokingly*]. By refusing me when I ask you to marry me! I've got to ask you. Gordon expects it! And he'll be so pleased when he knows you turned me down.

[*Footsteps approach*]

DARRELL. Hello, here comes Charlie. I must hurry. Nina, will you marry me?

NINA [*Sadly*]. No. Certainly not. Our ghosts would torture us to death! [*Forlornly*] But I wish I did love you, Ned!—I wish you loved me!—as we did a long time ago!

DARRELL [*Tenderly*]. That's the Ned to remember, Nina! Forget me! I'm going back to work. [*He laughs softly and sadly*] I leave you to Charlie. You'd better marry him, Nina—if you want peace. He's been waiting a long time.

MARSDEN [*Fading in*]. Do I hear my name taken in vain?

NINA. Dear old Charlie! Come here! [*Filter . . . With a strange yearning*] Peace! . . . yes . . . that is all I desire now . . . Charlie has found peace . . . he will be tender . . . as my father was when I was a girl . . .

Ned has just proposed to me, Charlie. I refused him. I don't love him any more.

MARSDEN. I suspected as much. Then whom do you love, Nina?

NINA [*Sadly*]. You, Charlie, I suppose. I have always loved your love for me. [*Wistfully*] It brings me peace.

MARSDEN [*Strongly*]. All my life I've waited to bring you peace, Nina.

NINA. I know . . . Do you want me to marry you, Charlie?

MARSDEN [*Humbly*]. Yes, Nina. I do.

DARRELL [*Amused*]. Bless you, my children! Bless you and—

[*His voice is drowned out by the drone of an approaching airplane . . . the drone grows louder*]

NINA. That's Gordon! . . . up there in his plane! . . . [*With anguish*] Gordon! [*Shouting*] Good-bye, dear! . . . [*Bitterly*] See, Ned! He's leaving me without a backward look!

DARRELL [*Joyfully*]. No. He's circling! He's coming back! [*The drone is very loud now as the plane is directly overhead*] He is going to pass directly over us! . . . See! He's waving to us!

NINA [*Frantically*]. Good-bye, Gordon! My dear son!

DARRELL [*With a last protest*]. Nina! Are you forgetting? He's my son too! [*Shouting up at the sky*] You're my son, Gordon! You're my son! [*Stops abruptly*] It's no use. He can't hear. He can't—

NINA [*With tortured exultance*]. Good-bye, Gordon! Fly up to heaven, dear. Fly with your love to heaven. Fly always! Never crash to earth like my old love, Gordon! Be happy, dear! *You've got to be happy!*

[*As the droning of the plane fades . . .*]

[*Music*]

ANNOUNCER

CREDITS

THE GUARDSMAN

Original Play
by Ferenc Molnar

Radio Adaptation
by Arthur Miller

CAST

FRANZ and THE GUARDSMAN	Alfred Lunt
MARIE	Lynn Fontanne
BERNHARDT	Everett Clark
MAMA	Viola Barwick
MAID	Geraldine Kay
COLLECTOR	Ray Suber
PEANUT VENDOR	Ray Suber

THE GUARDSMAN

Radio adaptation by

ARTHUR MILLER

I AM SURE that Alfred Lunt and Lynn Fontanne will never forgive me for what I did to this play. I remember watching them as they read before the microphone at the first rehearsal. A scene would go along as it was written in the original, and suddenly they would stop and glare at the script as though a louse had crawled over it. A new series of lines! A whole new scene! It was only after they had both grown rather exhausted that the very troubled look vanished from their faces. For you just don't fool around with a play like "The Guardsman," especially when the two people who stamped every line with their personalities are going to play it again, very much altered.

But it had to be changed because, as with every stage play transferred to the blind eye of radio, that half of the comic or dramatic effect which depends upon the audience's view of facial expression, physical movement, and sheer stagecraft, is lopped off automatically. And there is only one thing to put in its place—story. The Lunts did not take to that because their astonishing talent flourishes in the expression of nuance, pause, and the finest re-creation of life's ineffable details. When you have to be making story points every foot of the way those delicate effects tend to flatten out. Lesser artists would have settled for the story alone, but through the hardest work I have ever seen before the microphone, they managed to breathe into this replica much of the rhythm and personal excitement they gave the original on the stage.

As a job of work for me this was a beast. For the same reason, the play really demands that it never leave its single apartment set, and its moment at the opera. I suppose that is because Mr. Molnar's concept was so unified that he left very little to happen off stage that was more exciting than the events on the stage. Every reference in the play to something outside is rather carefully calculated to increase interest in what is happening at the footlights. Every strand of the story converges, at their points of interest, upon the area of the stage. This, of course, is as it should be in the theatre. But in radio, where an uninterrupted four-minute scene is eternity, that unity is something to be re-created on a wider physical base. Hence, the scene in the park, and the interruptions of the vendor, and so on.

More than any other this play illustrates the similarity of radio to motion-picture technique. In both, the story must never be lost sight of; in both, movement for its own sake is absolutely necessary; in both, economy of language is at a premium. Maybe the reason is that to compensate for the normal, intimate contact between actor and audience in the theatre, all these more superficial means of arousing interest must be used. With all its difficulties, however, this play had one great advantage from the point of view of an adapter: the scenes were mostly between two people. And that is always the best radio; or rather, second best. One person talking is better.

THE GUARDSMAN

ANNOUNCER

INTRODUCTION FOR THE THEATRE GUILD

[*Show music*]

ACT I

[*Music: Background*]

NARRATOR. In Vienna, once, there were two very famous stars. One was a man named Franz, and the other was a lady named Marie. And at the height of their fame they were married. And they lived, or tried to, in a sensible way. They had a maid named Liesl and a kind of housekeeper who was known all over Vienna as Mama, and a piano. Then Spring came. As our play begins Mama and Liesl were on their knees on one side of the living room packing costumes into a trunk, while on the other side, near the piano, the famous actor and [*Music: Sneak Chopin on piano*] his famous wife were conversing privately, while she played Chopin with dreams in her eyes.

[*Music: Piano*]

FRANZ. I asked you, Marie. Please don't play the piano. I am going away. Please stop playing.

MARIE. I thought you liked Chopin.

FRANZ. A wife does not play romantic music when her husband is going away.

MAMA [*Off mike*]. Are you sure you don't want the Princivalli costumes?

FRANZ. No, Mama, I don't want the Princivalli costumes, Mama.

MAMA. No, you're not going to play "Monna Vanna"?

FRANZ. I am not going to play "Monna Vanna." I have not done that show in three years. Therefore I do not take the costumes.

MAMA. All right . . . all right . . . all right!

MARIE. All right, all right! Will you two ever stop quarreling?

FRANZ. Every time I go on tour this same thing happens. Mama knows I don't play "Monna Vanna" but she pretends to be a driveling idiot just to make me nervous.

MAMA. Well, why don't you hit me? Go on, hit me!

MARIE. *Oh, Mama . . .* Mama!

FRANZ. Why does she tell me to hit her, Marie? Why does everyone try to make me more nervous than I am? Will you stop playing Chopin!

[*Doorbell*]

FRANZ. Now, what? [*Door opening*] Oh, Bernhardt. Come in, old man.

BERNHARDT. I hope I'm not interrupting anything important.

FRANZ. Just the usual argument.

MAMA. All I did was ask him if he wanted Princivalli costumes in the trunk.

[*Music: Piano stop*]

MARIE. Mama, will you listen to me? If you don't be quiet I'll throw you out.

MAMA [*Sadly*]. Do you hear that, Bernhardt? A nice way to talk to a mother. You're a critic. Is this justice?

BERNHARDT. It seems to me, Mama, that after nine years of being Marie's Mama you would be used to it by now.

MARIE. I give her twenty gulden a month for cooking. I give her seven for being Mama. You'd think a woman would appreciate . . .

FRANZ. Liesl, get my bags. Mama, close the trunk.

MAMA. The way he . . . !

FRANZ. Shut up! Sit down, Bernhardt. At least you can be comfortable.

BERNHARDT. How long is this engagement for, Franz?

FRANZ. Three nights. I play "Romeo," "Hamlet," and "Fire in the Opera House."

MARIE. Then you'll be home again by Friday?

FRANZ. Yes, dear. Friday.

MARIE. You're nervous.

FRANZ. I am nervous.

MARIE. Oh dear, you are just a little—unendurable.

FRANZ. I am just a little—unendurable.

MARIE. In that case it's wisest to leave you entirely alone.

FRANZ. It's wisest to leave me entirely alone.

BERNHARDT. Children, children!

MARIE. So it goes, Bernhardt.

BERNHARDT. What would your dear public think of this? Come now.

MARIE. In the theatre the playwright tells me what to say to my husband. At home I decide what he deserves from me.

FRANZ. That's the way she talks to me, Bernhardt.

MARIE. Yes, yes.

FRANZ. Day in, day out. Married six months—and we've come to this. Six months, Bernhardt!

BERNHARDT. I don't know. I haven't left her side for eight years and she's sweeter to me than ever.

FRANZ. It's easy for you—she doesn't love *you*—

MARIE. Oh, well—if you're talking of love—

FRANZ. I know, I know. You don't love me!

MARIE. Here he goes again.

FRANZ. Say it, sweetheart—you haven't said it today yet. Tell me that you no longer love me—keep on saying it—let me get used to it. I knew your love was not the kind to last very long, but I confess I scarcely looked for the end before September. This is only May, my dear. I had counted at least on June, July and even, possibly, August.

MARIE. May—Look at the buds outside. Oh how pretty!

BERNHARDT. Beautiful spring. Beautiful May.

FRANZ. You needn't encourage her, if you don't mind.

MARIE. It's a terribly beautiful month.

FRANZ. Why do you pretend to be crying?

MARIE. It's a feeling that comes over me sometimes. When the flowers bloom.

FRANZ. I see. The flowers. You have rose fever.

MARIE. I do not have rose fever.

FRANZ. Indeed not. I know what you're crying about—I know.

MARIE. If you know—why do you ask?

FRANZ. Let us separate then—let us get a divorce—let us confess honestly that this is the end.

MARIE. Stop walking up and down in front of me.

FRANZ. You go one way, I'll go another. That will be better than these everlasting lies, these hidden tears, these threatening [*Music: Chopin on piano*] eyes, this sulking in your corner, this—this Chopin music— this— Will you do me a great favor?

MARIE. What is it, dear?

FRANZ. Don't play Chopin.

MARIE. Why not?

FRANZ. Because Chopin is not meant for me.

MARIE. For whom then?

FRANZ. Chopin puts women in a mood—of romance—of longing, of desire of—of—in short, all the things that a decent married woman should not be thinking about. And I do not mean flowers.

[*Music: A harsh bang on the keys*]

MARIE. Oh, very well! Then I must not even do that now!

BERNHARDT. You'll make her cry again, Franz.

FRANZ. Nonsense. She's happy now. A martyr, a suffering angel—aren't you, you poor thing?

MARIE. If you knew how little I'm suffering you wouldn't be in such good spirits.

[*Door*]

LIESL [*Off mike*]. Excuse me, Ma'am, these came for you.

MARIE. Oh, what beautiful flowers! Was there any message?

LIESL. No, Ma'am.

BERNHARDT. Who could have sent them?

FRANZ. I don't ask questions any more, Bernhardt. She gets flowers all the time. This isn't the first by any means—Oh, no, my dear friend! Marie, darling . . . what is that you just took off that rose?

MARIE. What is what?

FRANZ. The envelope you found containing your admirer's card, with the declaration of his love. Give me that envelope!

MARIE. There was no envelope in the flowers.

FRANZ. There was. Give it to me at once.

MARIE. I will *not*.

FRANZ. I command you to give it to me.

BERNHARDT. Now Franz . . .

FRANZ. I want to know who the man is who expresses his admiration in red roses. This is the tenth bouquet at least—admiration has its limits!

MARIE. I will not give it to you.

FRANZ. Bernhardt, see her eyes flash! Look at her! She thinks she'll get out of it that way. I command you to give me that letter! Don't walk away from me, Marie!

MARIE. You are right. There was a letter. But I will not give it to you. Yes,

I know what name is on that card—but I will not tell it to you. Yes, the man who sent those flowers does admire me, does appreciate me, does love me, but I will not give you the letter. Now then.

[*Choppy heels on floor. Door slamming*]

FRANZ. Bernhardt . . . Spring has come!
BERNHARDT. Yes, Franz. Let's take a walk in the park.

[*Music: Up springy and down into*]

[*Birds in background . . . Footsteps at a stroll*]

BERNHARDT. I think the man who invented parks must have had trouble with his wife. You look calmer already, Franz.
FRANZ. It's merely exhaustion, my friend. Think of it married six months —turn around quick.

[*Fast walking*]

BERNHARDT. What's the matter? Where . . . ?
FRANZ. Keep walking, don't stop.
BERNHARDT. What's happened?
FRANZ. Nothing yet. Just walk.
CREDITOR [*Off mike*]. Just a minute! Please! Please!

[*All walking stops*]

FRANZ. Oh ho! Good to see you, old man. What can I do for you?
CREDITOR. What can he do for me? You know, sir, I hate to disturb a great artist like yourself, but I just happened to notice you, and—if you could let me have just a little bit on account. The whole day I've been calling on actors, and my boss is in a temper. The whole thing is only four hundred and sixty kronen. After all, sir, we can't make shirts if we don't get paid.
FRANZ [*Clears his throat*]. Would you like to see "Midsummer Night's Dream" tomorrow evening.
CREDITOR. I saw "Midsummer Night's Dream." You were elegant in that.
FRANZ. Yes, yes, I was rather good. "Salome" is playing the night after.
CREDITOR [*Weakening*]. "Salome?"
FRANZ. "Salome." Including the dance.
CREDITOR. Including the dance I would like to see "Salome."
FRANZ. Here's a pass for two. Next time allow the bill to reach a thousand kronen and you will get *four* seats.

CREDITOR. Thank you, sir. Good day to you. Good day.

FRANZ. Two seats for "Salome" and his bill goes up in smoke. Two seats for "Salome" and he is my slave. How powerful we are with those who matter to us least.

BERNHARDT. Here's a bench. Sit down.

FRANZ. Bernhardt, my life is at a crossroad.

BERNHARDT. I'm surprised at you, Franz. If you really must find out who sent the flowers, there are a thousand ways to do it without treating your wife like that. You know her—she'd rather cut her head off than tell you who sent them. The simplest way is to go and ask the florist.

FRANZ. Why should I ask him?

[*Peanut whistle approaching*]

BERNHARDT. You want to know who sent them, don't you?

VENDOR. Peanuts?

FRANZ. No peanuts.

[*Peanut whistle fading*]

BERNHARDT. Well if you know who . . .

FRANZ [*Continuing*]. I know who sent the flowers.

BERNHARDT. You know?

FRANZ. Of course I know!

BERNHARDT. Very well, then—who sent them?

FRANZ. I did.

BERNHARDT. What? You? *You* sent them?

FRANZ. Exactly. I sent them.

BERNHARDT. Are you crazy?

FRANZ. I am.

BERNHARDT. Well, I'll be hanged! [*In a change of tone*] You sent the roses? *Your* name is on the card?

FRANZ. No, it is not.

BERNHARDT. Whose is then?

FRANZ. I can't keep it to myself any longer. I've got to tell someone. Listen!

BERNHARDT. What's the trouble?

FRANZ. You know what Marie—that is, before we were married, she—

[*Peanut whistle approaching*]

BERNHARDT. I know—I mean I suspect at least.

FRANZ. Why should we be ashamed to speak of it? A man can't expect to find a wife—She had many admirers—very many. If I should count merely those I know personally—Hartung, Zellenberg, Krauss . . .

VENDOR. Peanuts?

FRANZ. No peanuts!

[*Whistle fading as*]

BERNHARDT. I made the inventory long ago, Franz. There were seven.

FRANZ. Not counting me?

BERNHARDT. Without you.

FRANZ. Pardon me! There were nine.

BERNHARDT. Seven!

FRANZ. There were nine. I cannot allow anyone to cast aspersions upon my wife—there were nine.

BERNHARDT. Make it nine then. The only thing we can be sure of is that I wasn't one of them.

FRANZ. I'm sorry, old man, but don't weep over it now. The point is, this is May, and when May comes that cool and apparently calm little woman is all aflame inside. New pastures beckon to her. In a word, I'm in for the same fate as all the others. The marriage ceremony was all in vain—he is coming—I hear his footsteps—coming nearer and nearer.

BERNHARDT. Whose footsteps?

FRANZ. The tenth. The eighth—anyway, the new man. I feel he is coming, he is coming as surely as spring.

BERNHARDT. Who?

FRANZ. That's the point. Who? What kind of man. We've talked it over calmly, very calmly.

BERNHARDT. Indeed.

FRANZ. She's explained it to me by the hour. Bernhardt, my wife is longing for a soldier.

BERNHARDT. Oh, come. A soldier.

FRANZ. I don't mean the ordinary Hussar type . . . Something different, Bernhardt, something foreign. He lives in her imagination. She told me. And she weeps that such men do not exist nowadays.

BERNHARDT. Weeps.

FRANZ. But I've thought it over, and such men do exist.

BERNHARDT. Where?

FRANZ. Did you ever notice one of those mysterious Guardsmen attached to the Russian Embassy? What if she should meet a man like that?

BERNHARDT. Well, what of it?

FRANZ. It would mean the end of me, of course; in my place would stand this nobody whom I could impersonate on the stage any minute. But if it's a Guardsman she wants she shall have him, she shall have him, Bernhardt.

BERNHARDT. You've decided, so to speak, to meet him halfway.

FRANZ. I have decided to meet him the whole way, Bernhardt. I will be that man myself; I will be the Guardsman.

BERNHARDT. What?

FRANZ. How many times in your own column have you said—a hundred different personalities live in one actor's soul? Very well, then, why shouldn't this Guardsman live within my soul? Either I am a good actor or I am not. This will be the supreme test.

BERNHARDT. Do you mean to tell me that you intend to act a part for your wife?

FRANZ. I have already begun. I have experimented with the costume, the makeup, the voice, step, carriage, and gesture. She will never recognize me.

BERNHARDT. Then what?

FRANZ. Then? Either she will yield or she will not yield. If she does not, I'll know once and for all that she is true to me. If she does yield, I will be very unhappy . . . but at least I will know. Anyway, I will have had one [*Peanut whistle*] sincere kiss from her.

BERNHARDT. I'm sure she'll recognize you, Franz.

FRANZ. She won't. I've already tested her. Last Tuesday I walked beneath her window.

BERNHARDT. In uniform?

FRANZ. In the long cloak, the tall fur hat, the beard and boots of a Russian Guardsman.

VENDOR. Peanuts?

FRANZ. No Peanuts!! She saw me from the window.

BERNHARDT. And?

FRANZ. Well, Bernhardt . . . she smiled.

BERNHARDT. Actually.

FRANZ. Actually. I sent her flowers with a card—I even have cards printed —Wassily Samsonov, that's my name. She brought the flowers home from the theatre. I made a terrible scene just as I did a few minutes ago. And you know, that little cat looked me straight in the eye and said they had been sent to the stagedoor by some silly girl.

BERNHARDT. Ts, ts!

FRANZ. Every day since, I've sent her flowers but she never brings them home any more. Then a letter came.

BERNHARDT. A letter?

FRANZ. From me. Asking if she had any objections to meeting me personally. The Guardsman.

BERNHARDT. Had she?

FRANZ. Here . . . look at this note. I keep it with me always. This is my wife's answer to the Russian Guardsman. Read it, friend.

BERNHARDT. "I have no objection."

FRANZ. I have no objection

BERNHARDT. Well, good Lord, what are you going to do?

FRANZ. I've done it. Last week I wired the manager of the theatre in Olmutz that I was available for three evenings.

BERNHARDT. Yes, you're leaving for Olmutz tonight.

FRANZ. Not precisely. Yesterday I sent my wife this letter. This is a copy. She's got the original hidden in the piano. Let me read it.

BERNHARDT. This is from the Guardsman.

FRANZ. Correct. The Guardsman. After she said she had no objections. Listen "Dear Madam. Great and revered artist. I see by the newspapers that your husband is to be away in Olmutz for several evenings. If nothing happens to prevent, would you have the great kindness to appear in your window at six o'clock tomorrow afternoon?" That's today. In about five minutes. "I will be watching from a cab near by. If you will pull back the curtain and look down into the street, I will pay my respects to you a half hour later in your own home, and I will be the happiest of men. I beg the honor of calling on the lady whose theatrical genius is your country's chief pride. Most respectfully, your humble Servant, Wassily Samsonov."

BERNHARDT. What about your engagement in Olmutz?

FRANZ. Called it off this morning. Come, let's get back to the house.

[*Walking*]

BERNHARDT. If you're not going to Olmutz why did you pack?

FRANZ. I am going to take my baggage, leave the house, go around the corner and drop it all at my tailor's. As far as she knows I am on the train to Olmutz.

BERNHARDT. Then?

FRANZ. Then I return to my own home in the first really great and serious part I have ever played in all my life. Hurry. It's almost six.

BERNHARDT. Franz . . . Franz . . . you're playing with fire!

FRANZ. Then at least let me warm my hands on the blaze. Come on, we'll run!

[*Music: Up and down and into*]

[*Piano playing Chopin*]

MARIE. Mama? [*Calls*] Mama, come in here!

[*Piano for a moment*]

MAMA. Oh, you look beautiful, Bebi—I was just washing the windows.

MARIE. What windows?

MAMA. In my room. I never get a good look at his face because my windows were dirty.

MARIE. My watch seems slow. What time is it?

MAMA. I've got three minutes to six. Oh that gown, Bebi, that . . .

[*Door opening*]

[*Music: Piano stops*]

FRANZ. Chopin, my dear?

MARIE. It's six o'clock, darling. You'll miss your train.

FRANZ. It's only two minutes of. I have plenty of time.

MARIE. Bernhardt, will you get him a cab?

FRANZ. I've arranged for a cab.

MARIE. I'm afraid you'll be late. I'll look at the clock in our room.

[*Walking away*]

FRANZ [*Calling after her*]. Yes, it would be a pity if I missed my train!

BERNHARDT [*Quietly*]. Which window is it, Franz?

FRANZ. The middle one by the piano. She's to draw the curtains apart.

BERNHARDT. What's the matter with you? You look sick.

FRANZ. I am in a cab down there in the street waiting with beating heart, wondering whether she will give me the signal.

BERNHARDT. Oh, come now, you know she won't.

FRANZ. Isn't it six?

BERNHARDT. About half a minute yet. Where's your uniform?

FRANZ. At the tailor's around the corner.

BERNHARDT. Well, don't worry, you won't have to use it. [*Clock chiming six*] See? It's just six now, and she's not anywhere near the window.

FRANZ. Oh, Bernhardt! She's such a true wife! She . . .

BERNHARDT. SSssh! She's coming!

MARIE [*Off mike approaching*]. Well? Where's your cab? It's six o'clock.

FRANZ. That's right, dear. It's six o'clock.

BERNHARDT. Exactly six. My watch has six.

MARIE. Six, yes.

FRANZ [*Happily*]. [*Slight pause*] Well, then, I'm off. Isn't she gorgeous, Bernhardt? Isn't she the most . . . What are you doing, darling?

MARIE [*Off mike*]. Just going to open the curtain. It's very dark in here.

FRANZ. Dark? I don't think it's dark in here at all.

BERNHARDT. Neither do I, frankly.

MARIE. Well, you're going anyway, so what's the difference?

[*Sound of draw-curtain parting*]

MARIE. Now, isn't that much better? I try to save him money on the electric bill and does he appreciate it?

FRANZ. I appreciate everything. Good-bye, sweetheart. Take care of yourself and don't forget me. I am not speaking to you from the window, dear. Please look at me when I am going away.

MARIE [*Absently*]. Yes . . . what is it?

FRANZ [*Ironically*]. I was bidding you good-bye, my wife. I said, "Good-bye, darling, take care . . ."

MARIE. Oh, yes. Good-bye. You haven't forgotten anything?

FRANZ. No, I haven't.

MARIE. Well, good-bye, you can go.

FRANZ. I am going even without your very kind permission.

MARIE. I didn't say it to offend you! What else can I say since you must go? I can't say, "Please don't go."

FRANZ. Indeed you can't. Imagine if I couldn't resist you and stayed?

MARIE [*Disgusted*]. Oh, please.

BERNHARDT. Children!

FRANZ. Then this is your farewell, Marie? All you have to say to me at the last minute?

MARIE. Good heavens! You'll be back in three days. You're not going to Siberia.

FRANZ. The journey to Olmutz may prove just as fatal as the journey to Siberia. What's the use—good-bye.

BERNHARDT. He's right, Marie. You don't even kiss him.

FRANZ. No thanks, Bernhardt. I do not accept kisses that are suggested by a third party.

MARIE. Come here, you fool. Give me a kiss.

FRANZ. I won't!

MARIE. Come here!

FRANZ. No!

MARIE. I *want* to kiss you, you foolish boy.

FRANZ [*Pretending stupidity*]. What. What is it you want?

MARIE. Kiss me.

FRANZ. Just as you like. [*Kisses*] God bless you.

MARIE. Do you call that a kiss?

FRANZ. Oh, for pity's sake!

MARIE. You child, you foolish boy!

FRANZ. You're torturing me!

MARIE [*With passion*]. Kiss me. Darling. [*They kiss*] Oh, Franz . . .

FRANZ [*Almost in tears*]. Sweetheart. Good-bye, good-bye. And all my thoughts be with you in my place.

MARIE. Yes. Don't be late, dear.

FRANZ. I'll rush home.

MARIE. I meant now—for your train.

FRANZ. She kisses me and thinks of time tables!

MARIE. But dear—!

FRANZ [*Imperiously*]. Help me down with my bags, Bernhardt!

MARIE. But Franz, I didn't mean—

FRANZ. Good-bye!

[*Music: Up and down and out*]

FRANZ. How do they get into these boots!

BERNHARDT. Here . . . push now. [*Effort*] There you are. It was very good of the tailor to leave you the key to his shop.

FRANZ. He's a fine fellow. Next week I will pay his bill. Where's my beard?

BERNHARDT. You have it on.

FRANZ. Oh. How do I look?

BERNHARDT. A Russian Guardsman. Let me hear you.

FRANZ [*In heavy Russian accent*]. Nizhny Novgorad bodolsky . . . I must compose my soul.

BERNHARDT. I can't stand it. I'm going back to see what she's doing.

FRANZ [*In his own speech*]. At six-thirty I'll be there. I want to be alone with her.

BERNHARDT. I'll be out by six-thirty.

FRANZ. Tell her I made the train all right.

BERNHARDT. Yes, Franz. [*Nervously*] I'm afraid you're going to regret this, Franz! You don't realize it, you look positively handsome!

[*Music: Up and down and out*]

MARIE [*Calling*]. Liesl! Liesl, come in here! Mama, is the hem in the back straight?

MAMA. Yes, Bebi, straight as an arrow to the heart. Oh, you are beautiful! You are superb, you are magnificent.

MARIE. It's not my fault that I'm beautiful, is it? Is it?

MAMA. Fault! My child, it's a blessing. A woman's got only one life to live, and when it's with her husband—

LIESL. You called me, Ma'am?

MARIE. Liesl, I shall want some tea. In tall glasses. Russian style. And fix yourself up a bit. How do you like my dress, Liesl?

LIESL [*Dutifully*]. It's lovely.

MARIE. What's the matter, Liesl?

LIESL [*Crying*]. Nothing, Ma'am.

[*Steps away . . . Door closing*]

MAMA. She's in love with your husband, Marie, that's what. [*Indignantly*] She ought to be ashamed of herself, having such thoughts in a respectable house like this, before my daughter!

MARIE. You don't like my husband do you, Mama?

MAMA. What do you expect of me? I'm to like the villain who robs me of my daily bread?

MARIE. What?

MAMA. In the old days, when you had so many gentlemen friends I used to chaperon you and see something of the social world. I had a social position. My heart cracks when I think of it.

MARIE. All right, Mama. Control yourself. You shall have your social position back again tonight.

MAMA. What, dearie?

MARIE. Instead of scrubbing the kitchen floor you shall go with me to the opera.

MAMA. Oh, you darling! You're alive again, you breathe again . . .

[*Doorbell*]

MARIE. Who's that? It's only twenty past six. Liesl, answer the door!

MAMA. Maybe he missed his train! I knew you could never trust him!

[*Door opening—Off mike*]

MARIE. Oh, Bernhardt. You're back.

BERNHARDT. Just to tell you that Franz made his train.

MARIE. That's splendid. Did he have to run?

BERNHARDT. No. He had plenty of time to spare.

MAMA. What are you sitting down for?

BERNHARDT. Mama, there is something invincibly distinguished about you, but I'll sit down in your presence anyway.

MAMA. Here's your hat.

BERNHARDT [*Asking*]. Unless you want me to go, Marie?

MARIE. I? Well, as a matter of fact I was about to lie down for a nap.

BERNHARDT. You're nervous, my dear.

MARIE. I? Nervous?

BERNHARDT. If I didn't know you better I might even say you want to get rid of me.

MAMA. Here's your hat!

BERNHARDT. What a charming creature you are, dear golden heart. I'll go when I'm ready.

MARIE. Bernhardt, you are a dear old idiot. [*Kisses him*]

MAMA. Don't misunderstand her when she kisses you. It was the same in my day. When I kissed a man, it meant that I wanted to get rid of him.

BERNHARDT. You are nervous, Marie.

MARIE. I?

BERNHARDT. Your eyes are shining, you are much prettier than you were a half hour ago. What is it, dear? Unless, of course, you're expecting someone.

MARIE. Granted I'm expecting someone, how does that concern you?

BERNHARDT. Not at all. But are you?

MAMA. Your hat is on your lap, should I put it on your head?

MARIE. Please, Mama. Yes, I'm expecting a caller, Bernhardt.

BERNHARDT. Oh. Going to the opera?

MARIE. I don't know. If it should be too late I may not go at all.

BERNHARDT. It's easy enough to get rid of a caller if you don't want him to stay.

MAMA. Yes, it looks like it. Here's your hat!

BERNHARDT. I expect to be at the opera myself, Marie. I'll drop by your box. May I?

MARIE [*Hesitating*]. Oh, yes, do. That'll be awfully nice.

BERNHARDT. I'll be running along then. It's always very nice to see you, Mama.

MAMA. I wish I could say the same.

BERNHARDT. You could if you tried as hard as I do. Good-bye, Marie.

[*Door closing*]

[*Half-hour chime of a clock*]

MARIE. Turn down the lights, Mama. Just leave the one on behind the couch.

[*Music: Chopin on the piano*]

MAMA. I'll leave you now, Bebi.

MARIE. Yes, Mama. Leave me now.

[*Doorbell*]

MAMA. The tea and glasses are on the table by the fireplace.

MARIE. Leave me, Mama.

LIESL [*Off mike*]. A gentleman to see you, Ma'am.

MARIE. Who is it?

LIESL. A general.

MARIE. Show him in.

MAMA. I'll be in my room, Bebi. [*Going*] This is the life! This is the glory of life! [*Fades off*]

[*Music: Just the piano for a moment*]

GUARDSMAN. Prodidje, pojalesta.

[*Music: The piano tinkles to silence . . . not an abrupt halt*]

MARIE [*She turns*]. Delighted. I appreciate the honor.

GUARDSMAN. I am Prince Wassily Samsonov. I kiss your hand.

MARIE. Charmed. Won't you sit down?

GUARDSMAN. I must beg a thousand pardons for seeking your personal acquaintance in this awkward fashion.

MARIE. Not at all. I wrote you I wanted to meet you. You have no need for excuses.

GUARDSMAN. I am terribly happy. I was very afraid.

MARIE. I hope you are gradually recovering. Will you have some tea?

GUARDSMAN. Merci. When I had the pleasure of coming in here you were playing Chopin, n'est-ce pas?

MARIE. Oui.

GUARDSMAN. You speak French so charmingly.

MARIE. De tout, de tout—Do you like Chopin?

GUARDSMAN. Ah, yes. He write so soft, so melancholicky. I see by the paper your distinguished husband is starring in Olmutz tomorrow.

MARIE. Yes. How many lumps?

GUARDSMAN. One.

MARIE. One.

GUARDSMAN. One. I think it is not manly to care for the sweets.

MARIE. My husband takes four lumps.

GUARDSMAN. Even without sugar the lot of the husband is sweet.

MARIE. You emphasize the word "husband" so oddly.

GUARDSMAN. I do not take husbands too seriously. Your husband is not still here, no!

MARIE. No!

GUARDSMAN. No, what I meant was—I regret that I must put in the pocket for the time being the pleasure of meeting your gifted husband. I am really a great admirer of his art.

MARIE. Oh, are you!

GUARDSMAN [*Fervently*]. Oh yes! He impersonates with such genius, such incomparable genius the—the higher life of the soul.

MARIE. Oh, yes! Lemon?

GUARDSMAN. No lemon. But it is easier to be artist with the very charmingly beautiful woman at one's side.

MARIE. You are making love to me already.

GUARDSMAN. May I say—I am happy you have recognized it. Do you regret it?

MARIE. I cannot regret what I cannot control.

GUARDSMAN. Then I may hope for the opposite of regret.

MARIE. Perhaps!

GUARDSMAN. With one little word you have make me happy. Your ear is so beautiful . . .

MARIE. Do you smoke? These are not very good cigarettes. My husband doesn't care for anything better.

GUARDSMAN [*Emphatically*]. These are very good cigarettes. With one little word you have make me very happy—a lonely soldier . . .

MARIE. Don't, don't take what I said so seriously.

GUARDSMAN. You destroy my little hope.

MARIE. I object to the word "hope."

GUARDSMAN. Please do not hurt me so. [*Passionately sad*] Vocnoyu Taspe von. Vocnogu Bosje moy.

MARIE. I beg your pardon. Are you angry with me?

GUARDSMAN. No, no! I had better go. My feelings they may carry me too far.

MARIE. Then this is farewell.

GUARDSMAN. After what I have done, what can it be but farewell?

MARIE. No, no, no! I am going to the opera tonight. Won't you call on me in my box?

GUARDSMAN. Yes, I will take the liberty of calling.

MARIE. We can continue our conversation in the anteroom. It is a little private room right off the box.

GUARDSMAN. My sincere thanks. Especially for the anteroom.

MARIE. I object to your thanks—and the misunderstanding.

GUARDSMAN. I bleed for shame. Vocnogu Bosje moy . . .

MARIE. Oh, no, no . . .

GUARDSMAN. I have insult the most gentle lady . . .

MARIE. I forgive . . .

GUARDSMAN [*She tries to interrupt this speech*]. It is impossible to forgive the beast I make of myself. But I do forgive you; I cannot bear to stand before you again, I . . .

MARIE [*Simply*]. I forgive you.

GUARDSMAN [*Beaten*]. You forgive me.

MARIE. Yes. The box is number 4 on the second tier.

[*Music*]

END OF ACT I

ANNOUNCER

COMMERCIAL

STATION IDENTIFICATION

> [*Ten second wait*]
>
> [*Music theme under*]

ACT II

ANNOUNCER

> [*Music*]

NARRATOR. It is evening in Spring in old Vienna. Marie and her mama have gone to the Opera where the Guardsman has been invited to call In reality the Guardsman is Marie's husband in disguise. The opera is about to begin, the lights dim down, Marie and Mama are settling down in their seats as the first notes of the overture are heard.

> [*Music: Operatic overture which moves into background*]

MAMA. Oh, Bebi, I love to sit in the boxes. You can look down and say anything to your friends in the orchestra and they can't hear you.

MARIE. If you don't behave, Mama, I'll take the price of your ticket off next month's salary.

GUARDSMAN. I beg your pardon, Madame.

MARIE. Excellency! How good of you to come!

GUARDSMAN. Spaziba.

MARIE. May I present, Prince Wassily Samsonov, my Mama?

GUARDSMAN. It is remarkable how much you resemble the mama.

MAMA. Most seem to think she looks more like her father.

GUARDSMAN. You did know her father?

MAMA [*Laughs loudly*]. Upon my word, Prince. Listen to him, Marie!

GUARDSMAN. I am afraid we disturb the audience, Madame. Could we leave Mama to enjoy the music? This way, Madame.

MARIE. Oh, you know the anteroom here.

> [*Music recedes and is shut out*]

GUARDSMAN. The first thing I learn about opera is how to get out. Ah—this is more lonely for us.

MARIE. You are not interested in opera.

GUARDSMAN. In you I am interested infinitely more.

MARIE. Life, life—is so sad. We've known each other only since six o'clock and yet it is already necessary to make certain matters clear.

GUARDSMAN. I am very sorry if there is anything in what I have said . . .

MARIE. No, no. I do not object to your saying nice things to me. I confess I need that as the field needs the rain.

GUARDSMAN. Well—then . . .

MARIE. But you are so revoltingly sure of the outcome.

GUARDSMAN. Pardon.

MARIE. I do not like it! I am a married woman. I have a husband. And I love my husband.

GUARDSMAN. Do you—do you . . .

MARIE. Why does this prosaic confession excite you?

GUARDSMAN. It excites me—it excites me very much. Everything about you excites me. Do you believe I can stand so near you, a woman with so warm blood and so pulsing nerve, and feel respect and esteem only? Is it possible?

MARIE. No, no.

GUARDSMAN. Then—if you think there is some other feeling beside esteem and respect—do you permit me to give it a name?

MARIE. If you give me time to think it over, then I may not allow it.

GUARDSMAN. Well, then I will give you time to think it over.

MARIE. I have thought it over. Yes . . . you may say it.

GUARDSMAN. This other feeling is love. But I respect the fact that you are in love with your husband.

MARIE. I did not say that.

GUARDSMAN. You did say it.

MARIE. No, I did not.

GUARDSMAN. That makes me very happy.

MARIE. It pleases you.

GUARDSMAN. May I—may I speak free?

MARIE. As freely as you like.

GUARDSMAN. Have you ever thought that you might sometime—forget your husband altogether?

MARIE. How dare you! Let go of my hand. Mama!

[*Quick few steps away and door closing*]

GUARDSMAN [*In his own voice*]. [*To himself*] Wonderful . . . wonderful woman!

[*Door opening*]

BERNHARDT. What are you doing on your knees?

GUARDSMAN. Bernhardt! She resisted me! Samsonov!

BERNHARDT. She is true to you.

GUARDSMAN. True. There is no doubt of it. And a woman who can be true to her husband when I am in pursuit will be true always. Oh, what peace of mind, what happiness to see her crush her feelings!

BERNHARDT. Congratulations. Excellent. Then you are sure.

GUARDSMAN. All I want now is to hear her speak those precious words, "leave me forever," then off with my wig and beard, and I will press my little one to me. [*Door*] [*Suddenly changing to his accent*] So then I say to the Czar, your Imperial Majesty . . .

[*Sound: Steps coming toward mike*]

BERNHARDT. Good evening, Marie.

MARIE. Oh, Prince, you've met Dr. Bernhardt?

GUARDSMAN. Just now. I have always read Dr. Bernhardt's writings.

MARIE. Do you know, Prince, why I have come back?

GUARDSMAN. No, why?

MARIE. Because I felt I had been a little too harsh with you.

GUARDSMAN. No, no.

MARIE. What?

GUARDSMAN. Well, maybe so.

MARIE. I should have said to you as calmly, as honestly as I now say it, that I could never, never, never deceive my husband. I beg your pardon for it.

GUARDSMAN. For being true to him.

MARIE. No—for not telling you at once.

GUARDSMAN. So now the time has come—I will make the confession myself. In the presence of this doctor . . . doctor . . .

MARIE. Bernhardt . .

GUARDSMAN. Doctor Bernhardt—with him as witness—I say there is nothing I would not do if you—if you—

MARIE. If I . . . ?

GUARDSMAN. You know what—I would say.

MARIE. I know, I know. But I want to hear you say it.

GUARDSMAN. Hear what? What do you want to hear?

MARIE. That there is no woman in the world—Oh, what do I want to hear? I want to hear you say you love me.

GUARDSMAN. Oh, dear God.

MARIE. Say it. We may never see each other again. Oh, Bernhardt, I'm behaving very badly, aren't I? Look at him, Bernhardt—He is no beauty, but at last—at last a man who is neither intelligent nor brilliant—he comes here and he doesn't know how to behave—but, dear old friend—at last—after all these years—at last a MAN.

BERNHARDT. Yes. Control yourself. Congratulations. I believe I'll take a look at the opera.

[*Footsteps away*]

MARIE. Prince, no man has ever forced me to say the things I have just said to you. I do not know what is happening to me. You do not know what is happening to you.

GUARDSMAN. No, you do not know what is happening to me.

MARIE. What's the matter? You were so ardent, so eager a moment ago and now, now you are afraid.

GUARDSMAN. I am mad. My happiness has turned my head. I do love you.

MARIE. Why are you putting on your coat?

GUARDSMAN. I cannot bear to stay since we cannot see each other any more.

MARIE. I meant no more tonight. Tomorrow, Prince. Tomorrow at five.

GUARDSMAN. Heaven help me!

MARIE. What?

GUARDSMAN. I say—heaven help me to exist without you until tomorrow—at five.

[*Music: Up and down into piano playing Chopin*]

MARIE. Liesl, come away from that window.

LIESL [*Off mike*]. Yes, Ma'am.

MAMA. You'll see him well enough when he comes, Liesl. It was a mistake to wash the windows, Marie. All she does is stand there looking out. I think she's also in love with the Prince now.

MARIE. What do you mean, also?

MAMA. Il ne faut pas que tu should try to keep it from your mama.

MARIE. That will do, mama. Liesl, go get the tea ready. Russian.

LIESL. Yes, Ma'am.

MAMA. It's only four o'clock, Bebi—and he won't be here until five. I think I'll fix myself up a bit.

[*Doorbell*]

[*Music: Piano stops*]

MARIE [*Calling slightly—Across the room*]. Whoever it is, I'm not home, Liesl . . . and I won't be back this afternoon.

[*Door opening off mike*]

MARIE. The idea, opening the door before Liesl answers it! Who . . . ? Well . . well . . . it's you.

FRANZ. My coming then is unexpected?

MARIE. Oh, for heaven's sake, stop acting. What's brought you back so soon?

FRANZ. I return two whole days earlier, and all you have to say is "What's brought you back so soon?" Is that all your greetings? Your kiss, your embrace?

MAMA. I think I'll go and put on my old clothes.

[*Door slam*]

FRANZ. Come, darling, greet me . . . greet me.

MARIE. I was just beginning to forget your sarcasm and your nagging. But now it's to begin all over again.

FRANZ. If you want me to, I can go back to Olmutz.

MARIE. Don't, don't! You are perfectly horrid. What happened? I thought you were signed for three performances in Olmutz.

FRANZ. The theatre in Olmutz has burned down.

MARIE. Burned down!

FRANZ. It will be in the papers tomorrow. I escaped within an inch of my life.

MARIE. Was anyone hurt?

FRANZ. Everyone was hurt. And now I am home to regain my strength—with my sweet little wife.

MARIE. You're in a very good humor.

FRANZ. Aren't you?

MARIE. Oh, yes. I am in good humor too.

FRANZ. Very well, then. I'm in good humor, you're in good humor, and everything is all right. I'm playing Hamlet tonight. At our theatre.

MARIE. You're going to stay home until it's time to go to the theatre?

FRANZ. Yes. I am still trembling. I was nearly consumed by a great flame last night. That is, in Olmutz. What did you do with yourself last evening?

MARIE. Nothing.

FRANZ. Must've been awfully boring.

MARIE. Yes, awfully.

FRANZ. Weren't you going to the opera?

MARIE. Oh yes. How silly of me. Of course—I quite forgot. That's so. I did go.

FRANZ. I suppose Bernhardt dropped in during the evening, as usual.

MARIE. Yes— he was there a little while.

FRANZ. Then you were alone most of the evening?

MARIE. No.

FRANZ. No?

MARIE. No, Mama was with me.

FRANZ. Otherwise you were alone all evening?

MARIE. How queer you are. If I tell you that I was alone—I was alone.

FRANZ. All evening?

MARIE. Well, Bernhardt was here—but you were still here of course.

FRANZ. No one else?

MARIE. No one else? Wait now—No.

FRANZ. I don't know, but I thought the concierge said something about a soldier.

MARIE. Really? Possibly a soldier came to see Liesl. We can ask her.

FRANZ. Never mind asking Liesl. One look from you and she'll confess the soldier came for her.

MARIE. Would she?

FRANZ. Yes, she'd even swear to it.

MARIE. Why should she swear to it?

FRANZ. Because if the soldier came to see you—

MARIE. Well!

FRANZ. I'm only joking. I've been riding in a smoking car all day—I'm full of bad jokes.

MARIE. And so, little by little our harmless questions have turned into a regular cross-examination. I was quite happy at first. I was quite touched. I thought you were interested in how I spent the evening— and now it appears that you have been suspecting me. And with a soldier! Very noble of you, I must say.

FRANZ. Oh, please—

MARIE. You must be out of your mind.

FRANZ. Please, please—It's the smoke, dear. First the theatre burns, and then all day in the smoking car . . .

MARIE. This is really too much. I want to know at once what is back of all this about a soldier. I'll call Mama and Liesl.

FRANZ. Liesl will tell the same lies as Mama, and Mama will tell the same lies as Liesl.

MARIE. I insist you tell me what you mean.

FRANZ. I mean that yesterday afternoon after I left a soldier was here.

MARIE. There might have been a regiment here. What had that to do with me? If Liesl wants to . . .

FRANZ. Let's agree that Liesl has confessed he came for her. We agree. Now . . .

MARIE [*Remembering*]. Oh, of course! It was the fireman.

FRANZ [*Ready to die*]. A fireman! !

MARIE. Yes. A fireman came to inspect the fire escape. The concierge mistook him for a soldier.

FRANZ [*Rocking with the blow*]. A fireman.

MARIE. A fireman. Why are you so surprised? Firemen are always interested in fire escapes. He even went up on the roof to inspect the chimney.

FRANZ. The chimney. He—he climbed up to the roof?

MARIE. That's right. Of course, when he came down I did have a glass of tea ready for him.

FRANZ. Of course. I don't accuse you of climbing up to the roof with him. The only difficulty is that firemen do not wear beards.

MARIE. Beards?

FRANZ. Beards. Guardsmen, however, always wear them.

MARIE. Guardsmen?

FRANZ. Guardsmen.

MARIE. Then all this—all this is not merely a joke?

FRANZ. No—it is not a joke.

MARIE. And you really—seriously—think that while you were slaving away earning money in Olmutz in a burning theatre—that I was entertaining soldiers?

FRANZ. Oh, my dear—entertaining soldiers.

MARIE. What did you say then? You said something much worse. And what are you doing now? You're thinking that I have deceived you.

FRANZ. Oh, for heaven's sake, don't get so excited.

MARIE. I who gave up her freedom—her whole life—her young and precious life for your sake . . . [*Weeping*]

FRANZ. But my dear . . .

MARIE. How can you do this to me?

FRANZ. This is really—

MARIE. You're killing my very soul. Someone has slandered me and you believe it!

FRANZ. Oh my dear—what nonsense.

MARIE. I can't stand it any longer. I feel that—that it's all over between us.

FRANZ. Don't say such things—you know how madly I love you.

MARIE. And yet you suspect me . . . You believe lies about me.

FRANZ. No, no. I don't believe anything wrong about you.

MARIE. I must go away. You believe malicious lies about my character.

FRANZ. No, darling, don't go! Stay with me! I do not believe them.

MARIE. With all your heart? You mean it honestly?

FRANZ. With all my heart—honestly.

MARIE. You love me and trust me?

FRANZ. I love you and trust you.

MARIE. Because it's all lies and slander. I was alone with Mama and I thought of your beautiful, ardent eyes—and I longed for you and wanted you with me. I loved you.

FRANZ [*Overpowered*]. My darling.

MARIE. *How* I must love you to be able to forgive you this. I do forgive you.

FRANZ. Forgive me, forgive me. I'm so—I'm so in love with you. Marie—why are you crying?

MARIE. Ah—if I could only tell you why I am crying!

[*Doorbell*]

MARIE [*Shocked*]. Someone is at the door.

FRANZ. Yes.

MARIE [*Moving off mike*]. I—I'd better do my face. I'll be in my room, if anyone wants me.

[*Door closing*]

BERNHARDT [*Off mike, coming in*]. Franz! What are you doing here? What's the matter?

FRANZ. I'm believing that I wasn't with her last night.

BERNHARDT. You weren't with . . . ? [*Laughs*] Perhaps you weren't! Is there anything you can't believe if it's necessary?

FRANZ. Never mind about that. I've got control of myself now. Where's that valise? Oh yes.

BERNHARDT. What in the world are you doing?

FRANZ [*Quietly*]. Now comes the moment when her lying is not going to help her any.

BERNHARDT [*Quietly*]. The uniform? Franz, you're not going to . . .

FRANZ. Hold that boot for me.

MARIE [*As though from next room*]. Who came, Franz?

FRANZ. Just Bernhardt! [*Sotto*] Quick, where's the beard?

MARIE. Why don't the two of you go to a café before we have dinner?

FRANZ. Spendid idea! Hurry and dress, dear, you'll come along?

MARIE. No, I'll rest here a while.

FRANZ. Not expecting someone, are you? [*Sotto*] Buckle my sword on, Bernhardt.

MARIE. That's a funny question.

FRANZ. Then why should I go out?

MARIE. Do go out—even for half an hour. Can't you understand? After this dreadful scene, I'm a wreck. Tell Bernhardt about the fire in Olmutz. The theatre in Olmutz burned down, Bernhardt.

BERNHARDT. You don't say.

FRANZ. Yes, and the fireman ended up 200 miles away drinking tea in my apartment.

MARIE. Oh, stop it!

BERNHARDT [*Sotto*]. Button the cloak, your pants will show.

FRANZ. Is the beard thick enough? Does it look real? It got wet in the rain last night. The curl seems to have gone out of it.

BERNHARDT. No, it's perfect. You're as Russian as the Czar.

FRANZ. Leave us now, Bernhardt. This scene I can't play before an audience. Come back later. Then . . . then we will all know.

BERNHARDT. Good-bye, then. And . . . and, oh, dear.

[*Walking away . . . Door opening . . . Closing*]

MARIE [*Still off mike*]. Franz? [*Pause*] Franz, have you gone?

FRANZ. Bernhardt went to get a table at the café. Come in here, sweetheart . . . for a moment, before I go.

MARIE [*Gayly*]. Coming, dear.

FRANZ. I can't seem to find that book I was reading . . .

[*Door opens*]

FRANZ [*Sliding into his Russian accent*]. And I love to discuss with the great critic the literature which I am always study so hard.

[*Her footsteps coming to him and toward the mike as . . .*]

It is perhaps a little early for me to arrive, but I could not keep away until five, Madam.

[*Her last step*]

MARIE. Good afternoon, Prince. I began to think you were not coming.

FRANZ [*In his own voice*]. What are you talking about? Are you trying out a part? Are you acting?

MARIE. No, my dear, you are doing the acting. Why, you're even in costume.

FRANZ. What do you think you're doing?

MARIE. Simply going on with our little comedy from where we left off last night—the comedy I've been playing for your sake since yesterday afternoon. If you wish we can keep it up, but I fancy we've had enough of it by now.

FRANZ. Now don't try to tell me you recognized me!

MARIE. You came in at that door yesterday at exactly twenty-nine minutes past six. At six thirty I had recognized you. At six thirty-one I was wondering whether I should laugh in your face—and at six thirty-two I had decided to play the comedy to the end.

FRANZ. That is not true.

MARIE. I see. You think you can play the Guardsman well enough to deceive me, but you don't think I am actress enough to play a much easier part—the woman who fell in love with the Guardsman.

FRANZ. You are not quite that good an actress.

MARIE. And you are not quite that good an actor.

FRANZ. You simply could not have recognized me! Whatever you may say, you simply . . .

LIESL. Please, Ma'am—there's a man outside.

MARIE. A man?

FRANZ [*Struck*]. A man? What kind of a man?

COLLECTOR. Excuse me, excuse me. I hate to disturb a great artist like yourself, sir, but couldn't you let me have just a little on account? The whole thing's only four hundred sixty kronen.

FRANZ [*In Guardsman's dialect*]. Artist . . . Artist . . . What do you take me for? I am Prince Wassily Samsonov, and if you . . .

COLLECTOR. Excuse me, sir, your own mother might not know you, your own wife might even mistake you for a minute, but you could put on all the uniforms and wigs and whiskers in the world and as long as you owe me money, I would know you. I'll have to give you back the tickets to "Salome." The boss wants his money.

FRANZ. Get out of here before I wrap this sword around your head! Get out, get out!

[*Door . . . Quick slam*]

MARIE. You see, dear? Even he knew you.

FRANZ. I haven't got my Guardsman's pants on.

MARIE. But your cloak covers you to your boot tops.

FRANZ. I don't care, *you* didn't know me. How did I give myself away? Prove it to me.

MARIE. You praised your own cigarettes.

FRANZ. That doesn't explain a thing.

MARIE. Your kiss. I really mean this seriously. You couldn't disguise your kiss. It was so entirely your own—it was impossible not to recognize it.

FRANZ [*Wilting*]. Yes—I was afraid you recognized my kiss.

MARIE. And your eyes.

FRANZ. My eyes?

MARIE. That sweet, warm, sad, look . . . You're looking at me that way now.

FRANZ. Then why didn't you tell me from the beginning?

MARIE. Because I wanted you to play the comedy out to the end. I did hope you'd have more courage than to rob us of this beautiful night.

FRANZ. Then you do love me?

MARIE. And you will never put me to the test again?

FRANZ. Never again. I am so in love with you. Why are you crying?

MARIE [*Weeping*]. Because you love me so—because I am just a bit ashamed of myself. Because I love you, Franz!

[*Door opening, off mike*]

BERNDARDT. May I come in? Are you on your knees again?

FRANZ. Bernhardt! She recognized me from the beginning!

BERNHARDT [*Laughs*]. Did you, Marie?

FRANZ. You look as though you didn't believe it.

BERNHARDT [*Playing for time*]. I not believe it?

MARIE. Of course he believes it.

FRANZ [*Realizing, with a bright laugh*]. I'll bet she told you all about it. Didn't she!?

BERNHARDT [*Weakly*]. Ah—ah—of course . . .

FRANZ. Then why are you looking at her that way?

MARIE. He's not looking at me any way. Oh, Franz, a rose by any other name—is still a rose. No beard, no boots, could ever hide the beauty of your soul.

FRANZ. Oh, Marie—you knew—you knew!

[*Chopin on piano*]

MARIE [*Laughs*].

FRANZ. Or did you? Marie, I command you! Stop playing Chopin.

[*Marie continues laughing into music*]

[*Musical curtain*]

ANNOUNCER

CREDITS

THE SILVER CORD

Original Play
by Sidney Howard

Radio Adaptation
by Erik Barnouw

CAST

(for radio performance)

CHRISTINA	Ruth Hussey
DAVID	Ralph Bellamy
HESTER	Beatrice Pearson
ROBERT	Elliott Reid
MRS. PHELPS	Estelle Winwood
DR. McCLINTOCK	A. P. Kaye

THE SILVER CORD

Radio adaptation by

ERIK BARNOUW

"THE SILVER CORD" was especially interesting to adapt to radio because it raised not only the technical problems generally present when a story is translated from one medium into another, but also problems of subject matter.

The play concerns a possessive mother and her two sons, Dave and Rob. One successfully frees himself from her; the other fails to.

Before the play, in the original version, Dave has been on a tour of Italy, Germany, and other European countries, arranged by his mother as preparation for the architectural career she has planned for him. He returns, to her chagrin, with a wife—Christina, an American girl-scientist who was pursuing her studies in biology at Heidelberg. Upon their arrival home the mother tries to break up the marriage. But Dave's eyes become opened to the unhealthy emotional pattern of the household and he breaks away. The younger brother Rob meanwhile fails in a parallel story, allowing the mother to break up his engagement with a girl called Hester.

Although the play deals frankly with a psychological subject from which most radio editors and producers would run as from the plague, this was not the real problem. The Theatre Guild has generally proceeded on the assumption that the radio audience could be treated on the same adult level as a Broadway audience, and has found no reason to change this attitude. The mother-son conflict was presented in a manner faithful to the play. No objection was heard, from network censors or home listeners.

The real problem was that the radio broadcast came only a few months after the end of World War II. It had been many years since Americans had toured and studied in Europe in the manner of David and Christina. The original play reflected reverence for architectural wonders since blown to bits and would have given the broadcast a dated feeling. Worse, the nostalgia for Italy and Germany would have raised resistances irrelevant to the theme of the play. In the adaptation, either the listener would have to be persuaded to think himself into a pre-Hitler frame of mind—a difficult feat—or changes would have to be made.

It seemed undesirable to make the play a period piece. The play's problems were as timely as always, and it seemed essential to present them as problems of current and immediate meaning. I finally decided, by some easy but important changes, to relate the play to the war, and make the radio version a kind of postwar-readjustment story. The elder son was returning not from an architectural tour but from war. The war had given him—as it gave many—a chance to escape from his mother. The girl was a biochemist who had been doing scientific war work in England. The second son had stayed home, a psychological 4F, almost hopelessly under his mother's influence. These changes affected only a few scenes. The play's basic conflict and all its great scenes fitted well into the revised pattern.

Technical problems that had to be solved included several common adaptation problems. In a stage play about a family it is almost inevitable that most of the action should take place in one room. All sorts of events that might more logically happen in a variety of settings are ingeniously, for the sake of economy and practical staging considerations, made to happen in one or two locales. But in radio, moving from one place to another is easy and costs nothing. Therefore it is possible and often advisable to unstitch the scenes as sewed together for the stage play and to stitch them together into a new pattern, more true to probability and more characterstic of the mobile radio medium.

The radio version starts not in the house, but in the car approaching the house, as Dave and Christina are on their way home. The argument as to whether Christina should occupy the same room as her husband takes place not in the living room but upstairs, as the new arrivals are being shown to their rooms. The mother talks Rob into jilting Hester not in the too-public living room, but in her own bedroom, as she rests on her chaise longue after a sham heart attack. Dave and Christina exchange words of love not in the living room but outdoors at night.

Except for the machinery of getting from one scene to another, and except for cuts made for speed, the radio version keeps as closely as possible to the brilliant dialogue of the original. Though the settings are sometimes different, important stretches of dialogue are preserved almost intact.

THE SILVER CORD

[*Signature register and fade. Applause simultaneous*]

[*Music down under*]

ANNOUNCER

INTRODUCTION FOR THE THEATRE GUILD

[*Music*]

ACT I

[*Car traveling at fair speed ... Several seconds of it ... Horn*]

CHRIS. Whoa ... take it easy, Dave.

DAVID. You don't know how it feels! Every landmark I see gives me an itchy toe. There's the old school I used to go to.

CHRIS. H-huh.

[*Car slows down a bit*]

DAVID. Now darling, keep your eyes open. As we get round this curve you'll see the pond.

CHRIS. Your own pond?

DAVID. Yep. Where Rob and I skated every year. And right next to that, the house. There—

[*After a moment, car slows further*]

CHRIS. David! It's beautiful! I love a Colonial house.

DAVID. Mother's full of tradition. Up to her ears ... you'll like Mother, no kidding.

CHRIS. Of course.

DAVID. Really, I'm *sure* you'll get along.

CHRIS. Why shouldn't we?

103

DAVID. And you'll like Rob, too.

CHRIS. Rob—didn't get in the service, did he?

DAVID. No, he was rejected for the draft. Kind of nervous, you know. Swell fellow, though. Well, here we are.

[*Car comes to halt . . . Car door opens*]

[*Light wind background*]

DAVID. Well, Mrs. Phelps.

CHRIS. I feel sort of . . . scared.

DAVID. You scared? Hah. Hand me that bag there.

CHRIS. Here you are.

[*Suitcase bumping . . . Car door closing*]

DAVID. Come on . . .

[*Footsteps up to house through following*]

DAVID. I'm kind of nervous myself. Shaking all over, I'm so excited.

CHRIS. It's cold, isn't it?

DAVID. Very cold.

[*Steps halt . . . Doorbell ringing*]

DAVID. Imagine . . . Over three years . . .

[*Door opens . . . Pause*]

HESTER. Hullo! You want Mrs. Phelps?

DAVID. Hey . . . who are you?

HESTER. Well I'm . . .

DAVID. Don't tell me! You're the girl my brother Rob's going to marry.

HESTER. Right! I'm Hester. And you're David!

DAVID. That's right! Gosh, I'm glad to know you. Hester, meet Christina My wife.

[*Door closes*]

HESTER [*Full of warmth*]. Hello, Christina.

CHRIS. Isn't this wonderful? Hello, Hester dear.

DAVID. Where's Mother? Where's everybody?

HESTER. Around somewhere. I was down here alone resting on the couch. I'm supposed to be having a breakdown.

CHRIS. Breakdown!

HESTER. They've declared me an invalid. Rob went out to skate but ...

CHRIS. On the pond?

HESTER. Of course. Only I don't see him anywhere.

[*Door banging off*]

ROB [*Off*]. Hester!

HESTER. Here Rob! In the living room! Come on in!

ROB [*Off, but arriving on at end of speech*]. They've been cutting ice, so the pond's full of holes! Hope nobody takes the short cut across the pond and ... [*Stops short*]

HESTER. Look, Rob.

ROB. DAVE!

DAVID. Rob!

ROB. Well, you old—

[*They both laugh with satisfaction*]

DAVID. Rob, this is Christina.

ROB. Oh, this is marvelous. Hello Christina. Welcome to our home.

CHRIS. Thanks Rob.

ROB. But aren't you way ahead of time? The afternoon train isn't due.

CHRIS. We decided not to bother with trains.

DAVID. When the boat got to New York we decided to get Chris's old car out of storage—

CHRIS. And Dave drove like a madman ...

DAVID. And here we are.

ROB. Hurrah for you!

HESTER. It's just grand! And don't they both look marvelous, Rob?

DAVID. But where's Mother?

ROB. Oh, in her room maybe, or—

MRS. PHELPS [*From upstairs*]. Da-vid! Dave, my boy!

DAVID [*Projecting to upstairs*]. Mother! Hello Mother!

MRS. PHELPS [*Still way off ... Her speeches continuous*]. Dave, my son! Where are you?

DAVID. Here, Mother! Here!

MRS. PHELPS [*A long fade in ... She arrives toward end of speech*]. Where are you, my boy? It's Mother, Dave. It's Mother. Oh David, my son, my son! To think I wasn't down here!

DAVID. We came earlier to surprise you, Mother. Chris thought that—

MRS. PHELPS. Oh, let me look at you, Dave. You *are* well, aren't you?

DAVE. I guess so. Look, Mother, I want you to meet—

MRS. PHELPS. Was the English climate *terribly* hard on you? And the V-bombs—did you suffer, Dave?

DAVID. Mother, you haven't said a word to—

MRS. PHELPS. And the crossing. Were you seasick? You must be careful not to take cold in this weather. Now David, you haven't been working too hard, have you?

CHRIS. He hasn't done a scratch of work since the war ended.

MRS. PHELPS. Eh?

CHRIS. We've been touring England, waiting for passage—

DAVID. Mother, I've been trying to make you take notice of Christina.

MRS. PHELPS [*Utmost warmth*]. Oh my dear Christina, I am sorry! Seeing this big boy again quite took me off my feet. Now let me look at *you*

HESTER. She looks lovely to me.

DAVID. And to me, too, Mother.

CHRIS. Hello, Mrs. Phelps.

MRS. PHELPS. Why Dave, she's splendid! Didn't I always say Dave would choose only the best? Dave, you *have* been working too hard. I don't like those circles under your eyes.

DAVID. Nonsense, Mother!

CHRIS. I think he looks pretty well.

MRS. PHELPS. But only pretty well. Oh Dave boy, this is too good to be true! After three whole years, and nearly six months married. Let me sit down! Let me sit here—and all of you cluster around me!

ROB. Here's a pillow, Mother.

MRS. PHELPS. And the smelling salts too, Robin.

ROB. Right here.

MRS. PHELPS. Oh, this excitement has quite laid me out! This is too wonderful! *My* war is won. I've won my two boys back again.

[*Music bridge: Emotional at first, then to bustly theme*]

[*Footsteps of several people on stairs, and bumping of suitcases*]

[*Some light ad libs*]

ROB. Here we are! Now where do these suitcases go?

MRS. PHELPS. I'll show you. [*Door opens*] Here, everybody, is David's old room. Just as he left it. Every day I've dusted in here, and said to myself: "David will be back, in his old little room, beside me."

DAVID. But Mother, you don't mean that Chris and I are . . .

MRS. PHELPS. Just a minute, David. There's something I want everyone to see. [*Drawer of chest pulled open*] Look, in this drawer.

ROB. Well, if it isn't his old blocks!

MRS. PHELPS. Do you remember those blocks, David?

DAVID. Do I?

MRS. PHELPS. The way you played with those . . . first showed me that you would be an architect. The foundation stones of David's career.

DAVID. Now, Mother, don't talk as if I'm an architect already. All I've done so far is camouflage factories so the Jerries wouldn't smash them.

MRS. PHELPS. You're *going* to be an architect now, aren't you?

DAVID. I'll try my darnedest.

MRS. PHELPS. Well, then! Now—everybody. Across the hall please.

[*Some slight stir and shuffle . . . Door opens*]

This little front room is for Christina!

DAVID. I say, Mother, can't we . . . ?

HESTER. Don't they want to be together, Mrs. Phelps?

MRS. PHELPS. I'm so terribly sorry, the guest room is being done over.

HESTER. But let them move into my room. It's so much larger and . . .

MRS. PHELPS [*Severely*]. We'll do nothing of the sort, Hester! Hester's here for a rest and I won't upset her. She's been dancing so much she's gone into a perfect decline! David can be quite comfortable in his old room and so can Christina in here, and it won't hurt them a bit.

CHRIS. Of course not.

HESTER. But gosh, I feel terrible that . . .

ROB. Now, Hester, if Mother has made all the plans you'd better let things be.

MRS. PHELPS. That's right, Robin!

DAVID. Well—

ROB. So which bags go in here?

DAVID. Just put those two in here for Chris for the time being. Our things are a little mixed, so . . .

ROB. Okay. [*Suitcases put down*] There you are, madam.

MRS. PHELPS. You'll be very comfortable in here, Christina. And now, I want Robin and Hester to supervise David, while I visit with my new daughter.

CHRIS. That'll be nice.

ROB [*Off, joshing*]. All right, come on Dave, we'll help you build something with your blocks.

DAVID [*Off, and fading*]. You dog, you, I'll—

[*Laughter of David and Rob cut off as door closes*]

MRS. PHELPS. Now, we two can have a chat. Let me really look at you. I've never seen a lady scientist before.

CHRIS. I hope I'm not so different from other women.

MRS. PHELPS. I've quite gotten over being afraid of you.

CHRIS. Afraid of me?

MRS. PHELPS. Can't you understand that? My big boy sends me a curt cable to say he's marrying a charming and talented biologist. But now that I know you, I'm *proud* to have you for a daughter.

CHRIS. You're being very nice to me.

MRS. PHELPS. It isn't at all hard to be nice to you, my dear. Now suppose you just lie down there, and rest, and I'll start unpacking for you.

[*Snap of suitcase being opened*]

CHRIS. Oh no, please, Mrs. Phelps, that can wait until some other time.

MRS. PHELPS. Now, dear, it's nice to have help with these things. I know. And you must be tired. Let your new mother— What's this?

CHRIS. What?

MRS. PHELPS. Is it medicine? You're well, aren't you, dear?

CHRIS. Of course! Oh, that's really a souvenir. It's what brought David and me together. It's a vial of penicillin.

MRS. PHELPS. Oh? How very scientific.

CHRIS. You see, I went to England to work on penicillin. One of the problems was to reduce it to a powder, so it could be shipped all over the world in little vials. Many of us worked hard on it, at a factory near Cambridge. And that's where I met David; he camouflaged the factory, as an English village. And that's how that vial brought us together.

MRS. PHELPS. How very nice! But I hope, for David's sake, that you also observed some cultural things in England, and not just science.

CHRIS. On our wedding trip, we took in all the landmarks!

MRS. PHELPS. Because, as a mother, I've always paid particular attention to my boys' cultural development. My boys learned their classics at their mother's knee. You read, I hope?

CHRIS. I can. I sometimes have to.

MRS. PHELPS. My dear, I only meant that I think it's so important, for David's happiness, that you should be what *I* call "a *reader*." Oh, it was very hard for me when David got the chance to go to England. But I said to myself: David must do his part. And he'll come back a complete man. Though I didn't actually look for him bringing you back, my dear, and coming home a married man!

CHRIS [*Laughs lightly*].

MRS. PHELPS. So I stayed home with Robin. Robin was rejected for the draft, you know. Nothing wrong with him physically, of course. Just the nervous type.

CHRIS. I see.

MRS. PHELPS. He's very sensitive and artistic. I've sometimes thought he should take up interior decorating, and decorate the houses built by David . . . Now tell me what your plans are . . . if you have plans, which I hope you haven't, because I've been making so many for you, such perfect ones.

CHRIS. We haven't many. But what we have *are* pretty definite.

MRS. PHELPS. Are they, really? What are they?

CHRIS. Well, we're going to live in New York, of course.

MRS. PHELPS. Why "New York, of course"?

CHRIS. It's by far the best place for Dave's work . . .

MRS. PHELPS. Oh, I can't agree with you, Christina!

CHRIS. And then, it's where my appointment is.

MRS. PHELPS. Your appointment?

CHRIS. At the Rockefeller Institute.

MRS. PHELPS. So that's why you're taking David to New York. You're thinking of your biology.

CHRIS. You can't blame me—so long as I think of Dave's work too. You must understand that.

MRS. PHELPS. I shall try to, my dear. Now you must try to understand me.

CHRIS. Of course. I want to.

MRS. PHELPS. Look at me . . . What do you see? Simply—David's mother. I can't say of you that you're simply David's wife, because clearly you're many things besides that. I think, as I look at you, that I belong to a dead age.

CHRIS. Oh come, Mrs. Phelps . . . I . .

MRS. PHELPS. But give us our due, Christina. We girls who did not go into the world to become streetcar conductors and lady scientists, we had our profession too, a great profession which I fear may vanish from the face of the earth: motherhood.

CHRIS. But Mrs. Phelps, I certainly don't—

MRS. PHELPS. Wait Christina! David was six, Rob only a little baby, when my husband died. I'd been married seven years, not very happily. I was pretty, too, as a girl. Very pretty.

CHRIS. I'm sure of it.

MRS. PHELPS. For twenty-four years, since my husband died, I've given all my life, all my strength to Dave and Rob. They've taken the place of husband and friends for me. Where do I stand, now? Rob has finished school and is marrying. David is married already. This is the end.

CHRIS [Puzzled]. The end?

MRS. PHELPS. Oh, I'm not asking for praise. I'm asking for something more substantial. I'm asking you, my dear, dear Christina, not to take all my boy's heart. Leave me, I beg you, a little part of it! Don't you think I've earned that much . . . as David's mother?

CHRIS. Mrs. Phelps—please don't think there's any problem here—

MRS. PHELPS. It's agreed, then, isn't it, that I'm not to be shut out?

CHRIS. Of course you're not!

MRS. PHELPS. Not by you, Christina. Nor by your work?

CHRIS. No, no!

MRS. PHELPS. Nor by anything?

CHRIS. You must know I appreciate all you've done for Dave. You must know that!

MRS. PHELPS. My dear, you're a very disarming person. I've known you ten minutes and unloaded my whole heart to you.

CHRIS. I'm proud that you trust me.

MRS. PHELPS. Thank you, my dear. And now . . . now that you know how I feel . . . now you won't take Dave to New York, will you?

CHRIS. But Mrs. Phelps!

MRS. PHELPS. Because that would be—crowding me out, setting me aside, robbing me . . .

CHRIS [Completely baffled]. Robbing you? Mrs. Phelps, you've no reason to think any such thing!

MRS. PHELPS. Well, it's nice of you to reassure me, and we don't have to worry right away. You'll have time to see how carefully I've worked everything out for David, and for you, too, my dear. And all I ask is that—

[*Firm knock on door and door opens at once*]

DAVID [*Fade on*]. Well, how are my two women getting along? Here, Chris, here is one of your nighties that was in my suitcase.

CHRIS. Thanks, dear—

DAVID. And—uh—have you got my toothbrush?

CHRIS. It's right [*Sound of toilet box opening*] in here with mine. Here, and here's your razor, too.

DAVID. Oh. Thanks. What do you think of this old lady, hmm? Pretty wonderful, isn't she?

CHRIS. Amazing, Dave.

MRS. PHELPS. And Christina is lovely. And very brilliant, I'm sure.

DAVID. You bet she is.

MRS. PHELPS. And while we're together, we three, I want to tell you all the arrangements I've made for you.

DAVID. Arrangements? What's all this? Are you still the old planner, Mother?

MRS. PHELPS. Of course. Christina, I happen to own a very large tract of wooded land here, most desirable for residences. You can see it out there, off to the left of the pond.

CHRIS. Oh . . . Yes . . . I see . . .

MRS. PHELPS. I've had many wonderful offers for it. But I've held on to it, ever since Dave chose his profession. Now we shall name it Phelps Manor, and open it. David will have charge. David will lay out the streets, design the gateways, build the houses and make his fortune, his reputation, and his place in the world!

DAVID. Now look here, Mother. This is all a bit sudden, isn't it?

MRS. PHELPS. David, with me to back you, there can't be any doubt about the outcome. Now isn't that better than New York, with its years of discouragement?

DAVID. There's certainly a difference.

MRS. PHELPS. Then we can consider it settled?

DAVID. Now, Mother, this isn't a thing we can decide on the spur of the moment.

MRS. PHELPS. What is there to think about?

DAVID. Well—

CHRIS. David has an offer of a job in New York, Mrs. Phelps.

MRS. PHELPS. A job?

DAVID. Yes. With Michaels. He's a big man. It could mean a fine start there.

CHRIS. And he's very interested in David.

MRS. PHELPS. I don't approve at all!

DAVID. And then Chris has her appointment, and—

MRS. PHELPS. Oh I'm sure we can work that out! . . . That's *very* easy! Christina, I am on the hospital board here, and— You do your work in a laboratory?

CHRIS. Usually.

MRS. PHELPS. I'll take you in the morning and show you *our* laboratory. It has a fine new microscope the High School didn't want any more. And an excellent gas stove, because it's also the nurses' diet kitchen. And you'll be allowed to putter around all you like, when it isn't in use by the real doctors. Now you *will* think it over—taking David to New York and ruining all his prospects?

DAVID. Now, Mother, Chris isn't taking me to New York. We're thinking of *both* our jobs; mine just as much as hers.

CHRIS. Mrs. Phelps, isn't it a choice for David between a sure success here, and his own achievement somewhere else?

DAVID. That's it exactly! And you see, Mother, our plans are pretty well laid out. Chris's job starts a week from today, and that's when we go to New York.

MRS. PHELPS. A week from today! No!

CHRIS. That's right.

MRS. PHELPS. No, no, I won't allow it!

DAVID. But look, we can't work this out now. We certainly appreciate this idea of yours, Mother. It's so generous that—well, it's like all the other fine things you're always doing for Rob and me. And Chris and I will certainly talk it over.

CHRIS. Of course we will.

DAVID. And now let's get ready for dinner. [*Fading*] Chris, if you want a bath, I'll be through in a few minutes. All right?

CHRIS. Right, darling

DAVID [*Off*]. The water is nice and hot, the way you like it!

[*Door closes*]

MRS. PHELPS. I think it's madness! It means—[*In despair*] it's all been for nothing!

CHRIS. What has?

MRS. PHELPS. All that I've done for David and given up for him and meant to him!

CHRIS. How can you say that?

MRS. PHELPS. I did so want to be friends with David's wife.

CHRIS. But can't we be?

MRS. PHELPS. Some day you'll have a child of your own and then you may know what it means, *if* . . .

CHRIS. If what?

MRS. PHELPS. If you don't sacrifice your child, too, to this work of yours.

CHRIS. Mrs. Phelps, I want terribly much to feel very close to you. Isn't that why we came here at once after we landed? Believe me, you and I value the same things. And you'll see that when I tell you—something David and I have saved till now to tell you—

MRS. PHELPS. Tell me what?

CHRIS. David and I . . . are going to have a baby.

MRS. PHELPS [*Gasp*]. Baby!

CHRIS. In about four months! . . . Mrs. Phelps, what's wrong? Are you all right?

MRS. PHELPS. My heart . . . It's not very strong.

CHRIS. Take this chair.

MRS. PHELPS. I'll be all right in a moment. I'll be all right . . . in a moment.

[*Music*]

END OF ACT I

ANNOUNCER

COMMERCIAL

STATION IDENTIFICATION

ACT II

[*Music*]

NARRATOR. Mrs. Phelps's momentary heart attack seems to have subsided, for now it is after dinner, and the family is having coffee and surveying the family collection of photographs.

[*Ad libs . . . They're all together, chuckling over family photos*]

[*Tinkle of coffee cups*]

ROB. Look at this one. Hah! Dave in his play pen!

DAVID. Let me see. [*Laughs merrily as he sees it*]

HESTER. Oh—marvelous.

CHRIS. This looks like Dave in a sailor suit.

DAVID. Uh—yeah! That's me all right.

MRS. PHELPS. Now put the coffee tray aside, and I'll tell you about the pictures.

ROB. All right, mother.

[*Slight tinkle as tray is moved*]

CHRIS. What were you doing in the sailor suit, Dave?

DAVID. Dancing the hornpipe, I think.

MRS. PHELPS. That was at Miss Briggs's dancing school.

CHRIS. Did Miss Briggs teach you to be graceful, Dave?

DAVID. She did indeed. As a boy I was a gazelle. But I got over it.

CHRIS. I'm just as glad. I've known one or two adult gazelles.

DAVID. Miss Briggs had red hair and castanets. Spain, she used to say, is the land of the dance.

MRS. PHELPS. Oh, every moment is vivid! This is David when he was ten weeks old.

CHRIS. Oh David!

HESTER. A darling baby! Did they always seat them on shells in those days?

MRS. PHELPS [*A bit coldly*]. It was a fashion like any other.

HESTER. David on the half shell.

[*Chris laughs*]

DAVID. I didn't always sit in shells. Mother's got one of me on a white fur rug.

MRS. PHELPS. It hangs over my bed till this day.

CHRIS. In the nude?

DAVID. No, in an undershirt.

HESTER [*Giggles*].

MRS. PHELPS [*Sternly*]. Fashions change.

CHRIS. I suppose they must. David wouldn't think of being photographed in his undershirt now. Let me see the picture again, Mrs. Phelps.

MRS. PHELPS [*With dignity*]. I think that's enough for this evening.

DAVE. Oh, come now, Mother, they were only kidding.

CHRIS. Please don't be angry, Mrs. Phelps. They're awfully interesting pictures.

MRS. PHELPS. Only interesting to me, I'm afraid.

CHRIS. Not at all. I loved them.

DAVE. Come on, let's see some more.

CHRIS. Show us some more, Mrs. Phelps. Are there many more?

MRS. PHELPS [*Still stern about them*]. Dave and Robin were photographed twice every month until they were twelve years old.

HESTER. Good grief! That makes over two hundred and fifty of each!

MRS. PHELPS. I never counted. I used to study their photographs, month by month. I could compare the expression at eight with that at eight and a half, and see the increased depth. I could study a picture of Dave playing with his blocks and point out those signs of architectural genius by which I decided to make him an architect.

HESTER. You mean you just up and decided?

MRS. PHELPS. Of course!

CHRIS. It seems a risky business.

MRS. PHELPS. What could be more natural?

HESTER. I know what Christina means. Look. I had some rabbits once, and I loved 'em. Suppose my family had studied pictures of me playing with my rabbits—and brought me up to be a lion tamer?

ROB [*Protesting*]. Now, Hester—

HESTER. What I say about children is: Have 'em, love 'em, and leave 'em be.

CHRIS. I'm not sure that isn't a very profound remark.

MRS. PHELPS [*Quietly furious*]. Robin . . . Put the pictures away, please.

ROB. Are you sure you don't want to go through the rest, Mother?

MRS. PHELPS. I'm afraid of boring Hester and Christina. They have higher interests, of course. Higher than husbands. Higher even than children, I suspect.

HESTER. Well of all the— [*She stops*]

MRS. PHELPS. What were you about to say, Hester?

DAVID. Uh, Chris, look! The kids are coasting down the long hill by moonlight. What do you say we go and watch them?

CHRIS. I'd love to.

DAVID [*Fading*]. It'll do us good! Come on!

CHRIS [*Fading*]. You'll all excuse us, won't you?

DAVID [*Off*]. I'll get your coat.

CHRIS [*Off*]. It's right here in the hall, David.

DAVID [*Off*]. Fine, let's go.

[*Door opening and closing*]

MRS. PHELPS. I think she might have had more consideration than to drag David out of doors in freezing weather.

HESTER. Mrs. Phelps, David dragged *her* out. Besides, they're in love, they want to be alone.

MRS. PHELPS. She might consider her husband's health.

HESTER. Why worry about anyone as husky as David? Besides, it's Christina and not David who's going to have a baby.

MRS. PHELPS. Hester!

ROB [*Shocked*]. Hester—of all things—what a way to talk to—

MRS. PHELPS. Never mind, Robin!

HESTER. I'm sorry I shocked you. But I had to say it.

MRS. PHELPS. Robin. I feel very old this evening. And very tired. Help me to my room, please.

ROB. Your heart isn't bothering you again, is it?

MRS. PHELPS. It may very well be. You'll excuse us, Hester . . . Your arm, Robin.

ROB. Yes, Mother.

MRS. PHELPS. That's it, my boy. Help your mother.

[*Music: Bridge*]

MRS. PHELPS. I'll just sit here for a while, in my chaise longue. Stay with me awhile. I'm lonely tonight, Robin.

ROB. Sure I'll stay, if you want me to.

MRS. PHELPS. There. Head in my lap. And let's have a real old-fashioned talk. This shows me something I've always suspected. You are *my* son David takes after his father.

ROB. You really think so?

MRS. PHELPS. Of course . . . [*Music out*] . . . Robin, has Hester decided where she wants to spend her honeymoon?

ROB. She doesn't care where we go.

MRS. PHELPS. I took such an interest in my honeymoon. Hester hasn't picked out her flat silver yet, has she?

ROB. I don't think so.

MRS. PHELPS. I can't understand it!

ROB. What?

MRS. PHELPS. Her indifference. It shocks me.

ROB. You think she is indifferent?

MRS. PHELPS. Has she made any decision about her new home?

ROB. She says anything will suit her.

MRS. PHELPS. *Normal* girls look forward to having their homes to receive their friends in.

ROB. She says I know more about that sort of thing.

MRS. PHELPS. Does Hester *have* many friends? Did she have lots of suitors besides you?

ROB. I suppose she had loads. Why?

MRS. PHELPS. One does wonder how much a girl has been sought after. But then, why should she have bothered with others when she thought she could land you? You are rather a catch.

ROB. Me?

MRS. PHELPS. Any girl would set her cap for you.

ROB. I don't think Hester did that.

MRS. PHELPS. Only—

ROB. Only what?

MRS. PHELPS. I can't help wondering if Hester's feelings for you are as strong as you think! And now, after what you've told me . . .

ROB. Well, it's too late to worry now.

MRS. PHELPS. It's never too late, Robin! It's not too late! Marriage is such an important step and you're so sensitive. It would be too terrible if you had to go through the disillusionment and disappointment of— Oh Robin, you must be saved from that! *Does Hester love you?*

ROB. She must, or she wouldn't have accepted me.

MRS. PHELPS. That isn't enough, Robin. *Do you love Hester?*

ROB. Why sure, I must. Who could help loving her? I mean . . . Good heavens, what do I mean? A man ought to marry and . . .

MRS. PHELPS. Either you don't love Hester or Hester doesn't love you.

ROB. She does love me.

MRS. PHELPS. I haven't seen her showing it.

ROB. Mother!

MRS. PHELPS. You're making a grave mistake to go on with this! These things are better faced before than after, Robin! Children come after, and then it's too late! Think before it's too late! And remember, the happiness of three people is at stake!

ROB. Hester's and mine and . . .

MRS. PHELPS. And mine! And mine! Only, I was wrong to say that! You must put my fate out of your mind, just as Dave has done. Let Dave find out for himself what he's done. Christina won't have time for home and children. But *you*, Robin, *you* can still be saved! You *will* face the facts?

ROB. You mean break with Hester?

MRS. PHELPS. At once . . . tonight . . . you have your chance.

ROB. Well if you think that . . .

MRS. PHELPS. Oh, thank heaven for this confidence between us! Thank God I've saved my boy! You'll see it won't be so bad to put up with your mother a little longer!

ROB. Of course not, Mother.

MRS. PHELPS. Oh, I've still plenty to give you! And I won't have to be lonely!

[*Music: Bridge*]

CHRIS. Dave. Hold me . . . hold me tight.

DAVID. You're shivering.

CHRIS. Yes.

DAVID. We'd better go in, darling. You'll catch a chill.

CHRIS. It isn't the cold. I'm scared, Dave.

DAVID. What about?

CHRIS. I'm not sure. I've never come up against anything like this before. And it scares me.

DAVID. What does?

CHRIS. I don't know how to tell you.

DAVID. What are you driving at?

CHRIS. David—do you look at me as apart from all other women? I mean, do you think of all the women in the world and then think of me quite, quite differently?

DAVID. I'll bite. Do I?

CHRIS. Please answer.

DAVID. Of course I do.

CHRIS. Because that's what being in love must mean. Don't you see how that feeling between a man and a woman is what keeps life going?

DAVID. Sure, but . . . what are you getting so worked up about?

CHRIS. I don't know . . . Perhaps we'd better go in.

DAVID. Yes . . . Getting mighty cold. Might get more snow.

[*They're walking slowly through the following*]

CHRIS. I feel a little better. Just talking with you. Alone.

DAVID. Look, Chris, don't get upset about anything. Mother gets funny ideas now and then, but . . . she's crazy about you. They all are . . . By the way, what do you think of Mother's plan?

CHRIS. About . . . Phelps Manor?

DAVID. That—and what she had in mind for you.

CHRIS. Puttering, when the "real doctors" aren't busy? What do you think of it?

DAVID. Well, New York is the real future for both of us, but—well, we might get that laboratory modernized, with Mother's influence, and then it might be fun to put up a development here. Of course Mother —when she gets an idea into her head—it sure is hard to get it out! What a spirited old lady she is, huh?

CHRIS. She's quite—remarkable.

DAVID. Well, maybe we can work things out some way, if—why honey, you're really shivering.

CHRIS. Yes!

DAVID. I hope you're all right.

CHRIS. Oh, darling!

DAVID. What?

CHRIS. Before we go in. Kiss me, kiss me, please!

DAVID. That's awfully easy. Oh sweetheart, I love you!

CHRIS. Oh, darling.

DAVID [*After moment's pause*]. Come.

[*Door opens*]

[*Furious hysterical sobbing of Hester starts off and builds through*]

DAVID. What's that?

CHRIS. It's Hester. [*Hysteria presently comes to mike*] Hester! Hester!

DAVID. Rob. What's wrong?

[*Door closing*]

ROB [*Fading in*]. I—I don't know. Hester, can't you pull yourself together?

CHRIS. Hester dear!

ROB. Can't you stop her?

DAVID. What started it, anyway?

CHRIS. Hester! Be quiet.

MRS. PHELPS [*Fading in*]. What on earth is all this noise?

DAVID. It's Hester.

ROB. She's upset. I was just . . . you know . . . Mother . . .

CHRIS. Hester! Stop it!

HESTER. Christina . . .

CHRIS. Open a window, Dave. Mrs. Phelps, will you give me your smelling salts?

HESTER. Tell Rob to go away! Tell Rob to go away!

CHRIS. Never mind Rob!

MRS. PHELPS [*Fading in*]. Here are my salts.

CHRIS. Thanks . . . Hester! Now stop it! Stop it, do you hear me?

HESTER. If you'd only send these awful people out! Take me away, Christina! Take me back to New York! I can't face them!

CHRIS. Now *stop* it!

DAVID [*Fading in*]. Here's some snow from the window sill. Rub it on her wrists and temples.

CHRIS. Fine.

DAVID. What brought this on?

MRS. PHELPS. Rob and she must have had a falling out.

DAVID. No ordinary one. Say—where did Rob go?

CHRIS. He went upstairs.

MRS. PHELPS. He's naturally distressed. I'd better go see how he is. Such scenes aren't good for him.

HESTER [*In a high strained voice*]. No, isn't that so, Mrs. Phelps?

MRS. PHELPS. Did you speak to me?

HESTER. Take the smelling salts to Rob with my love.

CHRIS. Hester, take it easy.

HESTER. There's something I want to ask you, Mrs. Phelps!

MRS. PHELPS. Tomorrow, my dear girl.

HESTER. There isn't going to be any tomorrow.

MRS. PHELPS. What?

HESTER. Rob has just broken our engagement.

DAVID. No!

CHRIS [*Staggered*]. Hester, what do you mean?

MRS. PHELPS. I'm immensely distressed, of course.

HESTER. He talked it over with you beforehand, Mrs. Phelps. He told me that much. So it's no use acting surprised.

DAVID. Now, Hester, really . . .

HESTER. Why did you make him do it?

MRS. PHELPS. I won't allow a hysterical girl to be rude to me.

HESTER. Why did you talk Rob into jilting me? Will you answer, please?

MRS. PHELPS. Such things are painful, but they're far less painful before than after.

HESTER. He quoted that one.

DAVID. Hester, please, let's calm down and . . .

HESTER. I want her to tell why she did it!

MRS. PHELPS. This is absurd!

HESTER. You've got to explain!

MRS. PHELPS. Isn't it enough that he found in time you weren't the wife for him?

HESTER. That isn't the truth!

CHRIS. Hester, darling!

HESTER. Can you tell me what he meant when he said the happiness of *three* people was at stake?

MRS. PHELPS. He must have been thinking of your happiness as well as his own and mine.

HESTER. What about your loneliness?

MRS. PHELPS. This *is* contemptible of you!

DAVID. Really, Hester . . .

CHRIS. This can't do any good, Hester.

HESTER. She's got to admit why she made Rob . . .

MRS. PHELPS. Very well! I did advise my son to break with you. Because he told me you neither love him nor make any pretense of loving him.

HESTER. That isn't true!

MRS. PHELPS. And I told him to risk anything . . . anything, rather than such an appalling marriage!

HESTER. I don't believe a word of it.

MRS. PHELPS. You may believe it or not.

CHRIS. Mrs. Phelps, you'd better let me handle this.

MRS. PHELPS. Willingly.

HESTER. I'm going. I'm going this minute.

MRS. PHELPS. There's a train at nine in the morning. It gets you to New York at twelve. I shall have the car for you at eight-thirty.

HESTER. May I have the car now, please?

MRS. PHELPS. There's no train tonight.

HESTER. I won't stay here. I'll go to the hotel in town.

MRS. PHELPS. You'll do nothing of the sort!

HESTER. You see if I don't!

MRS. PHELPS. You've got to think of appearances!

HESTER. Appearances are your concern. I'm going to the hotel.

MRS. PHELPS. It's full. It's sure to be full.

HESTER. I'll call them. Right now.

MRS. PHELPS. I forbid you.

HESTER [*Receiver . . . Hester jiggles receiver through*]. Will you take me, Christina, in your car? I'll call them right now. Hello? I want the Hotel, the Lakeview Hotel. Yes, the . . . [*Couple of dead jiggles of receiver*] The phone's dead.

MRS. PHELPS. I ripped the cord loose. You are the only person in the world who has ever made me do an undignified thing. [*Fading*] I shall not forget it. Goodnight. I am going to bed. David, will you come up and talk with me for a moment, please?

DAVID. Now, Mother, I can't come right now. I'll be up later.

MRS. PHELPS [*Off*]. Very well. I'll come in to see you. Goodnight.

DAVID. Hester, I'm terribly sorry about this. Really, I wish there was something I could do . .

HESTER. Take me to the hotel, David. Take me in the car.

DAVID. Now Hester, it *would* look strange to the hotel people. Surely you can stay overnight.

CHRIS. She'll stay, Dave.

HESTER. It wasn't true what she said! He did want to marry me!

CHRIS. Of course, dear.

HESTER. Oh Christina, you got to leave here too! You've got to get your baby away from this dreadful house! Awful things happen here!

CHRIS. Hester . . . calm down.

HESTER. You'll see. She's almost been driving me crazy! She'll do the same to you that she's done to me! You'll see! You'll see!

[*Music*]

END OF ACT II

ANNOUNCER

COMMERCIAL

ACT III

NARRATOR. It's an hour later now in the Phelps's home. Christina is still downstairs, trying to calm Hester, while Dave has retired to bed. Then . . .

[*Knock on door*]

DAVID. Yes? [*Door opens*] Oh! Hello, Mother.

MRS. PHELPS [*Fade in*]. I brought you an extra cover for this cold night.

DAVID. Oh. Well, thanks.

MRS. PHELPS. There! Oh, let me sit here a moment as I used to . . . so long ago.

DAVID [*Uneasy*]. I—uh—I wish Chris would come up.

MRS. PHELPS. Oh, David, try to get that horrid scene downstairs out of your mind! I need my big boy so! I face the greatest problem of my life. And you've got to help me.

DAVID [*Surprised*]. For Pete's sake, what's the trouble?

MRS. PHELPS. David. Are you sure you haven't *discarded* your mother?

DAVID. Good heavens, Mother! What put an idea like that into your head? Everything is the same as it always was. Why shouldn't it be?

MRS. PHELPS. Are you sure?

DAVID. Of course!

MRS. PHELPS. That's what I wanted you to say. Now put your hand in mine and tell me Christina is going to love me.

DAVID. She does already. Of course she does.

MRS. PHELPS. You are happy, aren't you?

DAVID. Couldn't be happier, since I found Christina.

MRS. PHELPS. I'm glad. Thank heaven that when your hour struck it didn't strike falsely, as it did for Robin! Of course, you and Robin are quite different. You are *my* son. Robin takes after his father. But David . . .

DAVID. Yes?

MRS. PHELPS. You mustn't be impatient with Christina if she seems, at first, a little jealous of our family. We've always been so close.

DAVID. Chris wouldn't be jealous over a thing like that. She's as level-headed as they come.

MRS. PHELPS. Jealous girls sometimes think things . . . morbid things.

DAVID. Morbid? Chris? I guess you don't know Chris, Mother.

MRS. PHELPS. I'm just asking you to be very understanding with her if, by any chance, she made the mistake of . . . well, of taking sides in what happened downstairs, for instance. Always be patient with her, David.

DAVID. Of course! Too bad about Rob and Hester.

MRS. PHELPS. She wasn't right for him, David. Not for Rob.

DAVID. Maybe not. Of course, you never exactly took to any of our girl friends, Mother.

MRS. PHELPS. I've only wanted you both to be patient . . . till the right one came. And now, good night, my boy.

DAVID. Good night!

MRS. PHELPS. I'll kiss you good night.

CHRIS [Off]. That's a pretty picture.

MRS. PHELPS. Oh come in, Christine. Nothing private. You're one of the family now.

CHRIS. Thank you.

MRS. PHELPS. Christina, whatever else you may have taken from me, you can*not* take from me the joy of feeling my son here, once more, in his old room, beside me.

CHRIS. I haven't meant to take anything from you, Mrs. Phelps.

MRS. PHELPS [Sweetly]. You know I was only joking. [Fading] Don't keep David up too late. He's tired. And you must be tired too, Christina. Good night.

[Door closes]

DAVID. You look pretty stern, Chris.

CHRIS. Do I?

DAVID. How's Hester?

CHRIS. Poor kid. I shouldn't be surprised if she were really in luck, Dave.

DAVID. You're probably right. But it isn't exactly up to me to say so. Come here, Chris . . . Sit down . . .

CHRIS. I'm such a tired girl, Dave . . . I want to be held on to and be told you love me, and that you enjoy loving me.

DAVID. That can all be done. Nothing has ever been so perfect for me as— these months with you.

CHRIS. I hate being so far from you tonight. Way on the other side of the hall.

DAVID. I don't like it myself. It's just one of Mother's quirks, always redecorating just at the wrong time.

[Lowers voice each time he mentions his mother]

CHRIS. She naturally wanted you near her.

DAVID. We'd better talk softly. Might keep Mother awake.

CHRIS. Dave . . . you remember what we were talking about this evening . . . outside . . . two people, a man and a woman, apart from all others. That's how marriage must feel, or it isn't marriage.

DAVID. Of course, and that's how we do feel . . . But why are you off on that again?

CHRIS. Do you realize, Dave, that the blackest sinner on earth is anyone who tampers with that feeling?

DAVID. If you say so, I'll say he is.

CHRIS. He!

DAVID. Huh?

CHRIS. Never mind . . . Your brother didn't feel that way about Hester, did he?

DAVID. Nor she about him, I guess.

CHRIS. I know better. I've had that child on my hands for the past hour. I've learned a lot, Dave.

DAVID. Look, Chris, don't get mixed up in this. Don't . . . "take sides."

CHRIS. Can I help it?

DAVID. It's not our business.

CHRIS. David . . . Hester goes tomorrow. When do we go?

DAVID. Well, I'd like to get away soon, but you know how Mother feels. She's been looking forward so long to our coming. And now this thing with Hester. I'm afraid she's in a kind of nervous state. I think we ought to take it easy for a few days, and not upset her.

CHRIS. She's bearing up!

DAVID. You can't tell. She's so darn game.

CHRIS. Is she?

DAVID. She always has been. I've seen her nurse Rob through one thing after another when . . . when she'd admit that she was twice as sick as he, with her heart and all. She said we were her job and she wouldn't give in.

CHRIS. It all kind of fits together, doesn't it?

DAVID. What does?

CHRIS. Weak heart and illnesses . . . and you having to go three thousand miles away from home to fall in love with me.

DAVID. What do you mean?

CHRIS. Dave! We've got to get out of here . . . tomorrow.

DAVID. What?

CHRIS. We've got to "take sides."

DAVID. Now look. I brought you here to meet Mother. I can't walk out now and leave her in the lurch.

CHRIS. Who comes first: your mother or me?

DAVID. Why ask such a question?

CHRIS. Because I love you. And I've got to find out if you love me. And I'm afraid . . . afraid . . .

DAVID. Chris, this is all nonsense.

CHRIS. No, Dave, listen: I've got to get this off my chest. Ever since we've been married I've come across queer rifts in your feeling for me, like arid places in your heart. One moment you're my perfect lover and the next, I'll find myself floundering in sand, and you nowhere to be seen. And now I know what keeps you. Your mother keeps you. I'm afraid of your mother's hold on you, David.

DAVID. Now, Chris, what kind of talk is this?

CHRIS. I've seen what she can do! And that's why this business of Hester's is a kind of test case, that may decide about *our marriage*.

DAVID. Chris, this is all absurd.

CHRIS. Is it?

DAVID. A man hasn't seen his mother for three years and he comes back and . . .

CHRIS [*Desperate*]. Your mother, your mother, always your mother! She's got you back! Dave, her big boy, who went away and got married! She's got you back!

DAVID. I won't stand for any more of this. A man's mother is his mother.

CHRIS. And what's his wife? Or doesn't she count?

DAVID. This is morbid rot! She warned me you'd be jealous!

CHRIS. *Did* she?

DAVID. But I never expected anything like this!

CHRIS [*Louder*]. Oh, Dave, what's going to become of me?

DAVID. I won't stand any more . . .

CHRIS. Hester's escaped, but I'm caught! I've got to face it! I'm going to have a baby by a man who belongs to another woman!

DAVID. Chris! Do you want Mother to hear you?

CHRIS. Do you think she hasn't!

[*Door opens*]

MRS. PHELPS. So . . .

DAVID. . . . You . . . *did* hear!

MRS. PHELPS. How could I help it? Now we know where we stand.

DAVID. Chris, can't you tell her you didn't mean it?

MRS. PHELPS. Of course she can't.

CHRIS. Of course not. I meant every word I said. And now I guess I'd better go . . . [*Fading*] I belong with Hester, now.

[*Door slams*]

DAVID. Chris! Mother, I'll straighten out everything in the morning, I swear I will. Chris is naturally upset about Hester, but—everything will be all right!

MRS. PHELPS. Dave, I'm on Christina's side.

DAVID. W—what?

MRS. PHELPS. I accept my fate. You have your own life to live with the woman you have chosen. No bonds bind you to me.

DAVID. Now, Mother—

MRS. PHELPS. I'm not complaining. I'm only sorry for one thing. To see you throw away your chance here, your great chance!

DAVID. But I haven't thrown— [*A scream by Christina, off, stops him*] What's that?

CHRIS [*Off*]. Rob! Dave! Dave!

MRS. PHELPS [*Overlapping Chris*]. It isn't a fire, is it?

[*Door opening fast*]

DAVID. Chris! Chris! What is it?

ROB [*Fading in*]. Say what's up? What's the trouble?

CHRIS [*Off*]. Dave, Dave! Come down, quick. [*Feet clattering downstairs . . . Chris goes on without pause, fading in*] Hester . . . I went into her room and she'd gone. Then I came to look downstairs. The side door was open and . . .

DAVID. Oh heaven.

ROB. What do you think happened?

CHRIS. I don't like to imagine.

[*Sneak in wind whistling*]

DAVID. She got away.

ROB [*Shouting out of the door*]. Hester! Hester!

CHRIS. I shouldn't have left her alone for a minute!

MRS. PHELPS [*Fading in*]. The little fool. Let her go!

CHRIS. No, we can't!

ROB [*Continuing to shout*]. Hester! . . .

CHRIS. We've got to go after her.

DAVID. Of course. Come on, Rob!

CHRIS. Dave, the pond!

ROB. Good lord! She took the short cut across the pond!

CHRIS. The holes in the pond! Quick, Dave, for heaven's sake!

DAVID. Come Rob.

ROB. I'm with you.

DAVID. Hurry, Rob.

MRS. PHELPS. Boys, come back! Come back! Dave . . . Rob!

HESTER. Rob . . . David—help!

DAVID [*Fading*]. There she is! In the water!

ROB. Hester!

DAVID. Hold on, Hester! We'll get to you, Hester! Hold on!

MRS. PHELPS. Boys! Boys! Come back! You'll catch pneumonia! I forbid it!

[*Music takes it away . . . Segue to peaceful theme*]

CHRIS. What do you think, Doctor?

DOCTOR. I think she was a lucky girl to have you here. You've done everything that was needed. She'll pull through nicely.

HESTER. She was wonderful, Doctor.

DOCTOR. I'm sure of it.

CHRIS. How soon do you think Hester can be moved?

DOCTOR. Go home, you mean?

CHRIS. Yes.

DOCTOR. Traveling might not be as bad for her as staying here. The sooner the better, I'd say.

CHRIS. I see what you mean . . .

DOCTOR. Good luck, Hester. You'll be all right.

HESTER [*Fading*]. Thank you, Doctor.

CHRIS. I'll see you to the door.

DOCTOR. Thanks.

[*Steps going downstairs during*]

CHRIS. Doctor . . . Do you think you ought to see Mrs. Phelps before you go?

DOCTOR. Why?

CHRIS. She keeps talking about her heart.

DOCTOR [*Chuckles*]. I'd rather not, if you don't mind. [*Steps arrive at bottom*] Between you and me, there's nothing wrong with that heart.

CHRIS. I suspected as much.

DOCTOR [*Confidentially*]. It would take an atom bomb to hurt it! Good-bye.

[*Door opening*]

CHRIS. Good-bye, Doctor.

[*Door closing*]

ROB [*Fading in*]. Was that the doctor, Chris?

CHRIS. Yes, Rob.

ROB. What did he say? How is Hester?

CHRIS. She's all right. She's pulling through fine.

ROB. Thank heaven. I've been worried stiff.

CHRIS. In fact, she's well enough to go home right away. Where's Dave?

ROB. He's putting danger signs around the pond.

CHRIS. Will you ask him to come upstairs when he comes in? [*Fading*] I'm going up to help Hester get ready.

[*Footsteps upstairs*]

ROB. Oh. Okay.

MRS. PHELPS [*Off*]. Robin!

ROB. Yes, Mother.

MRS. PHELPS [*Off*]. Was that the doctor?

ROB. Yes, Mother.

MRS. PHELPS [*Fading in*]. And he went without coming to look at me?

ROB. I guess he did. Hester will be all right, he said. She can go home today.

MRS. PHELPS. Well, there can't have been very much wrong.

ROB [*Worried*]. Mother . . . what are we going to do?

MRS. PHELPS What do you mean?

ROB. How am I going to face people? I'm so ashamed.

MRS. PHELPS. There's nothing to be ashamed of! It's clearer than ever that you did the right thing. The way Hester has behaved, I'm sure there's insanity in her family. And we'll just make that perfectly clear to everybody.

ROB. I suppose that would make it easier.

MRS. PHELPS. And after that . . . perhaps you and I could go on a trip.

ROB. Say, that'd be swell, if we could!

MRS. PHELPS. I know. We'll go to Florida, and you'll take a course at the University of Florida in interior decorating. Then when we come back perhaps my old dream can come true: my two boys working together!

ROB. That certainly would be something.

MRS. PHELPS. That is, if only Dave . . .

ROB. Yes, that's the problem.

[*Door opens*]

DAVID [*Off*]. Phew, it's cold. The pond will be frozen again by tomorrow if this keeps up.

[*Door closes . . . Fading in*]

What did the doc say about Hester?

ROB. She's leaving today.

MRS. PHELPS. There never was anything the matter with her.

DAVID. It's easy to see, Mother, that you don't often bathe in that pond in zero weather.

MRS. PHELPS. I hope I have more sanity. Robin, will you see that the car is made ready for Hester, whenever she wants it.

ROB [*Off*]. Sure. Right away.

MRS. PHELPS [*Drops voice*]. Dave . . .

DAVID. Yes, Mother.

MRS. PHELPS. I need you, Dave . . . What am I to do with Robin? I'm afraid you've got to help me with him.

DAVID. I'll do anything I can. But what's the trouble?

MRS. PHELPS. If I were well and able to stand the things I used to stand before my heart went back on me . . . and before my blood pressure got so high . . . I shouldn't trouble you. But as I am, and with Robin on the verge of a complete breakdown . . .

DAVID. But I haven't noticed anything about Rob.

MRS. PHELPS. Dave, he said things to me before you came in that no son of mine would dream of saying unless he had something the matter with him. I've got to get him away.

DAVID. What are you going to do?

MRS. PHELPS. Florida is the place. But he mustn't go alone. He can't face things alone. He's like his father. You're *my* son. That's why I turn to you.

DAVID. Why not go with him?

MRS. PHELPS. Because I'm not really well enough in case anything should happen. Oh Dave, do you think . . .

DAVID. What?

MRS. PHELPS. That Christina could spare you for a little? Just a few weeks? Just long enough to get Rob and me settled in some restful place? Do you think she would?

DAVID. Well, Mother, you know we have a lot of plans of our own. Chris has got to get to New York for her job. Of course this is important too, and . . . well, I could talk it over with her and . . .

CHRIS [*Off, arriving downstairs*]. Now's your chance. What do you want to talk over, Dave?

DAVID. Chris! What are you doing with the suitcases?

CHRIS [*Fading in*]. I've been packing. I'm going away with Hester. Are you coming?

DAVID [*Staggered*]. Now?

CHRIS. As soon as she comes down. I came down ahead to thrash out one thing for good and all.

MRS. PHELPS. To thrash out what, Christina?

CHRIS. Whether David is going on from this point as your son or my husband.

DAVID. Chris—you're not going to begin all that again!

CHRIS. Yes I am! Oh, I'd walk out without a word, even loving you as I do, if I thought this state of affairs made anyone in this family happy.

DAVID. What state of affairs?

MRS. PHELPS. You might let us judge our own happiness.

CHRIS. If you had any. But you haven't. You're all trapped . . . terribly, miserably trapped!

MRS. PHELPS. What we say in anger, we sometimes regret, Christina.

CHRIS. I'm not angry now—But I mean to strip this house and show it for what it is.

MRS. PHELPS [*Turning for help*]. Dave, I—

CHRIS. I mean to show you up, Mrs. Phelps! Then Dave can use his judgment.

DAVID. Chris! For heaven's sake. Can't I be both a good son and a good husband?

CHRIS. Not if your mother knows it, you can't!

MRS. PHELPS. If you'll excuse me, I will not stay to be insulted.

CHRIS. You'll lose him if you don't stay! . . . Oh, I know all about the legend of yourself as a great woman you've built up for thirty years for your sons to worship. But it hasn't taken me long to see that you're not fit to be anyone's mother!

DAVID. Chris, see here now . . .

MRS. PHELPS. Let her go on! She will explain that or retract!

CHRIS. Mrs. Phelps, why do you resent that I'm going to have a baby . . . David's baby . . .

MRS. PHELPS. I do not resent it.

CHRIS. And why did you bend every effort to separate Hester and Rob?

MRS. PHELPS. I did nothing of the sort!

CHRIS. Can you deny that your one idea is to keep your sons dependent on you?

MRS. PHELPS. I deny it all!

CHRIS. You may deny it till you're black in the face, but it's true. You belong to a type only too common, Mrs. Phelps . . . a type of self-centered, self-pitying, son-devouring mother.

DAVID. Chris!

MRS. PHELPS. Really, I—

CHRIS. Oh, there are normal mothers around; mothers who want their children to be men and women and take care of themselves; mothers who are people, too; who can look on their children as people and don't forever have to be holding on to them and tucking them up like everlasting babies. But you're not one of the normal ones, Mrs. Phelps!

DAVID. Chris! Please—I—

CHRIS. Look what you've done to your sons; you've destroyed Rob. You've swallowed him up until there's nothing left of him. Your crowning achievement was to make him unfit for military service—nothing wrong, just the nervous type. And Dave. You'd have swallowed him up too, if the war hadn't given him his chance to escape your clutches. And to think that some people actually admire your kind— you professional mothers!

MRS. PHELPS. I hope David sees the sordidness, the nastiness you offer him for his life. What can you offer David?

CHRIS. A chance to be himself. A chance to share with me the raising of his child. The solace and enjoyment of my love.

MRS. PHELPS [Revolted]. Ugh!

CHRIS. Can you offer so much?

MRS. PHELPS. I offer a mother's love! Which you scoff at!

CHRIS. Not within bounds. I hope my baby loves me. I know I'll love my baby. But if David lets me down, I hope I never turn to my children, as you did, Mrs. Phelps, for the romantic satisfaction I missed.

MRS. PHELPS. David, really—

CHRIS. *Why* did she separate us last night, David? Because she couldn't bear the thought of our being together!

DAVID. Chris, for heaven's sake—

CHRIS. And she couldn't bear that because, to this day, she refuses to believe that you're a grown man capable of desiring a woman!

DAVID. Chris!

MRS. PHELPS. No, no!

CHRIS. You find that revolting? . . . It is! . . . I can't wait any longer for your answer, Dave.

DAVID. Chris, please! Can't we calm down for a minute, and—

CHRIS. Is that your answer? Remember me, won't you, on Mother's Day! [*Calls*] Hester! Are you ready?

[*Hester's footsteps as*]

HESTER [*Running downstairs . . . Off*]. Coming. I'm all ready.

CHRIS. It's time to go. Here, I'll take one of those bags.

HESTER. Isn't . . . Dave coming with us?

CHRIS. I'm afraid not.

HESTER. Oh Christina!

CHRIS. Never mind. It can't be helped.

ROB [*Fading in*]. The car's ready, Mother. Any time Hester wants it.

CHRIS. We won't need it. We're going in mine. Straight to New York.

ROB. Hester, I don't know what to say . . .

HESTER. Don't say anything, Rob. I feel better, and my plans are complete. You know what I'm going to do? I'm going to marry an orphan.

CHRIS. Good-bye, Dave.

[*Door opens*]

[*Slight wind background*]

DAVID. Chris. You can't. It isn't fair to—

CHRIS. I'm sorry it's come to this. [*Choking*] It could have been so wonderful . . . [*Fading*] Come on, Hester.

DAVID. Chris! Don't go!

CHRIS [*Off*]. Good-bye!

DAVID. Chris! . . . [*Pause*] Mother. I'm sorry. I've made up my mind. I'm going too.

MRS. PHELPS. No, Dave! No!

DAVID. The silver cord is broken, Mother. We were trapped, and I never knew it. But now it's broken. I'm sorry, Mother. [*Fading*] Good-bye.

MRS. PHELPS. David, no, no, no! Come back! No Dave! DAVE! My boy! My boy! Come back!

ROB. Without even his coat . . . He's getting in the car.

[*Car door slams off and car starts off*]

MRS. PHELPS. Close the door . . .

[*Front door closes*]

Rob . . . *you* must always remember what David, in his blindness, forgot. That mother love suffereth long and is kind, envieth not, and is not puffed up, is not easily provoked; beareth all things; believeth all things; hopeth all things . . . At least, I think *my* loves does?

ROB [*Engulfed forever*]. Yes, Mother.

[*Music*]

ANNOUNCER

CREDITS

ON BORROWED TIME

Original Play
by Paul Osborn

Based on the Novel
by Lawrence Edward Watkin

Radio Adaptation
by Paul Peters

CAST

(for radio performance)

NARRATOR	Dwight Weist
TRIXIE	Brad Barker
SUSAN	Anne Burr
JIM	James Monks
GRAMPS	Walter Huston
PUD	Sarah Fussell
MELLETT	Ian MacAllaster
GRANNY	Leona Roberts
MR. BRINK	Glenn Anders
DEMETRIA	Dorothy Sands
MARCY	Frances Heflin
A BOY UP A TREE	Peter Griffith
DR. EVANS	Frank Lovejoy
MR. PILBEAM	Cameron Prud'Homme
WORKMAN	Ian MacAllaster
SHERIFF	John Girard
A BARTENDER	James Monks
GRIMES	Edwin Jerome

ON BORROWED TIME

Radio adaptation by

Paul Peters

Somebody, during one of the many radio meetings for "On Borrowed Time," complained that he could not understand what the play was all about. If he were to tune in that Sunday night, he insisted, on a silly story about an ass named Mr. Brink who got himself marooned up a tree, he would promptly turn it off.

We managed somehow to assuage this critic by assuring him that, since the story of "On Borrowed Time" had succeeded as a novel, a play, and a motion picture, he must be outnumbered a million to one. But our critic then protested he had no idea who Mr. Brink really was; and after accepting dubiously a filtered voice to sharpen the image of an anthropomorphic Death, he insisted he could not understand why Mr. Brink should pursue Gramps with such relentlessness. So, although Gramps is already 78 years old, we gave him a seismic palpitation of the heart as an extra kindly shove into the grave where, of course, he ultimately belongs.

A second critic, in the inevitable final conference just before the broadcast, would pause periodically and cry, "Now wait a minute. *I don't get the picture.* Just where is the apple tree in relation to the house? Where is the front gate in relation to the porch? How near is the tree to the fence?"

I don't remember whether we ever nailed that tree down in precisely the correct audible spot, but I would like to submit, in a genial mood, that all this passion for visual precision in a sonant medium is child's play and nonsense. Too often it only clutters up the script. Too often it assumes that the radio audience is so feeble-minded that listeners cannot even conceive that a house might have a garden and a garden might have a tree. Too often it reminds me of those gaudy Technicolor historical movies in which the burning of Atlanta is reproduced to the last scorched window sill, while the people, the emotions, the underlying ideas are stuck together with pure Scotch tape.

137

Wanting the visual focus of the stage, radio must, I suppose, use shorter scenes, break them up, shovel them about to keep the ear from napping. And since we can, by air wave, build a house in three words and furnish it in five, it would be foolish not to toss the action of "On Borrowed Time" from parlor to porch, from kitchen to garden, from basement workshop to upstairs bedroom.

Sometimes I wonder if, because in radio we can travel so freely, without tickets, soot, or taxes, we don't occasionally descend to a kind of biological bouncing about for the sheer sake of bounce. If the stuff were good, if the people were real, they could, for my money, stand talking on a dime for an hour and I would listen.

ON BORROWED TIME

ANNOUNCER

INTRODUCTION FOR THE THEATRE GUILD

ACT I

ANNOUNCER. This is the home of Dr. Jim Northrup's family in one of those quiet small American towns. Perhaps the nicest thing about the Northrup place is the cool, grassy yard, shaded by a gnarled old apple tree. Opposite the tree is a screen door leading to the comfortable living room, where Granny Northrup usually does her knitting; while Gramps Northrup, on a summer afternoon like this, is apt to be tinkering at his basement workbench on some gadget for his five-year-old grandson, Pud. Before long Granny will call . . .

GRANNY [Calling, off mike]. Juleyan!

GRAMPS. Oh, Hecate! There's your Granny!

PUD. Where's Hecate, Gramps?

GRAMPS. Where the woodbine twineth.

GRANNY [Louder, off mike]. Juleyan!

GRAMPS [Calling as he starts upstairs]. I'm coming. Hold your horses, can't you? [To Pud] Here, pal, hide my pipe under the workbench, will you? Whose afraid of the female of the species, howbeit more carnivorous than the male. Not us, not us. [Both are tramping lustily upstairs]

PUD [Chanting]. Carnivorous, not us. Carnivorous, not us.

[They reach the top and open the door]

GRANNY [Fade in] When you two get together over some gimcrack, you're as dead as a post.

GRAMPS. Was you calling, Nellie? Didn't hear you. Give us a kiss.

GRANNY. I hollered loud enough to wake the dead. I suppose you were too busy smoking that filthy pipe.

GRAMPS. Dr. Evans said one pipeful a day.

GRANNY. Smells to me like you been smoking six. Here, Trixie, you go out for a walk with your grandpa.

[*Trixie barks joyously*]

GRAMPS. I'll thank you not to claim kin to me with that flea bag.

GRANNY [*Shocked*]. Julian!

PUD [*Chanting gaily*]. I've got a bagful of fleas, I'll give you one if you say please.

GRANNY. There! Listen to that child. Turning your own grandson into a foul-mouth like yourself. If you don't mend your ways, Julian Northrup, I'm going to talk to Jim and Susan about sending Pud away to school.

GRAMPS. There ain't no school what'd take him. He's too little.

GRANNY. Demetria knows a nice boarding school in—

GRAMPS. Demetria! Great jumpin' Jerusalem! I might have known she was at the bottom of this. The old bird-stuffer.

GRANNY. Demetria's a fine Christian woman and I won't hear a word against her.

GRAMPS. She's a bird-stuffer!

PUD. What's a bird-stuffer, Gramps?

GRAMPS. It's just a bird-stuffer. Adam saw a dog, and it looked like a dog and he called it a dog. I saw your Aunt Demetria, she looked like a bird-stuffer and I called her a bird-stuffer.

GRANNY. You're poisoning that child's mind, Julian Northrup, and it's got to be stopped. It's got to be. [*Opens screen door*] I'm going up the street to visit a little with Demetria. [*Voice fading*] I'll be back soon.

[*Door closes . . . Phone rings*]

PUD. I'll answer it, Gramps. [*Ring is cut off by click*] Hello.

MELLETT [*Filtered*]. Dr. Northrup? This is Joe Mellett at Gainsville. It's coming, doctor—the baby's coming.

PUD [*Yelling*]. Hey, Pop. It's somebody called Joe Mellett. He's having a baby.

JIM [*Off mike, calling down*]. Tell him I'll be over in 20 minutes.

PUD. Can you wait 15 minutes, Joe?

MELLETT [*Filtered*]. Well, tell him to hurry—hurry!

>   [*Click as phone is hung up*]

PUD [*Calling*]. He says he's in a heck of a hurry, Pop.

>   [*Footsteps running down stairs*]

JIM [*Fading in*]. The *father* is always in a hurry. [*Calling*] Hey, Susan, want a ride? I'm driving to Gainsville.

SUSAN [*Off mike, calling back*]. I'd love it. [*Door opens and closes . . . Voice on mike*] Take care of Pud, will you, Gramps?

GRAMPS. Who else's taken care of that whippersnapper since he was born?

PUD. Whippersnapper, whippersnapper.

SUSAN. And stop using that crazy language. Pud repeats it.

GRAMPS. What crazy language?

SUSAN. You know what I mean. Come on, Jim. Good-bye.

>   [*Footsteps . . . Screen door opens and shuts . . . Dog barks*]

GRAMPS. Hey, you infernal behemoth, shut up.

PUD. Trixie, you're an infernal behemoth. Infernal behemoth. Infernal behemoth.

>   [*Trixie barks loudly, cross fading into bridge music*]

>   [*A car driving rapidly*]

SUSAN. Jim—!

JIM. You call this fast?

SUSAN. The road's slippery, darling. Oh—there's Granny and Demetria up ahead. They're waving at us. Jim, stop! Jim, listen to me!

JIM. Oh, all right. But I'll give you just one minute.

>   [*The car slows down with brakes squealing*]

>   [*Motor idles*]

SUSAN [*Calling out*]. Hello, Granny. Hello, Demmie!

GRANNY [*A sweet, tired old woman*]. Jim—Susan—I'm so frightened. There was a man following us.

DEMMIE [*A prissy, spinsterish, sharp woman*]. Now, Nellie, that's all nonsense.

JIM. What'd he look like?

GRANNY. Strange—awfully strange. And the way he looked at me with big, black eyes—like bottomless pits.

DEMMIE. I swear I don't know what's got into her. Must be the heat. I didn't see a soul.

JIM. You ought to be proud there's a man following you, Granny. Shows you're still in the running. Now you go home and lie down. That's orders. Doctor's orders.

DEMMIE [*Importantly*] Jim, I was hoping you'd be home. I want to talk to you—

JIM. About Pud. I don't want him going to a boarding school, Demmie. I've told you that. He's got a good home.

DEMMIE. Well, there's one person in that home whose influence on the boy—

JIM. Demmie, you're my wife's sister and for some strange reason, she's fond of you. So you're welcome at my house, though I wish you'd stop picking fights with Gramps. He's an old man and he's not very well.

DEMMIE. *I* pick fights with *him!* Why, last time—

SUSAN [*Tactfully*]. Granny, Jim's delivering a baby. I'm afraid we have to hurry.

GRANNY. Oh, dear, yes. Run along, Jim. Good-bye. Come home early.

SUSAN [*Voice fades as gears shift and car starts away*]. Good-bye, Granny. Good-bye, Demmie.

GRANNY [*After a little pause*]. Demmie! Look, there he is.

DEMMIE. Who? Where?

GRANNY [*Awed*]. That strange man who was following me. He's sitting in the back of their car!

[*Bridge music*]

[*Fade into outdoor early evening sounds: A cricket, some faint bird calls*]

PUD. Gramps, I'm hungry. Where's mom and pop staying so long?

GRAMPS. They went to Gainsville on account of that baby, remember? A baby's the dangedest contrariest thing there is.

PUD. Well, why ain't Granny here?

GRAMPS. Oh, you know what happens when your Granny and your Aunt Demmie get together! Better go inside now, pal. Grass is getting damp with dew. They'll all be coming home soon and get you your supper.

[*Footsteps . . . Screen door opens and shuts . . . Trixie barks*]

GRAMPS. No, Trixie. You stay out here. Go chase your tail in the grass. It'll do you good. I'll sit on this bench a while.

GRAMPS [*To himself, drowsily*]. Getting dark . . . Cold, too. I feel so—

[*Fading*]—so—[*Sighs*]

BRINK [*After a pause*]. [*He speaks very quietly, very precisely . . . His voice has an echo*] Mr. Julian Northrup, I believe?

[*Trixie whines*]

GRAMPS [*With a start*]. What's that? Did somebody say something?

BRINK. Most people don't hear me the first time.

GRAMPS. I felt tired all of a sudden and I must have—[*Sharp*] Say, who are you?

BRINK. You may call me Mr. Brink. I just dropped by to say that you must soon get ready to come with me.

GRAMPS. Where you goin'?

BRINK. Where the woodbine twineth. [*Trixie whines*]

GRAMPS. Where the wood . . . ? Say *I* just said that. I made it up. Now, look here, Mr. Brink. I don't know you. I don't know as I like you, either. Why should I go with you?

BRINK [*Gently*]. Because you're very old and you're tired. Oh, yes, you act hale and hearty, but I've watched you when nobody was looking. You're seventy-nine.

GRAMPS. Seventy-eight.

BRINK. My book says seventy-nine. It's almost time for you. Besides, Jim and Susan have come with me. [*Trixie whines*]

GRAMPS. Jim and Susan! You're crazy! They drove off to Gainsville this afternoon.

BRINK. People will call it an accident, but they came with me.

GRAMPS. Jim and Susan—went with you? Both of them went with you? Why? Why? When they're both so young? Poor Nellie, that's going to break her heart. And Pud—Somebody will have to look after Pud. You can't leave a little tyke like that alone. Demmie'll get hold of him—and she'll break his spirit. [*Resolute now*] Nope, I can't go with you, Mr. Brink. Even if I wanted to, I can't. Now you run along before I—[*A spasm seizes him ...He gasps in pain*] Oh-h-h ...

BRINK. You see. Your hour's close. The next time I come—

GRAMPS. No. I ain't going nowhere. You get out of here. You're trespassing. Now, go on, git! [*Pause, bewildered*] Well, I'll be . . . lollipopped. He's gone.

[*Trixie barks brightly again*]

GRANNY [*Fading in*]. Julian, who were you yelling at? I could hear you all the way to the front walk.

GRAMPS. I—there was a feller here.

GRANNY. I don't see anybody. You better come upstairs with me and get rest. I feel tired, too.

GRAMPS. All right, Nellie. I'll be up in a minute.

[*Screen door opens and shuts . . . Pud's footsteps running*]

PUD. Gramps, Gramps, who was that man?

GRAMPS. You saw him, Pud?

PUD. Sure. He went past the kitchen window. What'd he want?

GRAMPS. He wanted me to go with him.

PUD. Where?

GRAMPS. Where the woodbine twineth.

PUD. Oh, I know. You mean Hecate! Are you going, Gramps?

GRAMPS. Not on your life, I ain't. Not on your sweet life.

[*Bridge music*]

[*Fade into a child's phonograph record, maybe a* MOTHER GOOSE *song . . . After a moment, a door opens and closes*]

GRANNY [*Sharply*]. Pud, take that record off.

PUD. Why, Granny?

GRANNY. Because it ain't proper to play music in a Christian home so soon after a funeral.

PUD. You mean because Aunt Demetria says I'm a—a orphan.

GRAMPS [*Roaring*]. You hear that? Aunt Demetria! Why, that skinny old harpy—

GRANNY. Julian!

GRAMPS. Telling things like that to the boy. If I ever hear that—*poltergeist . . . !*

GRANNY. Julian! If you swear any more in front of—

PUD. I'm going to swear when I'm nine.

GRAMPS [*Warning*]. Ah-ah, Pud!

PUD. But you said I could, Gramps. I've learned all the words.

GRANNY. Julian! Did you tell that boy—?

GRAMPS [*Shouting*]. Quiet! I'm writing a letter.

GRANNY. Who are you writing to, Julian?

GRAMPS. Reverend Murdock. Looked kind of shabby when he was preaching that funeral sermon for Jim and Susan. So I'm sending him a check for $50. Now that's a good deed, ain't it, even if I say so myself.

PUD. Hey, Gramps, if you do a good deed, you can make a wish and it'll come true.

GRAMPS. Who says so, boy?

PUD. My picture book says so. Don't you remember? You read it to me— the story about the man who did good deeds and all his wishes came true?

GRAMPS. Must be so then.

PUD. All right, Gramps, make a wish, make a wish, make a wish. Wish me a whole truck load of chocolate bars. With almonds.

GRAMPS. No, we'll just hold that wish till the time comes. I'll think of something then—something colossal.

GRANNY [*Abruptly*]. Julian, it's just come to me.

GRAMPS [*Absently*]. What's that, Nellie?

GRANNY. Pud, take Trixie out for a walk.

PUD. But, Granny, Trixie don't want no walk. Marcy just brought her back.

GRANNY. Do as I say.

PUD. Oh, all right. [*Calling*] Come on, Trixie. Granny wants to tell Gramps something she don't want me to hear.

[*Dog barks, footsteps, screen door opens and closes . . . Barking fades*]

GRANNY. Julian, it wasn't an accident that killed Jim and Susan.

GRAMPS. Now, Nellie, you don't believe they smashed up their car on purpose?

GRANNY. I was just sitting here, asking myself why this cross had been put upon us. What had we done that was bad? And suddenly it was like—like hearing the voice of God. It's a judgment on us because of you!

GRAMPS. Me?

GRANNY. You and me both, Julian.

GRAMPS. Well, what've we been doing that's bad, Nellie? I can't think of nothing. Less you been up to something.

GRANNY. I've been closing my eyes to the way you're ruining Pud. We can't raise that boy, Julian—all by ourselves—we're too old.

GRAMPS [*Reassures her*]. Sure we can, Nellie. Same way we raised Jim. I'll keep teaching him to cuss and you'll keep teaching him not to.

PUD [*Off mike, shouting*]. Hey, Gramps, Gramps, somebody's stealing our apples again.

GRAMPS [*Rising, stamping toward door*]. Great Judas Priest! [*Screen door opens and shuts, footsteps on gravel*] Hey, you blasted young shikepoke!

PUD [*Off mike*]. Hurry, Gramps, he's coming down out of the tree.

GRAMPS. If I catch you, I'll give you such a tanning—

PUD [*On mike now*]. Gee, Gramps, he got away.

GRAMPS. I swear I wish that anyone who climbs that tree would have to stay there till I let him down.

PUD. Gramps! You know what you did? You made a wish.

GRAMPS. Huh?

PUD. A wish! You wished that anyone who climbed that tree would have to stay there till you let him down. [*Chants*] Gramps made a wish, Gramps made a wish, Gramps made a— [*Stops*] Cheesit, Gramps, here comes Aunt Demetria.

GRAMPS. Oh, Hecate!

[*Screen door opens and Granny calls*]

GRANNY [*Off mike*]. Oh, hello, Demmie. I seen you coming up the path. Come right in.

DEMMIE. Pud, darling, come here to your Aunt Demetria.

GRAMPS. The heck he will!

PUD. The heck I will! I hate you.

DEMMIE. Aren't you ashamed of yourself, teaching a child to talk like that? You whited sepulchre!

GRAMPS. Whited sepulch—! Why, you *woman of Babylon!* You—

PUD. You Poltergeist!

GRAMPS. That's right, boy. Come on . . . let's get out of [*Voice fading*] this company.

PUD [*Fading off mike*]. Hey, Trixie! We're going for a walk with Gramps.

[*Dog bark and footsteps fading*]

DEMMIE. You heard what he called me, Nellie. He called me—

GRANNY. I know. Revelations 17:5. Don't say it, Demmie. Come inside.

[*Screen door opens and closes . . . Footsteps*]

GRANNY. Sit down, Demmie. Sometimes I just don't know what I'm going to do. I wonder if you shouldn't bring Pud up?

DEMMIE. Well, Nellie, it ain't that I haven't thought about it. But I couldn't afford to. That is—not unless Jim left a will—

GRANNY. He did, Demmie. He left fifteen thousand dollars.

DEMMIE. Fifteen thousand! Oh-h!

[*A door opens and closes . . . Light footsteps*]

MARCY [*A cheerful young girl*]. Would you like some iced tea, Mrs. Northrup?

GRANNY. Yes, I would, Marcy. It's so hot. Bring some for Miss Riffle, too.

MARCY. It won't take more than a minute. [*Footsteps, door opens and closes*]

DEMMIE [*Tensely, whispering*]. Nellie, you don't mean to tell me you've got that Marcia Giles in this house?

GRANNY. She came in to help us after the funeral. Why?

DEMMIE. Well, her and that young Bill Murdock—carrying on just as brazen as you please. And you're allowing a person like that to be around where Pud is. Nellie Northrup!

[*Footsteps . . . Screen door opens and closes*]

GRAMPS [*Fading in quickly*]. Pud found a new mushroom—right under the privet hedge.

GRANNY. Be careful, Julian. That may be a toadstool.

GRAMPS. Well, that's what we're gonna find out. Pud's waiting till I bring the plant guide. Excuse me, Nellie, I'm in a hurry. [*Footsteps*]

DEMMIE [*Whispering loudly*]. Nellie! Tell him about Marcia Giles!

NELLIE. Oh, yes . . . Julian, wait a minute.

GRAMPS. Well, what is it?

NELLIE. It's Marcy, Julian. I'm afraid we'll have to get rid of her.

GRAMPS. I'd like to know why.

NELLIE. It seems—she's carrying on with young Bill Murdock.

GRAMPS. Good. Fine boy, Bill Murdock.

DEMMIE. And you're willing to have that kind of a girl in your house with Pud? Why, she's nothing more than a common, little—

GRAMPS. You're a liar.

GRANNY. Julian, don't you talk that way to Demmie. She knows what she's saying.

GRAMPS. What do you know? Tell me one thing.

DEMMIE. All right. I saw them—right in Milbaur Park.

GRAMPS. And what were they doing—right in Milbaur Park?

DEMMIE. Kissin'. Kissin'—like you never saw. Fair to make your blood boil. If they carry on like that in public, what must they do when they're alone?

GRAMPS [Angry]. Great jumpin' Judas! That makes me mad. That makes me so gosh-blamed mad . . . Nellie, if you listen to another word this old hellion says, you're a fool. I'm disappointed in you. I'm plain disappointed in you.

[He stamps out . . . Screen door opens and slams shut . . . Pause]

GRANNY [Tearfully]. Oh, dear. Oh, dear. [Then grieved] He can't call me a fool. He can't say he's disappointed in me.

DEMMIE. I don't see why you stand for it, Nellie. [Pause] Nellie, don't you think I should take Pud's things over with me now?

GRANNY [Sleepily]. Pud's things?

DEMMIE. Yes. And in the morning I'll go down to Lawyer Pilbeam's and have the papers drawn up.

GRANNY [With a start]. What papers?

DEMMIE. Why, about the will and the adoption and all—

GRANNY. Now, see here, Demmie. I didn't say anything about your adopting Pud. You're trying to put words in my mouth.

DEMMIE. You just said that I should bring Pud up.

GRANNY. If I did, I was wrong. Julian don't mean all the things he says. He's just a rough-spoken man. Oh [Sighs] dear, I just don't feel right. Must be the heat. Think I'll—go up to my room. [Dragging footsteps] You might tell Marcy to bring me up some iced tea, Demmie.

DEMMIE. Nellie, just look out that window. There's a boy going up that apple tree.

GRANNY [Going upstairs, voice fading]. Julian never catches them. He always hollers so's to give them time to run away. [Upstairs a door closes]

DEMMIE [*Angry footsteps*]. Well, I'll catch him. [*Opens and closes screen door . . . She yells*]. You nasty little thief; come down out of that tree and take the whipping you deserve.

BOY [*Off mike*]. I can't.

DEMMIE [*Yelling*]. Either you come down or I'll have the law on you.

GRAMPS [*Fading in*]. You'll do what?

DEMMIE There's a boy up that tree. I'm going to whip him for trespassing.

GRAMPS. Oh, you are! Thanks for telling me, Demmie. Because seeing as how there's *two* trespassers here, I'll begin with the one that's handiest. Give me that fence pale, Pud. There on the ground.

PUD. Here, Gramps. Now hit her. Hit her on the rump.

[*Trixie barks gleefully*]

DEMMIE. Julian Northrup—don't you touch me.

GRAMPS. Then git off my property.

[*Footsteps*]

DEMETRIA. You'll find out whose property [*Fading*] this is some day.

GRAMPS [*Yells*]. Now, you young whippersnapper. Why don't you come down off that tree?

BOY [*Off mike*]. Gee, mister, my britches is caught in behind.

PUD. Gramps, Gramps! Your wish! You see, he can't come down.

GRAMPS. What wish?

PUD. Your good-deed wish. Don't you remember?

GRAMPS [*Yelling*]. Rubbish! Listen, you piccalilli apple-stealer, you unloosen your britches and come down outa there just as fast as you can

BOY [*Off mike*]. But, mister, I—[*Then*] Gee, whizz! That's funny. They're loose now. Well, what do you know! [*Boy sliding down tree*] I'm coming!

GRAMPS. Now, then, young feller, I'm going to teach you not to steal.

BOY [*Pleading*]. Please, mister, I didn't steal nothing.

GRAMPS. Here! And here!

[*Sound of a little tussle*]

BOY [*Amazed*]. Why, they're apples! Ripe apples!

GRAMPS. And the next time you want some, don't sneak around the back. Ring the front bell and ask for 'em.

BOY. Gee, thanks, mister. [*Fading*] Well, so long.

PUD. That's another good deed, Gramps. That makes your wish twice as strong.

GRAMPS. Who says so?

PUD. My picture book said so.

GRAMPS. Must be true then. [*Calling*] Marcy! Marcy—come out a minute.

[*Screen door opens and closes*]

MARCY [*Slightly off mike*]. Yes, Mr. Northrup.

GRAMPS. Don't you know it's a sin to kiss men in Milbaur Park?

MARCY [*Off guard*]. But—but I didn't—I didn't kiss men in Milbaur Park. I kissed only one man in Milbaur Park.

GRAMPS. What'd you kiss him in the park for?

MARCY. Because we were in the park and . . . [*Nearly crying*] We didn't think anybody would see us.

GRAMPS. Don't you know Demetria's a born snooper? . . . I say, bring him up here and kiss him.

MARCY. Wh-what?

GRAMPS. Bring that Bill Murdock up here and kiss him. 'Stime, 'stime we had a little kissin' in this house again. How the heck's Pud gonna learn about kissin' if he don't never see any of it?

MARCY [*Cries now*]. Oh, Mr. Northrup!

GRAMPS. You in love with him?

MARCY. We've been engaged all summer.

GRAMPS. Thought I recognized the symptoms.

MARCY. Bill's got only one more year at Law School and then we'll get married. He took highest honors in his class last year.

GRAMPS. Tell that to Nellie, will you? And when you and Bill see Demetria in the park again, make Bill give you a big smacker right in front of her. Like this.

[*Loud smack*]

GRANNY [*Calling, far off mike*]. Marcy! Marcy! Where's my tea?

GRAMPS. You go and tell her Bill got highest honors.

MARCY. All right, Mr. Northrup.

[*Footsteps off . . . Screen door opens and closes*]

PUD. Gee, Gramps, I wish Granny would knit two bumps on the front of my sweater the way Marcy's got on hers.

GRAMPS. What?

PUD. Say, Gramps, I want to steal an apple, too. Boost me up the tree.

GRAMPS. You don't have to steal. Oh, all right. One—two—up you go!

[*Hoisting Pud into apple tree . . . Leafy rustle*]

PUD [*Off mike*]. You know, Gramps, I can't get down till you let me.

GRAMPS. Why not?

PUD [*Off mike*]. Because you wished *nobody* could come down till you let them. That was your good-deed wish. Then you did another good deed and that made it stick double.

GRAMPS. Did it? Well, now, I'm liable to keep you there all week. Maybe a hundred years. Depends on how I feel. I think I'll stroll down to Milbaur Park and pick up a few fossils for our collection.

PUD [*Off mike*]. Wait a minute. I'm coming with you.

[*Rustle of leaves*]

PUD [*In alarm*]. Gramps, I can't let go.

GRAMPS [*Laughing*]. Course you can't. You're going to hang on to that limb till I release you from my magic spell.

PUD [*Frightened now*]. Let me down, Gramps. Please! My arms is tired.

GRAMPS [*Laughing*]. Now, now, sonny. You can't go breaking my spell like that.

PUD [*Screaming in terror*]. Gramps, let me go! [*He cries*] Please, Gramps, please!

GRAMPS [*Tenderly*]. All right, let go, pal.

[*A rustle of leaves and a thud as Pud drops to the ground*]

PUD [*Sobs*].

GRAMPS. What's the matter, boy, what's the matter?

PUD [*Wailing*]. I couldn't let go.

GRAMPS. Of course you could.

PUD [*Sobbing more quietly*]. No I couldn't, Gramps. My hands wouldn't move. The tree was holding me.

GRAMPS. Now listen, you little puddlewhupper. That old apple tree couldn't hold nobody.

PUD [*Sniffling a little*]. Yes, it could, Gramps. You wished it could. Your two good deeds wished it double.

GRAMPS [*Slowly, full of wonder*]. You think so, Pud? You really think so? Golly, I'd like to get your Aunt Demetria up that tree. Wouldn't that be something!

[*Music*]

END OF ACT I

ANNOUNCER

COMMERCIAL

ACT II

[*Music*]

[*Fade into canary singing off mike . . . Footsteps go upstairs . . . Door is opened and closed . . . The canary now sings very brightly . . Rattle of glass on tray*]

MARCY. Here's your iced tea, Mrs. Northrup.

GRANNY [*Faintly*]. Oh, just set it down, Marcy.

MARCY. Is there anything wrong, Mrs. Northrup? You sound so—

GRANNY. I guess I'm just kind of tired, Marcy. I'll go to sleep in a minute . . . [*Pause*] Marcy, just see that Julian always has his pipe. Will you do that?

MARCY. Why, yes, Mrs. Northrup, but—

GRANNY. You're a good girl, Marcy . . . Now hand me my knitting.

MARCY. Here you are. Get a nice rest.

[*Door closes . . . Shimmer of music*]

[*Note sounds . . . The canary stops singing abruptly*]

BRINK [*With an echo*]. Don't you think you've done enough, Nellie Northrup?

GRANNY. That you, Julian? Why's it grown so dark? And the canary's stopped singing.

BRINK [*Echo*]. It's Mr. Brink. Don't you want to come with me now.

GRANNY. Come with you? Oh, I remember you now. You're the man who followed me the day that . . . See here, what call have you got to come buttin' into my bedroom and frightenin' my canary? It ain't proper.

BRINK. You'll feel better with me. You know—I'm not so bad as I'm made out to be.

GRANNY. Well, you might as well sit down and wait, then, 'cause I ain't goin' to stir till I finish this mitten. [*Her needles click quickly*] Julian says there won't anything keep his hands warm in winter but a pair of my mittens. Those boughten things you get at the store—they're no good. Julian's so headstrong, you know. He goes out in all kinds of weather.

BRINK. Are you ready now?

GRANNY [*Breathlessly*]. Wait . . . just a minute . . . I'm almost finished. [*Pause*] There . . . That's got it. Don't that red stripe look pretty with the grey?

BRINK [*Gently*]. Very pretty, my dear. Come now, give me your hand.

GRANNY [*Whispering*]. Yes . . . yes . . . my hand. [*She sighs a long sigh*]

[*The canary starts singing loud again . . . Cross fade into bridge music*] [*Sound of birds at twilight . . . A few crickets*]

[*Screen door opens*]

MARCY. Mr. Northrup! Mr. Northrup! Oh—there you are sitting under the tree. Don't you want to come inside now? It's getting dark. Supper's nearly ready.

GRAMPS [*Listless*]. All right, Marcy.

MARCY. Miss Demetria came over again this afternoon, Mr. Northrup. Asked about your health.

GRAMPS. Darned old she-dragon. Been over every day since Nellie's funeral. Just waiting for me to die.

MARCY. You've got to keep your strength up, Mr. Northrup. Besides, when you don't eat, Pud doesn't eat.

GRAMPS. That's what Nellie said. "Pud mimics everything you do . . . " . . . If only I'd got there in time, Marcy! We had words before she died—and I never got there in time to say I was sorry.

MARCY. She would have forgiven you anything, Mr. Northrup . . . Oh, I forgot. Here's your pipe.

GRAMPS. My pipe? I don't think I'll ever smoke any more, Marcy. Nellie didn't like it.

MARCY. But she did, Mr. Northrup. Just before she died, she took hold of my hand and said, "Marcy, see that Julian always has his pipe."

GRAMPS. Did she? Give me that pipe, Marcy.

MARCY. I'll go finish supper.

> [*Footsteps off . . . Screen door opens and closes . . . Match is struck*]

GRAMPS [*Calling*]. Pud!

PUD. Yeah!

GRAMPS. Gonna have supper in a minute.

PUD [*Calling back, off mike*]. I'm not hungry.

GRAMPS [*Tender*]. Gotta eat, boy. Hungry or not hungry. [*Dog barks*] Down, Trixie, down. There's only you and me and Trixie left now, Pud. The three of us got to keep up our strength.

PUD [*On mike now*]. You're gosh-darned right. That pipe taste good, Gramps?

GRAMPS. Better'n anything I know. You shouldn't cuss, boy.

PUD. Why shouldn't I? *You* do.

GRAMPS. I shouldn't either. Your Granny didn't like it. Let's you and me turn over a new leaf, huh, Pud?

PUD. What for?

GRAMPS. So your Aunt Demmie won't say I'm a bad influence on you and try to take you away from me.

PUD. Aw—we'll kill the old pucker-puss.

GRAMPS. Hush, boy. That's the *old* leaf. Go in and wash. Try some soap this time.

> [*Pud's footsteps . . . Screen door opens and shuts . . . Trixie barks*]

GRAMPS. No, Trixie, you stay out here. Marcy'll feed you later. [*Calls after Pud*] Call me when table's set. [*After a pause . . .*]

BRINK [*Echo*]. Good evening.

GRAMPS. Can't I ever shut my eyes without you butting in?

BRINK. I thought perhaps you'd like to come with me now.

GRAMPS. Can't do it. I got Pud to take care of. I'm all he's got now.

BRINK. I'm sorry, but you *have* to come. Just—*just give me your hand.*

> [*Wind vibrates*]

> [*Trixie whines*]

GRAMPS [*Breathless*]. Yes—my hand . . . No . . . not yet . . . not yet. [*Gasping a little*] Please, Mr. Brink—do me one favor before I go.

BRINK. Well?

GRAMPS. Couldn't I have one of those apples? Haven't even tasted them this year.

BRINK. Why, of course, you may.

GRAMPS [*Diffident*]. Would it be asking too much if you'd—get it for me? Not as spry as I used to be.

BRINK. Why, of course, I will. [*Leafy rustle*] Hmn. Guess I'll have to climb up. [*Sound of scrambling up tree*] Let's see—now wait a minute? There are some nice ones on the branch above [*Rustle*] That's better. Now, which shall it be? This one? [*Thud of apple*] Or this one? [*Another thud*]

GRAMPS [*Gleefully*]. I don't know as I want either of them, Mr. Brink. Because now I've got you up that tree, and by jumping Judas, you ain't coming down!

BRINK [*Shouting hoarsely*]. You don't know what you've done, old man You don't know what you've done.

GRAMPS [*Yelling over the elements*]. I know what I've done, all right. I've got you trapped, Mr. Brink. Tighter than a bolt in a monkey wrench. And you're going to stay right there till I let you go!

[*Theme music*]

STATION IDENTIFICATION

ANNOUNCER

[*Music*]

NARRATOR. Julian Northrup, or Gramps, has just tricked Death, in the beguiling person of Mr. Brink, up in an apple tree. Gramps wants to keep on living so as to bring up his orphaned grandson, Pud. But the boy's shrewish Aunt Demetria wants to bring up Pud herself and get Gramps out of the way.

[*Telephone bell ringing . . . Click of receiver*]

EVANS. Dr. Evans, talking.

DEMMIE [*Filtered*]. This is Demetria Riffle, doctor. I want you to meet me right away at Julian Northrup's house.

EVANS. But Miss Riffle—

DEMMIE. Something terrible's happened—and you're his doctor. I'll be waiting in the yard beside the apple tree.

[*A short musical chord fading*]

DEMMIE [*Filtered*]. Mr. Pilbeam, something terrible's happened to Julian Northrup—and you're his lawyer. I'll be waiting for you beside the apple tree . . .

[*A short musical chord . . . Fading into the off-mike sound of hammering and sawing*]

DEMMIE. Mr. Pilbeam—Dr. Evans . . . I want you to meet a friend of Julian's. His name is Mr. Brink. He's up in that apple tree.

EVANS [*After a pause*]. I don't see anyone up there.

DEMMIE. Oh, no. You can't see him, Dr. Evans. He's invisible.

PILBEAM. He's—*what*?

DEMMIE. He's invisible, Mr. Pilbeam. But Julian saw him and Pud saw him and when Trixie touched her nose to the tree, she fell over dead. That's why they're burying her now in Milbaur Park.

EVANS. That's not a very funny joke, Miss Riffle.

DEMMIE. What would you say if I told you I believed it was the gospel truth?

EVANS. I'd say you were crazy.

[*Off-mike hammering on wood*]

DEMMIE. Oh, you would! Well, Dr. Evans, I don't believe it, but *Julian* does. He said he's having those men build a seven-foot fence around that tree, because anybody who touched it would die. Touching that tree, in fact, is the *only* way anyone *can* die. There is no more death in the world, Dr. Evans, till Julian lets Mr. Brink come down out of that tree.

PILBEAM. Now, now, you don't think Mr. Northrup really believes that?

DEMMIE. I think his mind has snapped, Mr. Pilbeam. Julian Northrup is crazier than a loon.

PILBEAM [*Pause*]. Miss Riffle—if Julian Northrup should be insane, you'd have charge of Pud—wouldn't you?

DEMMIE. Naturally. I'm next of kin.

PILBEAM. That's what I thought.

DEMMIE. Mr. Pilbeam, I intend to get that boy away from this insane man's house before something terrible happens. Dr. Evans, there *is* a way of acting fast in such cases?

EVANS. If I think Northrup's crazy, I'll talk it over with the head of the state insane asylum.

[*Footsteps*]

PUD [*Quick fade in*]. Look who's back again, Gramps.

GRAMPS. With Pilbeam and Evans, huh? So you told them all about it? After I told you not to.

PILBEAM. Is it true, Northrup?

GRAMPS. Just as true as I'm standing here. I got him up there, all right. Now I've got to figure out what the heck to do with him.

EVANS [*After a pause*]. Look here, Northrup, can you talk to Mr. Brink?

GRAMPS. Sure.

EVANS. Then talk to him.

GRAMPS [*Calls up quietly*]. Mr. Brink, you're not mad at me, are you?

BRINK. I think I might be permitted a slight irritation.

GRAMPS. Say, I got an idea. Come here, Demmie. Mr. Brink, you see this old scarecrow? Her name is Demetria Riffle. Have you got her down on your book to snuff her out?

BRINK. Riffle? No.

GRAMPS. Well, Mr. Brink, I'm going to keep you up there till it's time for you to exterminate her. Them's the terms. [*Pause*] Well, you heard him, Demmie.

DEMMIE. Julian, I'm sorry for you. I really am.

GRAMPS. You mean you *didn't*—Pilbeam—Evans—*you* heard him?

EVANS. Sorry, Northrup.

GRAMPS [*Pleading*]. Didn't no one hear what he said?

PUD. He said I think I might be permitted a slight irri—irri—

GRAMPS. Irritation.

EVANS [*Footsteps in grass*]. Northrup, I want to show you something.

GRAMPS [*Yelling*]. Hey, there, keep away from that tree.

EVANS. I'm going to pick one of those apples and eat it for you.

GRAMPS [*Terrified*]. No. No, Evans—listen to me. Pud, give me that hammer.

PUD. This one, Gramps?

GRAMPS. You goll-darned fool—those apples are sure death. Take one more step toward that tree and I'll brain you!

[*Demmie screams . . . A moment of silence*]

EVANS. All right, Northrup. I just wanted to make sure you weren't joking . . . You going to be home tonight? I've got to talk to you.

GRAMPS. Sure, come any time. But leave that female Judas behind you.

[*Bridge music, fading into tapping on metal*] [*Far off mike, doorbell rings*] [*Door opens*]

MARCY [*Calling down softly*]. It's Dr. Evans. [*Tapping stops*] Mr. Northrup, I want you to know I'll do anything to help you and Pud.

GRAMPS. Thank you, Marcy.

MARCY [*Off mike*]. This way, doctor.

[*Footsteps down basement steps*]

GRAMPS. This is my workshop, Evans. Nowadays I—I just make things for Pud.

EVANS. By the way, you haven't met Willard Grimes, have you? I've been telling him about Mr. Brink and the apple tree.

GRAMPS. Now what'd you want to go and do that for?

GRIMES. Northrup, I was just going to ask you to come along with me and talk it over. Another fellow I'd like you to meet wants to hear all about it.

GRAMPS. Nope, reckon not, Mr. Grimes. You see, I don't want any more people knowing about this thing till I find some way of proving it. I figger that—

GRIMES. Oh, what's the use, Evans! [*Bluntly to Gramps*] Now get this straight, old man. I'm taking you to the state insane asylum.

GRAMPS. You're . . . you're taking me to the insane . . . [*A light dawns*] Demetria's behind this. Where is Demmie, Evans?

EVANS. Outside in the car.

GRAMPS. Waiting for Pud, eh? Look, Mr. Grimes, there ain't nothing wrong with me.

GRIMES. That's what we want to find out. If you're all right, you go home again. Now, are you coming along like a good fellow, or—

GRAMPS. Sort of looks like I gotta, don't it? [*A pause*] All right . . . all right . . . I'll come along. [*Footsteps*] Oh, wait, my badge. I've got to have my badge like I wear in parades. I'm a Spanish-American War veteran, you know.

GRIMES [*Humoring him*]. Fine. You couldn't march without your badge, now could you? [*Drawer opens . . . Clink of metal*]

GRAMPS. Here it is . . . Now, then, you fellers better set.

EVANS [*After a tense pause*]. Put that gun down, Northrup.

GRAMPS. Let me do the talking, Evans. First of all—I ain't going to no crazy house. Second—that old she-cat ain't getting Pud. But maybe— maybe I've got to prove to you what I said about a certain Mr. Brink

EVANS. It's useless, Northrup. Be reasonable . . .

GRAMPS. Wait a minute. Got your medicine kit with you?

EVANS. Yes . . . Why?

GRAMPS. Got anything in it—poison enough to kill a fly?

EVANS. As a matter of fact, I *have* a potassium cyanide solution—but—

GRAMPS. I'll make a bargain with you. And you'd best take it, too . . . cause if you don't I'm liable to go wild as all get out.

EVANS. Well, let's hear your bargain!

GRAMPS. Take the worst poison you got in that bag and put it in a tumbler Then catch a fly and put him in the poison. If the fly dies, I'll go to the insane asylum. If he don't, I stay here.

EVANS. Listen, Grimes, I know I can kill a fly. What do you say?

GRIMES. All right. It's a bargain.

GRAMPS. You get the poison, Evans. I'll get the glass. And Mr. Grimes, you catch a fly.

[*They move around . . . Clink of instruments in kit, clink of glass on table*]

EVANS. This stuff's strong enough to kill an elephant.

GRAMPS. You can use this tumbler. [*Gurgle of liquid in glass*] Where's the fly? Wait . . . here's one.

GRIMES. Got him?

GRAMP [*Pause . . . faint buzzing sound*]. Got him. Don't get so excited, little fly. Pretty soon, you'll be buzzing around good as new. In you go.

[*Tinkle against glass . . . Pause*]

GRAMPS. Ain't much of a swimmer, is he?

EVANS. I'll hold him under with the tweezers.

[*Tinkle of metal on glass*]

GRAMPS. Yeah, let him get a bellyful.

EVANS [*After a pause*]. I think he's had time enough.

GRAMPS. Take him out. [*Tinkle of tweezers on glass*] Lay him down on that paper on the workbench. [*Pause*] Looks kind of sick, don't he?

GRIMES [*After a pause*]. He's dead, Northrup.

GRAMPS. Wait a minute. Give this fly a chance.

[*A long pause*]

EVANS. Not a stir out of him.

GRIMES. All right, Northrup. A bargain's a bargain.

GRAMPS [*Tense*]. Look! He moved.

GRIMES. I don't believe it.

GRAMPS [*Excited*]. He's moving! . . . [*Pause*] Drunk as a coot, but he's crawling right across that danged piece of paper!

GRIMES. You didn't give him enough poison, Evans.

EVANS. I don't understand it. He had enough to kill a regiment.

GRAMPS. Well, *now* will you believe what I been telling you about Mr. Brink?

GRIMES [*Angrily*]. I don't know what kind of a trick this is, but I came to get him, and I will.

EVANS. Remember what you promised, Grimes.

GRIMES. What's a promise to a lunatic?

GRAMPS. So you don't believe it, eh? Even after I proved it to you!

GRIMES. You crazy fool, don't point that gun at me!

GRAMPS. Well, maybe there's another way of proving it. Evans, at this close range if I shoot Mr. Grimes right through the belly, he'd die, wouldn't he?

EVANS. Yes, but—

GRAMPS. Thank you, doctor, that's all I want to know.

[*Three shots . . . Thump of body on floor*]

EVANS. Good Lord! What have you done to him? He'll be dead in an hour.

GRAMPS [*A prayer*]. Stay up in that tree, Mr. Brink. If you come down now, I'm in a heck of a fix.

[*Music*]

END OF ACT II

ANNOUNCER

COMMERCIAL

[*Music*]

ACT III

ANNOUNCER. So great is Julian Northrup's love for his grandson Pud that he even succeeds in evading the dark visitor who some day comes to summon every mortal man. By ruse and by a miraculous power of his own, Julian imprisons Mr. Brink in an apple tree. The neighbors, of course, believe that the old man has lost his mind and should be removed to an asylum; and at last, in desperation, Julian has been forced to test his triumph over Death by shooting a man point-blank.

EVANS. I've asked you to drop into my office this morning, Pilbeam, because something's happened that will turn the world upside down —unless we stop it.

PILBEAM. You mean, Northrup?

EVANS. He shot Grimes last night. Shot him three times in the abdomen. Grimes had internal hemorrhages and it was an hour before I could get him to the hospital.

PILBEAM. What'd he shoot him for?

EVANS. He was experimenting.

PILBEAM. Experimenting! You mean he killed a man just to—

EVANS. He didn't kill him. *According to everything I know about medicine,* Grimes should have died. But he didn't. By some miracle he's still alive!

PILBEAM. That's funny.

EVANS. Funnier than you think, Pilbeam. I've been up all night trying to kill something. I've experimented with everything I could lay my hands on. Insects—bugs—stray cats—every dog I found. I couldn't kill a single thing. Nothing—except a mouse. *And you know how I killed it?* I tied it to the end of a fishing pole and touched it up against that apple tree.

PILBEAM. Good Lord! You mean what Northrup said about Mr. Brink was true?

EVANS. All I know is that the old man is not crazy. I've asked him to come here, too. Ought to be along any minute now.

PILBEAM. What are you going to do?

EVANS. I don't know. But if there is anything up in that tree, *it's got to come down*. It's got to come *down*.

[*Door opens, footsteps*]

GRAMPS [*Off mike*]. Oh, there you are. [*Fading closer*] Howdy, Pilbeam. Howdy, Evans. How's Mr. Grimes doing?

EVANS. Seems to be doing all right.

GRAMPS [*Chuckles*]. Glad to hear it. Nasty accident. Well, sir, what can I do for you?

EVANS. Sit down, won't you? [*Sound of sitting*] Northrup, I owe you an apology.

GRAMPS. Not at all. Wouldn't have any respect for you if you believed a thing like this right off. You're a *doctor*. My boy Jim was a doctor.

EVANS. Yes, I'm a doctor. Let me tell you about some of my patients, Northrup. I have a man who for ten years has been in constant pain. Yesterday I took the last chance and operated on him . . . it wasn't successful. He's in more pain now than he ever was. I hoped he would die last night. He didn't.

GRAMPS. Oh.

EVANS. Do you remember Mrs. Trenner, Northrup?

GRAMPS. The nice old lady who used to have all the dogs?

EVANS. She's been bedridden for three years. Hasn't a penny left—nothing to live for. Her only one idea is—to die. Well, that's two. And I'm just one doctor, one doctor in a little town. The world must be full of people like that.

GRAMPS [*Little pause*]. If you're hinting for me to let Mr. Brink down, you're on the wrong track, young fella.

EVANS. No more death. Think about it for a minute, Northrup. Nobody died last night. Nobody's going to die tonight. Or tomorrow night. Nobody's going to die—until Julian Northrup says they can. Five years from now the world will be so overcrowded, so full of disease and pain that it won't be fit to live in!

GRAMPS. You don't understand, Evans. I'm not doing this just because I want to. I'm not doing it for myself at all.

EVANS. You've got to let him down, Northrup.

GRAMPS. I've got to think of Pud. Pud can't get along without me.

EVANS. Well, think hard, Northrup. By the time Pud reaches twenty-five, you'll be—what? Ninety-eight—ninety-nine? You'd only be a nuisance to Pud.

GRAMPS. No, no. I wouldn't.

EVANS. Oh, yes, you would. Let Mr. Brink down *today,* Northrup. If you don't, I'm warning you, I'll do everything in my power to make you let him go!

[*Music: Bridge*]

DEMMIE. Sheriff, just read the decision at the end.

SHERIFF [*Reading in stumbling monotone*]. "It is the order of this Court that he be committed to the Gainsville Institution for the Insane, and that the custody of the child, John Gilford Northrup, be awarded to his aunt, Demetria Riffle."

GRAMPS [*Little pause*]. Well, doc, you kind of fixed me up good and proper, ain't you?

DEMMIE. Come, Pud, you're going with me now.

PUD. No, I ain't! I ain't! Let go of me, you she-cat.

[*Runs and hurls himself in Gramp's arms*]

Oh, Gramps . . . Don't let her take me, Gramps.

GRAMPS. I'd like to speak to Pud a minute, if you don't mind.

EVANS. All right. We'll wait outside. Come on, Sheriff—Miss Riffle . . .

[*Footsteps . . . Door opens and closes*]

GRAMPS. I'm going away, Pud.

PUD. Where, Gramps?

GRAMPS. Where the woodbine twineth.

PUD. You going with Mr. Brink? Take me, too, Gramps.

GRAMPS. Can't do that, boy. You got your whole life ahead of you.

PUD. Don't want my whole life ahead of me. I want to go with you. I love you, Gramps.

GRAMPS. Shouldn't love me that much, boy. You see, Pud, I been thinking it over. Maybe it ain't such a good thing for you to be living with me any more. Maybe your Aunt Demetria ain't as much of a poltergeist as we thought she was.

PUD. Don't you love me any more, Gramps?

GRAMPS. Sure, boy—but—It's just that I've got to go away now.

PUD [*Crying*]. You don't love me any more . . .

GRAMPS. Wait a minute, boy. Wait a minute . . .

PUD [*Fading*]. You don't love me any more. [*Running footsteps*]

> [*Door opens and slams*]

SHERIFF [*Off mike, calling*]. Well, what about it, Northrup?

GRAMPS [*Very weary*]. I'm coming.

> [*Footsteps, screen door opens and closes . . . Outside sounds*]

GRAMPS. Demmie, will you be good to Pud? Will you see that he gets some fun out of life?

DEMMIE. I will, Julian. I have wonderful plans for him already. I'm going to send him to Miss Ramsdell's school, in the fall.

GRAMPS. That's a girl's school!

DEMMIE. Not any more, Julian. They're going to have two little boys next year.

GRAMPS [*Ranting*]. You'll make Pud a sissy! By jumping Judas, you're *still* a poltergeist. I've changed my mind. I'm going to stay here and take care of Pud.

EVANS. Northrup! How can you take care of Pud if you're in the asylum?

GRAMPS [*Deflated*]. Oh. [*Pause*] Looks like you got me hog-tied, all right. Marcy, Marcy!

MARCY [*Off mike*]. Coming, Mr. Northrup.

> [*Door opens and shuts*]

GRAMPS. Marcy, pack Pud's things and give them to Miss Riffle, will you?

MARCY. To Miss Riffle? You think Pud's going to like that, Mr. Northrup?

GRAMPS. Can't help it, Marcy. I've reached the end of my rope.

> [*Footsteps on grass*]

GRAMPS [*Calls up to Brink*]. Well, Mr. Brink. Looks like the time has come.

> [*Wind sounds faintly*]

BRINK [*Slightly echoed*]. Yes, the time has come.

GRAMPS. I was going to let you down as soon as you got word that you could take Demmie. Don't suppose you got word in the meantime?

BRINK. No. There's been no call for Miss Riffle. There probably won't be for years.

GRAMPS [*Suddenly, after a pause*]. What's that? Did I understand you to say you were supposed to take her an hour ago?

BRINK. No, no. I said probably wouldn't take her for years.

GRAMPS. Well, I'll be! Why didn't you tell me, Mr. Brink? If you're supposed to take Demmie, too—

BRINK. But I am *not* supposed to take her.

GRAMPS. Well, this changes everything. Demmie, we'll go together. Just the two of us. Like old friends.

DEMMIE [*Terrified*]. Dr. Evans! There isn't anybody up in that tree, is there?

GRAMPS. Mr. Brink—I was wondering if you'd do me another favor? After you've taken Demmie, wouldn't you—just slip the sheriff in for good measure?

DEMMIE. Oh, no, no.

SHERIFF. Stop him!

BRINK. This is the wildest absurdity I ever heard. I have absolutely no authorization to take any of these people.

GRAMPS. Oh, thank you, Mr. Brink. I appreciate that. [*Pause*] Well, come on, you two. Demmie, you hang onto this arm. And Sheriff, you hang on to this one. I'll lead the way.

DEMMIE. You can't frighten me, Julian Northrup. I didn't hear a thing up in that tree. Not a blessed thing. And neither did anybody else.

MARCY [*Suddenly*]. Well, I did, Miss Demetria. I heard him. [*Stunned pause*]

GRAMPS. What? What's that, Marcy?

MARCY. I said I heard him. Just as plain as I hear you.

DEMMIE. What'd he say?

MARCY. He said if he could just come down, he'd take anybody Mr. Northrup asked him to.

MR. BRINK. That girl can't hear a word I say. She's the most inordinate liar I ever met.

DEMMIE. He didn't say he was going to take *me,* did he, Marcy?

MARCY. Oh, yes, he did, Miss Riffle. He said he was going to take you *first*.

BRINK. I never said any such thing.

GRAMPS. Hear him then, Marcy?

MARCY. Yes.

GRAMPS. What'd he say?—Now be careful.

MARCY. He said please hurry and let him down. Because the one he's really after is Miss Riffle.

GRAMPS. Yup. That's what he said. Let's get started. I'll say the magic words. Line up, you two. Here we go! Off to glory! [*Chanting*] Where the woodbine twineth—

BRINK. Stop that monkey business and let me down.

GRAMPS [*Chanting higher*]. Where the night-fire shineth . . .

DEMMIE [*Shrieks*]. Somebody stop him!

SHERIFF. We'll do anything you ask us to, Northrup. I'll tear up the court order. Look!

[*Tearing paper*]

It's torn. You don't have to go to the asylum.

DEMMIE. Julian, please!

[*A sudden silence*]

GRAMPS [*After thinking it over*]. All right. But you got to keep your hands off my boy, Demmie.

DEMMIE. I will, Julian.

GRAMPS. And keep the heck away from me, too.

DEMMIE. I'll keep the heck away from you, too.

GRAMPS. Now get out of here—all of you. Get off my property.

[*Footsteps*]

MARCY [*Ad libs*]. I never knew Miss Riffle could run so fast.

GRAMPS. Marcy, I love you. By Judas Priest, I love you. Now there's nothing in the world can stop us. Just you and me and Pud.

BRINK [*Echoed*]. Which world do you mean?

GRAMPS [*Calling back*]. What's that? I didn't quite understand, Mr. Brink.

BRINK. Of course not. My poor man!

MARCY. What'd he say, Mr. Northrup?

GRAMPS. He said, "My poor man." And I don't like the way he said it, Marcy. I don't like the way he said it.

[*Wind note fading into bridge music*]

[*Night sounds out of doors: Crickets, a bull frog . . . The apple tree rustles*]

BRINK [*Echoed*]. Pud? Is that you, Pud? Where've you been all evening?

PUD [*Tearful*]. Oh, hello, Mr. Brink. I ran away. Have Gramps and Marcy been looking for me?

BRINK [*Evasively*]. I wouldn't know. What'd you run away for?

PUD [*Tearful*]. Because Gramps doesn't love me any more.

BRINK. But you're not big enough to run away, my little man.

PUD. I am so. And I'm not your little man. I'm not your little man at all, so there. I'll spit in your eye.

BRINK. I'm afraid you might find that difficult. You couldn't reach me.

PUD. I could too.

BRINK. You'd be afraid.

PUD. I'm not afraid of anything.

BRINK. Why, you're even afraid to climb this tree.

PUD. I am not. I climbed that tree before you got up it and I climbed down again. That's more than you can do.

BRINK. But you couldn't climb it now, at night. Why, you can't even climb that fence.

PUD. That's easy. I can do it with one hand.

BRINK. It's a high fence—but let's see you do it.

PUD. All right.

[*Wind higher . . . Faint thunder in distance . . . A whippoorwill sounds shrilly . . . Sound of Pud climbing fence*]

BRINK. Try over on this side. It's easier.

PUD. There, see! What'd I tell you?

BRINK. Splendid! I never thought you could.

PUD. Golly, I can see far from the top of the fence.

BRINK [*Whispering*]. Can you see me?

PUD. Yes. What makes your voice so whispery, Mr. Brink?

BRINK [*Softer, more seductive*]. Look at me!

PUD. Gee, you've got funny eyes, Mr. Brink. They make me dizzy.

BRINK [*Hypnotic*]. Look at me again. That's right. Keep looking at me [*Wind shrieks . . . An owl hoots*] Now—give me your hand. Lean forward and give me your hand. Just a bit more . . . lean toward me a little bit more . . .

PUD [*Screaming*]. I'm falling, I'm falling. Gramps—Gramps!

[*He crashes to the ground*]

[*Into bridge music*]

[*Fade into off-mike sound of rain . . . Clink of instrument on glass*]

PUD [*Sobbing*]. Gramps, my back hurts.

EVANS. Now this is going to stick you, Pud. Just a bit, like a needle. Then it won't hurt so much. [*Pause*] There.

[*Again clink of metal on glass*]

GRAMPS. Well, doc? He'll be all right, won't he?

EVANS. Northrup—he'll never be able to walk again.

GRAMPS. Never be able—to walk—again. Oh no, to drag around all your life? I can't let that happen to him. Never. Come along with Gramps, Son. [*Sound of lifting body off bed . . . Pud whimpers*] There, there. I'll hold you so it doesn't hurt.

EVANS. Northrup, where are you going with the boy?

GRAMPS. Wait here, doc. [*Footsteps*]

EVANS. But Northrup—

[*Screen door opens and closes . . . Heavy rainfall up . . . Bullfrog croaks . . . Footsteps in rain*]

GRAMPS [*Calling quietly*]. Mr. Brink.

BRINK [*Echoed*]. Oh, it's you.

GRAMPS. Why did you do it? Why did you do it?

BRINK [*Gently*]. My poor man, I didn't mean to hurt the boy. It was an accident that he fell off the fence. I planned to *take* him. It was the only way out. Already there is so much anguish in the world because you kept me here, and every hour makes it worse.

GRAMPS. Mr. Brink, will you take us both now?

BRINK. Gladly.

GRAMPS. Come on down, then.

[*Wind blows harder . . . Rain pours . . . Brink coming down tree*]

PUD [*Sobbing*]. Gramps, my back hurts so—

GRAMPS. Just a minute, boy. [*An owl hoots*] Here's Pud, Mr. Brink.

BRINK [*Closer*]. No, you first. Just—touch my hand.

[*Suddenly, the rain stops, the wind subsides*]

GRAMPS [*Bright and cheerful*]. Well, well! He was quite a load before, but now he's light as a feather. Take Pud, Mr. Brink.

BRINK [*Echo gone*]. Yes—now—

PUD [*Brightly*]. Hello, Mr. Brink! Are we dead, Gramps?

GRAMPS. Must be. I feel like a two-year-old. How about you?

PUD. I feel like a two-year-old, too, Gramps.

BRINK. Come along, now. We have to hurry. I'm way behind schedule.

GRAMPS. Where we going?

BRINK. You'll find out.

PUD. Anyhow, we'll be there together, won't we, Gramps?

GRAMPS. You're darned right, we will. You're darned tootin' right.

GRANNY [*Calling off mike*]. Juleyan! Juleyan! Do you have to use such
language in front of the boy?

GRAMPS. Well, what the heck do you know about that! Nellie ain't changed.
She ain't changed at all.

[*Music*]

ANNOUNCER

CREDITS

AH, WILDERNESS!

Original Play
by Eugene O'Neill

Radio Adaptation
by Arthur Arent

CAST

(for radio performance)

NAT MILLER	Walter Huston
RICHARD	Jack Kelk
NARRATOR	Eugene O'Neill, Jr.
TOMMY	Teddy Rose
MRS. MILLER	Katherine Raht
MILDRED	Judy Parrish
ARTHUR	Richard Widmark
AUNT LILY	Eda Heinemann
SID	Walter Kinsella
MR. MACOMBER	Will Geer
WINT	Tony Barrett
BELLE	Dennie Moore
BARTENDER	Frank Lovejoy
MURIEL	Susan Douglas
SALESMAN	Russell Collins

AH, WILDERNESS!

Radio adaptation by
ARTHUR ARENT

WHAT MAKES IT a pleasure to adapt to radio any play by Eugene O'Neill is the fact that every scene in it is sure to have a beginning, a middle, and an end. This is more extraordinary than it sounds, since many plays (some successful ones included) are so woodenly contrived that any effort to break them down for purposes of radio adaptation results in chaos and the subsequent building of a brand new structure. All O'Neill's scenes, however, build to their curtains with an awesome inevitability heart-warming to the adapter.

The dominant motif of "Ah, Wilderness!" being nostalgia, it was necessary to create this mood at the outset. Thus the Narrator speaks of "blacksmiths and Merry Widow hats and zithers and black lisle stockings with lace openwork." His speeches are musically underscored with "Bedelia," a song of the period. He then introduces the Miller family one by one, as they come into the parlor after lunch, thus evoking the easy informality of the period, and, more particularly, this household.

Since the play was written in four acts, a certain shifting of scenes was inevitable, the new act curtains giving them a slightly different emphasis. But with the exception of Dick's scene with his sister Mildred, which I arbitrarily set in his bedroom for purposes of variety, no relocation of scene was necessary.

By and large, so solid and inevitable was the line of this play that it required less juggling and rearranging than any I have ever adapted. As proof of this, the only changes made in rehearsal were a minute and a half cut from the running time and the insertion, at Lawrence Langner's suggestion, of the bluefish episode.

AH, WILDERNESS!

ANNOUNCER

INTRODUCTION FOR THE THEATRE GUILD

ACT I

[*Music: A few introductory chords and then it segues into "Bedelia." . . . The melody seeps in, and then, as the strings take over, the music fades underneath until cue*]

NARRATOR. Tonight we turn back the pages of time for a nostalgic hour. It is the year 1906, in the United States of America. Teddy Roosevelt is in the White House, there's a blacksmith on every Main Street, and the automobile is a luxury item. The women are wearing Merry Widow hats, chatelaine bags, and black lisle stockings with lace openwork. And the men? Ah, the men have discovered peg-top trousers, those strange indispensables you can climb into only by removing your shoes. There is a pug dog and a zither in every home. And the title on the sheet music on every piano is . . . "Bedelia" . . .

[*Music: Up . . . Two young, fresh voices,—a boy's and a girl's— are heard singing the words*]

NARRATOR. And now that we've established the color and the period, I'd like you to meet the Miller Family. They live in a large small town in Connecticut, where Nat Miller is the owner and publisher of the local newspaper . . . First, there's Tommy, the youngest . . .

[*Running footsteps approach*]

TOMMY [*Calling*]. Aw, I don't want any more milk, Ma. And I said excuse me and you said all right . . . Can I go out and play now, Ma?

MRS. MILLER [*Off*]. [*Correcting him*] *May* I go out and—

TOMMY [*Quickly*]. May I?

MRS. MILLER. Yes. But you set off your crackers away from the house, remember!

TOMMY [*Joyfully*]. Yes, ma'am. [*Door slams . . . Approaching footsteps*]

NARRATOR. This is Mildred and Arthur. Two more of the Miller children.

MILDRED. *Children?*

NARRATOR. I beg your pardon, Mildred. Of course you're not a child any more. Er—how old are you?

MILDRED. Fifteen and four months.

NARRATOR. Of course. Er—suppose you describe yourself.

MILDRED. Well, I'm tall and rather slender. I've got a nice nose and gray eyes and—er—well, I think I'm attractive.

NARRATOR. What are you wearing?

MILDRED. I've got on high black shoes with French heels, a long black pleated skirt, very full at the bottom, and a white shirt waist. My hair is up, of course.

NARRATOR. Thank you . . . What about you, Arthur?

ARTHUR. *I* am a sophomore at Yale.

NARRATOR. Thank *you*. [*Footsteps approach . . . Voices ad libbing*] And here, unless I am mistaken, are Mrs. Miller and Aunt Lily . . .

MRS. MILLER. Goodness, Tommy's left the screen door open! The house will be alive with flies! [*Door slams shut*]

LILY. Well, you can't expect a boy to remember to shut doors on the Fourth of July.

[*Mandolin tuning up*]

MRS. MILLER. That's you all over, Lily. You'll have that boy spoiled to death in spite of me. Phew, I'm hot. Aren't you? This is going to be a scorcher. Arthur, get up and let your Aunt Lily sit down. Take your mandolin over to the window seat.

ARTHUR [*Gallantly*]. Certainly. Aunt Lily, my chair.

LILY. Thank you, dear.

[*Arthur begins to play "Waltz Me Around Again, Willie" on the mandolin . . . Footsteps approach*]

NARRATOR [*Over the music*]. And here come the gentlemen—Mr Nathaniel Miller, himself, and Uncle Sid Davis. Nat has just turne fifty. He's a little stoop-shouldered now from reading copy, and his hair—well, let's call it thin.

NAT. What's the name of that piece, Arthur?

ARTHUR. "Waltz Me Around Again, Willie."

SID. Sure. I know that one. [*Sings*]

> Waltz me around again, Willie,
> Waltz me around again, dear, etc.

NARRATOR [*Over the singing*] Uncle Sid is Mrs. Miller's brother, but he is *NOT* married to Aunt Lily. There's been talk about it for twenty years now, but Aunt Lily won't have him because—well, you'll hear about that later. [*Song up and out as chorus is finished*] Well, I guess that's about everybody, except Richard.

NAT. Arthur, where *is* Richard?

ARTHUR. He's still in the dining room, reading a book. Gosh, he's always reading now. What's got into him, anyhow?

NAT. He reads his schoolbooks, too, strange as that may seem to you. That's why he came out top of his class. I'm hoping before you leave New Haven they'll find time to teach you reading is a good habit.

ARTHUR. Sure, but not the way he does it. I believe in moderation.

NAT. That'll be enough out of you . . . Sid, you coming to the Onondaga Club picnic with me this afternoon?

SID. You bet.

MRS. MILLER. Sid, you'll be careful, won't you?

SID. Oh, sure.

MRS. MILLER. We're going to have dinner in the evening tonight, you know —the best shore dinner you ever tasted, and I don't want you coming home—well, not able to appreciate it.

LILY. Oh, he'll be careful today, won't you, Sid?

SID. Lily, I swear to you if any man offers me a drink, I'll kill him—that is, if he changes his mind. [*They all laugh*] Want to come with me to the fireworks display at the beach tonight, Lily?

LILY [*Flustered*]. I—I'd like to, Sid, thank you. Only not if you come home—you know.

SID. Nat, your sister's got an evil mind. She reads evil into everything I do—even before I do it.

MRS. MILLER [*Quickly*]. That reminds me, Nat. You've got to speak to Richard. It's about those evil books he's reading. I found some more in his closet. You've got to give him a good talking-to.

NAT. Do I have to? On the Fourth of July?

MRS. MILLER. That's got nothing to do with it. When it comes to a heart-to-heart talk between a father and his son the time of the year is irrelevant. You've got to talk to him. Right *now!*

SID. What's he reading? Nick Carter or old Cap Collier?

NAT. No, he passed that period long ago. Poetry's his red meat nowadays —love poetry. Socialism, too, I suspect. Well, might as well get him on the carpet. [*Calls*] Richard! [*No answer, louder*] Richard! [*A bellow*] Richard!

ARTHUR [*Topping him*]. Hey, Dick, wake up! Pa's calling you!

DICK [*Off*]. All right. I'm coming. [*Pause . . . Then footsteps approaching*]

DICK. Did you want me, Pa?

NAT. I'd hoped I'd made that plain.

DICK. I didn't hear you, Pa. [*Dreamily*] I was off in another world.

MILDRED. Yah, yah, yah!

ARTHUR. Did you hear that, everybody? *He was off in another world!* [*Imitating him*]

NAT. What were you planning to do today, Richard? Going out to the beach with your sister?

DICK. That silly skirt party! I should say not!

MILDRED. He's not coming because Muriel Macomber isn't. I'll bet he's got got a date with her somewheres.

DICK. You shut up! . . . I thought I'd just stay home, Pa—this morning, anyway.

NAT. Help Tommy set off firecrackers, eh?

DICK [*Great dignity*]. Father, I am seventeen years old. A man of seventeen does not spend his time with firecrackers . . . Besides, I don't believe in this silly celebrating the Fourth of July—all this lying talk about liberty—when there is no liberty.

NAT. Hmmmn.

DICK [*Dramatically*]. The land of the free and the home of the brave! Home of the slave is what they ought to call it—the wage slave ground under the heel of his master, starving, crying out for bread for his children, and all he gets is a stone. I tell you, the Fourth of July is a stupid farce!

MILDRED. My, My!

NAT. Hmmn. Them are mighty strong words, son. You'd better not repeat such sentiments outside the bosom of your family or they'll have you in jail.

SID. Yup, and throw away the key.

DICK. Let them put me in jail! No, you can celebrate your Fourth of July. I'll celebrate the day the people bring out the guillotine. *That's* what this country needs! Plenty of guillotines! [*Reciting*] "The days grow hot, O Babylon! Tis cool beneath thy willow trees!"

MRS. MILLER. There you are, Pa. That must be from one of those awful books he's reading!

NAT. What books are they, son?

MRS. MILLER. I'll tell you. There was one by that Oscar Wilde. The Picture of—of . . .

DICK. "The Picture of Dorian Gray." One of the greatest novels ever written in the English language.

MRS. MILLER. Then there was a play by that Irishman, Bernard Shaw.

DICK. The greatest living playwright in the English language.

MRS. MILLER. And poems by a man named Swin . . . Swin . . .

DICK. "Poems and Ballads," by Algernon Charles Swinburne. Just the greatest living poet in the English language! He—he tells the truth about real love.

MRS. MILLER. Love! Why—why some of the things I simply couldn't read they're so—so *indecent*. All about—well, I can't tell you before Lily and Mildred. And he just got a new one yesterday. The Rubay— What is it Richard?

DICK. "The Rubáiyát of Omar Khayyam." That's the best of all!

NAT. Oh, I've read that, Mother. Got a copy at the office.

LILY. I—I've read that, too. At the library. I like—some parts of it. [*Shyly*]

> The moving finger writes, and having writ,
> Moves on: nor all your Piety nor Wit
> Shall lure it back to cancel half a Line,
> Nor all your Tears wash out a Word of it.

MRS. MILLER. Why, Lily, I never knew you to recite poetry before!

DICK. Good for you, Aunt Lily. But that isn't the best. The best is:

> A Book of Verses underneath the Bough,
> A Jug of Wine, A Loaf of Bread—and Thou
> Beside me singing in the Wilderness—

[*Loud knock on door*]

NAT. Now who in the world can that—

ARTHUR. It's Old Man Macomber! I can see him through the window.

NAT. Dave? Now what in thunder does that boring old idiot— [*Excitement and speeded tempo to end of scene*]

SID. Excuse me, I was just leaving.

ARTHUR. Me, too. I got to catch the 9 o'clock trolley.

MILDRED. Wait for me, Art. Wait till I get my hat.

MRS. MILLER. Nat, you get rid of him the first second you can. I want to talk to you about—

NAT. Why do *I* have to listen to the old buzzard? Why is it always I who—

MRS. MILLER. He's your biggest advertiser, dear, that's why.

NAT. Don't you think I know that? If he weren't, know what I'd do? I'd take him by the seat of his pants and— All right, everybody, clear out. If that old battle-axe's got something to complain about, he's come to the right party this time. I'm just about fed up with his—You come back as soon as he leaves, Richard. I'm not through with you yet. [*Door opens*] Come in, Mr. Macomber. [*Door shuts*] Sit down . . . Have a cigar.

MACOMBER [*Acidly*]. You're forgetting. I never smoke.

NAT. So I was. Well, I'll smoke alone then.

MACOMBER. I'll come to the point at once. I regret to say it's something disagreeable—disgraceful would be nearer the truth—and it concerns your son Richard!

NAT. Oh, come now, Dave, I'm sure Richard hasn't—

MACOMBER. And I'm positive he has. You're not calling me a liar, I hope.

NAT. No one said anything about a liar. I only meant you're surely mistaken if you think—

MACOMBER. I'm not mistaken. I have proof of everything in his own handwriting.

NAT [*Sharply*]. Let's get down to brass tacks. Just what is it you're charging my son with?

MACOMBER. With being dissolute and blasphemous. I charge him with deliberately attempting to corrupt the morals of my daughter Muriel.

NAT. Then I'm afraid I will have to call you a liar, Dave.

MACOMBER. I thought you'd get around to that, so I brought some of the proofs with me. Have a look at 'em. I've a lot more at home.

NAT. What are they, letters?

MACOMBER. You might call them that. Can you deny they're in your son's handwriting?

NAT. No, I can't.

MACOMBER. Anyways, Muriel's confessed he wrote them to her. Go on, read one. Out loud.

NAT [*Reading*].

> My life is bitter with thy love; thine eyes
> Blind me, thy tresses burn me, thy sharp sighs
> Divide my flesh and spirit with soft sound—

Why, that's Swinburne.

MACOMBER. Exactly! And that's one of the *mild* ones! Evidently you've been too busy to take the right care about Richard's bringing up or what he's allowed to read. But that's your misfortune and none of my business. But my daughter Muriel is my business, and I can't and I won't have her innocence exposed to the contamination of a young man whose mind, judging from his choice of reading matter, is as foul—

NAT [*Controlling his temper*]. Why, you darned old fool! Can't you see Richard's only a fool kid who's just at the stage when he's out to rebel against all authority, and so he grabs at anything radical to read and wants to pass it on to his girl and boy friends, yes, and his elders, too, to show off what a young hellion he is! Here, take this stuff back. It doesn't mean anything to me—that is, nothing of what you think it means. If you believe this would corrupt Muriel, then you must believe she's easily corrupted!

MACOMBER. Now you're insulting my daughter. I won't forget that.

NAT. I'm not insulting her. I think Muriel is a darn nice girl. That's why I'm giving her credit for ordinary good sense.

MACOMBER [*More sharply*]. Well, I knew you'd prove obstinate, but I certainly never dreamed you'd have the impudence to—

NAT. What *did* you dream I'd do?

MACOMBER. Give him a hiding he'd remember to the last day of his life! You'd ought to do it for his sake, if you had any sense—unless you want him to end up in jail!

NAT. Dave, I've stood all I can from you! You get out! And get out quick before I—

MACOMBER. I'm going. But there's one thing more. Here's a letter from

Muriel for your son. It makes plain how she feels about him. I hope he heeds what's inside, for his own good and yours, because if I ever catch him hanging around my place again I'll have him arrested! And don't think I'm not going to make you regret your insults. I'm taking the advertisement for my store out of your paper.

NAT. Go ahead and sue! When I get through there won't be a person in town who'll buy a dishrag in your place! *Now get out!* [*Door slams*] Hey, you forgot your letters! [*Pause*] Hmmmn ... Looks like they're *all* Swinburne! ... Hmmmn ... [*Reads*]

> That I could drink thy veins as wine, and eat
> Thy flesh like honey, that from face to feet
> Thy body were abolished and consumed,
> And in my flesh thy very flesh entombed!

Hmmmn, this stuff *is* kind of warm—too darned warm, if you ask me! Certainly not the kind of thing to be sending to a decent girl. Hmmmn. I thought the boy was just stuck on her—the way one gets stuck on a decent girl at his age ... I wonder—I wonder if maybe— [*Angrily*] By the Lord, if that's true I'll give him a hiding he'll never forget! [*Shouting*] Richard, come in here!

[*Footsteps approach*]

DICK. Yes, Pa?

NAT. Look here, son. I'm going to ask you a question, and I want an honest answer. I warn you beforehand if the answer is "yes" I'm going to punish you and punish you hard because you'll have done something no boy of mine ought to do. But you've never lied to me before, I know, and I don't believe, even to save yourself punishment, you'd lie to me now, would you?

DICK [*Quietly*]. I won't lie, Pa.

NAT. Have you been trying to have something to do with Muriel—something—you know what I mean. [*Pause: Then*]

DICK [*Shocked*]. No! What do you think I am, Pa? Why, I—I love her! I'm going to marry her—after I get out of college! She's said she would. We're engaged!

NAT [*Relieved*]. All right. That's all I wanted to know, son.

DICK. I don't see how you could think—Did that old idiot Macomber say that about me?

NAT. Shouldn't call your future father-in-law names. 'Taint respectable. It's these letters you wrote.

DICK. What lett—Oh, Swinburne! They're beautiful, aren't they?

NAT. A little strong, I'd say. By the way, here's one from her to you. Better be prepared for a bit of a blow, son . . . Well, see you at dinner tonight . . . [*Footsteps receding . . . Door slams . . . A pause . . . Then the sound of an envelope being opened, another pause*]

DICK [*Reads, slowly*]. Mr. Richard Miller. This is to let you know that I have no wish to see you ever again anywhere, anytime. Please do not make a nuisance of yourself by trying to get me to change my mind as my eyes have been opened to your true character. Very truly yours, Muriel Macomber. [*Long pause, then*] The little coward! I hate her! She can't treat me like that! I'll show her! I'll show her! [*Then: sobbing*] Muriel! *Muriel!*

[*Music*]

MRS. MILLER. I do hope Nat and Sid aren't going to be late for dinner. [*Sighs*] But I suppose with that darned picnic it's more likely than not. I see you've got your new dress on, Lily.

LILY [*Embarrassed*]. Yes, I thought—if Sid's taking me to the fireworks tonight—I ought to spruce up a little.

MRS. MILLER. Lily, why don't you change your mind and marry Sid and reform him? You love him and always have—

LILY [*Stiffly*]. I can't love a man who drinks. [*Then*] Essie, it's sixteen years since I broke off our engagement.

MRS. MILLER [*Angrily*]. Sixteen years!

LILY. But if he kept his promise and stays sober and takes me to the fireworks tonight—then—[*With agitation*] He must! It's our last chance! I know it!

MRS. MILLER. Well, dear, I hope you're right. Good gracious, if I'm not forgetting! I've got to warn that Tommy against giving me away to Nat about the fish. He knows, because I had to send him to market for it, and—

LILY. Essie, what *are* you talking about?

MRS. MILLER [*Guiltily*]. Well, you know how Nat carries on about not being able to eat bluefish.

LILY. I know. He says there's a certain oil in it that poisons him.

MRS. MILLER [*Chuckling*]. Poisons him, nothing! He's been eating bluefish for years—only I tell him each time it's weakfish. [*Footsteps*] Ssssh.

DICK [*Dejected*]. 'Lo, Ma, Aunt Lily.

MRS. MILLER. Oh, it's you, Richard. Feel any better, dear?

DICK. It doesn't matter. Nothing matters.

LILY. Dick, you really mustn't let it upset you this way. Things like this come up all the time. *I* know.

DICK. Things like what, Aunt Lily?

LILY. You and Muriel.

DICK. Oh, her! I wasn't even thinking about her. I was thinking about life. Aunt Lily, life is a joke! And everything comes out all wrong in the end!

MRS. MILLER. Richard, I think you must be hungry.

DICK. I'm not hungry a bit! Food! That's all you think of in this house!

MRS. MILLER. Well, somebody's got to think of it. And that reminds me: it's time to put the—er—weakfish in. Coming? Lily?

LILY. Yes, Essie. [*Footsteps receding . . . Door slams . . . Pause*]

DICK [*To himself*]. A fine thing . . . the world torn up . . . civilization in its death rattle . . . and all they think of is food. [*A low whistle is heard*]

WINT [*Off*]. Hey, Dick! . . . Psst! Open the screen door. Let me in. [*Door opens*] It's me. Wint Selby.

DICK [*Respectful*]. Oh, hello, Wint. Come on in. [*Door closes*]

WINT [*Low*]. Keep it quiet, Kid. I don't want your folks to know I'm here. Tell your brother Art I want to see him a second—on the Q.T.

DICK. Can't. He's up at the Rands'. Won't be home before ten, anyway.

WINT. Darn, I thought he'd be here for dinner. Gosh, that gums the works for fair.

DICK. What is it, Wint? Can't I help?

WINT. I might tell you if you can keep your face shut.

DICK. Oh I can.

WINT. Well, I ran into a couple of swift babies from New Haven this afternoon, and I dated them up for tonight, thinking I could catch Art. But now it's too late to get anyone else and I'm nearly broke, and I can't afford to blow them both to drinks.

DICK [*Eagerly*]. I've got eleven dollars saved up. I could loan you some.

WINT. Nix, Kid, I don't want to borrow your money, but you're a good sport . . . Say. Say have you got anything on for tonight?

DICK. No.

WINT. Want to come along with me? [*Quickly*] I'm not trying to lead you astray, understand. But it'll be a help if you would just sit around with Belle while I'm with Edith. See what I mean? You don't have to do anything, not even take a glass of beer—unless you want to.

DICK. Aw, what do you think I am—a rube?

WINT. You mean you're game for anything that's doing?

DICK. Sure I am.

WINT. Ever been out with any girls—I mean, real swift ones?

DICK [*Lying*]. Aw, what do you think? Sure I have! Say, don't worry about me.

WINT. Okay, I wouldn't ask you if I didn't know you were coming down to Yale next year. I don't want to lead you astray.

DICK. I've been around.

WINT. Well, you be at the Pleasant Beach House at half-past eight, then. The back room. And bring some cloves to take the booze off your breath. So long.

DICK. So long, Wint. See you right after dinner tonight!

[*Music*]

[*Dishes, etc. . . . . Over it Sid is heard singing "In the Sweet Bye and Bye" at the top of his lungs*]

TOMMY. I'll have more lobster, Ma.

MRS. MILLER. All right . . . Hush, Sid. You not only come home late to dinner but in a state of . . . of . . .

SID [*Jovially*]. Good-fellowship, that's the word for it.

MRS. MILLER. And after you promised Lily!

LILY [*Coldly*]. Oh, never mind me, Essie. My feelings are of no consequence.

MILDRED. Ma, can I have some more lobster?

MRS. MILLER. Certainly, dear. Richard?

DICK. No, thanks, Ma.

MRS. MILLER. But you've hardly eaten a thing, and that little you've bolted as though you were in an awful sweat to get some place!

DICK. Me? In a sweat to—Where would I be going?

MRS. MILLER. Well, maybe I'm imagining things. Nat? How about you?

NAT. No, thanks. I'll have some of that other. It—er—isn't bluefish by any chance, is it, my dear?

MRS. MILLER. Of course not. You know we never have bluefish, on account of you.

NAT [*Gravely*]. Yes, I regret to say, there's a certain peculiar oil in bluefish that invariably poisons me.

[*A loud peal of laughter from Tommy*]

MRS. MILLER. Stop that, Tommy! Stop that this inst . . .

TOMMY [*Choking*]. I—I can't help it, Ma!

NAT. Well, I must say I don't see what's so darned funny about my being poisoned.

SID [*Drunkenly*]. Aha! Nat, I suspect a plot! This fish looks blue to me —very blue—Aha! Look at your wife! Regard that guilty expression! Can it be this woman has been slowly and systematically poisoning you all these years? Can it?

NAT. Oh, give us a rest you darned fool! A joke's a joke, but—[*Hurt*] Is this true, Essie?

MRS. MILLER. Yes, dear, it is true, if you must know. You've eaten bluefish for years and thrived on it and it's all nonsense about that peculiar oil.

NAT [*Deeply offended*]. Essie, kindly allow me to know my own constitution! Now I think of it, I've felt upset afterward every darned time I've had fish! Here, take it away. I can't eat this!

MRS. MILLER. Well, don't then. Have some lobster. How about you, Sid?

SID [*Singing, at the top of his lungs*]. "In the sweet bye and bye" [*Spoken*] No, thanks. [*Singing*] "We will meet on that beautiful shore"—

MRS. MILLER. Mercy sakes, Sid! Can't you stop singing?

SID. No ma'am. When I feel good I want the world to know! [*Singing*] "Work and pray, while you—"

TOMMY. Lookit, lookit! Uncle Sid's eating the claw—shells and all!

MRS. MILLER. Sid, do you want to kill yourself? Take it away from him, Lily!

LILY [*Coldly*]. I am not responsible for your brother's actions, Essie.

SID. That's right. She's not responsible. Wouldn't take the responsibility as a gift. Lily doesn't *like* responsib—

NAT. Sid, I think you'd better go up to bed for a while.

SID. Bed? Yes, maybe you're right . . . But first there is still a duty I must perform. No day is complete without it . . . Lily, I regret I am too drunk to take you to the fireworks this evening. I regret it very, very much. And now, I ask you, Lily, once and for all. Will you marry me? [*Pause*]

LILY [*Tensely quiet*]. No, Sid, I won't.

SID. Right. Don't blame you at all. [*Sings*]

> In the sweet bye and bye
> We will meet on that beautiful shore;
> Work and pray, while you may
> We will meet in the sky bye and bye. [*Fades*]

[*Door closes*]

NAT [*Laughing*]. That Sid! He's a case. Darned if you can help laughing at him even when—

LILY [*Tense*]. That's it. Sid's a case . . . Everybody laughs . . . encourages him! . . . that's been his downfall . . . everyone always laughing, everyone always saying what a card he is, what a case, what a caution, so funny . . . and he's gone on doing it . . . and we're all responsible . . . making it easy for him . . . we're all to blame . . . and all we do is laugh!

MRS. MILLER. Now, Lily, now, you mustn't take on so. It isn't as serious as all that.

LILY [*Bitterly*]. Maybe—it is—to me. Or was—once. [*Contritely*] I'm sorry, Nat. I'm sorry, Essie. I—I'm not feeling so well tonight. If you'll excuse me I'll go in the parlor and lie down on the sofa.

[*Footsteps receding*]

MRS. MILLER. Poor Lily! Why, Richard, you haven't had your ice cream yet! Where are you going?

DICK. I don't want any ice cream, Ma.

NAT. Your mother asked you where you're going?

DICK. Oh, for a walk, I guess. See you later. Good night.

MRS. MILLER. Don't come home late, dear, and be careful! What with all those fireworks going off and everything— !

DICK. Don't worry about me, Ma. Nothing can happen to me.

[*Music*]

END OF ACT I

ANNOUNCER

COMMERCIAL

STATION IDENTIFICATION

ACT II

[*Music*]

NARRATOR. Well, we're still back in 1906, and it's still the Fourth of July. It's evening, now. Dad and Mother and Aunt Lily are in the parlor. Uncle Sid has gone upstairs to sleep off his—high spirits. And Dick? Well, young Richard, having just been thrown over by his best girl, has set his feet firmly along the path to ruin. To help out a friend, he has consented to be the fourth party in a blind date—with two swift babies from New Haven. We see him now at the Pleasant Beach House—a notorious waterfront dive. And with him is, yes, one of the swift babies. Her name is Belle . . . [*Fades*]

[*A player piano grinding out "Bedelia"*]

DICK. So this is the Pleasant Beach House! Gee!

BELLE. This is it. And my name is Belle, remember?

DICK. 'Course I do. I—I wonder where my friend Wint disappeared to?

BELLE. Stop worryin'. He'll be back. So will Edith. [*She giggles*] Drink up your beer, why don't you? It's getting flat.

DICK. I—I let it get that way on purpose. I like it when it's flat.

BELLE. Then how about loosenin' up and buyin' me another drink?

DICK. Certainly. Excuse me. I—I was thinking of something else. Have anything you like. Bartender, see what the lady will have—and have one on me yourself.

BARTENDER. Say, you're a sport, all right! I'll have a cigar. What'll you have, Candy Kid? The same?

BELLE. Uh—huh.

BARTENDER. What's yours, mister? Another beer?

DICK. A small one, please. I'm not thirsty.

BELLE. Say, kid, I don't know what to make of you. You've got me guessing. Don't you know fillin' up on beer'll only make you sleepy? Have a man's drink!

DICK. All right. I was going to. Bartender, bring me a sloe-gin fizz.

BELLE. And make it a real one!

BARTENDER. Comin' up. [*Footsteps receding*]

BELLE. Say, dearie, are you sore at me?

DICK. Me? Of course not. What ever gave you that idea.

BELLE [*Seductively*]. You see, it's this way with me. I think you're one of the sweetest kids I've ever met—and I could like you such a lot if you'd give me a chance—instead of acting so cold and indifferent.

DICK. I'm not cold and indifferent. [*Tragically*] It's only that I've got—a weight on my mind.

BELLE [*Impatient*]. Well, get it off. You'll feel better.

[*Footsteps approaching*]

BARTENDER. Here y'are. That'll be forty cents—with the cigar.

DICK. Here's a dollar. Keep the change.

BARTENDER. Thank you, sir.

DICK. Don't mention it.

[*Footsteps receding*]

BELLE. Well, here's how! Bottoms up! . . . That's the stuff! . . . Gee, you got pretty hair. Honey Boy, I'm crazy about you! [*Calling*] Bartender, another round—the same!

DICK. I—I'm crazy about you, too.

BELLE. Then how about a little kiss?

DICK. I—I've sworn off all that.

BELLE. What do you mean you swore off *all that*?

DICK. I took an oath I'd be faithful.

BELLE. Till death do us part, eh? Well, well!

[*Footsteps approaching*]

BARTENDER. Here's your pleasure.

DICK. Here's a dollar. Keep the change.

BARTENDER. Thank you, sir.

DICK. Don't mention it. [*Receding footsteps*] Well, bottoms up! Gee, that's good stuff, all right.

SALESMAN [*Jovial*]. Well, well! Good evening.

BELLE. Hello.

SALESMAN. Mind if I join the party? I'm just a lonesome bachelor tonight and—

BELLE. There's no party here, Mister. Not that I ain't tryin'.

SALESMAN. That sounds—er—hopeful.

DICK [*Drunk*]. Let's have another drink! Bartender!

BELLE. You've had enough . . . Listen, kid. Here's an old friend of mine, Mr. Smith from New Haven . . . We're old friends, aren't we, Smitty?

SALESMAN. Definitely.

BELLE. Kid, I'm going over and sit at his table for a while. And you better go home.

DICK. I'm never going home! I'll show them! [*Recites*]

> But I wouldn't do such, 'cause I loved her too much,
> But I learned about women from her!

SALESMAN. Say, this is rich! Attaboy, young feller! Give us some more!

DICK. Belle, I have something to say to you.

BELLE. I don't want to hear it.

DICK. You—you oughtn't to lead this kind of life. It isn't right—for a nice girl—like you. Why don't you reform?

SALESMAN [*Guffaws*]. Say, that's rich—that's rich, that is!

BELLE. Shut up, the kid's in love! Tell us about it, Honey.

SALESMAN. Yeah, who is she? What's her name?

DICK. Her name—her name—I cannot tell you her name.

SALESMAN. Why not?

DICK. It is gone, gone with the rest of her.

BELLE. What's the matter, is she dead?

DICK. In a manner of speaking. She has ceased to be.

SALESMAN. What happened to her?

DICK. I killed her.

BELLE & SALESMAN. *What?*

DICK [*Reciting*].

> Yet each man kills the thing he loves,
> By each let this be heard,
> Some do it with a bitter look,
> Some with a flattering word,
> The coward does it with a kiss,
> The brave man with a sword.

DICK [*Tragically*]. I did it with a kiss. I'm a coward. A coward, do you hear! Oh Muriel, Muriel . . . I feel . . . awfully . . . sleepy . . . Muriel . . . dear . . .

BELLE. That's right, kiddo. Have yourself a little snooze.

[*Music*]

MRS. MILLER. Oh, I do wish Richard would come home!

NAT. There now, Mother, he'll be in any minute now. Don't worry about him.

MRS. MILLER. What time is it now?

NAT. Only a little past ten.

MRS. MILLER. Why, you said that an hour ago! Nat Miller, you're telling me a fib, so's not to worry me. You let me see that watch!

NAT. Well, it's a quarter to eleven. But that's not so late—when you remember it's the Fourth of July!

MRS. MILLER. Oh, I just know something terrible's happened to him!

MILDRED. Ah, Ma. Dick only sneaked off to the fireworks at the beach, you wait and see.

TOMMY [*Sleepily*]. Where's Dick?

MRS. MILLER. He hasn't come in yet, dear. [*Suddenly*] My gracious, in all the excitement I was forgetting you're still up! Go up to bed this minute!

TOMMY [*Yawning*]. I'm not sleepy.

NAT. Did you hear what your mother said?

TOMMY. Okay. I heard. 'Night, everybody.

VOICES. Good night, Tommy.

MRS. MILLER. What time is it?

NAT. Now, Mother, I just told you a minute ago—

MRS. MILLER. I don't see how you can take it so calm! Here it is midnight, you might say, and our Richard still out, and we don't even know where he is.

MILDRED. I hear someone. Bet that's him now, Ma.

MRS. MILLER. You give him a good piece of your mind, Nat, you hear me! You're too easy with him, that's the whole trouble! The idea of him daring to stay out like this!

[*Footsteps approaching*]

SID. Hello.

MILDRED. Oh, it's Uncle Sid.

NAT. Hello, Sid. Had a good nap?

SID. Nat and Essie—and Lily—I—I—want to apologize—for coming home —the way I did—there's no excuse—but I didn't mean—

NAT. Of course, Sid. It's all forgotten.

MRS. MILLER. We know how it is with picnics, Sid. You just forget it.

SID [*Desperately*]. Lily—I'm sorry—about the fireworks. Can you—forgive me? Lily? [*No answer*]

SID [*Breaking down*]. You're right, Lily—right not to forgive me! I'm no good and I never will be! I'm a no-good drunk!—no good to myself or anybody else!—if I had any guts I'd kill myself, and good riddance! —but I haven't—I'm yellow, too!—a yellow, drunken, bum! [*He sobs*]

LILY [*Very much moved*]. Don't cry, Sid! I can't bear it! Of course I forgive you! Haven't I always forgiven you? I know you're not to blame—*Don't,* Sid! [*Door slams . . . Pause, then*]

MILDRED. It's Dick!

MRS. MILLER. Oh, thank Heaven! thank Heaven!

[*Footsteps approaching*]

RICHARD [*Drunk*]. Greetings, Mother, Father, relatives . . . I greet you on this auspicious and patriotic occasion . . .

MRS. MILLER. Dear Lord, what's happened to him! He's gone crazy! Richard!

SID. Crazy, nothing. He's soused!

ARTHUR. He's drunk, all right . . . you've got your nerve! You fresh kid! We'll take that out of you when we get you down to Yale all right, all right!

RICHARD.

> Yesterday this Day's Madness did prepare
> Tomorrow's Silence, Triumph, or Despair.
> Drink! for—

NAT. Richard! How dare—!

MRS. MILLER [*Hysterical*]. Don't you strike him, Nat! Don't you—!

SID. Steady, Nat! Keep your temper. No good bawling him out now! He don't know what he's doing.

NAT [*Half ashamed*]. All right—you're right, Sid.

DICK. "And then—I will come—with vine leaves in my hair!"

[*A loud sardonic laugh*]

MRS. MILLER. Richard! You're intoxicated!—you bad, wicked boy, you!

DICK. "Speak the speech, I pray you, as I pronounce it to you, trippingly on the tongue. But if you mouth it as so many of your players do, I had as lief . . . had as lief . . ." Ma! I feel rotten!

MRS. MILLER. My poor boy!

SID. Let me take care of him. I know this game backwards.

NAT. Yes, Mother, you leave him to Sid.

SID. Come on, Old Sport! Upstairs we go! Your old Uncle Sid'll fix you
up. He's the kid that wrote the book!

[*Music*]

END OF ACT II

ANNOUNCER

COMMERCIAL

ACT III

[*Music*]

NARRATOR. Well, it's the next day now, July fifth. Nat Miller has broken
a precedent and come home during the day—for one specific purpose.
He has promised Mrs. Miller he will punish their son Richard for
coming home—er—intoxicated, the night before . . . [*Fades*]

NAT. Darn it, Mother, I'd ought to be back at the office!

MRS. MILLER. You can't go back without talking to him. It's your duty—!

TOMMY. What has Dick done? Why is everybody scared to tell me?

NAT. Young man, I've never spanked you yet, but that don't mean I never
will! Now, skedaddle! . . . By the way, Mother, where is Richard?

MRS. MILLER. He's still in bed. [*Quickly*] But you needn't think I haven't
punished him. I've given him pieces of my mind he won't forget in
a hurry. And I've kept reminding him his real punishment was still
to come—that you were coming home from the office on purpose—
and that then he'd learn that you could be terrible stern when he
did such awful things.

NAT. Hmmmmmmmm.

MRS. MILLER. And that's just what it's your duty to do—punish him good
and hard! The idea of him daring—But you be careful how you go
about it, Nat. Remember he's like you inside—too sensitive for his
own good. Shall I go up now and tell him to get dressed, you want
to see him?

NAT. Yes! I can't waste all day around here!

MRS. MILLER. Now you keep your temper, Nat, remember!

[*Footsteps receding*]

NAT. Darn women, anyway! They always get you mixed up. Their minds simply don't know what logic is! [*Calling*] Sid! Oh, Sid!

[*Footsteps approaching*]

SID. Yes, Nat?

NAT. Sit down, I want to talk to you . . . Sid, this thing with Dick is a darned sight more serious than Essie has any idea. [*Intently*] There was a woman with him last night. At the Pleasant Beach House!

SID. That dive!

NAT. They were seen together. That's just the sort of darned fool thing he might do to spite Muriel. I've got to have a straight talk with him —about women and all those things. I ought to have long ago.

SID. Yes, you ought.

NAT. I've tried to a couple of times. I did it all right with Arthur—but heck, with Richard I always get sort of ashamed of myself and can't get started right. You feel, in spite of all his bold talk out of books, that he's so darned innocent inside. [*Footsteps*] Oh, hello, Mother.

MRS. MILLER. I'm sorry, Nat, but he was sound asleep and I didn't have the heart to wake him.

NAT. Well, I'll be double-darned! If you're not the—

MRS. MILLER. Now don't lose your temper at me, Nat Miller! You know as well as I do he needs all the sleep he can get today after last night's ructions!

NAT. Well, I'll be eternally—Here I come home especially to—and you don't even—*because he was sound asleep!*—No use talking, you certainly take the cake! I'll see you at supper!

[*Door slams*]

MRS. MILLER. Well! I never saw Nat so bad-tempered.

SID [*Chuckling*]. Bad temper, nothing. He's so tickled to get out of it for a while he can't see straight!

[*Music*]

MILDRED. Psst! Dick! It's me. Mildred!

DICK. Go away. Can't a man have any privacy even in his own bedroom?

MILDRED. I've got something for you. Guess what!

DICK. Don't bother me. I'm in no mood to play riddles with kids.

MILDRED. Oh, well, if you're going to get snippy! And you pretend to be in love! If I told Muriel that!

DICK. Is it—from her?

MILDRED. Uh-huh. A letter. I was walking past her house just now when she threw it down to me. Here it is. [*Letter being opened*] Gee, it must be nice to be in love like you are—all with one person.

DICK [*Excited*]. Gee! Do you know what she says? That she didn't mean a word in that other letter! Her old man made her write it. And she loves me and only me and always will, no matter how they punish her!

MILDRED. My, I'd never think she had that much spunk.

DICK [*Gleefully*]. And she's going to try and sneak out and meet me tonight! [*Loftily*] I don't know whether I'll consent to keep this date or not.

MILDRED. Well, I know. You're not allowed out, so you can't keep it.

DICK. I'm going to sneak out, right now. You tell Pa and Ma after I've gone so they won't worry—like last night.

MILDRED. All right. But what'll you do till nighttime? It's ages to wait.

DICK. What do I care how long I wait! I'll think of her—and dream! I'd wait a million years and never mind it—for her . . . The trouble with you is, you don't know what love means!

[*Music*]

MURIEL. Tell me what happened, Dick—from the beginning.

DICK. Well, Muriel, after I read your first letter, I didn't want to live any more. Life seemed like a tragic farce.

MURIEL. I'm so awfully sorry, Dick—honest I am! But you might have known I'd never write that unless—

DICK. I thought your love for me was dead. I thought you'd never loved me, that you'd only been cruelly mocking me, to torture me!

MURIEL. Dick, I'd never! You know I'd never!

DICK. I wanted to die. I sat and brooded about death. Finally I made up my mind to kill myself.

MURIEL [*Excited*]. Dick, you didn't!

DICK. I did, too. I thought, "When I am dead, she will be sorry she ruined my life"

MURIEL. If you ever had! I'd have died, too! Honest, I would!

DICK. But suicide is the act of a coward. That's what stopped me. [*Change of tone*] And anyway, I thought to myself, she isn't worth it.

MURIEL. That's a nice thing to say!

DICK. Well, if you meant what was in the letter, you wouldn't have been worth it, would you?

MURIEL. But I've told you a dozen times, Pa made me—

DICK. So I said to myself, I'm through with women. They're all alike.

MURIEL. I'm not.

DICK. And I thought, what difference does it make what I do now? I might as well forget her and lead the pace that kills, and drown my sorrows! You know I had eleven dollars saved up to buy you something for your birthday, but I thought, she's dead to me now, and why shouldn't I throw it away? [*Quickly*] I've still got almost five left, Muriel, and I can get you something nice with that.

MURIEL [*Excited*]. What do I care about your old presents? Tell me what happened.

DICK. After it was dark I sneaked out and went to a low dive I know about—a secret house of shame. They let me into a secret room behind the barroom. There wasn't anyone there but a Princeton senior I know—he belongs to Tiger Inn, and he's fullback on the football team—and he had two chorus girls from New York with him, and they were all drinking champagne.

MURIEL. Dick Miller! I hope you didn't—

DICK [*Carelessly*]. I had a highball myself. Then I noticed one of the girls—the one that wasn't with the fullback—looking at me. She had strange-looking eyes. And then she asked me if I wouldn't drink champagne with them and come and sit with her.

MURIEL. She must have been a nice thing! And—did you?

DICK. Why shouldn't I, when you'd told me in that letter you'd never see me again?

MURIEL [*Tearfully*]. But you ought to have known Pa made me—

DICK. I didn't know that then. She had yellow hair—the kind that burns and stings you!

MURIEL. Did you get drunk?

DICK. Only a little at first. But you ought to have seen me when I got home! I was on the verge of delirium tremens!

MURIEL. Oh! . . . Did you kiss her?

DICK. No, I didn't.

MURIEL. You did, too! You're lying and you know it! You did, too!

[*In a frenzy*] I hate you! I wish you were dead! I'm going home this minute! I never want to lay eyes on you again! And this time I mean it!

DICK. Muriel! Wait! Listen!

MURIEL. I don't want to listen! Let me go! If you don't I'll bite your hand!

DICK. I won't let you go! You've got to let me explain! I never—*OUCH!* [*Pause, then, slowly*] All right. Go if you want to—if you haven't the decency to let me explain. I'll go back to her of the yellow tresses that burn and sting!

MURIEL. See, that's what I mean! [*Then*] Was she—very beautiful?

DICK. Yes—but not as beautiful as you.

MURIEL. Do you—love her?

DICK. No. I love you.

MURIEL. I—I'm sorry—I hurt your hand.

DICK. It was nothing. [*Then*] Muriel?

MURIEL. Yes?

DICK. Can I—can I—kiss you?

MURIEL. Will it wash off—her kisses—make you forget—for always?

DICK. Yes.

MURIEL. Then—all right—Dick. [*Pause*] The moon is beautiful tonight, isn't it?

DICK. Not as beautiful as you. Nothing is . . . Won't it be wonderful after we're married? Gosh, but I love you! Gosh, I love you—darling!

MURIEL. I love you, too—sweetheart! [*Pause*] Where'll we go on our honeymoon, Dick? To Niagara Falls?

DICK. That dump where all the silly fools go? I should say not! . . . No, we'll go to some wonderful place! Somewhere out on the Long Trail—the trail that is always new—on the road to Mandalay! We'll watch the dawn come up like thunder out of China!

MURIEL [*Happily*]. That'll be wonderful, won't it?

[*Music*]

MRS. MILLER. My, but I'm glad Mildred told me where Richard went off to. I'd have worried my heart out if she hadn't. But now, it's all right.

NAT. I'd hardly go so far as to say that. Just because we know he's all right tonight doesn't mean last night is wiped out. He's still got to be punished for that.

MRS. MILLER. Nat, I've told you how sorry he was, and how he said he'd never touch liquor again. It didn't make him feel happy like Sid, but only sad and sick, so he didn't see anything in it for him—that's what he said.

NAT. Well, if he's really got that view of it driven into his skull, I don't know but I'm glad it all happened. That'll protect him more than a thousand lectures—just horse sense about himself . . . Still, I can't let him do such things and go scot-free. And then, besides, there's another side to it . . .

MRS. MILLER. What do you mean, another side?

NAT. I mean—er—discipline. There's got to be some discipline in a family. I don't want him to get the idea he's got a stuffed shirt at the head of the table—

[*Door closes*]

MRS. MILLER. That's Richard now.

[*Footsteps approaching*]

DICK [*Walking on air*]. Hello.

MRS. MILLER. Hello, Richard.

NAT. Hello, Son.

MRS. MILLER [*Whisper*]. Goodness, he acts queer! Nat, do you suppose he's been—?

NAT. No. It's love, not liquor, this time.

MRS. MILLER. Richard! What's the matter with you? Why are you sitting down over there in the dark?

DICK. Huh?

MRS. MILLER. Your father's been waiting to talk to you.

NAT. You better leave Richard and me alone for a while, Mother.

MRS. MILLER [*Apprehensive*]. Well—all right. I'll go sit on the piazza. Call me if you want me . . . [*Door closes . . . A pause*]

NAT. Sit down over here, Richard . . . Well, how are the vine leaves in your hair this evening?

DICK [*Shamefaced*]. I don't know, Pa.

NAT. Turned out to be poison ivy, didn't they? [*Kindly*]

DICK. I know I was a darned fool.

NAT. You sure were—not only a fool but a downright, stupid, disgusting fool! It was bad enough for you to let me and Arthur see you, but to appear like that before your mother and Mildred! And I wonder if Muriel would think you were so fine if she ever saw you as you looked and acted then. I think she'd give you your walking papers for keeps. And you couldn't blame her. No nice girl wants to give her love to a stupid drunk!

DICK [*Suffering*]. I know, Pa.

NAT. All right. Then that settles—the booze end of it. [*Sharply*] But there is another thing that's more serious. How about that woman you were with at the Pleasant Beach House?

DICK [*Flabbergasted*]. You know—?

NAT. Did you—that is—did you—?

DICK. No, Pa, I didn't.

NAT. How'd you happen to meet this lady, anyway?

DICK. I can't tell that, Pa. I'd have to snitch on someone—and you wouldn't want me to do that.

NAT. No. I suppose I wouldn't. Hmmn. Well, I believe you—and I guess that settles that. [*Pause, then, self-consciously solemn*] But listen here, Richard, it's about time you and I had a serious talk about—hmmn—certain matters pertaining to—and now that the subject's come up of its own accord, it's a good time—I mean there's no use in procrastinating further—so here goes. [*Pause*] Richard, you have now come to the age when—Well, you're a fully developed man, in a way, and it's only natural for you—I mean, pertaining to the opposite sex, it's only natural for you—Here's what I'm driving at, Richard. There are girls and girls—I mean, your whole life may be ruined if—I mean, there are some who—I mean, they're apt to be whited sepulchres, and your whole future life may—I mean—do you see what I mean—[*Giving up*] Oh, heck, I suppose you boys talk all this over among yourselves and you know more about it than I do. I'll admit I'm no authority. I never had anything to do with such women and it'll be a heck of a lot better for you if you never do!

DICK. I'm never going to, Pa. [*With shocked indignation*] I don't see how you could think I could—now—when you know I love Muriel and am going to marry her. I'd die before I'd—

NAT. That's the talk! By George, I'm proud of you when you talk like that, Son! There's nothing more to say and we'll forget it, eh?

[*Pause*]

DICK. How are you going to punish me, Pa?

NAT. I *was* sort of forgetting that, wasn't I? Well, I'd thought of telling you you couldn't go to Yale—

DICK. Don't I have to? Gee, that's great! Muriel thought you'd want me to. I was telling her I'd rather you gave me a job on the paper because then she and I could get married sooner . . . Gee, Pa, you picked a lemon. That isn't any punishment. You'll have to do something besides that.

NAT. Then you'll go to Yale and you'll stay there till you graduate, that's the answer to that! Muriel's got good sense and you haven't!

DICK. All right, Pa, if you say so.

NAT. I do say so. And now we're finished, you better call your Mother.

DICK [*Calling*]. Ma!

[*Door opens*]

MRS. MILLER. My, it's a beautiful night. The moon's way down low—almost setting.

NAT. I noticed it. Don't believe I've ever seen such a beautiful night—with such a wonderful moon. Have you, Richard?

DICK. No! It was wonderful—down at the beach— [*Stops*]

NAT [*Quietly*]. I can only remember a few nights that were as beautiful as this—and they were so long ago, when your mother and I were young and planning to get married.

[*Pause*]

DICK [*Note of surprise in his voice*]. Yes, I'll bet those must have been wonderful nights, too. [*Then*] You sort of forget the moon was the same way back then—and everything.

NAT [*Huskily*]. You're all right, Richard. [*Blows his nose*]

MRS. MILLER. You're a good boy, Richard.

[*Pause*]

NAT. Better get to bed early tonight, hadn't you, Son?

DICK. I couldn't sleep. Can't I go out on the piazza and sit for a while— until the moon sets?

NAT. All right. Then you better say good night now. I don't know about your mother, but I'm going to bed right away. I'm dead tired.

MRS. MILLER. So am I. Kiss me good night, dear.

DICK. Good night, Ma.

MRS. MILLER. Good night. Don't stay up till all hours now.

DICK. Good night, Pa.

[*Pause, then*]

NAT. Why, Dick! [*Another pause and the door is heard closing*] Hmmmn. First time he's done that in years. I don't believe in kissing between fathers and sons after a certain age—seems mushy and silly—but that meant something! . . . And, Mother, I don't think we'll ever have to worry about his being safe—from himself—again. I—I guess no matter what life will do to him—he can take care of it now.

[*Music*]

ANNOUNCER

CREDITS

THREE MEN ON A HORSE

Original Play
by John Cecil Holm and George Abbott

Radio Adaptation
by Arthur Miller

CAST

(for radio performance)

ERWIN	Stuart Erwin
PATSY	Sam Levene
MABEL	Shirley Booth
AUDREY	Betty Breckenridge
CLARENCE	J. Scott Smart
HARRY	Frank Lovejoy
FRANKIE	George Tyne
CHARLIE	Millard Mitchell
MR. CARVER	Edwin Jerome
DELIVERY BOY	James McCallion
ANNOUNCER	James McCallion

THREE MEN ON A HORSE

Radio adaptation by

ARTHUR MILLER

IT MAY BE because I rarely write comedy myself that I enjoyed adapting this play so much. Originally it was one of the funniest plays ever written, so it was a delight to add a few private jokes of my own, for if they didn't get laughs I could blame it on the original author; if they did I could claim credit for them myself.

Structurally the play did not present as great a problem as "The Guardsman." That play was one that is completely comfortable in its setting, whereas most plays are hard to keep within those iron bounds. "Three Men on a Horse" is one of the latter, for in nearly every scene of the original, reference is made to the world outside; people are constantly arriving from definite places and going to definite places. Thus the problem of enlarging the physical scope of the play merely required the adapter to follow the logic of the play's own movement.

The curious thing about this play is that scenes which were hilarious on the stage became unwieldy and overlong when an attempt was made to transfer them as such to the microphone. I found it necessary constantly to cut and shorten—the interesting thing about radio drama and stage drama. The radio, for some reason I do not pretend to understand, demands that the story being told always be in motion, always discernible, never for a moment allowed to recede from the consciousness of the listener. On the stage, however, it is possible and often desirable that elements which are not strictly story-advancing material be written into a scene. I suppose that stage allows for more embroidery because the characters themselves are visible and possess in themselves a narrative interest. Whether this is the explanation or not, it is the reason for my conclusion—taken after much labor in the radio vineyards—that really fine radio drama or first-rate radio comedy is an impossibility. For the story element of a play, although of decisive importance to its structure, is but the skeleton upon which the more attractive values of dramatic literature are hung.

This limitation of radio is not, to my mind, the result of the arbitrary half-hour or hour time-allotment. If we had been given two hours to put on this play we would still have had to rewrite it to bring up the story at every turn of the dialogue. Again I say that I do not know why this must be so, but it is. Luckily, in the case of "Three Men on a Horse," the play had a strong story as well as funny words. The story was really comic and was embedded in the very nature of Erwin and his dilemma. And the audience laughed because it was a funny story, not so much because the lines were sharp.

THREE MEN ON A HORSE

ANNOUNCER

INTRODUCTION FOR THE THEATRE GUILD

ACT I

[*Music: Into background*]

PATSY. Boy, have I got a story. I'll tell it to you. And you'll see what I mean when I say, life is peculiar. It ain't even peculiar, it's—it's worse. I'm standin' in front of you, a man who could have been a millionaire. But *multi* . . . multi, but what's the difference, and I don't mean from stealin'. I mean from straight honest labor, from bettin' on the horses. To make a long story short, me and my buddies, Frankie and Charlie, and my girl Mabel, we go down to the Jamaica track one day with our last forty bucks. Five minutes later we got ten bucks left.

[*Sneak ad lib crowd milling around*]

[*Music: Out*]

PATSY [*Continuing*]. We're standing in front of a pari-mutuel window with a ten spot between us. The last race begins in a couple of minutes. We look at each other, little Frankie and big Charlie and Mabel and me.

FRANKIE [*A high piping voice*]. Patsy, listen to me. Big Sneeze looks good to me.

PATSY. But Charlie, but Frankie, if we lose this ten spot we ain't got no supper tonight.

MABEL. That's right, Patsy, darling, don't bet any more. All I got left is two cans of chicken à la king in my room.

CHARLIE. What's wrong with chicken à la king?

207

MABEL. What's wrong! I'm beginning to cackle, that's all.

PATSY. Save the chicken à la king. We may have to trade it in for tomorrow's racing form.

CHARLIE. What'll we do with ten bucks, Patsy? We ain't in business with ten bucks, you might as well put it on something.

FRANKIE. Sure, we got the train tickets home. Big Sneeze looks awful good to me, Patsy.

PATSY. What do you say, Mabel? Lay it on?

MABEL. All right, but don't ask me to hock my dresses again.

FRANKIE. If worse comes to worst Patsy can hock his solid gold belt buckle.

PATSY. Again my buckle! Every time a horse looks good to him I walk around holding up my pants.

CHARLIE. Hey, the windows are closing!

FRANKIE. Lay it on Big Sneeze, Patsy! Hurry up. Big Sneeze!

PATSY. Big Sneeze, OK, OK! Big Sneeze. [*Inspired*] Say . . . I suddenly got the same feelin' as you, Frankie! Ten bucks on Big Sneeze! On the nose.

[*Music: Up: One excited bar of horse race music . . . A very short bridge which thins out, leaving . . .*]

[*Gallop of many hooves fading . . . as . . .*]

PATSY. The upshot is, the next morning I go across the street from the hotel and when I come back, I am holding up my pants.

[*Music: In sadly and into background*]

PATSY. But what I am getting at is this to show you how peculiar life is. At that very same minute that I am returning from the hock shop, a man named Erwin who lives in Ozone Heights is getting ready to leave for his office. Now at the time I'd never heard of no Erwin in Ozone Heights, but I know now he is a very nice fella. Forty bucks a week, a vacuum cleaner, a lawnmower, and a six-room house—that type fella. The kind of house exactly like every other house on the block. You know, the kind of block where everybody's got a dog so at night they can find which house is theirs.

[*Music: Up a beat and down into background*]

PATSY [*Softly, as though in a room*]. This morning the sun was shining—the way it does in the suburbs . . . Erwin comes into the living room looking for his hat, and he sees his wife. She is crying. She is crying, and unbeknownst to me—that is, without me knowing it, my life begins to gradually turn upside down, inside out.

[*Music: Out*]

ERWIN. What's the matter, dear? Something in your eye?

AUDREY. I'll be all right, Erwin.

ERWIN. What's the matter, Audrey? Can't you tell me? I'm late for work . . .

AUDREY. You were going to stay home from the office one day this week.

ERWIN. Yeah, but not today, sweetie. How in heaven's name am I going to turn out sixty-seven Mother's Day greetings? They just have to be in today.

AUDREY [*Hopefully*]. You could write them in the country.

ERWIN. You know I've never been able to write in the country. The birds and the butterflies distract me.

AUDREY. But, Erwin, you . . .

ERWIN. Wait! How's this? "The birds and the butterflies send you a greeting. It's spring and today in mem'ry we're meeting." Mother's Day Number 11. I'll call that "To Mother on Mother's Day."

AUDREY [*Sobs*].

ERWIN. What's the matter with you, Audrey?

AUDREY. Erwin—you don't love me any more.

ERWIN. Why? What's happened?

AUDREY. I'm going to wait till my brother gets here. I just phoned him to come over.

ERWIN. Then I'm getting out. Every time you get mad at me you call your brother. Why do you do that, Audrey?

AUDREY. He understands things . . . he's a businessman, not a poet.

ERWIN. Businessman! Look out the window at his forty-six houses—it took a world war to get people to buy them. My greeting card verses are read from Asbury Park to Seattle, war or peace!

[*Door opening*]

Gee, Clarence, I wish you'd ring before you come into my house.

CLARENCE [*A big Rotarian*]. I built this house.

ERWIN. But I bought it.

CLARENCE. At that price it was a gift. What's the matter, Sis? You look all upset. Has he been doing anything to you?

AUDREY. Oh, Clarence . . . I sent Erwin's suit to the cleaner's this morning . . .

CLARENCE. You needn't say more, Sis. Erwin, your cleaning bills are entirely too high, and I insist . . .

AUDREY. No—I mean I found this little notebook in the inside pocket.

ERWIN. Oh, *that!*

AUDREY. Clarence, look at these names. Shirley, May, Lena Wee, Nelly Squeeze . . .

CLARENCE. Erwin!

ERWIN. But listen!

AUDREY. Not one or two, Clarence, but pages of them. Look at these phone numbers . . . Jamaica 6-6-2-3-1.

ERWIN. But darling . . . !

CLARENCE. What is this, a harem?

ERWIN. It's no harem, it's only a hobby!

AUDREY. Only a hobby . . . [*Cries*]

ERWIN. They're all horses, dear.

CLARENCE. Horses! What do you do, call them up when you're lonely?

ERWIN. No, no . . . I just dope them out.

CLARENCE. Well, *that's* a new word for it. But you happen to be married to my sister!

ERWIN. Now listen to me! One day I came across a racing paper on the bus and I found out that the fellow who doped them out wasn't so good. So the next day I did it for fun and I've been keeping track of them in that book. It's just to pass the time. Like some people do crosswords.

CLARENCE. Crosswords do not have telephone numbers!

AUDREY [*Sobs*]. Oh, Erwin!

ERWIN. They're not telephone numbers, sweetheart. See? "Jamaica 6"—that's the sixth race at Jamaica. And then 6-2-3-1. That's the order I thought the horses would finish. On this other page is the way they actually did finish.

CLARENCE. You mean you guessed all of them right?

ERWIN. [*Naïvely*]. Sure, Clarence. Once in awhile I miss, but usually . . .

AUDREY. What's this number? 896.50—

ERWIN. That's what I made the week of January 20th—$896.50.

AUDREY. You made that and never told me?

ERWIN. Oh, I'd never bet on a horse, sweetie. This is all on paper, like a game.

CLARENCE. Erwin, you've been winning money since January, and nobody but you knows about these secret bank accounts.

ERWIN. I have one bank account!

CLARENCE. Suppose you die . . . a bus crash . . . a horse kicking you . . .

ERWIN. Horses don't kick me!

CLARENCE [*Topping him*]. Think of Audrey! Where are you keeping your money?

ERWIN. In Audrey's pocket. And I don't want you telling me what to do any more either, Clarence.

CLARENCE. Sure, what do you care if my sister walks around without a rag on her back, you . . .

ERWIN. She's got plenty of rags on her back!

CLARENCE. Listen, listen, how proudly he says it. His wife walks around in rags and he . . . !

ERWIN. Oh shut up!

AUDREY. Erwin!

ERWIN. Where's my hat? I'm getting out of here.

CLARENCE. Betting is immoral, Erwin! Especially secret betting. You'd think you'd give me a little tip sometime so *I* could make a few dollars. After I practically gave this house to you!

ERWIN. You didn't give me this house and there's always water in the cellar.

AUDREY. Erwin, you'll hurt Clarence's feelings!

ERWIN. And the water in the cellar ruined my whole fishing outfit and now I won't be able to go fishing this year!

[*Door opening*]

AUDREY. Where are you going, Erwin?

ERWIN. To the office, to make money to buy more of those 14.98 rags for your back.

AUDREY. No, Erwin. I want you to spend everything for a new fishing outfit.

CLARENCE. He's got enough socked away to buy a whole river.

ERWIN. Sure I have. Don't believe me, darling, believe Clarence. He knows everything. He's the only builder in New Jersey who builds houses with fishing privileges in the cellar.

AUDREY. Erwin!

ERWIN. Goodbye!

[*Door slam*]

[*Music: Up and down and out*]

[*Telephone*]

HARRY. Lavaliere Hotel. Cocktail Lounge. Yeah, this is Harry. Yeah, the bartender. Wait a minute. [*Calls*] Hey, Frankie, hey, Charlie . . . Gus wants to know if you're goin' to place any more bets today.

FRANKIE. We're still dopin'.

HARRY. Gus? They're still dopin'. Yeah, they'll call you later.

[*Phone hangs up*]

HARRY. Hey, look, you guys. I don't mind you usin' the bar for an office but make believe you're drinking in case the boss comes in.

CHARLIE. All right, set up a small beer.

HARRY. Oh, afraid of drowning, heh? How about you, Frankie?

FRANKIE. I'll have an extra straw. We're waiting for Patsy. He's gettin' his belt buckle hocked. We'll have money in a couple a minutes.

CHARLIE. Yeah, and Mabel is hockin' her dresses and her bracelet.

FRANKIE. Yeh, boy, it's a good investment to give Mabel a present. She's always so nice about hockin' it for you.

CHARLIE. Well, let's get down to some figuring here. I think the third race ought to be Rose Cross.

FRANKIE. Yeah, Rose Cross looks pretty good—

HARRY. Hey . . . hey . . . move down to the end of the bar. Here comes a customer.

[*Unsteady footsteps approaching*]

FRANKIE [*Sotto*]. What's he drunk or something? Hey—I think he's cryin'.

CHARLIE [*Moving away*]. Let him cry, we got the third race to dope out.

HARRY. Yes, sir, what'll you have?

ERWIN. I've been so sad all day. What's good for forgetting?

HARRY. Forgetting? Well, none of it'll help you remember anything. How about a Scotch for you, Mister?

ERWIN. Fine. You know, I should be at the office now. But I'm not there.

HARRY. No, that's right. You ain't.

ERWIN. Her brother thinks he's so smart. He can't even build a house without water in the basement.

HARRY. That's the way it goes. Some can and some can't.

ERWIN. And now I can't take my fishing trip.

FRANKIE [*Off mike*]. Maybe we should pass up the third race. What looks good in the fourth?

ERWIN. What are those fellows doing at the end of the bar?

HARRY. They're tryin' to decide on a horse to play. They live in the hotel.

ERWIN. Do you think they'd mind if I gave them a horse?

HARRY. They'd never remember to feed it.

ERWIN. I mean a tip. On the third race.

HARRY. Oh . . . Well, I think it might be better if they made the choice theirselves . . . because if they lost they wouldn't feel so good.

ERWIN. You mean they wouldn't like me?

HARRY. You got the idea.

FRANKIE. Do what you like, Charlie. I'm going to wait for Patsy. Maybe he'll have something.

CHARLIE. Well, I'm playin' Rose Cross.

ERWIN. Oh, no!

CHARLIE. What's that?

ERWIN. Don't play Rose Cross. Semester's going to win the third race.

CHARLIE. Semester, eh? Look, Bud, Semester ain't won a race since they invented horseshoes. I'm going to use the phone, Harry.

ERWIN. But Semester's going to win.

[*Phone dial*]

FRANKIE. Don't bother him, he's phonin' the bet.

ERWIN. But I have it right here. Third race, Semester. See? In my little black book.

FRANKIE. Look, buddy. I know you got it from the horse's mouth. But you shouldn't oughta believe what a horse tells you.

CHARLIE. Hello, Gus? Charlie. A dollar to win and one to show on Rose Cross in the third.

ERWIN. No, Semester, Semester!

FRANKIE. Shut up, you're holdin' up production.

CHARLIE. Well, squeeze me in, will ya, Gus? Ok, Rose Cross. [*Hangs up*]

CHARLIE. The race is startin'. We nearly didn't make it.

FRANKIE. Patsy! We been waitin' for you. Harry—get out the rope for Patsy's pants.

PATSY. I been all over town tryin' to raise fifty. Soon as they see me holdin' up my pants nobody knows me. Mabel's out tryin' to raise something, too.

FRANKIE. Charlie just put two bucks on Rose Cross.

PATSY. Where'd you get two bucks, Charlie?

CHARLIE. I promised to run the elevator tonight.

ERWIN. I was telling them to play Semester, but they didn't.

PATSY. Who's this?

CHARLIE. Just some drunk.

ERWIN. Semester in the third. Hasty Belle in the fourth . . . Oh, my—I don't feel so good.

HARRY. Right over there, bud. Keep goin' straight and turn to the left.

ERWIN [*Off mike*]. Oh, my . . . I—

HARRY. And step on it, please!

[*Phone rings*]

CHARLIE. That's Gus. I'll get it.

[*Phone being picked up*]

CHARLIE [*Off mike*]. Hello? Yeah, Gus. What's that? Say that again.

HARRY [*During the above speech*]. Here's the rope for your pants, Patsy. I had a little time so I braided it for you.

CHARLIE. OK, Gus. Yeah. Thanks. [*Phone hangs up*] What do you know?!

PATSY. What? What do I know?

CHARLIE. Semester.

FRANKIE. Semester won?!

CHARLIE. Yeah.

PATSY. So what about it?

FRANKIE. Well, didn't you hear him?

PATSY. Who?

FRANKIE. That square, that drunk. He's been tryin' to give us Semester for the last ten minutes.

HARRY. He kept opening this little book.

PATSY. Gimme that book, Harry.

FRANKIE. Lemme see.

PATSY. Don't crowd, don't crowd! You bother me. Gee—he's got them all figured out here. Hey! He had Brass Monkey for the first. Brass Monkey came in. He had Fairweather and Semester—they came in. He picked every race!

CHARLIE. Aw, he maybe wrote them down after the races was run.

HARRY. Nuts. I heard him say Semester before the race even started.

PATSY. Who is he, Harry?

FRANKIE. Maybe he's a handicapper.

PATSY. Now you know a guy with them outatown clothes ain't no handicapper.

HARRY. He said something about working in an office. And some water in the cellar or something.

PATSY. Look at this. Hasty Belle in the fourth. And he's got selections for all seven races today.

FRANKIE. What'd you get on your belt buckle, Patsy? Maybe we lay two bucks on Hasty Belle.

PATSY. Two bucks nothin'. We're layin' the roll. Here's eighteen bucks, Charlie. Take it around to Gus. The works on Hasty Belle. I'm goin' into the men's room and keep him there till the race is over.

FRANKIE. But how do we know it ain't a racket?

PATSY. If it is I never heard of it.

FRANKIE. Then it ain't a racket. But he looks awful dumb, he looks like a hick, Patsy!

PATSY. A hick, eh? Frankie, go to the public library and look up a picture of Daniel Boone. That's the biggest hick in the world to look at. And that man discovered fur.

[*Music: Up and out*]

FRANKIE. Come on, Harry, a small beer. I got four cents.

HARRY. They don't come that small. On your income why don't you take up jelly beans?

FRANKIE. But as soon as Hasty Belle wins we'll all have plenty of money. Charlie just laid eighteen bucks on the nose.

[*Door opening*]

MABEL [*Off mike*]. Hello, boys.

CHARLIE & FRANKIE. Hiya, Mabel.

MABEL. Patsy told me to meet him here. We had some business to talk over.

FRANKIE. That's all right, Mabel. We know where you been.

MABEL. Kinda embarrassing to me, always to be hockin' things. But it's all over now. All I've got left is the dress I'm wearing. My mother, poor thing, she was right. She said, put your money in gold inlays, and keep your mouth shut. Where's Patsy?

FRANKIE. He's in there.

MABEL. Where?

FRANKIE. There.

MABEL. Oh.

FRANKIE. He's talkin' business with a friend.

MABEL. In there?

FRANKIE. Well, the guy don't feel so good. He just dropped in to tip Patsy off on some fixed races so Patsy could get straightened out.

MABEL. You mean he fixes the races?

[Door opening]

MABEL [Continuing]. Hello, Patsy, I'm back.

PATSY. Boy, is that guy sick. How'd you make out, Mabel?

MABEL. Well, I went to this place on 8th Avenue like you told me and I unwrapped the dresses which was very good as you recall and he says they wasn't and I says they was and he says that ain't the question. He says they might be worth $40 but that they was only worth $8 to him and I says that wasn't the right attitude to take and he says never mind the attitude, will you take the eight bucks?

PATSY. Did you take it?

MABEL. Yeh. Then I asked somebody on the street where I could sell a parasol with a gold head and they said I would have to have an analysis and I said I wouldn't do that.

PATSY. That's a good girl. Charlie, here's eight bucks. Go around to Gus and lay it on More Anon in the fifth race.

CHARLIE. But we don't know the results of the fourth yet or anything. How do we know . . .

PATSY. I know a lot now. I been talkin' to him.

FRANKIE. I'll place the bet on the phone.

MABEL. I'm going up to my room, Pats. My feet hurt. Gee, it's swell about this friend of yours fixin' the races so we can get a roll again.

[Phone dialing in background]

PATSY. Heh?—Yeah, it's swell. See you later, sweetheart.

MABEL. But be sure you win, heh? Cause if I have to hock what I got on, it won't be nice . . . I mean in case I have to go anywhere.

[Door closing]

FRANKIE. Hell, Gus? This is Frankie. Sock eight bucks on the nose—More Anon in the fifth. [Off phone] Hey, Patsy.

PATSY. Yeh?

FRANKIE. It's post time for the fourth. Gus'll give me a blow by blow of the race if I hold on.

PATSY. Hold on. Here's nickels. What's the final odds?

FRANKIE. Hasty Belle is 4-1.

PATSY. 4-1—Terrific. Terrific.

[*Door opening*]

Hullo, Erwin. How you feel now, Erwin? Fellas, his name is Erwin.

CHARLIE. I knew it would be something like that.

ERWIN. I think I feel a little bit better now.

HARRY. Yeah, you're a much healthier shade of green now.

PATSY. You sit right down in this chair and rest yourself, Erwin. Harry, draw Erwin a nice glass of beer in a clean glass.

HARRY. At last. Somebody's gonna drink something.

CHARLIE. I hope Erwin don't have to leave soon.

PATSY. Erwin is not leavin'. He's stayin' here till he gets straightened out. And you want to know something, fellas? Erwin picks horses for a hobby.

CHARLIE. A hobby! You mean he ain't even a pro?

PATSY. He's better than a pro. He always picks winners.

CHARLIE. How do we know he ain't a nut? You know how a guy can get about horses.

ERWIN. I'm not a nut. I was valedictorian at Samuel Gompers High . . .

FRANKIE. Yeah, I'm here, Gus. Shut up you guys, the race is on.

PATSY. Shut up, everybody.

FRANKIE. Go ahead, Gus, give it to me. Yeah? They're at the quarter.

ERWIN [*Quietly*]. What is this?

PATSY [*Aside*]. Horse race. Drink your beer nicely.

FRANKIE. Yeah, Gus, go ahead. Joybird's leading . . . then Little Lie . . . Post Script . . . Where's Hasty Belle? Gee—Hasty Belle's last.

CHARLIE. A hobby, a hobby!

FRANKIE. Joybird still up at the half . . . who? Little Lie's taking the lead . . . now Post Script . . . neck and neck . . . yes . . . still that way?

CHARLIE. And Mabel's got no more dresses.

PATSY. Shut up. Go ahead, Frankie, where's Hasty Belle?

FRANKIE. They're in the stretch . . . [*To Patsy*] He's past . . . he's past . . .

PATSY. Who's past?

FRANKIE. Who's past, Gus? Joybird? Hasty Belle passing Joybird! What? Talk louder, Gus! OK.

[*Phone hangs up*]

FRANKIE. She won.

PATSY. Who won?

FRANKIE. Hasty Belle.

PATSY. Hot dog! You hear that, Erwin!

HARRY. Lemme in on the next race, Patsy!

CHARLIE. And you told me it was a hobby, Pats! What're you always kidding me for?

ERWIN. Well, I'm glad to have met you fellows.

PATSY. Where you going?

ERWIN. Oh, I have to be at the office.

PATSY. You mean you work?

ERWIN. Certainly, how could I make a living without working?

PATSY. But what do you do with your money from the horses?

ERWIN. I told you, I never bet. It's just a hobby, like crossword puzzles. Well, so long . . .

PATSY. Now wait, wait. Uh—you'll lose your job, Erwin. You can't go to no office looking like that.

ERWIN. But I've got to. I'll be late for Mother's Day.

CHARLIE. He'll be late for what?!!

PATSY. What're you screamin' for, Charlie? If the man says he's gonna be late for Mother's Day, he gonna be . . . What do you mean, Erwin, you'll be late for Mother's Day? Harry, another beer for Erwin.

HARRY. Comin' up!

ERWIN. I have to get my verses written.

PATSY. Oh, you're a song writer.

ERWIN. No. Greeting card verses. For Mother's Day. So I'll run along now, and I'm very happy to . . .

[*Phone rings*]

FRANKIE. I'll get it.

[*Phone unhooked as*]

PATSY. Just wait one minute, Erwin.

FRANKIE. Frankie speakin'. Yeah, Gus. Yeah? How much? Ok, thanks.

[*Phone hangs up*]

FRANKIE. More Anon took the fifth race. We made 735 bucks!

HARRY. The guy's a walkin' genius!

PATSY. Genius! He's better than a genius, he's brilliant, he's . . .

CHARLIE. Two in a row—it ain't human!

ERWIN. Well, so long, fellows.

PATSY. Now, wait a minute, Erwin. Why don't you sit down and relax?

ERWIN. Yes, but I—

PATSY. People who work in offices have gone home already.

ERWIN. But Mr. Carver'll be there waiting for me.

FRANKIE. You'll be late. When I went to school it was always better to be absent than late.

ERWIN. Not at Samuel Gompers. At Samuel Gompers . . .

PATSY. Erwin, look. We're horse bettors. Everything we make we'll give you 10 per cent. Just keep pickin' them for us. What do you say?

ERWIN. But my job . . . I've got a job.

PATSY. We'll call your boss and tell him you won't be in today. Believe me, Erwin, you look like you were run over with ice skates. What's the number, Erwin?

ERWIN. B. O. 4-7652. But what'll you tell him? He doesn't know you.

[*Phone dialing*]

PATSY. What's the boss' name again.

ERWIN. Mr. J. G. Carver. But look . . . now Patsy . . .

PATSY. Hello? Mr. Carver, please.

ERWIN. I don't think I want to go through with this, I—

PATSY. Hello, Mr. Carver. [*Sotto*] What's your last name, Erwin?

ERWIN. Trowbridge.

PATSY. Are you serious?

ERWIN. Yeah, that's my name. But look . . . I can easily go to work now.

PATSY. Mr. Carver, Erwin Trowbridge won't be in today. He got sick on his way to the office . . . yeah, terrible. We been workin' over him. He's in the drug store now. Me? I'm the soda jerk. Jerk! Fact is, I'm the pharmastist! What's the matter, you never been in a Pharmasty? Yeah, like—like with malteds. Wait a minute. Hold the wire. Erwin, he says as long as you make sure to have your work in tomorrow— it's jake with him.

ERWIN. Oh, I'll have it definitely.

PATSY. Mr. Carver? He says he'll have it in definitely. My address? It's no use giving you my address. I'm moving the store tonight. To Boston!

[*Phone hangs up*]

[*Music: Up and under to background*]

END OF ACT I

ANNOUNCER

COMMERCIAL

STATION IDENTIFICATION

ACT II

[*Music: Continuing in background*]

PATSY. Well, as you could imagine, after two hours with Erwin pickin' the horses for us, we got a strong smell of Palm Beach and twenty years of breakfasts in bed. Me, I take a short walk to the hock shop for my belt buckle. Mabel comes trotting back from her favorite broker with her five dresses and says to me . . .

MABEL. Gee, Pats, it feels just like old times. Ain't it nice of Erwin to fix the races for us.

PATSY. I didn't have the patience to explain to her. Besides, it wouldn't make no sense to Mabel anyway. She used to dance in the Follies and got hit in the head with a champagne bottle. But despite all the dough Erwin is making for us he don't feel so good so he sleeps all night in my room to sober up which is all right. We had him locked in anyway. Meantime over across the river the Ozone Heights excitement is really going on.

[*Music: Out*]

AUDREY. Oh, Erwin, my Erwin. Where are you . . . where are you?

CLARENCE. Will you stop that wailing, Audrey? That worm isn't worth it. I told you not to marry him, didn't I? Remember what I said to you? I said—"Don't marry him" . . . One look at him and I knew he'd never make Kiwanis.

AUDREY. But what's happened to him? He never stayed away all night in his life.

CLARENCE. A married man playing horses! It's disgraceful. I help him along—let him have a house on easy payment plan—does he come to me with a good thing? No—he . . .

[*Phone*]

AUDREY. Oh, maybe that's him! Hello? Oh, Mr. Carver, I've been trying to call you all morning. Hasn't he come to work again? Oh, my . . . Where? A drug store? You mean he's sick? All right, I'll call you if I hear anything.

[*Phone hangs up*]

Hello? Operator? Give me the police, hurry.

CLARENCE. What happened?

AUDREY. Erwin collapsed in a drug store. And his 65 Mother's Day verses are due in today and Mr. Carver says they're moving the store to Boston!

[*Music: Up and out*]

[*Door opening*]

FRANKIE. Ssh! He's still sleeping.

MABEL. I guess he drunk too much last night. Look—his verses are all over the floor.

PATSY. Wake him up, Frankie. He's gotta dope out today's races.

FRANKIE. Erwin? Erwin, wake up. Wake up . . . He was writin' them verses till three this morning.

ERWIN [*Waking*]. Oh . . . oh, my head . . . what time is it?

PATSY. Twelve o'clock noon.

ERWIN. Noon! Why didn't you wake me? Mr. Carver's got to have my verses today or he'll fire me! Where are my clothes?

PATSY. You ain't going anywhere, Erwin. Frankie, pick up the verses and take them over to Erwin's office.

ERWIN. That'll be fine. Meanwhile I can get dressed. Tell Mr. Carver I'll be there in an hour. And gee—I've got to call my wife.

MABEL. He's so devoted. It's like he wasn't married or something.

PATSY. Sit down on the bed, Erwin. I want to remind you, you got an agreement with us. You were going to pick the horses for us today.

ERWIN. But I've got a job, I—

PATSY. In my breast pocket, Erwin, I got one hundred and twelve dollars for you.

ERWIN. For me? You mean just from picking the horses?

PATSY. That's right, Erwin. Ten per cent of what we made yesterday. Today you stand to double it if you stick with us.

MABEL. Sure, we'll make you rich, Erwin, and vica versus, I hope.

ERWIN. Well, gee . . . I never realized I could actually make that much betting the horses.

MABEL. That's the beauty part of it, Erwin.

PATSY. So get dressed and start dopin' out the races. Go in the other room.

ERWIN [*Going away*]. Boy! With that much money I could tell Clarence to go to . . .

[*Door closing*]

PATSY. All right, come on, everybody, pick up the verses. There's one under the bed, Charlie. Gee—get a load of this:

> "Why was it that I chose to roam
> Cross land and sea so far from home?
> If that be life—my Mother dear,
> I send this card of Love and Cheer."

Mother's day Number 37. That kicks you, y'know? That goes right through my heart.

MABEL. If a guy said something like that to me I'd—I'd—

PATSY. Yeh, I know. Fellas—I feel we oughta do something big for Erwin. That Carver, his boss, that big salami . . . payin' him a fast forty a week for genius stuff like this, for regular Shakespeare merchandise. It's a shame!

FRANKIE. It's a rookin'.

PATSY. The world should see stuff like this. They oughta be put in barrooms, poolrooms, railroad stations, calendars—Wait, I got it.

CHARLIE. What?

PATSY. Liebowitz! Jake Liebowitz, the printer next door who does all them classy post cards for the five and ten. Get him on the phone, Mabel.

[*Phone dialing as*]

PATSY. Frankie, take these verses down to Liebowitz right now. I'll
explain to him on the phone.

FRANKIE. OK, I'll shoot right over.

[*Door opening and closing*]

MABEL. He's on the phone, Pats.

PATSY. Gimme that. Hello, Jake? Patsy. Well you ain't that busy. Listin,
I want a special job done on verses . . . verses . . . not nurses,
verses! You know, poetry verses like "Roses are Red" . . . yeah.
About a thousand, and Jake, I want them on shiny paper with lace
maybe. I want them nice, so we hang them in poolrooms and bars.
Frankie'll have them there in two minutes. Don't leave before you
get them. O.K.

[*Phone: Hang up*]

MABEL. Gee—you're liable to make Erwin famous, Patsy. I love an illiterary
atmosphere.

[*Door opening*]

ERWIN. Well, I'm off. Did Frankie take my verses to Mr. Carver?

PATSY. You don't never have to worry. You have nothing to worry about.
I just sent your verses to Jake Liebowitz . . .

ERWIN. Who is Liebowitch?

PATSY. A big printer. He's going to print your verses and sell them all
over the country. Barrooms, poolrooms . . .

MABEL. Liebowitz'll put Mother's Day on the map, Erwin.

ERWIN. What right have you to do a thing like that?

PATSY. But Erwin . . .

ERWIN. I'm going to lose my job now! If you think this is funny . . .

PATSY. But you'll make big dough out of them now. And you can tell Mr.
Carver to take his forty a week and . . .

ERWIN. But I can't lose my job. Mr. Carver is the only boss I ever had and
I like to work for him. Get back my verses, Patsy, or . . .

[*Sound: Door opening*]

FRANKIE. Boy, I nearly missed Liebowitz, but he's got the verses.

PATSY. Frankie, go over and get them back.

FRANKIE. Hey now, look . . . I can't get them back now. They're gone—

ERWIN. Gone? What's happened to my verses!

FRANKIE. Nothing. Liebowitz was gettin' into a cab when I got there. His daughter is having a baby in the hospital, so I congratulated him and he took the verses with him in the cab.

ERWIN [*Beginning to fall apart*]. And Mr. Carver is waiting for my verses!

FRANKIE. I'll get them back tonight, maybe. Why don't you dope the horses, Erwin, and get your mind off it?

ERWIN. Horses! How can I think of horses with my sixty-five Mother's Day verses riding around in taxicabs? You'll ruin me, you'll . . .

PATSY. All right! Frankie, get in a cab and try all the West Side hospitals. Charlie, take the East Side . . .

CHARLIE. There's a million Liebowitzes!

PATSY. Find Jake and don't give me no arguments!

[*Door opening and closing*]

PATSY. It'll all turn out okay now, Erwin. Now here's the racing form. Just . . . What's he got his eyes closed for?

MABEL. He fainted about a minute ago.

PATSY. Fainted!

MABEL. Sure. He's a genius. Most geniuses faint a lot.

PATSY. The races start in an hour. I'm going down and try to find Liebowitz. Call the bar and get a bottle of rye. If he won't drink, spill some on his face. Don't let him out of here till I get back, and if he wakes up keep it literary.

[*Music: Up and into vamp music from the radio*]

MABEL. How do you feel now, Erwin? Should I turn the radio off, maybe? I want it to soothe your head.

ERWIN. I'm going to call my wife and get out of here . .

MABEL. No, wait, Erwin. [*Click*] Let me show you the dance I used to do in the Follies.

ERWIN. Were you in the Follies?

MABEL. Oh, sure. I did a specialty. Of course I'm a little bigger now . . you know . . . but I used to come out with a sort of a sheet on . . . here, I'll show you with this bed spread . . . See? I'd have it draped on like this. And then I'd sort of sing—do you want to hear it?

ERWIN. I'd love to.

MABEL [*Sings "Siam"*].

MABEL. And then I go into my dance. Course this is just a rough idea and the sheet kind of drops off for my finish. How do you like my kicks?

[*Dance—sound of tearing*]

MABEL. Gosh, my dress—oh Erwin, I'm dizzy all of a sudden. Catch me, Erwin, I'm going to fall . . .

ERWIN. Just relax, Mabel, and lie down now . . .

[*Door opens*]

PATSY. Erwin, I got your verses back. What do you call this?

ERWIN. Oh, Patsy!

PATSY. Get outa that bedspread, Mabel, and go back to your room.

MABEL. But I just got dizzy . . .

PATSY. I'll get you dizzy, you little monkey . . . go on . . .

MABEL. But Patsy dear . . .

PATSY. Get out!

[*Door slam*]

ERWIN. You shouldn't treat her that way. She only wanted to . . .

PATSY. This is gratitude for everything I done for you! I no sooner turn my back and you're feedin' drinks to my girl . . . I oughta mobilize you!

ERWIN. But she only . .

PATSY. I know what she only! What do you take me for, a sucker?

ERWIN. Well, give me my verses anyway.

PATSY. I'll give your verses.

[*Sound: Harsh rip of paper*]

Here's your verses . . .

ERWIN. Don't, don't tear them!

PATSY. Here's your verses.

[*Sound: Harsh rip*]

ERWIN. Stop! Please!

PATSY. Nobody makes a sucker out of Patsy!

[*Music: Up and out*]

FRANKIE. So where is he now?

PATSY. In the other room. Cryin' his eyes out about his verses. What a dope I am.

MABEL. You should have more faith in me, Pats. I'm getting too heavy to start two-timin' you.

PATSY. I couldn't help it. I lost my temper. What a dope!

CHARLIE. Well, you better bring him around, Patsy, is all I can say, or we'll all be makin' the trip to the hock shop before the week is up.

PATSY. Mabel, Frankie, come with me. We'll try to apologize.

[*Door opening*]

ERWIN [*Sobbing*].

PATSY. Erwin? Erwin, my friend. My beautiful, wonderful, dear friend Erwin, I'm sorry. I lost my temper. Listen, Erwin . . .

ERWIN. The way you treated her. You ought to be ashamed.

MABEL. He is ashamed, Erwin. But I forgive him. He's just strung very high.

PATSY. We picked up all the pieces, Erwin. If you want, we'll copy out the verses on new paper. I apologize. It's just I'm so crazy for Mabel that when I seen her wrestlin' around with you, I . . .

ERWIN. Well, all right, Patsy. As long as you'll have them recopied.

PATSY. Sure. Because we got the highest respect for your genius. And I would like to give you your 10 per cent. Here, Erwin. A hundred and twelve bucks.

ERWIN. Heh? Gee . . .

PATSY. Of course, if you saw your way clear to dope out some horses right now we would be willing to bet our roll on anything you say, and you might have a thousand bucks tonight . . .

ERWIN. A thousand . . . !

PATSY. I don't like to say it, but we did nurse you back to health . . .

FRANKIE. Like you was a baby, almost . . .

ERWIN. Gee, fellows, I'm . . . I'm sorry. I . . . Where's the racing form?

PATSY. You're sittin' on it. [*Now rapidly*] O.K., fellas, get the elevator boy and the chamber maid and everybody get to work copying Erwin's verses. Frankie, Mabel, come on, let's get the pieces together. Here's a sharp pencil, Erwin.

ERWIN. All right, I'll try.

PATSY. Everybody start copying the verses and be quiet so Erwin's brain can work on the racing form. Try to hurry, Erwin, we only got about half an hour before the first race.

[*Music: Up in dream manner—Erwin is thinking . . . Bring up very soft, high strings, and hold in the background as*]

MABEL [*Quietly*]. He's such a sweet little fellow. Look at him. What a talent! I betcha I could be a writer except whenever I think I get hungry before anything comes out.

PATSY. Don't talk so much, you're bustin' up his thoughts. Keep copying the verses.

FRANKIE. These pieces are all mixed up. I got this one straight exceptin' one word down here in the corner.

[*Music: Fade out*]

CHARLIE. I got an extra word on mine. What do you need?

FRANKIE. Something to rhyme with—let me see—"We trudged our way on Sundays"—something to rhyme with Sundays. The piece is missing.

CHARLIE. No, the word I got left over is "bluebirds."

FRANKIE. How about "undies"? That rhymes with "Sundays."

PATSY. Erwin wouldn't want to use that.

MABEL [*Whispering*]. Hey, Erwin's got something. He just wrote something on a piece of paper and stuck it under his pillow.

PATSY. Got a selection, Erwin?

ERWIN. It's no good. It's . . . Don't bother reading it, Charlie, it's no good. Put it back under the pillow.

CHARLIE. "Equipoise."

FRANKIE. That's the one I was going to pick.

ERWIN. But it doesn't count, I tell you.

PATSY [*Suspiciously*]. Why don't it? You wrote it down, didn't you?

ERWIN. Yes, but just to get the feel. It's no use. I can't figure them out just sitting here. I've always done them on the bus.

PATSY. Sure, no wonder he can't figure them sittin' on that lousy bed. Come over here by the window, Erwin. Here, sit down on the chair. [*Window opening*] There . . . see the fresh air comin' in? It's just like a bus, ain't it?

ERWIN. Well . . .

PATSY. Try . . . concentrate. You're on the bus, see? The buildings are passing by . . .

FRANKIE. Fares, please . . . have your fares ready . . .

CHARLIE. Next stop the Hoboken Ferry . . .

MABEL. Does this bus stop at Bergdorf-Goodman's? [*Sotto*] Not that I'm getting off there of course . . .

PATSY. Concentrate, Erwin . . . Here, we'll rock the chair for you . . . [*Chair rocking*] Whee!—here we go around a corner.

ERWIN. It's no use, Patsy, I can't do it. The only way is for me to get on the bus to Ozone Heights.

FRANKIE. How about a taxi?

PATSY. If Erwin says a bus, it's a bus. Frankie, you and Mabel take Erwin home on the bus. Erwin, drop in and see your wife, but call your selections back here as soon as you get into the house.

ERWIN. That'll be fine. Let's go. Oh, my poor Audrey . . .

[*Door opening*]

PATSY. And Erwin, no looking out of windows. Just horses.

MABEL. Come on, Erwin dear.

PATSY. And treat him nice, Frankie. Buy him a soda with ice cream.

[*Music: Up and into background*]

PATSY. Well, Frankie and Mabel took Erwin home on the bus. And sure enough passing the Flatiron Building, he gets an inspiration, and the minute he gets home, he calls me.

ERWIN [*Filter mike . . . The phone*]. Hello, Patsy? I got some selections on the bus. For the first race, Sunador, second Frolic, third Motto, fourth Mr. Khayyam. I'll figure the other races on the way back to the hotel. Good-bye.

PATSY. Then he turned to Audrey and throws her a big hug—he loved that Audrey. But he lives up to his promise and gets back on the bus to New York. But at the same time in the hotel, we are still copying his torn verses, when suddenly the door opens.

[*Music: Out*]

[*Door opens*]

CARVER. Who's in charge here?

PATSY. Who are you?

CARVER. I'm Erwin Trowbridge's boss, J. G. Carver, and I know my rights. I've just come from Erwin's house and his wife says he's living with you here. You've been stealing his verses!

CHARLIE. Stealing what!

CARVER. I ain't afraid of you fellows or any other greeting card company in the United States.

PATSY. Charlie, throw the gentleman into the street, will you?
CHARLIE. Let's go, Bo . . .
CARVER. Take your hands off me!

[*Door opens*]

I've been in business since 1898! You can't do this to J. G. Car—

[*Door slams*]

[*Phone*]

PATSY. Hello? Yeah, Gus. Swell. Call you back.

[*Sound: Hang up*]

PATSY. Charley? Motto took the third. That means we got three winners for today.
CHARLIE. What do you want to do now?
PATSY. I want to take everything out and put it on Mr. Khayyam in the fourth.
CHARLIE. There's only one thing bothers me, Patsy. Remember when Erwin was figuring the races on the bed before? He wrote down "Equipoise" for the fourth and he hides it under the pillow. Now he gives us Mr. Khayyam. Why'd he change it?
PATSY. He was just warmin' himself up with Equipoise. Like a pitcher winds himself up.
CHARLIE. Yes, but Equipoise is a great horse. I don't like it, Patsy. I think he's tryin' to pull something on us.
PATSY. But why? Why would Erwin do anything?

[*Door opens*]

MABEL. Hello, Pats. Gee, you oughta see Erwin's house.
PATSY. Where is he?
MABEL. He's comin' up with Frankie. Gee! What a house! A regular porch to sit on, and grass, and a second floor with beds in it . . . And Patsy, Erwin says he wants to sell it.
PATSY. OK, buy it. We're tryin' to decide on the fourth race.
MABEL. Patsy, don't you think we ought to get married if we're going to live in a house?
PATSY. You can get married any day. I got a four-horse' parlay on the fire and they don't come up often. Charley . . .

MABEL. Patsy, I think we ought to buy this house before everything blows us back into the hock shop again.

PATSY. Why, what do you mean? Why should anything happen?

MABEL. I don't know, I been so nervous all day I shook a rhinestone out of my bracelet.

[*Door opens*]

ERWIN. Hello, fellas, are my verses copied?

PATSY. Here you are, Erwin. All in A-1 condition. And we won the first three races.

ERWIN. Well, isn't that fine!

PATSY. About this Mr. Khayyam in the fourth, Erwin . . .

ERWIN. Say, this is terrible! These verses . . . these aren't my words at all.

PATSY. Why not?

ERWIN. Well, listen!

> "I wonder if the old church stands
> Where we trudged our way on Sundays;
> I recall how we sat with folded hands
> . . . So now I don't ever get drunk no more on
> Tuesdays or Mondays."

PATSY. That's no good, huh?

MABEL. Of course not. It should be, "Now I don't get drunk *any* more."

CHARLIE. We lost the last line and I put that one in.

ERWIN. Mr. Carver would drop dead if he saw this!

MABEL. What you cheapskates ought to do is hire some first-class poet so Erwin wouldn't have to worry so much.

PATSY. When Mr. Khayyam comes in we'll hire Longfellow.

MABEL. You can't hire Longfellow . . . he's way up in Boston or some place.

CHARLIE. And anyway, how do we know Mr. Khayyam ain't goin' to come in last?

ERWIN [*Laughs*]. Yes . . . that would be awful, wouldn't? [*Laughs*] That's pretty good, Charlie.

PATSY. Wait a minute, Erwin. We can't lose, can we?

ERWIN. "I recall how we sat with folded hands" . . . I can't remember that last line . .

PATSY. Forget the poetry for a minute, will ya? We cant' lose, can we, Erwin?

ERWIN. Well, no—I don't think so.

PATSY. Mr. Khayyam was your selection, wasn't he?

ERWIN. Oh yes, that's the horse.

CHARLIE. Then why did you write Equipoise and stick it under the pillow before?

ERWIN. Just to see how it looked on paper. I wasn't sure.

PATSY. Oh, so you wasn't sure.

ERWIN. I'm surprised at you fellows. You took care of me yesterday when I was sick, but now you're getting greedy.

PATSY. I notice you took your 10 per cent all right.

ERWIN. Well, of course . . .

PATSY. Of course. You wouldn't by any chance be thinkin' about crossin' us up, would you, Erwin?

ERWIN. How could you think such a thing of me!

PATSY. Well . . . OK, boys . . . Frankie, here's eleven thousand bucks. Sock it all on Mr. Khayyam.

FRANKIE. Eleven thousand . . . Don't let me touch it. Stick it in my pocket.

PATSY. Take it down to Gus. Hurry up . . . No, wait. How much you betting, Erwin?

ERWIN. Oh, I wouldn't bet.

CHARLIE. What do you mean? Which way wouldn't you bet?

ERWIN. I wouldn't bet on anything. That would spoil it.

MABEL. Sure. Erwin explained that to me.

PATSY. Shut up, Mabel. Erwin, I thought maybe you ought to bet on this particular nag. If he's good enough for us to put our shirts on he's good enough for you, too. So just give your bet to Frankie and he'll take it to Gus with ours.

CHARLIE. That's right, Erwin, give Frankie some dough.

ERWIN. Well, it'll spoil all my fun, but . . . here's two dollars, Frankie.

FRANKIE. Two dollars!

PATSY. What are you, kiddin'?

ERWIN. No, I'm serious—I think he'll win.

PATSY. We're layin' down eleven thousand bucks and you want to play a deuce. You can't think much of the horse.

ERWIN. All right, make it ten dollars.

PATSY. Frankie didn't hear you.

ERWIN. Then fifty.

PATSY. Frankie still didn't hear you.

ERWIN. What do you want?!

PATSY. Every nickel you got on you. All your 10 per cents. Hand it over.

ERWIN. Well, all right, but . . .

PATSY. Here you are, Frankie. Put that on Mr. Khayyam for Erwin— right on the nose.

[Door opens]

ERWIN. Wait, Frankie. Fellows, I never bet in my life. And I know that once I do I'll never be able to pick winners on the bus again . . .

FRANKIE. After this race we'll be able to *buy* a horse.

ERWIN. But what'll I do going home on the bus every day?

PATSY. You'll do cross-word puzzles. And, Erwin, if Mr. Khayyam don't come in today you'll have a word for "dead pigeon," and brother, it'll start with "E" like in "Oiwin."

[Music: Up and out]

END OF ACT II

ANNOUNCER

COMMERCIAL

ACT III

[Music: Bridge into a dance band in background]

PATSY. We're sittin' around the radio waitin' for the race to begin. To say the least, with eleven thousand bucks on Mr. Khayyam, my heart is beatin'. I don't like the look on Erwin's face neither. It's blank. Who knows what he's thinkin'? Maybe he purposely let us win so now we'd sink everything on Khayyam. The minutes go by. Frankie is so nervous he keeps combin' his hair—while he's still got it. Charlie is already sneakin' hotel envelopes into his pocket—chewin'-gum money. And Mabel is sittin' with her eyes closed—in case she faints. I can almost hear the chicken à la king comin' to life in the closet . . . if we lose this race we're clean.

ERWIN. Are you sure this is the station that broadcasts the race?

MABEL. Yeh, it'll be on in a minute. I like that station. They have the most commercials, about food and all. Whenever we come back from the hock shop we like to turn it on. You know, in ten minutes you can listen to a complete meal on that station.

PATSY. Stop talkin' about hock shops. Erwin, you wouldn't cross us up, would you? I'm gettin' panicky, Erwin . . .

CHARLIE. You shouldn't 've sent Frankie down with the cash.

[*Door opens*]

CLARENCE. There he is!

ERWIN. Clarence! What are you doing here?

CLARENCE. You low-down cheat! You couldn't come out and fight me like a man! You . . . you . . .

PATSY. Who is this, Erwin?

ERWIN. My brother-in-law. Clarence, meet . . .

CLARENCE. He pretends he knows all about horse races. He comes home before and leaves a list of selections on the floor. I bet my shirt today and he cleaned me out with that list!

ERWIN. What list, Clarence . . . ?

CLARENCE. The list you left on the floor in your house. You knew I'd pick it up sooner or later! You're such a sneak you think everybody else is!

ERWIN. Oh, I know what he means . . .

PATSY [*Suspiciously*]. Yeah, Erwin? What does he mean? Explain, Erwin.

ERWIN. Well, on the way home before, Frankie thought that being on the bus would help *him* make the right selections, like it helps me. But he got them all wrong. And I guess he left the list home.

CLARENCE. That's a lie! You . . .

PATSY. Charlie, throw the gentleman into the street.

CHARLIE. Let's go, Bo . . .

[*Door opening*]

CLARENCE. Erwin! You little double-crossing, Mother's Day crook! I'm cleaned out!

[*Door slam*]

PATSY. So you'd double-cross your own brother-in-law, Erwin?

CHARLIE. I told you we shouldn't put everything on Mr. Khayyam.

MABEL. Erwin wouldn't cheat anybody. No kiddin', Patsy, he's too . . .
he's too . . . ignorant.

[*Door opens*]

FRANKIE. Well, I put the works on Khayyam. Gus had to share it with
another booky. He couldn't handle 11 g's.

RADIO ANNOUNCER [*Filter*]. Sorry we couldn't tune you in earlier, ladies
and gentlemen . . .

PATSY. The race . . . shut up, everybody!

RADIO ANNOUNCER. . . . We'll pick up the fourth race which is now going
on. And a great race it is, folks. They're coming to the quarter now,
War Glory, Good Advice, Ladies' Man and Mr. Khayyam in that
order.

CHARLIE. I told you, Khayyam's a stinker!

ANNOUNCER. At the quarter now . . . Ladies' Man moving up . . . yes,
past Farino, past Farino. Good Advice is holding that lead, jockey
Meade using his head. There they are at the half, Good Advice, War
Glory, Mr. Khayyam.

FRANKIE. He's back in third place!

ANNOUNCER. Mr. Khayyam driving now—rushing in there. Ah, there's a
tumble, a spill!

PATSY. If that's Khayyam . . .

ANNOUNCER. Chase Me stumbled, throwing the jockey. But he's all right.
Yes, he's getting up. A great jockey, tough as they come. There they
are at the three-quarter pole now. Mr. Khayyam leading now.

MABEL. He's leading, Pats!

ANNOUNCER. Ladies' Man coming up—War Glory right behind. There
they come fast into the stretch. Looks like a little shoving in there . .
no, no, it's all right, I guess. At the stretch now coming down there
with a rush, at the home stretch Eq . . . Equipoise . . . *Equipoise!* . .
who's been 'way behind is surging up to Mr. Khayyam; neck and
neck now, fighting it out, two great horses, what a RACE! Ladies and
Gentlemen, he's passing . . . no, not quite . . . wait a minute . .
Yes . . . yes, that's the finish. Equipoise wins.

PATSY. Equipoise!

ANNOUNCER. He trailed all the way but he wins in a terrific burst of speed.
Mr. Khayyam second and Sun Archer third in the money. Thos

who backed Equipoise had something to be thankful for today. But he's a fine horse . . . and . . .

[*Radio switched off*]

ERWIN. Well. That's too bad, isn't it?

CHARLIE. Yes, it's just too bad, Erwin.

MABEL. I'm sick, y' know? I'm sick to the stomach. Look at my hand shaking.

PATSY [*Angering*]. What've you got to say, Erwin? Not that it matters, naturally.

ERWIN. Well, I guess the handicappers were right. They all thought Equipoise would win. [*Tries to laugh*] I guess that's what makes it interesting. And memorable, too.

PATSY. Oh sure. We're going to give you something real memorial, Erwin.

MABEL. Boys . . . what're you goin' to do?

ERWIN. Now, wait a minute, fellows.

PATSY. This is one horse race you ain't never gonna forget, Erwin.

[*Humph. He hits Erwin*]

ERWIN. Now, wait a minute!

CHARLIE. Let me get a crack at him!

MABEL. But gee, Mr. Khayyam won most of the race!

PATSY. Frankie, turn on the radio loud in case somebody hears this in the hall!

MABEL. Don't! Don't hit him again!

ANNOUNCER [*Off mike*]. There's a big confusion down there. I'm trying to find out what happened. What excitement! My man is down there now trying to find out what happened and my wire is open so stand by, everybody . . .

PATSY. Keep Erwin on the floor, Charlie.

PATSY. He knew all the time Equipoise was going to win!

ERWIN. I didn't, I swear I didn't know . . . !

FRANKIE. Shut up! Something's happening!

ANNOUNCER. No bets are being paid pending an official announcement. Looks like a disqualification to me.

PATSY. What?!

ANNOUNCER. Well, well . . . I was all wrong, folks, I was all wrong. Equipoise may not have won after all. The judges have been in a huddle down there at the stand, and boy! What excitement . . . wait a minute, folks . . . what is it, Perry?

MABEL. That must be Perry Mullins, the cop.

PATSY. Shut up!

ANNOUNCER. Oh, here's the latest announcement just put into my hands. Equipoise has been disqualified. Mr. Khayyam declared the official winner—Sun Archer second, and Ladies' Man . . .

[Radio switched off]

PATSY. Erwin! Erwin, what are you doing on the floor?

ERWIN. You make me good and mad.

PATSY. That's it, Erwin, get up. I'm awful sorry . . .

ERWIN. You make me so mad I could . . .

[Humph. He hits Patsy]

PATSY. What're you hitting me for? We won, didn't we? Hey, get him off me!

CHARLIE. Stop hittin' Patsy! Cut it out! Erwin, cut it out!

[Door opening]

AUDREY. Oh, Erwin!

MABEL. Erwin! Your wife is here!

ERWIN. [Panting]. My wife? Why, Audrey . . .

AUDREY. Erwin, I'm so lonesome. Can't you come home now?

ERWIN. Right away, dear. I was just having a discussion with my friends here.

AUDREY. Mr. Carver called me and I rushed over in a taxi. He's outside Erwin, and he's asked me to plead with you to give him a hearing You owe so much to Mr. Carver . . .

ERWIN. Oh, sure. Mr. Carver! Come in, Mr. Carver.

[Sound: Footsteps . . . Halt]

CARVER. Erwin . . . have these men a contract with you?

ERWIN. Oh no, no, they just . . .

CARVER. Who gave you your start, Erwin? Who taught you to rhyme Remember in the beginning . . . "tremendous"? How long yor worked on "tremendous" until I gave you "tenderness"! Who taugh you everything you know about Mother's Day? And Saint Patrick' Day, and St. Valentine's?

PATSY. Erwin, what do we do for the fifth at Jamaica?

ERWIN. Don't interrupt Mr. Carver.

PATSY. But we got nothing for the fifth . . .

ERWIN. Don't interrupt!

AUDREY [*Admiration*]. Oh, Erwin!

CARVER. I'll have your office repainted, Erwin, and fix the window so it opens. And I'll put your name on the door, and I'll give you sixty dollars a week. Make it seventy-five.

ERWIN. Gosh, Mr. Carver!

PATSY. Listen, stick with us, Erwin, and you'll make that much per hour.

MABEL. We could buy him his own bus, even.

ERWIN. I'm afraid I can't, Patsy. I won't be able to dope them any more.

PATSY. But why, why, Erwin? You don't want to go back to the salt mines, do you? That Mother's Day drudgery? That poetry mill?

ERWIN. You made me bet, Patsy. I could only do them when it was for fun.

PATSY. Well, make believe you didn't bet. We'll even go so far as not to give you your winnings.

MABEL. You could even charge him.

ERWIN. No, Patsy. It's like when you hear somebody else's problem, you know, just how to solve it for him. But when it's your problem, you never are sure of the answer. Can't you see it, Patsy?

PATSY. But look what you stand to make, Erwin!

ERWIN. No, Patsy, it was pretty much an accident that I picked Mr. Khayyam.

PATSY. Accident!

ERWIN. I *really* had the feeling for Equipoise. But I began not to trust my feeling, so I took Mr. Khayyam instead. See, it was only a game before, but now so much would be at stake I couldn't trust myself to do it again.

PATSY. All right, Erwin. Then let me apologize for beating you up before. It's just I got so mad that you missed, because, after all, money aside, it was a beautiful thing for me, seeing a man gettin' inspirations like you did. And I got mad for your sake that the spell was broken. I mean . . . well, what I'm trying to—What's the matter? What're you holding your head for?

MABEL. He's got that look on him again.

ERWIN. Quick, a pencil!

PATSY. Here, here. What, Erwin? A horse? Remember, it's the fifth at Jamaica. Just say it, say it, Erwin, and I'll take it down! I promise not to let you make a nickel on it!

ERWIN. Uh . . . let me see now . . .

> "The race is o'er
> We've won, my lad,
> Love and Kisses
> To dear ol' Dad!"

PATSY. But Erwin, the fifth!

ERWIN [*Proudly*]. Father's Day . . . Number 1.

MABEL. Don't be sad, Pats; remember, you still got me—and them two cans of chicken à la king in my closet.

[*Music up to finish*]

ANNOUNCER

CREDITS

PAYMENT DEFERRED

Original Play
by Jeffrey Dell

Based on the Novel
by C. S. Forester

Radio Adaptation
by Gerald Holland

CAST
(for radio performance)

WILL MARBLE	Charles Laughton
ANNIE MARBLE	Elsa Lanchester
WINNIE	Susan Douglas
PROSPECT	Herb Rawlinson
HAMMOND	Gale Gordon
JUDSON	Franklin Parker
GROCER	Eddie Mar?
CONSTABLE	Eddie Mar?
JIM	Bill Johnston
DOCTOR	Joe Kearn?
NARRATOR	Gayne Whitman
MADAME COLLINS	Maria Manto?

PAYMENT DEFERRED

Radio adaptation by

GERALD HOLLAND

HAVING SEEN Charles Laughton in the original New York production some fifteen years before, I was delighted with the assignment to adapt "Payment Deferred" for the Theatre Guild on the Air. The play introduced Mr. Laughton to American audiences and his performance was still vivid in my mind. Reading the play over again, I seemed to be able to recall every gesture and inflection of this great actor, and so in fitting the play into the limits of one hour on the air, I was careful to preserve as much as possible of the original.

Of course, as in the case of all radio adaptations of plays which run as much as three times as long in the original script, lines and sound have to be devised to make up for the lack of sight in the audience. It was impossible to transfer to radio the complete chilling picture of the bank clerk, Will Marble, as he sat in his chair at the window—staring out into the garden that held his terrible secret. But references could be made to it and with a line here and there, Mr. Laughton made it very effective on the air.

In the original play, all the action took place in the Marble living room. In the radio version, it was possible to give movement to the story by showing Marble as he was refused credit at the neighborhood store and in the garden on that stormy night when he buried the body of the young nephew from Australia. The listener heard Marble panting over his grisly task, his gasp as the policeman discovered him and offered to throw a light in the yard—and his terrified protests that deferred payment for his crime then and there.

The scene that begins with the arrival of the nephew from Australia and ends in his murder was one of the most exciting of the original play and happily it was also capable of being transferred almost intact to the air—with the addition of sound that sharpened the action.

The original play opened with a prologue and closed with a flash back

241

to that scene wherein a real-estate agent is showing the now notorious house to a prospective tenant. Here again was a fortunate circumstance because both scenes, with the always necessary cuts, could be preserved for the radio version.

But the success of the radio version was definitely assured when the Theatre Guild was able to cast Mr. Laughton in his original role. The same mounting sense of horror came over the air as it came across the footlights fifteen years before and sent the nightly audiences away, a little fearful of the shadows of alleyways, but convinced that they had seen a memorable performance by one of the greatest of living actors.

PAYMENT DEFERRED

ANNOUNCER

INTRODUCTION FOR THE THEATRE GUILD

ACT I

[*Music: Up and under*]

NARRATOR. There is a house for rent at Number 53 Malcolm Road, Dulwich, England. It is a shabby house on a shabby street. Once it was the home of William Marble, bank clerk. At present, the shutters are closed, and the paint on its weather-beaten exterior is chipping off. Standing on the porch, a real-estate agent, accompanied by a prospective tenant, is unlocking the front door.

[*Key in lock*] [*Door creaks*]

HAMMOND. Step right in, sir.

PROSPECT. Quite dark in here, isn't it, Mr. Hammond. Spooky.

HAMMOND [*Laughing*]. I suppose it is. Half a mo till I open the shutters.

[*Footsteps and window raised, shutters opened*]

PROSPECT. Ah, that's better. I've never been in a house where there's been a murder committed. I've half a mind to take it—it has a kind of attraction for me.

HAMMOND. If you're quick, it's yours for the asking.

PROSPECT. You knew him, didn't you, Mr. Hammond?

HAMMOND. Will Marble? Knew him for years. Rented him this house myself. My own place is right next door.

PROSPECT. One can imagine the idea creeping into his brain . . . his mind gradually becoming fascinated. That little bottle of poison just outside there in the hall cupboard.

243

HAMMOND. If you ask me what was at the bottom of it, I'd say it was his wife. Probably nagging at him 'till he didn't rightly know what he was doing. I'll take my oath she drove him to it.

PROSPECT. Really?

HAMMOND. I should say it all started two years ago or more. They were on their uppers—the poor devil was at his wits' end. [*Fade*] There wasn't a shop around here would give 'im any more credit and he'd borrowed to the limit from everybody down at the bank where he worked—

[*Music: Bridge*]

[*Mantel clock striking eight . . . Breakfast dishes rattling*]

WILL [*Peevishly*]. It's a fine state of affairs, Annie, when a man can't have eggs for his breakfast.

ANNIE. Well, since you've been allowing me only 40 shillings for the house, dear . . .

WILL. That's it, blame me! Perhaps if you were a better manager . . .

ANNIE. If I were a better manager . . . ! I don't think that's quite fair, Will, I really don't.

WILL. Next, you'll be throwing it up to me again about my losing our savings in that investment!

ANNIE [*Quietly*]. I never did, Will.

WILL. Well, look at us . . . stony broke, owing money all over the place.

ANNIE. Don't get so worked up, Will.

WILL [*Suddenly deflated*]. I know, I'm a failure—go on—say it!

[*Footsteps off*]

ANNIE. Be quiet, Will, here comes Winnie!

[*Door opening*]

WINNIE. Good morning, Mother . . . Father.

WILL. Good morning, Winnie.

ANNIE. Come sit down to your breakfast, dear.

WINNIE. I'm not hungry. Just some toast.

WILL [*Gruffly*]. You might braid your hair before you come to the table.

WINNIE. I've time enough for that before school.

WILL. Hrmmmmmmph!

[*Pouring tea*]

ANNIE. Mrs. Hammond was saying only last night, Will, over the wall . . . She doesn't know what to do about the cost of living herself . . . She said—

WILL. I don't care for Mrs. Hammond's opinions! The point is what *we* can afford, and it's pretty clear from the bills we can't make both ends meet.

ANNIE [*Timidly*]. You know some of the bills are yours, dear.

WILL [*Coldly*]. Meaning what, my girl?

ANNIE. The chemist's bill. All those photography things you bought. Films and hypo and cyny-ide of something.

WINNIE [*With her mouth full*]. Oh, Mum, that's his photograph stuff with the red label. It's poison.

WILL. Cyanide? [*Thoughtfully*] Yes, I'd forgotten . . . looks as if it might come in useful . . .

ANNIE [*Shocked*]. Will, what do you mean?

WILL. What I say. It looks as if we may need a drop before we're through. It's soon over so I've heard.

ANNIE. Oh, how can you say things like that, dear? Before Winnie, too.

WILL. Well, it may come to it yet. It's getting too much for me, Annie. I can't get away from it all for a single second. I lay awake at night . . .

ANNIE. Yes, dear, I know.

[*Chair pushed back from table*]

WILL [*Bitterly*]. Now, I've got to go down to the bank and count someone else's money all day. It's ironic, that's what it is.

ANNIE. Never mind, dear, something will turn up.

WILL. I'm not one to believe in miracles. Goodbye!

ANNIE & WINNIE. Goodbye!

[*Door closes*]

WINNIE. All he ever talks about any more is money, money, money! I'm fed to the teeth with it!

ANNIE. Winnie, you should be ashamed! You've no idea how hard your father works . . . how kind he is really . . . he's not himself these days . . . You don't know how proud he is . . . [*Voice breaking into sobs*]

[*Music: Up and under for montage*]

[*Bank atmosphere . . . Typewriters and voices in background*]

WILL. Judson, old boy, I don't like to ask—but I was wondering if you might let me have a fiver for a day or so . . .

JUDSON. But this is only the third of the month.

WILL. Yes, I know—but something unexpected came up—I'd pay you back in a day or so . . .

JUDSON. I couldn't do it, sorry . . .

WILL. Well, look here, old man—if you could just let me have—

JUDSON. Not a shilling—is that plain enough?

WILL [*Low*]. Thank you.

[*Music: Up and under*]

GROCER. There'll be no more groceries on credit, Mr. Marble. That's my last word on the subject.

WILL [*Hotly*]. I must say that's a pretty high-handed attitude.

GROCER. And what's more, if you don't settle up at once, I'll—

WILL. You'll get nowhere threatening me, Mr. Evans!

GROCER. You had plenty of warning.

WILL. Well, my man, I'll see you don't get a penny!

GROCER. There are laws to see that I do, Mr. Marble!

WILL [*Quarreling*]. You wouldn't take it to court . . . !

GROCER. Wouldn't I? As a matter of fact, I've already started action, Mr. Marble!

[*Silence for a second . . . Then hurried footsteps to door . . . Door opens and slams*]

GROCER [*Muttering*]. Humph! Him and his bowler hat and city clothes and not a shilling in his pocket!

[*Music: Up and then slowly fade out for*]

[*Rhythmic tapping against table leg through*]

WILL [*Muttering*]. Four and eight twelve . . . three's fifteen . . . and two . . . [*Bursting out*] For Heaven's sake, Winnie! Stop kicking the table and go to bed.

[*Tapping stops*]

WINNIE. Sorry, Father.

WILL. Lord knows, I've got enough with these infernal bills without that noise!

ANNIE. Poor Will!

WINNIE [*Sighing*]. I want so to move from this horrible neighborhood.

ANNIE. Winnie, be still!

WILL. I can't raise a penny anywhere—and with Evans about to take it to court—Well, if the bank gets wind of it, my job wouldn't be worth that! [*Snaps his fingers*]

ANNIE. After twenty years' service?

WILL. It would mean the end of us, Annie!

ANNIE. No!

[*The door bell rings . . . It's an old-fashioned hand bell rung with a turn of a crank*]

WILL. Good Lord, who's that!

ANNIE. It's probably just Charlie Hammond, dear!

WILL. No—you know how he rings! Evans hasn't wasted much time!

WINNIE. Shall I answer it, Mother?

ANNIE. Yes, dear, see who it is—now, Will, don't look like that—[*Winnie's footsteps*]

[*Door opens off*]

JIM [*Off*]. Is Mr. Marble at home?

WINNIE [*Off*]. Will you come in, please—he's in the living room . . .

JIM [*Off*]. Oh, thanks, miss.

WILL [*In a frightened whisper*]. That's not Charlie—it's Evans' man. I know it! . . .

ANNIE. Wait now . . .

WINNIE [*Fading in*]. Right in here, sir . . . Father, it's somebody for you.

WILL [*Shaken*]. For me?

JIM. Oh! Good evening! Sorry if I scared you. You look as if you'd seen a ghost! Mr. Marble, isn't it?

WILL. Yes.

JIM. Good! [*Coming on mike*] Found you first shot. I don't expect you know me.

WILL. No . . . I . . . I don't think so.

JIM. Well, it's some time since you saw me last. I was about four, I think . . . My name's Medland.

WILL. Medland!

JIM. Yes, Jim Medland. My mother was your older sister, wasn't she?

WILL [*Realizing he is reprieved*]. Not . . . not Win's boy? Good Lord! You must excuse me. Gave me a bit of a turn, you coming in sudden like that. Here, let me introduce you. This is Annie . . . your aunt, I mean.

JIM. How do you do?

ANNIE. Nicely, thank you. This is a surprise!

JIM. Yes. I'm sorry to burst in on you like that without letting you know, but I've only just landed from Australia.

ANNIE. I'm sure we're very pleased.

WILL. Winnie, hear that? Here's a new cousin for you. [*To Jim*] This is our girl.

JIM & WINNIE [*Together awkwardly*]. How do you do?

WILL. We named her after your mother, you know.

JIM. Oh, yes?

WILL [*Awkwardly*]. Well . . . you must sit down for a bit and tell us all the news.

JIM. Yes, rather. I'll just go and get rid of my taxi.

WILL. Taxi?

JIM. Yes. He's waiting. I wasn't sure I'd got the right place.

WILL. Oh, I see.

JIM [*Fading*]. Shan't be a moment.

> [*Door opens and closes off*]

WILL. Taxi, eh?

ANNIE. Oh, Will! He . . . he might be able to help us!

WILL. I know. I know. Did you see that coat? Worth a tidy sum, that. Besides, you can't get over here from Australia unless you've got a wad of dough.

ANNIE. Oh, Will, do you think he would lend us money?

WILL. Perhaps, but I've got to handle it very carefully. Now, listen to me, Annie, you two clear out after a bit, will you, and just leave this to me!

ANNIE. All right. What about the whiskey, dear? You'll have to offer.

> [*Door closes off*]

WILL. I'm not wasting whiskey on a mere boy! Look out! Here he comes!

JIM [*Fade in*]. I say . . . does it always rain like this in England?

WILL [*Laughing*]. No . . . not quite always. Here, Jim, sit by the fire and get warm.

JIM. Thank you.

WILL. Well, and how's your mother after all this time?

JIM. Mother died . . . six months ago.

WILL. I say! I'd no idea. That's terrible, that is.

JIM. She never really got better after the shock of father's death.

WILL. Tom dead, too? You don't say that? Well, upon my soul! That is rough and no mistake. Any of your father's family here?

JIM. No, you're the only relatives I have in the world—so far as I know. I thought I'd look you up right away.

WILL. Yes . . . and quite right, too.

JIM. I thought you'd know the best hotel to stay at.

WILL [*Judicially*]. Well, that depends, of course . . .

JIM. Someone on the boat said the Carlton wasn't bad.

WILL. The Carlton, eh? Yes, well, you might do worse. A good deal worse. Of course, it isn't exactly what I should call cheap. But I suppose that doesn't matter much in your case.

JIM. I'll give it a run for a day or so while I have a look around.

WINNIE [*Timidly*]. Have you seen many kangaroos?

JIM. Yes, rather! I've hunted them quite a bit.

WILL [*Forcing a jocular tone*]. Kangaroos! What will she be thinking of next? [*Jim laughs*] Did you ever know such a kid?

ANNIE. Winnie, school tomorrow. Better get to bed.

WILL [*Feigns surprise*]. Not bedtime already, surely? Well, Winnie! Haven't you got a kiss for your old father, then?

WINNIE. Good night, father.

JIM. Good night, Winnie.

WINNIE [*Shyly*]. Good night.

[*Footsteps*]

WILL. By the way, Annie, what about a bit of supper for our young nephew here?

ANNIE. I'm afraid we haven't anything very . . .

JIM. Oh, please, don't worry about me. I had something before I came down. I'd like to smoke, though, if I may?

ANNIE. Why, of course.

WILL. Here, have one of mine.

JIM. You try one of mine.

WILL. I don't mind. I say, that's a nice case you've got. Hmmmm—sort of combination, isn't it—cigarette case and wallet. I call that very neat.

JIM. Yes, birthday present. It's rather well made.

WILL. Well lined, too!

JIM. Those are Australian cigarettes . . . [*Will laughs*]

JIM [*Realizing*]. Oh! The money, you mean . . . ?

WILL. Well, it's rather a lot, isn't it, for a young man to be carrying about on him?

JIM [*Coolly*]. Oh, I don't know.

WILL [*Laughs excessively*]. Not for you, eh? Don't you bother to sit up, Annie, if your head's bad. I expect Jim will excuse you if you feel you'd rather go on up.

JIM. I say, I'm awfully sorry. I didn't realize you were feeling rotten. I'll go . . .

ANNIE. No, no, please . . . you stay and talk to Will for a bit. He so seldom gets anyone fresh to talk to. I'll just say good night now, if you don't mind.

JIM. Of course not.

ANNIE. You'll come to see us often, won't you?

JIM. I'd like to, thanks.

ANNIE. Good night.

[*Door closes*]

WILL [*Heartily*]. Well, Jim! What are your plans—going to stay over here—for good, I mean?

JIM. Yes, provided I get a job which suits me. Why?

WILL. I was thinking you'll probably want to invest your capital, that's all.

JIM. Oh, my money's nearly all tied up.

WILL. Did your mother ever tell you anything about my job, I wonder?

JIM. Yes, I think so. To do with a bank, isn't it?

WILL. Yes, that's right. The County National, foreign exchange department. Been in it all my life. Buying and selling money, you know. It's a bit of luck for you that you turned up just the moment when I might be able to do you rather a good turn.

JIM. Me? Er . . . how do you mean?

WILL. Well, through my job I get bits of information that don't reach everybody. I got a tip that the franc is going to be stabilized. Rise like the very devil!

JIM. I'm afraid it's all rather like Greek to me.

WILL. It's simple enough! Francs are going up—anybody who buys them now will make a small fortune.

JIM. What's it got to do with me?

WILL [*Slightly menacing*]. Well, you've got the capital. And I've got the knowledge. It seems to me we ought to be a pretty strong combination.

JIM. Oh, I've really very little money that I can touch, and, what's more, I don't think I'd be interested.

WILL [*Desperately*]. You don't object to making money, do you?

JIM. No, perhaps not, but . . . well, the truth is, I don't much like the sound of it.

WILL. Perhaps I haven't made it clear enough.

JIM. No, it isn't that. It's just that I don't want to have anything to do with it.

WILL [*Frantically*]. Look here! Don't you be a young fool! I know a devil of a lot more about this game than you do and I tell you it's the chance of a lifetime. You take my advice and think it over before you . .

JIM [*Firmly*]. It wouldn't be any use. I'm quite certain now.

WILL [*Almost a whine*]. I say, you're not resenting what I said just now, are you?

JIM. Oh, let's forget it! . . . I must be moving.

WILL. You . . . you can't go like that. I mean, I shall feel you're fed up about what I've been saying.

JIM. Oh, please . . . don't let's talk about it any more.

WILL. But I *must* explain. I've had a bit of trouble lately over . . . well, I don't see why you shouldn't know . . . over money. You see I've got Annie and the kid to think of, and if I don't find a hundred pounds pretty quick it means the poorhouse for the three of us. You're old enough to understand what that means to anyone who's always kept himself respectable.

JIM [*Greatly embarrassed*]. I'm . . . I'm sorry.

WILL. I think the shame of it would kill me. I wonder, if . . . if I might ask you a great favor. There's no one else I can go to. Will you lend me . . . a hundred . . . just for . . . just till the end of the month? I swear I'll pay back every penny!

JIM. I . . . I really don't have it to spare.

WILL. I just don't know which way to turn, straight I don't!

JIM. I'm afraid I must say good night.

[*Chair moving back*]

WILL [*Frantically*]. Wait! But I can't let you go like this. I . . . I never should forgive myself.

JIM. It's all right.

WILL. But I should feel that you would never want to come here again.

JIM. Well, to be candid, I'm not very keen. You see, I came down here looking forward tremendously to seeing my own people . . . the only ones I've got, and from practically the first you've done nothing but try and get money out of me, one way or the other. I'm sorry to have to talk to you like this, but . . .

WILL [*In a decisive tone . . . Quietly*]. You're quite justified.

JIM [*Surprised*]. I say. I'm awfully sorry I . . .

WILL. No, you were quite right. It's not much use me apologizing. I've behaved very badly.

JIM. Forget it, please. I really must go.

WILL [*Pause*]. I do ask one thing, though, before you leave. Have a drink with me. [*Urging*] Just to show there's no ill feeling, eh?

JIM. There's no ill feeling.

WILL. Oh, come then, you need a nip before you go out in that weather.

JIM. Well . . . all right.

WILL. That's the way! Sit down half a minute while I get the whiskey.

JIM. It will have to be rather a quick one.

WILL [*Fading*]. The bottle is just out here in the hall cupboard. Won't be a moment.

   [*Door opens*]

WILL [*Off*]. Take a look at that photograph on the table. Do you know anybody there?

JIM. Is this your wedding picture?

WILL. Right! And proud as a peacock in those days, I was. Nothing fazed me then. The world was my oyster, no mistake. [*Fading in*] Life's a rum business anyway you look at it . . . Well, never mind. Here's your drink.

JIM. Oh, thank you.

WILL. Well . . . [*With effort*] . . . drink up!

   [*Clink of glasses*]

JIM. Cheerio!

   [*Music: Up dramatically . . . Then down . . . Then segue into simulation of sound of digging in earth*]

[*Downpour of rain . . . A clap of thunder . . . Rumbling away . . . Marble's heavy breathing*]

CONSTABLE. Hello there, in the garden! What's going on?

WILL. Huh—it's—it's me, Constable—Marble!

CONSTABLE [*Laughing*]. Well, doing a bit of gardening on a night like this!

WILL [*Makes a horrible attempt to laugh*]. Lost something—my wallet—dropped it as I came in!

CONSTABLE. Oh—wait a minute, I'll give you some light.

WILL. No! No!

CONSTABLE. I'll throw my torch in there.

WILL [*Hastily*]. Never mind—I found it! I found it just as you came along. I was just going into the house.

CONSTABLE. Found it, eh? Well, that's luck—good night, Mr. Marble! [*Fade*] Better get out of those wet clothes.

WILL. Yes . . . yes . . .

[*Music: Up and fades out entirely for*]

ANNIE [*Fading in, calling*]. Will! Will, whatever happened last night?

WILL [*In terror*]. What are you talking about! What do you mean!

ANNIE. Your clothes—they're full of mud—and they're hardly dry yet. Did you fall?

WILL. Yes . . . I took young—young Medland to get a taxi—I came in the back way and I—I fell in the garden. It was pouring.

ANNIE. Oh. It was awfully nice of the boy to lend you money. We must try to pay him back as soon as possible, Will.

WILL. Of course. In time . . .

[*Doorbell*]

WILL. Who—who's that!

ANNIE. I don't know who it could be so early in the morning—Will, what's the matter—are you having a chill . . .

WILL. I felt a bit queer—it's nothing.

ANNIE [*Fading*]. I'll see who it is.

[*Door opens*]

HAMMOND [*Off*]. Ah, Mrs. Marble!

ANNIE [*Off*]. Hello, Mr. Hammond—come in . . .

HAMMOND [*Fading in*]. Well, well—Hullo, Will—how goes it . . .

WILL [*With relief*]. Oh, it's you, Hammond . . .

HAMMOND. And who did you think it was—Lloyd George? [*Laughs excessively*] Well, I see you started digging your garden.

WILL. What!

HAMMOND. Been doing a bit of work out there, haven't you. Those weeds—

WILL. I haven't touched them—it must be that dog of Kingston's. It's always straying about . . .

HAMMOND. Hah! Better hire him then—clean the garden for you cheap, eh?

WILL [*With vast relief*]. Yes, that's right.

ANNIE. How is your real-estate business, Mr. Hammond?

HAMMOND. Oh, fair, Mrs. M—no cause for complaint. By the way, I recently secured a new tenant for that vacant shop at the corner.

ANNIE. Oh! The new dress shop?

HAMMOND. That's right. Madame Collins is the proprietor. A foreigner.

ANNIE. French, isn't she?

HAMMOND. Yes—married this Collins chap. He's in a nursing home. Bit of a looker, she is. Better keep an eye on Will, here. [*Laughs*] [*Marble laughs weakly*] Look, Will—what I dropped in to see you about. We've got a property on our books that would suit you two down to the ground—out in the country a bit—you'd like that, wouldn't you, Mrs. M?

ANNIE. Oh, yes, I would if—

WILL. We're not moving!

HAMMOND. Lower rates—not much farther to the city . . .

WILL [*Exploding*]. I don't care if it's Buckingham Palace, rent free! I don't want it—that's plain enough, isn't it?

HAMMOND. No need to jump down a fellow's throat!

WILL. All right, I'm sorry—Only don't keep on about moving—we shall never leave here . . .

HAMMOND. I was only trying to be helpful—Well, I'll be going along—good-bye, Mrs. Marble.

ANNIE. Good-bye, Mr. Hammond . . .

HAMMOND. Good-bye, Will . . .

WILL. Good-bye, Charlie—I'm sorry . . .

HAMMOND. Oh, no harm done . . . [*A pause*]

[*Then door opens and closes off*]

ANNIE. Will, you were pretty hard on poor Mr. Hammond . . .

WILL. Get me a glass, Annie—I want a whiskey.

[*Music: Bridge*]

[*Door opens and closes off*]

WILL [*Calling*]. That you, Annie?

ANNIE [*Off*]. Yes, dear.

WILL. Where have you been. It's after six.

ANNIE [*Fade in*]. Winnie and I just walked to the cleaner's, and called in for your suit.

WILL. Well, hurry up and get your things off. I've got something to tell you . . .

WINNIE. What's this book, Father?

WILL [*Harshly*]. Put that book down!

WINNIE. "Medical Jurisprudence."

WILL. Put that book down, do you hear?

WINNIE. It's such a queer sounding name.

WILL. Well, it doesn't concern you.

WINNIE [*Mystified*]. All right, Father.

ANNIE. What did you want to tell us, Will?

WILL. Oh, nothing really to get excited about, I suppose . . . It's only that . . . I've pulled off a little deal . . . merely a matter of finance which, of course, wouldn't interest you.

ANNIE. But . . . Will, what is it? Have you made some money?

WILL. Yes, a little. Ha! The right side of thirty thousand pounds, shall we say?

ANNIE [*Staggered*]. Thirty thousand!

WINNIE. Father!

WILL. I made investment in Francs . . . and this one came off.

ANNIE. But . . . Will, how *can* you have made all that?

MARBLE. You don't believe me, eh?

ANNIE. Well, dear . . . I hardly know what to think . . . It's all so sudden. I can't understand.

WILL. It's not so difficult. Just a question of knowing the right time to buy and having the guts to chance it. We're rich, Annie.

ANNIE. Oh Will, this isn't a joke is it?

WILL [*Laughing*]. Joke! No fear! You can have anything you want, what will it be?

ANNIE. You know what I've always wanted.

WILL. And what's that?

ANNIE. A little house in the country.

WINNIE. Oh yes, Father, can we?

WILL [*Hoarsely*]. No! You can't!

ANNIE [*Surprised*]. Well I'm sorry dear, only . . .

WILL. You can have anything . . . except *that!* As a matter of fact, I've fixed up this afternoon to buy this place.

WINNIE. But Father, you know I hate this place!

ANNIE. Winnie—run along—I want to talk to your father.

WINNIE [*Fading*]. Oh, why can't we move now! [*Pause*]

ANNIE. Will.

WILL. Yes.

ANNIE [*Making the plunge*]. Will, couldn't you tell me?

WILL. Tell you?

ANNIE. All about it, I mean.

WILL [*Slightly uneasy*]. About what? I don't know what you're talking about, Annie.

ANNIE. My dear, I'd never blame you . . . whatever you've done—really I wouldn't

WILL. How do you mean . . . whatever I'd done—?

ANNIE. Will, can't you trust me? It frightens me not knowing . . . I'd rather you told me . . . everything.

WILL [*Getting really alarmed*]. I . . . I don't know what you're driving at.

ANNIE [*Feeling that he does*]. I couldn't help guessing, dear. You've looked so worried and that jumping so when anyone knocked . . . Oh, don't you see?

WILL [*Trembling*]. What have you guessed?

ANNIE. Dear . . . I tried to think that it wasn't that . . .

WILL [*Whispering*]. What?

ANNIE. I tried to pretend to myself that it was all my imagination, but all the time I . . . I knew . . . I just thought if you *could* talk to me about it . . . it might . . . help. There's one thing, Will . . . Does anyone suspect?

WILL. Annie . . . Annie . . .

ANNIE. All right, dear, we won't talk about it . . . I only felt that if the Bank sent anyone here when you weren't in, I shouldn't know what to . . .

WILL [*Incredulously*]. The Bank? The Bank, did you say?

ANNIE. When they find the money's gone, I mean. Yes, dear, I guessed. I mean, a man in your position . . . thousands of pounds like that but I understand, Will. The temptation . . . [*Marble is now half laughing, half sobbing*]

ANNIE. Dear, why do you look like that? I was bound to know sooner or later, wasn't I? . . . I . . . Will! Don't dear! Don't! What is it? What have I . . . What have I said?

WILL. You'll . . . be . . . the . . . death of me . . . Annie!

ANNIE. What do you mean, Will?

WILL [*Laughing hysterically*]. You really don't think I'm a thief, do you! It's so funny.

[*Music: Up and out of his hysterical laughter*]

[*Music: Up to finish*]

END OF ACT I

ANNOUNCER

COMMERCIAL

STATION IDENTIFICATION

ACT II

[*Music: Up and under*]

NARRATOR. Well, it is now a few weeks later, and William Marble's worries about money are over. But there is a little less poison in a certain bottle that Mr. Marble keeps in the cupboard for his photography. There is a place in the garden that looks as if someone had been digging there. And there is no trace at all of the rich young nephew from Australia . . .

[*Music: Fade out for*]

ANNIE. Will? Stop staring out the window at the garden and listen to me. Won't you be going to work this morning?

WILL. No.

ANNIE. Will it be all right—I mean for you to stay home today?

WILL. I've quit the job.

ANNIE. You've quit! You're not going to work any more?

WILL. Not for the County National! Twenty years of being ordered about like a blooming dog is quite enough for yours truly. I'm independent now. [*His voice rising*] I can do as I please! Do you hear! I won't be ordered about by anybody!

ANNIE. Will, I'm worried about you.

WILL. Worried about me? Why? Why should you be worried about me?

ANNIE. Well, you seem so nervous, dear. You seem to have something on your mind—

WILL. Something on my mind—what do you mean—what do you mean by that.

ANNIE. I didn't mean anything, Will—it's just that you do nothing but sit in that chair all day long. Dear, can't I help in any way?

WILL [*Same vein*]. The bills are all paid, aren't they! That's what we wanted, wasn't it? Money? Well, we've got money so I'll thank you to leave me alone!

ANNIE [*Quietly*]. All right, Will . . . would you like some tea, dear?

WILL. No!

ANNIE. All right.

WINNIE [*Fading in*]. Hullo, mother! Hullo, father!

ANNIE. Hello, Winnie—where have you been?

WINNIE. Shopping! Look, father, what I got with the money you gave me!

WILL [*Dully*]. What is it?

WINNIE. Green garters! Gladys Brown's got some and she thinks she's everything. Wait until she sees these!

ANNIE [*Amused*]. Oh, Winnie!

WILL [*Chuckles a little*]. A little money makes a difference, eh, Winnie?

WINNIE. Does it though! It's so much more fun being rich!

WILL [*Laughs*]. What a kid!

WINNIE. Oh, there are ever so many more things I want to get . . . a hat, a coat, dresses and—

ANNIE. You have a good warm coat, Winnie—you don't need another one . .

WINNIE. Oh, but Mother! That old one I have is not what they're wearing at all—I want to get one like Gladys has—

ANNIE. Winnie, there's no need to be extravagant.

WILL. Oh, let the kid get what she wants, Annie!

WINNIE. Thank you, father!

ANNIE. But Will, I don't think it's right. When she has a perfectly good coat.

WILL [*Breaking in angrily*]. We've got the money and what difference does it make if she has one coat or half a dozen! I can pay for them, can't I?

ANNIE. Yes, Will, it wasn't that—I just don't think Winnie should get into expensive habits—that's all.

WILL. I won't have any more about what I can afford and what I can't afford, do you understand? I won't have it!

ANNIE. Will, there's no need to fly off the handle. I only said—

WILL. It's enough to drive a man dotty! [*Fade*] I won't have any more of this money talk!

ANNIE [*Calling after him*]. Will, where are you going!

WILL [*Shouting—Off*]. I'm going out!

[*Sound: Door opens and slams*]

[*Music: Bridge into*]

[*Sound: Strolling footsteps*]

HAMMOND. Mind if I walk along with you, Will? Beautiful day, isn't it?

WILL. I'm just going to Hudson's grocery, Charlie.

HAMMOND. Hudson's. Aren't you trading with Evans any more?

WILL. No. He got nasty about a bill and he'll never get another penny's business from me . . .

HAMMOND. Is that a fact? Well, I don't blame you, Will—you've got the laugh on him since you made that killing in francs . . . you can get all the credit you want now, eh?

WILL. I suppose.

HAMMOND. You seem rather glum, old boy.

WILL. Oh. I've been a bit off my feed lately.

HAMMOND. Yes—oh, I say—Look—here comes something to cheer you up!

WILL. What's that?

HAMMOND. It's that French dressmaker I told you about! That Madame Collins! Not half bad, eh? I'll introduce you.

WILL. I'd rather you didn't.

HAMMOND. Nonsense! [*Laughs*] [*Drops to whisper*] Oh, she's a cute
   trick all right . . . and does she know it! [*Clears his throat—Then
   up*] Well, well,—good afternoon, Madame Collins!

MADAME. Ooh! Mr. Hammond!

HAMMOND. That's right! Madame Collins, I'd like you to make the
   acquaintance of my friend, Mr. William Marble.

WILL. How do you do.

MADAME. Not the *celebrated* Mr. Marble!

HAMMOND. That's right!

WILL [*Laughs a little*]. Don't know about the celebrated part.

MADAME. Oh, but yes—every one in the neighborhood talks about the
   Mr. Marble . . . who made a fortune in francs.

WILL. Wouldn't say a fortune exactly . . . [*Laughs*]

HAMMOND. Oh, Will did himself very well, he did.

MADAME. To me it is wonderful how you men of finance know just what
   is going to happen! How do you do it, Mr. Marble!

WILL. I'm afraid that's rather a long story—matter of information, you
   know—knowledge of conditions, that sort of thing . . .

MADAME. It must be fascinating—to me at least with my little shop—and
   no one to advise me.

WILL. If ever I can be of service in the way of investments, I'd be very
   glad—

MADAME. Would you, Mr. Marble? Oh, that would be wonderful! And
   perhaps you will come to see my little shop?

WILL. Why, yes . . . [*Laughs a little*] Perhaps I will . . .

   [*Music: Bridge into*]

   [*Music: Up and under for montage*]

WILL. Waiter, you can bring us the bill now.

WAITER [*Off*]. Yes, sir—right away.

WILL. Enjoy your dinner?

MADAME. Oh, but it was perfect! One can see that you are accustomed to
   dining in great style, no?

WILL. Oh, I don't know—I don't go out often. Cigarette?

MADAME. Thank you—oh, such a beautiful case! A present from a lady?

WILL. No, I bought it myself.

MADAME. Come now—you do not expect me to believe such a story!

WILL [*Flattered, laughs*]. No, really! I say, Madame Collins, I don't know
   your first name.

MADAME. And should you?

WILL. I'd like to—

MADAME. Very well—it is Marguerite—but my friends call me Rita.

WILL. Including me?

MADAME. If you like . . .

WILL. I do . . . Rita. I say, you're quite beautiful, you know . . .

MADAME. You think so?

WILL. Yes, lovely.

MADAME [*Whispering*]. Be careful . . . Not in here.

WILL. I can't resist kissing you.

MADAME. Mr. Marble! You should not have done that.

WILL. I'm sorry . . .

MADAME. You are a very naughty man!

WILL. Well, if I am, it's your fault . . .

MADAME. Oh—so it is my fault—and why?

WILL. You're so—so—oh, I don't know. You're wonderful, Rita! I never met anyone like you!

MADAME [*Laughs*]. And how many ladies have you told that!

WILL. No, I mean it—I've got to see you again—tomorrow night?

MADAME. Ummmmm—perhaps.

[*Music: Up and under . . . Segue into cafe orchestra off*]

[*Sound: Rapping of knife against water tumbler*]

WILL. Where is that miserable waiter of ours! [*Raps again*]

MADAME. He will be along—is there such a hurry—you have just finished your drink.

WILL. I want another.

MADAME. Maybe you drink a little too much?

WILL. I'm all right.

MADAME. You seem so nervous. Is anything wrong?

WILL. No, nothing's wrong. Look here, Rita, we can't go on like this meeting in barrooms and restaurants. I've got to see you alone where we won't have to worry about people—you know how people talk—

MADAME. And where would we meet?

WILL. My house! Will you come, Rita?

MADAME. Come to your house? And how would your wife like that?

WILL. I've fixed that. I'm sending her away with the kid for a holiday—they'll be gone three weeks. We'll have the house to ourselves.

MADAME [*Laughs*].

WILL. What are you laughing at?

MADAME. Oh, you amuse me—you great, big strong man of affairs—no sooner have you thought of something and—voila, c'est arrangé! [*Pretending indignation*] I have nothing to say about the matter!

WILL. I'm sorry—I rather thought you'd like to come—I only meant—

MADAME [*Breaks in*]. Oh, but I only tease you! [*Low*] Yes, of course, I would like to come to your house! Send them away, darling—send them away quickly!

[*Music*]

[*Sound: Clink of glasses—pouring*]

WILL. Drink, Rita?

MADAME. No—

[*Sound: Tosses it off and pours another*]

MADAME. Should I not turn on the lights?

WILL. It's much nicer like this.

MADAME. Eh bien, mon cheri . . . What are you thinking about?

WILL. Eh? Oh, nothing in particular.

MADAME. But you must be. You have been just standing there—staring out the window. Is there something so interesting in the garden?

WILL [*Quickly*]. What do you mean?

MADAME. My goodness—I don't mean anything—I just wondered why you were so quiet.

WILL. I suppose I have been thinking. They'll be home tomorrow. Our last evening.

MADAME. You have missed them very much?

WILL. You know I haven't, Rita. These three weeks have been—wonderful. Rita, you don't know what it's meant—you coming in like this. At times I've almost managed to forget.

MADAME. That you have a wife?

WILL. No—not that.

MADAME. What then?

WILL. Oh, nothing—just that I—[*Stops short*]

[*Sound: A window flung up*]

WILL [*Yells*]. Get out of that garden! Get out, do you hear me! You filthy little beggar!

MADAME. What is it?

WILL. Kid from next door—chasing his ball! [*Yells*] Get out of there!

MADAME. He won't hurt anything!

WILL. I'll show that young puppy! [*Fading*] I'll teach him to stay off my property!

MADAME. Don't! The boy is doing no harm!

[*Sound: Door slams off*]

[*Music: Reprise to "Pick and Shovel" theme*]

[*Sound: Door opens and closes off*]

WILL [*Fades in panting*]. Little devil! Maybe that will teach him to stay out of my garden! Dirty little beggar!

MADAME [*Frightened*]. You struck him!

WILL. Well, that will teach him! . . .

[*Sound: Bottle and pouring . . . Tosses off the drink . . . Music out*]

WILL [*Breathing heavily*]. Well—why are you looking at me like that?

MADAME. I don't know—I do not understand—I am a little frightened.

WILL [*Trying to cover up now*]. Why, Rita—why are you frightened?

MADAME. You fly into such rages.

WILL. I just don't want people running over my property! The little mucker had no business out there.

MADAME. But is it any reason to get in such a state? I think maybe I will go now.

WILL. No, Rita! Don't go—don't leave me alone tonight—our last night. I'm sorry—I'm just a little upset, that's all. Please stay—let me get you a drink. I'm quite myself now.

MADAME. If I stay—will you do something for me?

WILL. Anything, Rita.

MADAME. You will help me?

WILL. Of course—any way I can. What is it?

MADAME. Darling, it is my shop—I must have three hundred pounds for my shop.

WILL. What! Three hundred! Good Lord!

MADAME. If I do not get it quickly I must be made bankrupt . . .

WILL. Yes, but three hundred!

MADAME. Oh, what a fine lover. You say you love me and—

WILL. I'm not made of money, you know.

MADAME. You have plenty of money for everything but me! Look at this house, it's furnished like a palace.

WILL. Do you expect me to live the way we used to in a miserable hovel?

MADAME. Other times you were not so stingy with your money—begging for a kiss—like a little puppy dog. Very well, forget the whole thing —I will go—and perhaps it is best I do not see you any more!

WILL. Rita, Rita—don't go! Look here, I don't say but what I might be able to—manage a little toward it anyhow. There's no sense in having a row.

MADAME. Who has a row? Mon Dieu, I do not have a row!

WILL. It's all right then? Kiss me, Rita?

MADAME. Well—all right—you do love me, you bad boy?

WILL. Yes, Rita—I do—

MADAME. And you will help me?

WILL [*Laughs*]. Oh, you're marvelous, Rita. You always get your way. Yes, I'll help you.

MADAME. You will give me the money tonight? A check?

WILL [*Going off mike a little*]. Yes, I suppose so—but Rita, I can't keep this up, you know—

[*Taxi coming to a stop in street*]

MADAME. It's only that poor little shop—

WILL [*Interrupting*]. Oh, Good Lord!

MADAME. What is the matter now!

WILL. Taxi just drove up! It's Annie and Winnie!

MADAME [*Exclamation of dismay*].

WILL. Rita, get out of here—quick—the back way—hurry, for heaven's sake!

MADAME. I must get my hat and things.

WILL. There on the chair! Hurry, Rita!

[*Sound: Doorbell*]

MADAME. I am going! Do not forget—tomorrow the check, my darling!

WILL. Get out, get out!

[*Sound: Doorbell again*]

WILL. Coming, coming! Just a minute . . .

[*Sound: Door opens*]

WINNIE. Well, hello, father! We're home!

WILL. Oh, hullo, Winnie—didn't expect you until tomorrow. Is your mother coming in?

WINNIE [*Laughs*]. Well, of course, she's coming in! She's just paying the taxi—oh, goodness, what a mess this living room is!

WILL. I was going to straighten up this evening. Did you have a good holiday?

WINNIE. Oh, yes . . . Father! Look! Isn't that someone going through our garden? .

WILL. Garden! No, couldn't be— !

WINNIE. But father, it is someone going out the back gate! Why, it's Madame Collins!

WILL [*Loudly*]. No! No, it couldn't be! She hasn't been in here. She hasn't been in this house.

ANNIE [*Fading in*]. Hello, Will, what a mess the place is in!

WILL [*Irascibly*]. Why didn't you let me know you were coming home today?

ANNIE. It doesn't matter, does it? Aren't you glad to see us?

WILL. Of course, only—

ANNIE. I thought we should hurry back. You see, Winnie found an article in the paper.

WINNIE. In our hotel reading room, Father.

ANNIE. About your nephew, young Mr. Medland.

WILL. Medland! What about him?

ANNIE. I thought you should learn of it right away.

WILL [*Shaken*]. What is it? Give me that paper.

[*Sound: Rustle of newspaper*]

ANNIE. See? It's an advertisement—solicitors asking information as to the whereabouts of James Colville Medland of Brisbane, Australia. Will, this may explain why we never heard from him again.

WILL [*Flaring up*]. Well, what do you expect me to do about it?

WINNIE. Father, he's missing! Anything might have happened to him!

WILL. The boy may be off on the continent for a trip. He could be a hundred places. If he's disappeared, it's none of our business, I tell you!

ANNIE [*Meekly*]. I only thought Will, since he was our relative and so kind to us—

WILL [*Flaring up*]. You've all you can do to mind your own affairs!

[*Sound: Crumpling of newspaper*]

WILL. Now, I don't want to hear any more about it. You get your hat and coat off and calm down. I'll take your bags upstairs.

[*Sound: Footsteps*]

ANNIE. I'm so worried about your father.

WINNIE. I should think you would be! He's acting so queer! And drinking!

ANNIE. Winnie!

WINNIE. Well, he *is* drinking an awful lot, mother! Look at the bottles!

ANNIE. I know . . .

WINNIE. And why does he keep reading this same old book?

ANNIE. What book?

WINNIE. This one on medical jurisprudence—all about poison and murder trials!

ANNIE. I—I don't know.

WINNIE. Just listen to this, mother. He's even marked the page [*Reads*] ". . . Death is practically instantaneous, and after death . . ."

ANNIE. Oh, don't, Winnie!

WINNIE. It's the same book he bought before we went away. You really ought to do something about Father.

ANNIE. Yes . . . Run along, Winnie, and start unpacking . . . I'll be up in a few moments.

WINNIE [*Fading*]. All right, mother.

[*Sound: Door closes*]

[*Sound: Slight pause . . . Then sound of pages in book being turned*]

ANNIE [*With dawning realization*]. "After death the body often retains the appearance of life. It is some time before rigor mortis sets in, the cheeks being red and the muscles continuing to flex . . ." [*Sharp intake of breath*] "Death is practically instantaneous" . . .

[*Sound: Door opens*]

WILL [*Sharply*]. Annie! Annie, what are you doing with that book!

ANNIE [*After a pause*]. Jim Medland . . . Oh, no, Will! [*In hoarse crescendo*] No, no, no, NO!

[*Music*]

END OF ACT II

ANNOUNCER

COMMERCIAL

ACT III

[*Music: Up and under*]

NARRATOR. A year has passed now since the stormy night that William Marble poisoned his rich young nephew, Jim Medland. Marble still sits at the window and stares out into the garden where Medland lies buried. He cannot put the murder out of his mind, and yet his horrible secret is a little easier to bear now . . . because he does not bear it alone . . .

[*Music*]

[*Sound: Cup . . . Pouring, etc., at the table*]

ANNIE. You've hardly had anything to eat, Will.

WILL. No . . . I don't feel I can eat, Annie . . . I was just thinking. A year ago I thought money would solve everything. We haven't got much out of it, have we? Fat lot of use it's been, really.

ANNIE. No . . . except that it's given Winnie a good start.

WILL. I'm not even sure of that. She's not the same girl, Annie—giving herself airs—and the people she runs around with. They're not our sort. She'll be looking down on us directly. What time does she get here?

ANNIE. She should be here any moment.

WILL. When is she going back to school?

ANNIE. Why, dear, she's not going back—I told you—she's going to work for Mr. Cammans, the photographer.

WILL. Oh, yes. That means she'll be here all the time.

ANNIE. Of course, Will—this is her home. Don't you want her?

WILL. No, I don't. I can't help it, Annie. These last three weeks she's been away with those friends of hers we've gotten along so well. We don't want anybody else.

ANNIE. It has been more like it used to be before . . .

WILL. You've been fine, Annie. I don't know how you stuck it. It must have been awful for you. It was keeping it all to myself that made me feel like that. God, you don't know!

[*Sound: Door opens and closes off*]

ANNIE [*Calling*]. Is that you, dear?

WINNIE [*Off*]. Yes.

ANNIE. Come in, Winnie. Did you have a nice time with your friends?

WINNIE. As good as you can have without the right clothes.

WILL. What's wrong with your clothes?

WINNIE. Oh, Father, you're impossible! Mother, my hair's a mess. I can't do a thing with this new permanent.

ANNIE. It looks very pretty, dear.

WILL [*Wistfully*]. I always liked your hair the way it was.

ANNIE. Your new silk frock has come from the shop.

WINNIE. Oh, that! Oh, by the way, mother, I won't be taking that photography job. I found a better place.

ANNIE. Winnie!

WILL. Where?

WINNIE. Oh, I met someone . . . at Paula's. A man. He's got a friend who runs a ballroom in Regent Street, where they give lessons. He said he could get me a job.

WILL. What as?

WINNIE. As a dancing partner, at first. Afterwards I might be taken on as an instructress.

WILL. You can get it out of your head at once! I know what ballrooms in Regent Street mean.

WINNIE. I'm going to do it—no matter what you say.

WILL. Here—you be careful what you're saying or—!

WINNIE. I won't. You always do everything you can to stop me having any fun.

WILL. Don't be ridiculous! This fellow can't be any good getting you into a place like that.

WINNIE. Don't you dare say anything about him! He's a jolly sight better than you are!

ANNIE. Really, Winnie . . . your own father . . .

WINNIE. Ask him then! Ask him about that Frenchwoman! Madame Collins.

WILL. Shut up! You little fool . . .

WINNIE. I won't, I won't shut up! She was here in this very house when we came back from Bournemouth last summer!

WILL. Shut up!

WINNIE. You know she was. I didn't know then what it meant. I do now and I'm leaving this rotten house for good.

WILL. You devil!

WINNIE. Good-bye, mother!

[*Sound: Quick footsteps . . . Door opens and slams*]

ANNIE [*Calling*]. Winnie! Come back!

WILL. She'll be back, Annie.

ANNIE. I'm going after her.

[*Sound: Footsteps*]

WILL [*Calling*]. You can't go out in that rain, Annie!

[*Sound: Door opens off . . . Rain*]

ANNIE [*Off*]. [*Calling*] Winnie! Winnie!

[*Music: Up and out*]

[*Sound: Rain*]

ANNIE. She's gone, Will, she's gone! I couldn't stop her!

WILL. Come in, Annie—you're wet through—

[*Sound: Door closes*]

ANNIE. Will . . .

WILL. Yes, dear?

ANNIE. What made Winnie say that about . . . Madame Collins? Will, she *wasn't* here, was she?

WILL [*Nervously*]. Of course not. She's off her head. Talking wild . . .

ANNIE. What ever made her think of Madame Collins? She went back to France nearly a year ago. I can't imagine what Winnie was thinking.

WILL. She'd say anything.

ANNIE. But she must have . . . had . . . some reason . . .

WILL. Well, if she had, *I* don't know anything about it. You don't think I'd . . . let you down, Annie?

ANNIE. No, I know you wouldn't really, but . . . but . . . Oh, Will, I couldn't bear to think that . . . that you'd been untrue to me. If I thought that . . . I don't think I could go on. I'd kill myself.

WILL. Annie! There's never been anything . . . I swear!

ANNIE. Oh, I know, dear, really. I'm just silly. I trust you, Will, always.

WILL. Annie . . . you're drenched . . . you'll catch a chill! I'm putting you to bed—you mustn't get down sick, Annie . . .

[*Music*]

DOCTOR. Your wife's not at all well, Mr. Marble. You should have a nurse in.

WILL. I won't have strangers wandering about this house! I mean to say— I'll take care of her.

DOCTOR. You don't look any too fit yourself, Mr. Marble. You should have help.

WILL. I'm quite all right, Doctor! I don't want anybody in—I'll take care of Annie. She's just worried about our daughter.

DOCTOR. No word from the girl?

WILL. Not a word—that's what's got poor Annie down—that and running out in the rain the night Winnie left.

DOCTOR. Well, you get the medicine, give her plenty of fruit juice—and for heaven's sake, man, take care of yourself, too.

WILL. I'll be all right . . .

DOCTOR. Well, at least try to get some sunshine—sit out in the garden in the afternoon . . .

WILL. The garden? Yes . . . yes, doctor . . .

[*Music*]

[*Sound: Door opens and closes*]

[*Sound: Mantel clock strikes nine*]

WILL. Annie—are you awake!

ANNIE. Yes, Will.

WILL. How do you feel this morning?

ANNIE. Just terribly weak.

WILL. I'll get you some more fruit juice.

ANNIE. I don't really want any, Will.

WILL. But the doctor said so, Annie . . . and I'll fix the hot water bottle.

ANNIE. You've been so kind, Will . . .

WILL. We've got to get you well—

ANNIE. Has there been any word, Will,—of Winnie? [*Plaintively*] It isn't like her to run away.

WILL. She'll be back, Annie.

[*Pause*]

ANNIE. Why ever did she say that about Madame Collins, Will?

WILL. Madame Collins!

ANNIE. I don't understand.

WILL. Never mind. Winnie was just talking a lot of silly nonsense.

ANNIE. I don't know what I'd do without you, Will.

WILL. Annie, try not to worry—just you get well. I'll squeeze the oranges now . . . Anything else you want?

ANNIE. No . . . Only please don't leave me for long . . . Somehow I can't bear to be alone any more.

WILL. I know, Annie . . . I know . . .

ANNIE. I start imagining . . . such horrible things . . . If we could only get away from here.

WILL. Poor Annie . . . Try to sleep a little if you can . . . I won't be long.

[*Sound: Door closes*]

[*Music: Bridge*]

[*Sound: Doorbell . . . Footsteps . . . Door opens*]

MADAME. 'Ello, Cheri.

WILL [*In hoarse whisper*]. Rita! What are you doing here?

MADAME. Let me in, please.

[*Sound: Door closes*]

ANNIE [*From upstairs*]. Who is it, Will?

WILL [*Calling*]. What? Oh, nobody, Annie, it's only the paper boy with the paper.

[*Sound: Living room door closes*]

WILL. You must go away at once. My wife . . . She's ill. Terribly ill. She's upstairs now.

MADAME. Well?

WILL. She'll hear you! She mustn't know you're here! It would upset her . . . she couldn't stand the slightest shock!

MADAME. But I 'ave come from the continent on purpose to talk to you.

WILL. Well, I'm not going to listen. I've finished with you. I wish I'd never set eyes on you!

MADAME. Listen to me! The last time you sent any money was before Christmas . . . I write three letters to which you do not answer. I tell you 'ow I must 'ave money.

WILL. I'm sick to death of the whole business. Being bled by a rotten . . . a dirty little blackmailer! And you won't get another penny out of me.

MADAME. No? Suppose I say to you that I must 'ave five 'undred pounds?

WILL. You can say it. You won't get it . . .

MADAME. P'raps you think differently if I say I must tell some things to your wife?

WILL. What?

MADAME. I might 'ave to tell her about three weeks when she was at Bournemouth . . .

WILL. You couldn't! She wouldn't believe you! Besides, she's ill, I tell you. If she had a shock like that, she . . .

MADAME [*Triumphantly*]. So? She 'as never found out anything? Thank you, that is what I wish to know.

WILL. You devil!

MADAME. Now, we 'ave wasted a long time. You will write for me a check.

WILL. I can't do it . . . I . . . Rita! . . .

MADAME. 'Ere is a pen. Sit down!

WILL [*Pleading*]. Rita . . .

MADAME. Where is your book? Now . . . you will write a check for "Bearer" for five 'undred pounds.

WILL. But—

MADAME. And if you do one thing to stop it—you know what will happen. If it is there, you will not hear from me again.

WILL. This can't go on, you know. Soon, there won't be anything for you to get. Then, I suppose you'll be satisfied.

[*Music*]

ANNIE [*Calling weakly*]. Will . . . Will . . . Where are you, Will? I'm frightened . . . [*She coughs and then struggles for breath*] You've been gone so long.

[*Sound: Bed springs creak*]

ANNIE [*Whimpering*]. I've got to find you, Will . . . Will, where are you? Will, I'm coming down.

[*Music: Up and down*]

[*Sound: Bare footsteps on stairs*]

[*Out of music on cue*]

ANNIE [*A little cough and her labored breathing as she approaches the door*]. [*Then the voices of Marble and Madame behind the door . . . Note: These lines are muffled*]

WILL. I wish to heaven I'd never laid eyes on you—I hope I never see you again . .

MADAME. Now, now—is that a nice way to talk? To your Rita?

WILL. Get away from me . . .

[*Sound: The door knob turns and the door opens a little bringing the voices right on mike*]

MADAME. You forget easily, darling. Me—I shall never forget. I think of the afternoons . . . Just at this time . . . when you sit in the old chair waiting. And while you are looking out into the garden I creep in and put my hands to cover your eyes . . . then you jump out of the chair and hold me in your arms . . . remember?

ANNIE [*A sharp intake of breath and*]. [*Whispering*] Oh no!

[*Sound: Door closes quietly*]

[*Music: Bridge*]

WILL. I'll write this check, Rita, and then you must go.

[*Sound: Pen scratching under*]

MADAME. Now that is my darling . . .

[*Sound: Tearing out of check*]

WILL. REMEMBER, this is the last time!

MADAME. Of course!

[*Sound: The doorbell*]

WILL. Good Lord! That's the doctor—he mustn't find you here—get out the back way—

MADAME. I will go now—and remember, do not try to stop this check . . .

WILL. For God's sake, get out!

[*Sound: Doorbell again*]

MADAME [*Mockingly*]. Good-bye, my darling!

WILL. Get out! [*Up*] Coming—just a moment! Coming!

[*Sound: Door opens*]

DOCTOR. You didn't hear my first ring.
WILL. I was squeezing some fruit juices—come in doctor . . .

[*Sound: Closes door*]

DOCTOR. Everything all right?
WILL. Yes, quite. She's a bit brighter today.
DOCTOR. I thought for a moment she was worse. You look flustered.
WILL. I'm all right.
DOCTOR. Has she had her lunch?
WILL. Yes, I fetched her tray.
DOCTOR [*A pause*]. What about you?
WILL. Me?
DOCTOR. You're not looking too good. See here, old man you don't want to get down just as we're getting her well . . .
WILL. No—
DOCTOR. I'll go up and see her now . . .

[*Music: Brief*]

[*Sound: Footsteps on stairs . . . Off*]

DOCTOR [*Off calling*]. Mr. Marble! Mr. Marble!

[*Sound: Hurried footsteps*]

WILL. Yes, Doctor. Doctor, is anything wrong?
DOCTOR [*Off*]. Yes.
WILL. Is she . . . is she bad again?
DOCTOR [*A pause*]. [*Calling*] She's dead!
WILL. Dead! Dead! How can she be . . . !
DOCTOR [*Fading in*]. It must have just happened—not more than a few minutes . . .
WILL. Annie!

DOCTOR. She appears to have been—poisoned.

WILL. Poisoned?

DOCTOR. Is there any poison in the house?

WILL. No—no, at least where she could get it!

DOCTOR. What poison was in the house?

WILL. Cyanide—I had it for my photography—I've had it some time.

DOCTOR. Where did you keep it?

WILL. Here—in this cupboard at the foot of the stairs—she couldn't have got is possibly . . .

DOCTOR. Is this the bottle?

WILL. Yes—but it was half full . . .

DOCTOR [Sniffs]. When did you give her the fruit juice last?

WILL. About . . . three quarters of an hour ago. Why?

DOCTOR. Did you see her drink it?

WILL. Yes. There can't have been anything in that. I took it upstairs and didn't leave her until I brought the glass down with the other things.

DOCTOR. Where is that glass?

WILL. It's here on the tray with the other things . . . No—it's not! But it was here! Did you take it?

DOCTOR. I got *this* glass from beside her bed.

WILL. But there was only the one glass! I brought it down! It was there on the tray. [A pause] Doctor . . . [Pause] She couldn't have got downstairs alone . . .

DOCTOR. I know that, too, Marble.

WILL. Then . . . how did the glass . . . get upstairs?

DOCTOR [Pointedly]. That's what *they'll* want to know . . .

WILL [Pause]. [Starts a low, horrible laugh] You . . . [Laughing low] You think . . . you think I killed *HER*? [His laughter builds hysterically] [Calling] Annie! Annie! Annie!

  [Music: Builds to climax and out for]

HAMMOND [Fade in]. The old story, my friend—him carrying on with another woman and the two wanting the wife out of the way. The judge himself said there couldn't have been a plainer case—the motive was there—they proved the poison was in the cupboard—they proved she couldn't have got it herself . . . they hanged him, of course.

PROSPECT [Abruptly]. I'll take the place . . . About the garden, it's in a shocking state. I never saw so many weeds. It'll take a lot of digging to root them out.

HAMMOND. Yes, and if you ask me, I should say that you would have to dig pretty deep.

[*Music*]

ANNOUNCER

CREDITS

DEAD END

Original Play
by Sidney Kingsley

Radio Adaptation
by Paul Peters

CAST

(for radio performance)

SPEAKER at cornerstone celebration	Henry Sharp
GIMPTY (Peter Quinn), a young architect	Richard Conte
ANGEL . . . Michael Artist	
TOMMY . . . Danny Leone	
SPIT . . . Harlan Stone	the Dead End Kids
T.B. . . . Arnold Stang	
FREDDIE . . . Ronald Liss	
A BOY from the 2nd Avenue gang	Jerry Boyer
PHILIP, a fat boy who lives in the fine apartments	Alastair Kyle
DOORMAN to the East River Apartments	Jay Velie
BABY-FACE MARTIN, a gangster	Alan Baxter
HUNK, his dumb bodyguard	Maurice Gosfield
MRS. MARTIN, Baby-Face's aged, drab mother	Agnes Young
FRANCEY, the girl Baby-Face once loved	Ann Thomas
DRINA, Tommy's older sister	Joan Tetzel
KAY MITCHELL, the girl from the East River Apts.	Anne Burr
JACK HILTON, Kay's fiance	John Flynn
MR. GRISWALD, Philip's father	Dwight Weist
A POLICEMAN	Henry Sharp
FIRST G-MAN	John Flynn
SECOND G-MAN	Dwight Weist

DEAD END

Radio adaptation by
Paul Peters

THE FIRST PROBLEM, patently, is one of time. A Broadway play runs roughly 120 minutes. A Theatre Guild on the Air script runs roughly 50. More than half the original drama, then, must go.

So you start by stripping the story to the bone. Sometimes, alas, when you take off the verbal flesh, you find great segments of skeletal void—three vertebrae missing, the pelvis dislodged, or a femur going nowhere and supporting nothing—and frantically you shore it up with baling wire and lath. The shoring is usually done in that chaotic haste that accompanies all radio as inseparably as fleas accompany a dog; and if anybody touched the makeshift structure after the broadcast, I have an idea that over the mike would sound the brittle, hollow clatter of tumbling bones.

In stripping a play to its basic story another problem arises. Frequently, for lack of time, you must excise a scene that adds no narrative progression but subsists solely by grace of charm, wit, atmosphere, character, or other elements which, no matter how engaging, are purely literary embellishments. Now, someone, in the course of those conferences without which no broadcast can be made, is bound to rise and say, "I saw it on Broadway and you left out that wonderful bit where . . . " Or, "Oh, you can't omit that line about the girl who . . . Why, that was the funniest line in the play!"

The ones that get away, it seems, are always the funniest.

So you twist a hunk of dialogue or you break your story line to insert a scene for the purpose of retaining a gag which now no longer seems funny.

Stripped to its understructure, "Dead End" is revealed as half a dozen stories: what we used to call the collective play. A savage slum aroma holds them together. On Broadway the ponderous realism of Norman Bel Geddes' production was an important atmospheric factor in the play's great success.

Some of the stories, for sheer time limitation—50 minutes instead of 120—had to be omitted. Some were dropped because, as one discerning script critic said, "On the radio, you can't tell the kids apart." I don't know what the adapter, rewriting feverishly in the nights between one rehearsal and the next, can really answer to this.

Of the individual stories, some are good, some are not so good. The slum boy Tommy, for instance, is vital and moving; even the dialogue here has color and life. Tommy's fate is neatly integrated into the story of Baby-face Martin, the gangster, who—though a more conventional figure—is deftly fitted into the two excellent stories of Mrs. Martin and Francey, his fallen school-day sweetheart. But the story of the nice young architect never goes beyond "Hello, good-bye, I'm leaving, I've left"; and by no amount of tinkering could it be improved. Some of the tinkering, I fear, stands out like a piece of sandpaper; but for part of this filler I am not really responsible.

DEAD END

ANNOUNCER

INTRODUCTION FOR THE THEATRE GUILD

ACT I

[*A band plays gaily, fading somewhat as the narrator speaks*]

NARRATOR. This is the dead end of a New York street which runs into an old abandoned wharf on the East River. If you listen, you can hear the tugboats chug and the ferryboats whistle. [*A distant chug and whistle . . . A boat bell rings*] As so often happens in this great metropolis, rich and poor live side by side. To the left of the Dead End towers the white magnificence of the East River Terrace, New York's finest apartment house. It has now grown a little mellow with age, a little grimed with city soot—but the iron gate to its garden still opens in the rear to the dead end street. A few yards beyond the gate stands a diner called, as usual, the Coffee Pot. Across the street, where once stood a row of tenements and abandoned old houses, the ground is now cleared. Before this clearing a crowd has gathered. [*Distant sound of crowd, some applause*] A band is playing. [*Band up*] On a platform draped with bunting a speaker is talking. [*Distant drone of speaker's voice, no words distinguishable*] It is a big day for the Dead End neighbors, rich and poor alike. They are waiting for someone. The speaker, sensing this, says . .

[*Speaker's voice up quickly*]

SPEAKER [*Echo*]. . . . and so I give you your neighbor and friend, the dreamer whose vision has made this project possible—I give you— Peter Quinn!

[*Cheer and applause . . . They die off . . . A tugboat whistles*]

GIMPTY [*Speaking with an echo*]. I'd rather you called me Gimpty.

[*Crowd murmurs . . . Some laughs*]

That's the name you've known me by—you people among whom I've lived most of my life—with whom I've shared my joys and sorrows. This is a day of joy for me and my wife. For today, on this spot, the dream we both nourished for so many years is about to come true. Who among you does not remember when this place was a slum so hideous that it twisted the souls of the boys who once played in that Dead End street? Do you remember those boys? Some of them stand among you now—grown men. Some of them wear uniforms. But back in 1933, at the height of a great depression, when the banks were shut and men sold apples on street corners, I sat in the sun on the wharf, because I had no office . . . and as I worked on the drawing board in my lap, I would watch those boys dive into the scummy river and listen to their [*Fade*] tough tenement talk . . .

[*A drawn-out tugboat blast . . . River sounds . . . Splashes of water . . . Fade in of boys' voices*]

ANGEL. Howza wawda, Tommy? Cold?

TOMMY [*Fading in*]. Naw. It's duh nuts. Look out, I'm coming out. [*Splash*] Yew trew wid yur shoe-shining, Angel?

ANGEL. Yeah. I didn' git no customers all mornin'. Boy, am I gonna make a hole in dat wawda. Watchout below!

[*He screams and dives . . . Splash*]

SPIT [*Fade in*]. Dat dive stinks. Watch me. I'm gonna do duh backjack. Hey, T.B., watch me. [*He screams and dives . . . A great splash*] How wuzzat?

T.B. Aw, Spit, yew dive like a floozy. Watcha holding yur nose for?

SPIT [*Splashing*] I'm comin' out and knock yew in a eye.

T.B. Oh, yeh?

TOMMY. Lay offa T.B., yuh hear me, Spit? Pick on a kid what kin fight back. T.B.'s got a cough.

SPIT. Aw-w-w-w.

TOMMY. Yeah, aw-w-w-w. If yuh wanna know whose leader a dis gang, start sumpm. Just start sumpm.

GIMPTY [*Fading in*]. Shut up, Tommy. Everybody knows you're leader of the gang.

TOMMY. Hi, Gimpty.

SPIT. Hey, Gimpty, yuh got a butt?

GIMPTY. No . . . You used to be a nice kid, Tommy. What's happened to you? Your sister's worried about you, too.

TOMMY. Aw, Drina—she's tryin' to make a sissy out a me . . . Besides, don' let 'er kid yuh, Gimpty. When she comes down heah, it ain't me she's lookin' fuh. She wansa see yew.

GIMPTY. Me? You're crazy!

TOMMY. She's godda mash on yew. I can tell.

GIMPTY. Ah, you're full of hot air, Tommy.

TOMMY. Hey, watcha drawin', Gimpty?

GIMPTY. Houses.

TOMMY. Gee! . . . [*Yelling*] Hey, Spit, looka heah! Gimpty drawing houses.

SPIT [*Off mike*]. I'm coming.

[*Splashes and drip of water*]

TOMMY. Ony I don' understand—whatsa good a houses on paper?

GIMPTY. You've got to draw them on paper before you can build 'em.

SPIT [*Fading in*] Aw, go wan. He puts 'em on paper cause he's godda gimp in his leg an' can't build 'em.

[*An iron gate opens with a clang*]

T.B. [*Calling, fading in quickly*]. Hey, Tommy! Tommy, lookit what's comin' out a duh fancy joint.

TOMMY. Yeah, dat's 'at fresh li'l kid, Wee-wee. What dey usin' duh back door fuh, T.B.?

T.B. They fixing duh street in a front of dat house. Gas main broke or sumpm. Yew know—[*He makes a fierce noise*] . . . it's a air drill.

PHILIP [*Off mike*]. Doorman, where's our chauffeur?

DOORMAN [*Off mike*]. He's on the corner with the cab drivers, Master Philip. Shall I get him?

PHILIP [*Off mike*]. Yes. Father wants him. Hurry up.

[*Footsteps away*]

TOMMY [*Calling*]. Hey, kid! Hey, Wee-wee! What ah yuh, a boy 'r a goil?

SPIT. He's a goil, cantcha see?

PHILIP [*A little off mike*]. I'm a man. [*The boys razz him*] And I can name all the Presidents of the United States. That's more than you can do.

T.B. Tommy kin. I bet yuh a dollar Tommy kin.

PHILIP. Put up your dollar. Here's mine.

T.B. Gosh—a whole live dollar! Go on, Tommy, show 'im—show 'im, Tommy.

PHILIP. Washington, Adams, Jefferson. Now let's see your Tommy name the next three.

TOMMY. Er—Madison—er—Harrison—

PHILIP. Wrong.

TOMMY. Well, who cares, anyway. Yuh li'l sissy, I'll spit in yuh eye an' drown yuh. Hey, what's 'at junk yuh got in yuh mout'—like a hawse?

PHILIP. It's a brace to make my teeth straight.

TOMMY. Wh-a-a-at? Why, I could do dat with one wallop.

PHILIP. You try and you'll be arrested.

TOMMY. Look what's gonna arrest me, fellahs!

PHILIP. Did you ever hear of Judge Griswald? He's my uncle.

T.B. Yeah? Didja ever hear a Judge Poikins? He sent me to rifawn school.

SPIT. Hey, Tommy, waddya say we give 'im duh woiks?

TOMMY. OK. Let's mobilize 'im.

     [*Running footsteps*]

PHILIP [*Frightened, shrill*]. Don't you touch me. Don't you—! . . . Doorman! Doorman!

DOORMAN [*Fading in, bellowing*]. Get away from here, you scum! Go on, beat it, or I'll call the police. Come inside, Master Philip. [*Iron gate opens . . . Voice fades*] Your chauffeur said he's . . .

     [*Iron gate bangs shut*]

TOMMY [*Yelling after them*]. Wait till I git yew, Poicy. I'm gonna fix yer wagon. [*Low*] Hey, guys, we gotta git dat kid away from deah. D'ja see dat dollar? Wow! We gotta git 'im.

SPIT [*Mocking Philip*]. Ya-a-a-a-ah, the sissy! Dat's my uncle! Dat's my brace!

TOMMY. Shad up, Spit! Quit hollerin' an' tink a how we gonna git some dough.

T.B. If we had a nickel we could all go to Schultzie's an' while I wuz buyin' a chocolate bar, yew guys could steal sumpm.

[*Fade in with slow footsteps*]

Looka dem two guys comin' down a street. Maybe dey'll buy a shine fum yuh, Angel. Dey got dough, I bet.

ANGEL. Yeah. Boy, lookit dem close! Flashy, huh?

TOMMY. Go wan, Angel. Git duh lead out a yur pants.

[*Running footsteps*]

ANGEL [*Calling*]. Hey, mister, yuh want a shine?

MARTIN [*Tough, flat voice*]. Go on, beat it!

ANGEL. Yew—duh oduh guy—yew want a shine, doncha?

HUNK. Whatsammatuh, yuh cockeyed? Can't yuh see we got one?

MARTIN. Hey, wait a minute, runt. Wanna run a errand fuh me?

ANGEL. Sure. Wheah?

MARTIN. Right up de block—number 418—Mrs. Martin—fourth floor. Tell her a friend a hers wants a see her here.

ANGEL. O.K. 418. [*Footsteps fading with voice*] Fourt' floor . . . Mrs. Martin.

TOMMY [*Yelling*]. Come on. Les go swimmin'. Last one in 's a rotten egg.

[*Screams and splashes*]

HUNK. Let's go back to St. Louis, boss. It ain't safe heah.

MARTIN. Whatsamattuh? Yew afraid? I tol' yuh what I come heah faw. I want to see my mudder an' Francey. Besides, I like dis ol' wharf . . . It reminds me a when . . . when I wuz a kid. Yew go tuh that ol' tailor shop I tol' yuh about on a cornuh. Ask duh old man wheah Francey is. Go on and stop bellyachin'. I'll wait heah fuh yuh.

[*Gimpty's lame footsteps approach*]

GIMPTY [*Fade in*]. Excuse me—but don't I know you from somewhere?

MARTIN. No.

GIMPTY. I could've sworn I—

HUNK [*Menacing*]. He said no, didn't 'e? Now go wan, beat it.

GIMPTY [*Snapping his fingers*]. I've got it. Martin. Baby-face Martin!

MARTIN. I ain't Martin, you louse.

GIMPTY. Don't you recognize me, Marty?

MARTIN. O.K. Yew ask fer it an yuh git it.

[*Cocked gun noise*]

GIMPTY. Put that gun away, Marty. I'm Gimpty. Don't you remember Gimpty?

MARTIN. Sh! Shat up! My name's Johnson. Git it? Johnson.

GIMPTY. We were kids here. I was one of your gang. You don't have to worry about me.

MARTIN. Yeah. You wuz that funny little lame kid who used to mind my clothes when I went swimmin'. Kin yuh keep yur lip buttoned up?

GIMPTY. I always used to, didn't I?

HUNK. Lissen, boss, you can' trust nobody.

MARTIN. He ain't nuttin' to worry about. Go where I tol' yuh. Beat it.

HUNK. OK. [*Voice fading*]. It's yer funeral as well as mine.

GIMPTY. Say, Marty, what did you do to your face?

MARTIN. Operation. Plastic, dey call it . . . I guess yuh read about me, huh?

GIMPTY. You're the headliner these days.

MARTIN. Now you're talkin'! . . . Hey, dat's somethin' new over there, ain't it?

GIMPTY. East River Terrace. One of the swellest apartment houses in town. You have to have blue blood and a million bucks to live in there. This iron gate leads to the garden. You can see the private dock for yachts over there.

MARTIN. Well, what do yuh know? . . . Flossy, huh? Say, what's your racket, Gimpty?

GIMPTY. I'm an architect.

MARTIN. What's dat?

GIMPTY. I design houses.

MARTIN. Yuh don' say! Little Gimpty, an look at 'im. A architect. Well, I always knew you'd come trew. Not like dese udder slobs. Yuh must be in a big dough, huh?

GIMPTY. Nine out of ten architects are out of work. There's a depression on, remember?

MARTIN. So what's a good a being a architect?

GIMPTY. Don't ask me . . . Strictly speaking, I'm not even an architect. Before you're an architect, you got to build a house, and before anybody'll let you build 'em a house, you got to be an architect.

MARTIN. An fer dat yuh had to go to high school?

GIMPTY. College, too. Six years . . . Say, Marty, how smart is it for you to come back here?

MARTIN. I ain't here. I'm out West. Read da papers . . . You want to know sumpin? I ain't see my old lady 'n seven years. 'At's one reason why

I come back. Boy, seven years! Since a day I come out a reform school.

GIMPTY. You've sure gone a long way since ... I never could quite believe it was you, Marty ... To kill eight men!

MARTIN. Say, watcha tryin' to do? Tell me off, you punk?

GIMPTY. You know better than that.

MARTIN. I'm not so sure. Maybe yuh'd like dat reward at's up fuh me. Fawty-two hundred bucks is pretty big dough fer a joik like yaw.

GIMPTY. You can trust me, Marty.

MARTIN. "Couldn' quite believe it was yew!" Whacha tink I wuz gonna do—hang aroun' 'dis dump fer Santy Claus to take care a me? Look a yew. Six years yuh went tuh college and what a yuh got? I ain't like yew punks, freezin' and starvin'—for what? Peanuts? Yeah, I got mine, but I took it.

GIMPTY. Aren't you ever scared?

MARTIN. Me? What of? Yuh can't live faever ... An—sure—deah's times when I git da jumps ... An' times when I git a terrific yen tuh stay put an ... say, yew remember that kid, Francey? She wuz my goil when we wuz kids.

GIMPTY. Oh, yeah. I remember.

MARTIN. Ey don' make no more like her. Gee, I got a terrific yen to see dat kid again.

ANGEL. All I'm asking is a dime, mister.

HUNK [*Fading in*]. I tol' yuh nuttin' doin'. Now go wan, beat it.

ANGEL [*Fading in*]. Aw, yuh cheapskate! Yuh ought tuh gimme a dime, anyhow. I went deah for yuh, didn't I?

MARTIN. Did yuh git her address, Hunk?

HUNK. Yuh mudder ain't home. Duh kid said huh door wuz locked.

MARTIN. Nah—Francey. What about huh?

HUNK. Duh ol' geezer in a tailor shop said 'e didn't know, but 'e gimme da address of some aunt a hern. She might know.

MARTIN. Well, go and git it. Go wan—hurry up! Grab a cab.

HUNK. Wheah'll yew be?

MARTIN. In dat Coffee Pot on a cornuh. Make it snappy. [*Voice fading*] Remember what I tol' yuh, Gimpty. Keep yer lip buttoned up.

ANGEL [*Yelling after them*]. Pikers! Yuh cheap pikers!

GIMPTY. Shut up, Angel. And stay away from those guys, you hear?

ANGEL. Ah, what faw?

GIMPTY. Because they're not going to do you any good. Keep away from them, that's all.

[*Splashes . . . Drip of water*]

TOMMY [*Fading in*]. Hey, Angel, didja git any dough?

ANGEL. Naw. They're couple a cheapskates . . . Hey, guys, heah's 'at new kid 'at moved in a block.

SPIT. Wheah, Angel? I don't see 'im.

[*Footsteps slowly fading in*]

ANGEL. Come on, hurry up! He's comin' down a street. Better git out a duh wawda.

T.B. Wow! It's cold. [*Coughs*] My T.B.'s coming back.

SPIT. Aw-w-w! Yew an' yur T.B.

TOMMY. Shad up, Spit! [*Calling*] Hey, yew new kid. Come heah. [*Footsteps slow down*] Come on, don' be so slow . . . Whatsya name?

FREDDIE [*Fade in*]. Freddie. Freddie Miller.

TOMMY. Wanna belong tuh are gang?

FREDDIE. Yeah, shuah.

TOMMY. Got any dough? Yuh godda be ineetiated.

FREDDIE. I god tree sants.

TOMMY. Gimme it. [*Pause*] 'At's all yuh got?

SPIT. Soich 'im.

FREDDIE. Yuh don' haf tuh. I'll toin my pockets out for yuh. Look. Deah ain't no more.

TOMMY. Listen, yew. If yuh wanna belon' to dis gang, you godda git a quartuh.

FREDDIE. Wheah ahm gonna git a quatuh fum?

SPIT. Yuh kin snitch it fum yuh ole lady, cantcha?

FREDDIE. Dat's a sin tuh steal.

TOMMY. A-a-ah, yuh sissy! Come on, gang. [*Footsteps*] Guard dis dough, Spit.

FREDDIE [*Calling after them*]. Hey, yew. Gimme back my tree sants. I don' wanna hang out wid youse.

SPIT. Scram, punk, scram.

FREDDIE [*Bawling, running after them*]. Gimme back my tree sants.

SPIT [*Low*]. Les mobilize 'im, Tommy. Wadda yuh say?

TOMMY Ok. [*Footsteps stop*] Hey, yew, kid—wanchur money back? Well, come and git it.

[*Freddie's footsteps approach falteringly*]

SPIT [*Yelling*]. Grab 'im, Tommy. Grab 'im.

TOMMY. I got 'im!

T.B. On a groun'. Trow 'im on a groun'.

TOMMY. Gimme some a dat dirt, Angel.

ANGEL. Rub it in 'is face, Tommy. Rub it in.

[*Freddie howls . . . The boys laugh . . . Running footsteps fade in . . . Three sharp slaps . . . The noise stops . . . Silence except for heavy breathing*]

DRINA. Tommy, let him up. I'll slap you one. Let go, I say. Tommy! All right, kid, you can get up now.

[*Freddie rises, sobbing*]

TOMMY. Aw, scram, will you, Drina?

DRINA. Wait till I get you home, Tommy, I'll scram you.

TOMMY. Aw, git out a heah or I'll bust yuh one.

DRINA. That's fine talk, Tommy—bust you one. What are you scratching your head for? You buggy? Come on home. I'm gonna wash your hair in kerosene.

[*Freddie sobs again*]

DRINA. Well, what are you cryin' about? Did they hurt you or somethin'?

FREDDIE. Dey took my tree sants.

DRINA. Tommy, did you take this boy's three cents?

TOMMY. I did not.

DRINA. Who did? Who's got that money?

T.B. Not me.

ANGEL. Don' look a me.

TOMMY. Spit, giv 'im back his tree cents.

DRINA. Oh, so you're the one, Spit. I might have known it. Come on, fork over.

SPIT. Try 'n make me, yuh floozy.

DRINA. I'll crack you—you talk like that!

[*A resounding smack*]

SPIT. Aw, I'll sock yuh inna—

TOMMY. Doncha hit 'er, yuh louse. Dat's my sistuh! Give 'er dat dough. Go wan!

SPIT. Aw-w-w . . . Here.

DRINA. Here's your money, kid. You're new around here, aren't you? Well, you look like a nice boy. Stay away from these bums. They're no good.

SPIT. Come on. Les go swimmin'. Last one in's a rotten egg.

[*Screams and splashes*]

DRINA [*Yelling*]. Tommy! Tommy! Come out of that water. You can't go running around with a head full of livestock.

TOMMY [*Splashing, off mike*]. Aw-w-w. I'll come when I'm good 'n ready. Quit bodderin' me!

DRINA. Dog-gone you, Tommy!

GIMPTY [*Fading in*]. You've sure got a tough job on your hands, Drina.

DRINA. Hello, Gimpty. What are you going to do with a kid like that?

GIMPTY. As long as you live around here, I don't know.

DRINA. It's not that he's dumb, either. His teacher says he's one of the smartest she's got. But he plays hooky all the time.

GIMPTY. It's this neighborhood. It's no good for kids.

DRINA. It was different when Mom was alive. She could handle him. Between the two of us we used to make enough money to live on a decent street. Boy, the minute I start working full time again, I'm going to move out of here so fast!

GIMPTY. Me too, Drina.

DRINA. You drawing again, Pete? Can I see it?

GIMPTY. If you want to. It's a new idea in community housing.

DRINA. Hmn. I like all that open space around the buildings—with trees and grass and everything. Yeah, those sure are pretty houses, Pete.

GIMPTY. But what's the good? Is anybody going to build them?

DRINA. What's the matter with *you?* Why don't *you* build 'em?

GIMPTY. With what?

DRINA. Well, supposing you had to wait—five years—or maybe ten years. If you believed in those houses, they'd be worth fighting for, wouldn't they?

GIMPTY. I believe in them all right, but—

DRINA. You know what, Pete? You need the right woman beside you.

GIMPTY. Like who, for instance?

DRINA. Oh, I don't know. I bet there's plenty that would be willing.

GIMPTY. What good would she be—the right woman beside me?

DRINA. For one thing, she'd see that you fight.

GIMPTY. You think so, Drina?

DRINA. I know it.

GIMPTY. As a matter of fact, Drina, I have got some pretty big plans. Some day I want to tear this block of tenements down and put up my houses instead. You see, I figure that the neighborhood a kid grows up in has a big effect on the kind of life he leads. I've seen this neighborhood do terrible things to kids. Baby-face Martin lived around here once—a little wild, but a good kid. This place made a murderer out of him. Yeah. When we were in school they used to teach us that evolution made men out of animals. They forgot to tell us that it can also make animals out of men.

DRINA. Gee, Pete, I like to hear you talk. [*Calling*] Hey, Tommy! Come here a minute.

[*Splash*]

TOMMY [*Calling off mike*]. What faw?
DRINA [*Calling*]. I want you to hear this.

[*Drip of water*]

TOMMY. Hear what?
DRINA. All about evolution.

[*Drip of water*]

TOMMY [*Fading in*]. Evilushin'? What's 'at?
GIMPTY. Well, it's like this, Tommy. A thousand million years ago we were all worms in the mud—and evolution made us men.
DRINA. And women, too.
TOMMY. Ah, I wusn't even born a tousan' million years ago.
GIMPTY. No, but your great, great, great, great, great, great, grandfather was. And evolution turned him from an animal into a man.
DRINA. Gee, that's nice. It's like God.
GIMPTY. It is God. Once it made dinosaurs—animals as big as that house.
TOMMY. As big as that? Wow!
GIMPTY. Then it didn't like its work, so it wiped them out.
TOMMY. Boy! I'd like to see one a dem babies.
GIMPTY. Once evolution gave snakes feet to walk on. Then it took 'em away. Evolution says: "Now men—I made you walk straight, I gave you reason, I gave you dignity, I planted a God in your heart. Now let's see what you're going to do with them. If you can't do anything with them, I'll take them away and men will crawl on their bellies like snakes—or die off altogether like dinosaurs."

[*Iron gate opens and shuts*]

TOMMY. Hey, Gimpty, deah's yuh goil friend comin' out a dat gate.

KAY [*A pleasant, young voice, fades in*]. Hello, Pete.

GIMPTY. Oh, hello, Kay. You know Drina McGrath.

KAY. Hello.

TOMMY. Yew live in 'at joint?

DRINA. Tommy, mind your own business.

KAY [*Laughing*]. Yes, I do live in that joint.

TOMMY. What are yew—a millionairess?

KAY. No.

TOMMY. Den what a yuh doin' comin' out a deah?

DRINA. Tommy, stop being so nosy.

GIMPTY. Will you beat it, kid? Scram! Get out of here!

DRINA. Yeah. And head for home, Tommy. I'm gonna wash that mop of yours.

TOMMY. Hey, Gimpty—'at evilushin' guy, did 'e make bugs too?

GIMPTY. Yeah.

TOMMY [*Fading slowly*]. Yuh heah dat, Drina? God makes bugs an' yew wanna kill 'em. Is 'at nice? So long . . .

[*He scrams and dives*]

[*Splash*]

KAY [*Laughing*]. He's very logical.

DRINA. Yeah. That part's all right, but he's lousy, too—and that part isn't. I don't know what to do with that boy. [*Fading*] I swear, I just don't know.

[*Footsteps up the street . . . A pause . . . River sounds, a boat whistle . . . Distant splashes and cries from the swimming boys*]

KAY. Oh, Pete. Last night I was talking to Jack's friends. I—I thought they might find some work for you. [*Snap of purse lid*] This man gave me his card. He said you might come up and speak to him.

GIMPTY. Gee, Kay, thanks. Hmn—Del Block—he's a good architect. [*He laughs*] You want to know something funny? Last night I was going around the house like a chicken with its head chopped off—and mom asked me why . . . so I told her.

KAY. Told her what?

GIMPTY. About you. How we'd got to talking here and meeting every day and what great friends we've become. Kay, I told her that I—I worshipped you.

KAY. You didn't?

GIMPTY. Well, I do. Do you mind?

KAY [*Touched*]. Mind? You fool. Did you tell her *all* about me? About me and Jack, I mean.

GIMPTY. Yes. She said you sounded like a very real person.

KAY. I'd like to meet her some time . . . Why not now?

GIMPTY. Er—I'm afraid she's out for the afternoon. But—er—maybe I can get her to come down here day after tomorrow—huh?

KAY. I may be leaving tomorrow.

GIMPTY. Tomorrow?

KAY. Jack's taking a little party on a fishing trip. He invited me to go along.

GIMPTY. How long will you be gone?

KAY. About three months.

GIMPTY. That's a long time.

KAY. Yes.

[*Iron gate clangs open*]

HILTON [*Fading in*]. Why the back way? What's happened in front?

DOORMAN. I'll tell you, Mr. Hilton. You see, the gas main . . .

KAY. Hello, Jack.

HILTON. Kay! What are you doing out here?

[*Gate shuts*]

KAY. Oh, I just came out . . . This is Mr. Quinn, Jack . . . Mr. Hilton. Peter's a fine architect. You ought to see his designs.

HILTON. How do you do?—What a day I've had, Kay, arranging things at the office. But everything's all set now. The boat's in shape. We're ready to shove off, Kay.

[*Splash*]

TOMMY [*Fading in, panting, off mike*]. Hey, Gimpty, watch me do a backjack. Yew, too—Gimpty's goil friend . . . watch my backjack. [*Yelling, fading*] Wheee!

HILTON. Say, what's going on here?

KAY. Nothing.

HILTON. Come on, let's go in.

KAY. I have a headache. I want to stay out a few minutes.

HILTON. We've a million things to do. Come in and take an aspirin.

KAY. You go ahead. I'll be right along.

HILTON. I'd like to know what the big attraction is out here.

KAY. Please don't make a fuss.

HILTON. Then stop acting like a prima donna. I've been tearing around all day like a madman, and I come home to find you behaving like a cheap—

KAY. Jack!

HILTON. All right. Stay there. [*Footsteps . . . Gate clangs open and shut*]

GIMPTY. Is that the guy?

KAY. Yes . . . He's not really as bad as that. He's just—so darn jealous.

GIMPTY. If it were anybody else, all right. But you—he can't treat *you* like that.

KAY. He really loves me. He wants me to marry him. Pete, I've known what it means to scrimp and worry and never be sure from one minute to the next. I've had enough of that . . . Let's get away from here. Couldn't we go to your place?

GIMPTY. No. We couldn't. You wouldn't like it, Kay. I lied to you before. My mother's home all right. But the truth is—I'm ashamed to let you see the place. It's a dump—a dump, I tell you. Now you know.

KAY. Oh, Pete—that's silly. [*Fading*] Come on. We'll go there now.

[*They walk up the street . . . You hear Gimpty's limp*]

[*A tugboat whistles . . . Splashes*]

TOMMY [*Fading in*]. I'm comin' out. Drina'll be hollerin' huh head off. You comin', guys?

T.B. [*Off mike*]. Shuah.

SPIT. I'm coming.

ANGEL. Wait fuh me.

[*Splashes . . . Footsteps*]

FREDDIE [*Fading in*]. Hey, yew! Tommy!

TOMMY. What? Oh, it's duh new kid. So yuh come back, huh? Whatcha want?

FREDDIE. I snitched a quartuh fuh yuh.

TOMMY. OK., Freddie. OK. Give it heah. Now yuhr inna gang, see?
[*Calling*] Lissen, yew guys, anybody gits funny wid Freddie, gits
funny wid me, see?

FREDDIE. Gee, tanks, Tommy.

TOMMY. See? He loins fast. Remember de foist time I moved roun' heah?
I wuz wearin' white socks and I wouldn't coise or snitch nuttin', so
yuh all taught I wuz a sissy. I had to beat duh pants off a yuh, before
yuh let me inna gang.

[*Iron gate clangs open . . . Footsteps*]

PHILIP [*Slightly off mike*]. There they are, Daddy. Those boys that
wanted to hit me.

TOMMY [*Yelling*]. Aw, shat ap, you tub a lard.

GRISWALD [*Yelling off mike*]. You touch him again and I'll break your
neck.

TOMMY [*Yelling*]. Aw, nuts to yew, faw eyes.

GRISWALD. Next time, Philip, you hit them back.

[*Footsteps . . . Fading slowly*]

I'm going to buy you a set of gloves and teach you how to box.

PHILIP [*Fading*]. Will you, Daddy? Oh, that would be such fun.

TOMMY. Come 'ere, guys. I gotta scheme how we kin git dat kid.

ANGEL. Yeah?

SPIT. How?

TOMMY [*Lowering voice*]. Foist we git 'im inna hallway.

T.B. What hallway?

TOMMY. Dat empty house across a street.

SPIT. An' nen . . .?

[*Footsteps*]

MARTIN [*Fading in*]. Hey, yew kids seen 'at udduh guy I wuz wid? Duh
short one named Hunk?

TOMMY. Naw. 'E ain't bin aroun'.

[*Footsteps*]

NEW BOY [*Fading in*]. Hey, *youse!* Whoza leaduh uf dis gang?

TOMMY. Me. What about it, you runt? Wanna make sumpin out a it?

NEW BOY. Da Secon' Avenoo gang sent me ovah heah. Dey wanna know if
yew guys wanna fight deir gang.

TOMMY. Sure. OK. Felluhs? Yuh wanna fight da Secon' Avenyoo gang?

[*Cries of approval*]

NEW BOY. OK. Dey said on deir block, Satiday.

TOMMY. OK. Satiday, felluh? [*Cries of approval*] Faw o'clock? [*Cries of approval*] OK. We'll be up deah Satiday faw o'clock an' boy yew tell 'em we'll kick duh stuffin' out a dem.

NEW BOY. Yeah? Yew stink on ice.

TOMMY. Yeah, yew too. Lissen, tell 'em no bottles or rocks, yuh heah? Just sticks 'n bare knucks. Flat sticks. No bats.

NEW BOY. Sure. Dey gonna kick do pants off a yuh.

TOMMY. Oh, yeah? Now git outa heah befaw I bust yuh one. Scram!

[*Footsteps running*]

NEW BOY [*Yelling back, off mike*]. Aw-w-w, nuts tuh yew!

MARTIN [*Fading in*]. I bet yew kids are gonna lose 'at fight.

TOMMY. Who sez so?

MARTIN. I do. 'Cause yuh don't know how to fight a gang. If you lissened to me, I could give yuh some pointers.

TOMMY. Les hear yer pointers.

MARTIN. Well, foist ting is tuh git over dere oiliyuh 'an yuh said, see? [*Limping footsteps approach*] Hi yuh, Gimpty.

GIMPTY [*Fading in*]. Hello, Mar—Hello, Johnson.

MARTIN. If you git dere oiliyuh, dey won't be ready fuh yuh, see? 'En I tell yuh watcha wanna do. Tree aw far a youse gang up on a guy. Den one a yuh kin git behin' 'im an slug 'im wid a stockin' fulla sand. An' if ey're licking yuh, pull a knife on 'em.

TOMMY. Gee, it ain't fair. We made up no knives.

GIMPTY. Say, what are you trying to tell these kids?

MARTIN. Shut yer trap. Listen, kid—ere ain't no fair an' ere ain't no square. It's winnuh take all. It's easier tuh lick a guy by pullin' a knife.

GIMPTY. Tommy, don't listen to that stuff. You'll get in trouble.

MARTIN. Lissen, Gimpty—yew lookin' fer a sock in a puss?

GIMPTY. No . . . but I'm not going to have these kids—

MARTIN. Yur not gonna what? Bettuh hold yer lip. [*Casually*] Whattsa-mattuh, kid, ain't yuh got a knife?

TOMMY. Angel's godda knife. He kin loan it tuh me.

ANGEL. Nuttin' doin'. Yuh won't give it back.

SPIT. Give Tommy 'at knife, or I'll crack yuh one.

FREDDIE. Look, I jus' give Tommy a quatuh. Why dontcha sell 'em 'at knife, Angel? Whaddaya say?

ANGEL. Aw right. Lessee duh quatuh foist.

TOMMY. Here.

ANGEL. Aw right. Here's a knife.

GIMPTY. Look, Tommy—you don't know what you're doing. Give me that knife. [*A little tussle*] Give it to me.

MARTIN. Leave 'im alone. Git out a heah, yuh monkey. Go on, git!

GIMPTY. You think I'm going to stand here and watch you make criminals out of these kids? Tommy, I want that—

[*A vicious slap*]

MARTIN. Now maybe yuh'll loin to keep yer trap shut. I don't like guys 'at talk out a toin. Beat it.

GIMPTY. All right. All right, Johnson.

[*He limps away*]

MARTIN. Member what I tol' yuh, kid. Pull a knife on 'em. Ey'll squeal an' run away, every time.

[*Music*]

END OF ACT I

ANNOUNCER

COMMERCIAL

ACT II

[*Fade in with river sounds and tugboat whistle . . . Iron gate clangs*]

SPIT. Pst! Tommy! Deah's Wee-wee.

TOMMY [*Whispering*]. Yew know what a do, T.B.?

T.B. [*Whispering*]. Sure. I stop 'im and ast 'im sumpin.

TOMMY. What do you ask him?

T.B. Gee, I don't know—

TOMMY. Ast 'im about his watch. He's always showin' it off . . . Spit, when we git inside duh empty house, yew hold da door . . . Angel, yew and me'll stand on duh sides an' grab 'im . . . Yuh got it straight?

SPIT. Got it.

ANGEL. OK.

TOMMY. Aw right, when I give duh word, yuh scatter. [*Loud*] Guess I'll run up tuh Foist Avenyu, felluhs. [*Fading*] Any a yew guys comin' along?

ANGEL [*Fading*]. Naw. I godda go home.

SPIT [*Fading*]. Me, too. So long, Tommy.

[*A ferry boat chugs by*]

T.B. [*Calling*]. Hey, Wee-wee, what time is it?

PHILIP [*Off mike*]. Half past four.

T.B. Tanks. Gee, dat's a nice watch yuh got deah. What kin' is it?

PHILIP [*Off mike*]. It's called a chronograph. [*Fading on mike*] You want to see it?

T.B. Boy, 'at almost as nice as 'n Ingersoll? Wanna hear sumpin? [*Coughs . . . Then proudly*] 'At's a T.B. cough. I got T.B. I bet yew never knew a kid wid T.B. before.

TOMMY [*Yelling off mike*]. Hey, fellahs, come on in 'is empty house. I got sumpin to show yuse.

SPIT [*Off mike, yelling back*]. What izzit?

ANGEL [*Off mike*]. I'm comin'

TOMMY [*Yelling off mike*]. Ain't yew comin', T.B.?

T.B. Sure. [*Quietly to Philip*]. Yew wanna come, Wee-wee? [*Yelling*] Hey, Tommy, kin I bring Wee-wee?

TOMMY [*Yelling off mike*]. Nah, he can't come. Dis is ony fuh da gang.

T.B. [*Yelling back*]. Aw, why not? He's a good kid. [*Quietly to Philip*] Come along, Wee-wee. I'll make 'em letcha in.

[*Footsteps*]

TOMMY [*Off mike, but closer*]. Don' bring dat sissy ovuh heah, I tell yuh.

[*A door shuts*]

T.B. Too bad dey won' letcha see it, Wee-wee. Boy, it's sumpin great. Great. Yuh nevuh seen anythin' like dat.

PHILIP. Well, I don't care. My father and I are driving to the country.

T.B. [*He bangs on a wooden door*]. Hey, fellahs, let 'im come 'n see it, will yuh? He's OK. [*Bangs on door*] Open a door, Tommy.

[*A bolt is thrown back . . . Door opens*]

TOMMY [*Reluctantly*]. Well . . . awright. I guess we kin let 'im in, huh, fellahs?

SPIT. Aw, I don' know.

ANGEL. Awright, let 'im in.

T.B. Well, yuh comin', Wee-wee?

PHILIP. I'm expecting my father and the chauff—

T.B. [*Curtly*]. All right. It's yuhr loss. Close a door, Tommy.

[*Door bangs shut . . . Bolt clicks*]

PHILIP. Wait! [*Banging on door*] Open the door, I'm coming in. Open the door!

[*Bolt flies open . . . Door opens*]

TOMMY. Now yuh talkin', kid.

[*Door bangs shut . . . Bolt flies shut*]

PHILIP [*Screaming, slightly off mike*]. Let me go! [*Crack*] Ouch! Let me out of here. Let me out of here.

[*Crack, crack . . . He screams*]

[*Bridge music*]

[*Footsteps going up squeaking wooden steps . . . Fade in with off mike sound of scrubbing clothes on washboard . . . Knock on door . . . Scrubbing stops*]

MRS. MARTIN [*Flat voice, off mike*]. Who izzit?—Well, yuh comin' in 'r ain't yuh?

[*Door opens slowly and closes*]

MARTIN [*Fading in*]. Hello, Mom. Still washin' clothes, huh?—It's me, Mom . . . I had my face fixed.

MRS. MARTIN. Yuh no good tramp. What're yuh doin' here?

MARTIN. Ain'tcha glad to see me, Mom?

[*A sudden wet slap across the face*]

MRS. MARTIN. That's how glad I am.

MARTIN. 'At's a great hello—slappin' me in a face widda wet wash.

MRS. MARTIN. Yuh dog! Yuh stinkin' yellow dog yuh!

MARTIN. Mom. Wot kin' a talk is 'at?

MRS. MARTIN. Don't call me mom. Yuh ain't no son a mine. What do yuh want from me now?

MARTIN. Nuttin'. I jis wanted tuh see yuh, 'ats all.

MRS. MARTIN. Then git out a here. Before I crack yer face again. Git out a here.

MARTIN. Why, yuh ole tramp, I killed a guy fer lookin' at me de way yew are.

MRS. MARTIN. Yeah. You're a killer awright. You're a murderer . . . sure. Ain't I got troubles enough with the cops and the newspapers botherin' me? Just leave me alone, will you? Yuh never brought nothin' but trouble. Just go away an die—but leave me alone.

[*The scrub board sound again*]

MARTIN. You need any dough, mom?

MRS. MARTIN. Keep yer blood money.

MARTIN. Yuh gonna rat on me . . . gonna tell a cops?

MRS. MARTIN. No. They'll get yuh soon enough.

MARTIN. Not me. Not Baby-face Martin.

MRS. MARTIN. Baby-face. Baby-face . . . [*She begins to sob*] I remember when yuh wuz a baby . . . I should a smothered yuh in yer crib—murderer! Now git out a here—go on git! [*Door is opened and slammed shut . . . She sobs bitterly*] Just leave me alone, leave me alone . . .

[*Bridge music*]

STATION IDENTIFICATION

NARRATOR. From an old wharf at the Dead End of a New York waterfront street, Peter Quinn, an unemployed architect, watches with troubled eyes the life of this neighborhood, where squalid slum and swank apartment house stand face to face. His particular concern is focused on young Tommy McGrath, whose leadership over the tough Dead End Kids makes him an apt pupil for the vicious teachings of gangster Baby-face Martin . . . But now . . . in the corner diner, Quinn sits with Kay, the girl from the swank apartments . . .

[*Fade into juke box jazz playing softly off mike . . . Rattle of dishes*]

GIMPTY. Two more coffees, Joe. Here . . . [*Ring of coin on counter*]
You know what I did this morning, Kay? I went around to see Del
Block about that job.

KAY. What happened?

GIMPTY. Well, we had a nice chat. He showed me some of his work—good
stuff. [*Laughs*] Then he asked me if I knew where *he* could find a
job. Can you picture that? In the year 1933 a guy who built some of
the finest skyscrapers in New York asking *me* where to find a job!
No wonder they're singing: "Brother, can you spare a dime?"

KAY. Pete, this neighborhood is getting you down. It's not good for a man
as sensitive as you. Can't you move away?

GIMPTY. Where? How?

KAY. I wish I could help you.

GIMPTY. You do help me, Kay. You'll never know how much. Listen,
Kay—I know this is crazy—but if I *could* find a job or something—
will you marry me?

KAY. First I want you to know that I love you, Pete . . . That is, as much
as I'll let myself love anybody. But I'm going away with Jack tonight.
Because if I stay, you and I will only end by making each other
miserable. We'd better call it quits now, Pete.

GIMPTY. You don't have to go with him, Kay. Nobody can make you.

KAY. Don't, Pete. I know I'm right. [*Sound of rising*] I've got to pack my
things now.

[*Footsteps*]

GIMPTY. Don't go with him, Kay. I love you. [*Sliding door opens and
shuts . . . Juke box music blends into street sounds . . . Footsteps
as they walk along street*]

GIMPTY. I'll do anything to make you stay. Isn't there some way—something?

KAY. What could we do, Pete? It's hopeless . . . Will I see you on the
wharf tonight before I leave?

[*River sounds fade in: A high tugboat whistle*]

GIMPTY [*Tortured*]. I don't know. Kay, listen to me—

KAY. Here's the gate. [*Footsteps stop*] Good-bye, Pete.

GIMPTY. Kay . . . !

KAY. Try to come tonight.

[*Footsteps . . . Iron gate clangs open and shut . . . A pause . . .
A boat whistles*]

MARTIN. Hey, Gimpty—dat's some pretty fancy-lookin' skirt you got deah.
High class, huh? [*Sniggering*] Yuh havin' fun wid 'er? . . . Well,
fer cryin' out loud, whassa matter? Can't you talk?

GIMPTY. Cut it out, Martin.

MARTIN. Lissen. yuh joik, why don't yuh git wise to yuhself? Dose dames
is easy.

GIMPTY. I said—cut it out.

MARTIN. Look what wantsa fight wid me. [*Laughing*] Crooked-leg
Gimpty!

GIMPTY. Years ago I used to think you were something—but you're rotten,
see? When I think of what you taught those kids yesterday, I want
to see you wiped out!

MARTIN [*Screaming*]. Why, yew lousy—! [*A vicious crack*] Now maybe
you'll shut up!

GIMPTY. That's all you can do is reach for your gun, isn't it? Well, why
don't you shoot? That would bring the cops running, all right. It
would bring them right to you, wouldn't it?

MARTIN. You bettuh watch yur step, Gimpty! Or you'll wind up wid a
gimp in yur neck as well as yur leg.

GIMPTY. I'm not afraid of you, Martin. I'm not afraid of you or that gun
any more. It's *you*, Baby-face, who better watch out.

[*Bridge music*]

[*The iron gate opens and clangs shut*]

GRISWALD. All right, Philip. Now stop crying. Tell Daddy what happened.

PHILIP [*Sobbing*]. They beat me with a stick and took my watch away.

GRISWALD. I swear I'll send that whole gang to jail. Would you know them
if you saw them, son?

PHILIP. Yes, Daddy.

[*Splashing of water*]

T.B. [*Fade in*]. Wow! Izzat waddah cold! My teet 'r knockin, Tommy.

TOMMY [*Fade in*]. Yeah. Yuh lips 'r blue.

T.B. I bettuh git dressed befaw I start coughin again.

PHILIP. There they are, coming out of the river. That Tommy—he's the
leader.

[*Running footsteps*]

GRISWALD. Now, you little thief—you're going to get what's coming to you.

TOMMY. Hey, yew! Le' go a me, will yuh? Whassa big idee?

GRISWALD. What makes you think you can beat this boy and get away with it?

PHILIP. He's the one that took my watch, Daddy.

TOMMY. I did not, yuh fat li'l joik.

GRISWALD. Give me that watch or I'll break your neck.

TOMMY. I ain't got it. Lemme go!

GRISWALD [*Shouting*]. Doorman! Doorman, call an officer. I'm going to have this thief arrested. [*Iron gate clangs open*] Get the police, doorman.

DOORMAN. Yes, sir. [*Door clangs shut*] [*Cab whistle is blown off mike*]

TOMMY. Aw, mister, don't toin me ovuh tuh da cops, will yuh? Oh, yuh joik—yuh're breakin' my ahm. Hey, felluhs, help me! Gimpty, help me!

GIMPTY [*Fading in*]. Listen, you're hurting that kid. Let him go.

GRISWALD. Hurt him? I'll kill him.

TOMMY [*Strangling*]. Hey, mister, yer chokin' me! Look out—I godda knife.

GIMPTY. Tommy! Drop that knife.

TOMMY. I'll stab yuh, mister. Lemme go or I'll stab yuh.

[*A grunt from Tommy ... A cry of pain from Griswald ... Running footsteps*]

PHILIP. Daddy, he got away. [*Then screaming*] Ooh, Daddy—your hand! it's bleeding!

[*Iron gate clangs open and shut*]

DOORMAN. What's the matter?

GRISWALD. Catch that boy! Well, go on—run after him. He stabbed me.

DOORMAN [*Fading*]. Yes, sir.

[*Off mike a cab whistle is blown*]

GIMPTY. Are you hurt? Can I help?

GRISWALD [*Caustic*]. Isn't it a little late for that now? Give me your handkerchief, Philip.

PHILIP. Here, Daddy.

[*Footsteps*]

POLICEMAN. What's wrong?

GRISWALD. I've been stabbed in the hand, officer. By one of these young hoodlums out here. I want that boy arrested.

POLICEMAN. Sure. Do you know who he was?

GRISWALD. How would I know who he was? . . . I feel sick. I'm going in to call a doctor. But I want that boy caught and arrested, you understand? [*Fading*] Come on, Philip. [*Gate sound*]

POLICEMAN [*Calling after him*]. I'll do the best I can. [*Pause*] Who does that guy think he is, anyhow?

GIMPTY. Haven't you heard, officer? That's the great Charles Griswald. He's Judge Griswald's brother.

POLICEMAN. Oh, that's different. You know any of these kids he was talking about?

GIMPTY. Me? No. [*Footsteps lightly fade in*] Hello, Drina.

DRINA [*Fading in*]. Say, Pete, have you seen—

GIMPTY [*Cutting her off quickly*]. Sorry I can't help you, officer. It might be any one of a million kids in this neighborhood. Maybe you'd better forget it.

POLICEMAN. Not if he's Judge Griswald's brother. [*Voice fading*] I'll ask around inside.

[*Gate sound*]

GIMPTY. Drina, tell Tommy to keep away from here for a while.

DRINA. Why? What's he done?

GIMPTY. Just tell him to keep away.

DRINA. Gosh, I don't know what to do with that boy! [*Tugboat whistle*] . . . Say, Pete, can I ask you something?

GIMPTY. What is it, Drina?

DRINA. There's a fella I know always asking me to marry him. And I've been wonderin' if maybe I ought to—for Tommy's sake. He's got money . . . What do you think?

GIMPTY. If he's got money—sure. Why not?

DRINA. That doesn't sound like you.

GIMPTY. No? How do you know what's going on inside of me?

DRINA. Don't you think I know how it feels to be in love—and want somebody you can't get?

GIMPTY [*Looking at her for first time*]. Hey, you're a smart girl . . . You're pretty, too.

DRINA. Ah, don't give me any of that taffy. You don't even know I'm alive. I hate to see you butting your head against a stone wall.

GIMPTY. What are you talking about?

DRINA. You know. Sure, she's beautiful. Pete, she's not for you.

[*Gate opens and shuts*]

POLICEMAN [*Fading in*]. Well, I got something to work on, anyway. They heard the other kids call him Tommy. Hey, girl, you know a kid named Tommy something?

DRINA. No. No, I don't . . . What'd he do?

POLICEMAN. Pulled a knife on some high muck-in-muck in there.

DRINA. Was the man hurt?

POLICEMAN. Oh, just a cut in the hand. But boy, is he boined up! Not that I blame 'im. Kin you picture a kid like that pullin' a knife! Where do they loin dat stuff?

DRINA. Yeh. Where do they learn it? Right here on this street . . . that's where they learn it. I just remembered—I got to go home. [*Fading*] So long, Pete.

GIMPTY. Yeah, in this neighborhood they learn everything . . . Say, officer, tell me something. Supposing a guy knew where Baby-face Martin was.

POLICEMAN. He'd be lucky. There's a reward for that cookie. Forty-two hundred bucks.

GIMPTY. I wasn't thinking about the reward. What I wanted to know was . . . how could a guy go about reporting him.

POLICEMAN. Phone the Department of Justice. They'd be down here in a minute. [*Suddenly*] Hey, wait a minute. Do you know where Baby-face Martin is?

GIMPTY. Colorado, the newspapers say.

POLICEMAN. Yeah. Well, I guess I better start hunting this Tommy squirt. But I'm telling you, Mac, whoever turns Baby-face Martin in is taking an awful chance. [*Footsteps, voice fading*] He's a killer.

[*Music: Fade into the roar of the elevated, the honk of autos*]

HUNK. Dis must be de joint, chief. Yeah—722—dat's duh number dat aunt of Francey gave me. She said it wuz unner duh Elevated.

MARTIN. Gee, what a dump.

HUNK. It's worse'n a dump, if you ask me.

MARTIN [*Sharp*]. Shad up. Keep a lookout while I go inside. [*Footsteps up stone steps . . . A doorbell rings sharply . . . Impatiently again . . . The door is flung open*]

FRANCEY [*A harlot's voice*]. Hey, what's a idee, keepin ringin 'at bell? You goin' to a fire or sumpin?

MARTIN. Francey! Gee, what's come ovuh yuh, Francey? You look—

FRANCEY. How do yew know my name? Who are yew? [*Pause*] Well, fuh th' love a Mike! It's Marty! Yuh done sumpm to yuh face.

MARTIN. Plastic, dey call it.

FRANCEY. Gee, I'm glad to see yuh, Marty. Come on inside. [*Footsteps . . . Door closes*] Here, dis way. Dis is my room. [*Door opens and closes*] [*An El train roars by*]

MARTIN. Hey, what kind a joint is dis?

FRANCEY. It's a house. I live heah, 'at's all.

MARTIN [*Low*]. Francey! Francey! Gee, I bin wantin to see yuh, Francey.

FRANCEY. No. Don't kiss me, Marty.

MARTIN [*Sharp*]. Whassamattuh? Aint I good enough fuh yuh?

FRANCEY. It ain't dat. It's me. I—I ain't feelin good, so I don't want yuh to kiss me, dat's why.

MARTIN. I ain't nevuh fuhgot da way yew kiss.

FRANCEY [*Wistfully*]. I ain't neithuh. [*She laughs*] Aw, go wan. Yew wid all yer fancy dames. I read about yew—inna noospapuhs. Where do I come off?

MARTIN. Dey ain't got nuttin', dem dames—no guts, no fire. But yew— yew bin in my blood, Francey. Ever since we wuz kids . . .

FRANCEY [*Wistful*]. An yew bin in mine . . . if you wanna know.

MARTIN. Remembuh de nights we used to sit down deah on duh wharf?

FRANCEY. Yeah, I remembuh. Da sky used to be full a stars an I wuz fulla dreamy idees. I wuz fourteen then, goin' on fifteen.

MARTIN. Come heah. Come to me.

FRANCEY. Ony don't kiss me.

MARTIN. Come closuh.

[*An El rumbles by*]

FRANCEY. Marty . . . Gee, what a couple a crazy kids we wuz den. Gonna get married we wuz. I bought a ring at da five and dime.

MARTIN. Yeah. Ony we didn't have money fuh de license. Gee, it seems like yestiddy.

FRANCEY. Yestiddy? It seems like a million years . . . Marty, lissen. Yew godda go way an' hide. I don't want 'em to git yuh.

MARTIN. Whatsa diffrince wheah I go? Ey got thuh finger on me . . . But I'll tell yuh what . . . I'll scram out a heah if yew come with me.

FRANCEY. Ah, what do yuh want me fer? I wouldn't be good fuh yuh.

MARTIN. I know what I want.

FRANCEY [*Laughing crazily*]. Yeah. Dis is a pipe dream I'm havin'. I'm Minnie de Moocher, kickin' a gong aroun'.

MARTIN. Lissen. I got de dough now, kid. We kin do it.

FRANCEY. But I'm sick, Marty. Doncha understand—I'm sick.

MARTIN. What's a matter wid yuh? If I got da dough, couldn't a doctuh fix yuh up?

FRANCEY. It's too late now. [*Shrill*] I can' go wit' yuh. Can't yuh tell by lookin' at me? Ain't yuh got no sense? Now stop askin' me.

[*A pause . . . An El rolls by*]

MARTIN. Why didncha git a job?

FRANCEY. Dey don' grow on trees.

MARTIN. Why didncha starve foist?

FRANCEY. Why didnchou?

MARTIN. What a sucker I yam! Twice in one day. First my mudder'n den yew! I shouldn' a come back . . . Heah's twenny bucks. Buy yuhself sumpn.

[*Crackle of money*]

FRANCEY. Baby! Dat's some roll yuh got. Yuh cud choke a hoss on 'at. Couldn't yuh spare me anudder twenny?

MARTIN. Say, what'd yuh call dis? Fuh two bits, I'd knock yuh—

FRANCEY. Awright, Marty—But—will yuh do me a favor? Fuh old times' sake?

MARTIN. What?

FRANCEY. Will yuh kiss me—here, on a cheek. Please—jus' once . . . Tanks, Marty. [*Door opens*] Good-bye.

[*Door slams open and shut . . . Fade into bridge music*]

[*Fade in with river sounds*]

HUNK. What we hangin' aroun' dis burg fuh, Marty? Too many people know yuh heah. Les go back to St. Louis, whaddaya say?

MARTIN. Sh. I'm thinkin'. [*A tugboat blast*] Yuh know, Hunk—der's a pile a tin in 'at flossy apartment house.

HUNK. So what?

MARTIN [*Low*]. Maybe we kin pull a snatch—kidnap one a dese rich kids —Dere's one called Wee-wee—

HUNK [*Low*]. We're too hot.

MARTIN [*Low*]. Wassamattuh, yuh scared? Stop yuh yammerin' and fin' out about de mugs in dat joint. Specially 'at Griswald guy. We gotta move fast.

HUNK [*Low*]. OK. Yuh duh boss.

[*Footsteps away*]

MARTIN [*Calling after him*]. Make it snappy. I'll be waitin' heah.

[*Pause . . . Steamship horn . . . Gimpty limps over*]

GIMPTY [*Loudly*]. Hello, Baby-face!

MARTIN. Whaddaya mean, yellin' my name out like 'at?

G MAN [*Fading in*]. Get your hands up, Martin. The Department of Justice wants you.

MARTIN. I ain't Martin. My name's Johnson. Wanna see my driver's license . . . ?

G MAN. Keep your hand out of that pocket . . .

[*A shot . . . A cry . . . A thud*]

MARTIN. I guess dat'll hol' yuh a while, flatfoot! As fuh yew, yuh Gimpty rat—

[*A machine gun sputters*]

GIMPTY. That got him all right. Where'd he get you, detective?

FIRST G MAN. In the side.

SECOND G MAN [*Fading in*]. Are you hurt bad, Bob? Can you sit up?

FIRST G MAN. I should have plugged him right away, Jerry. You don't give a snake like that a break.

SECOND G MAN. Anyway, we got Baby-face Martin, Bob. The department will cite you for this.

[*Running footsteps . . . Clang of gate*]

ANGEL [*Fading in*]. Hey, lookit, Spit! Duh G Men is here!

POLICEMAN [*Fading in*]. What's going on here? Who's shootin'?

SPIT [*Fading in*]. Boy, dey sure made chop-meat out a dis guy!

SECOND G MAN. It's all right, officer. Department of Justice. We had a machine gun set up on the terrace.

ANGEL. Hey—dat's duh guy whose shoes I shined!

GIMPTY. You'd better get this man to a hospital, officer.

POLICEMAN. Break it up, you kids. This ain't no circus.

DOORMAN [*Fading in*]. Hey, officer! Grab that boy. He's one of the gang that stabbed Mr. Griswald.

POLICEMAN. Where? This one?

ANGEL. Cheesit, Spit. [*Voice fading*] Look out for duh cop.

POLICEMAN. Oh, no, you don't. Stand still or I'll slug you one.

SPIT. Lemme go! I didn't do nuttin'.

POLICEMAN. Oh, no? You just beat up a boy and stabbed his father, didn't you?

SPIT. Aw, I didn't have nuttin' to do wid it. It wuz a kid named Tommy McGrath.

POLICEMAN. Tommy McGrath, huh? Where does he live?

SPIT. On Foist Avenoo between Fifty-toid and Fifty-fawt.

POLICEMAN. All right. Come on. [*Fading*] Show me where he lives and I'll let you go.

SECOND G MAN [*Calling after him*]. Hurry up with that ambulance, officer.

POLICEMAN [*Off mike, fading*]. Soon as I get to a telephone.

GIMPTY. Your partner's going to be all right, isn't he, detective?

SECOND G MAN. Sure . . . Say, you're Peter Quinn, aren't you?

GIMPTY. Yes.

SECOND G MAN. Well, thanks for the tip, Quinn. Come over to the office tomorrow and get the reward.

GIMPTY. No, thanks. I didn't turn him in for the reward.

[*Music*]

END OF ACT II

ANNOUNCER

COMMERCIAL

ACT III

[*Music in full*]
[*Riverboat sounds . . . Distantly, voices talking, laughing, an.
jazz music . . . Close up, crackle of a bonfire*]

ANGEL. . . . An' all of a sudden da shots come . . . [*Imitating shots*] . . .
a-a-a-a-a-a-a . . .

T.B. Da papuhs said dey foun' twenny gran' in 'is pockets.

ANGEL. Boy, he musta bin a smaht guy.

SPIT. Baby-face? Sure. He was tops. Public enemy numbuh one. Boy, he
had guts. He wasn't ascared a nobody. He could knock 'em off like
dat. [*Imitating tommy gun*] A-a-a-a-a. Boy, like nuttin'.

T.B. Gee, what I couldn' do wid twenny gran'. Why, I *bet* you could buy
a boat like dat un on a private pier.

ANGEL. Gee, dey got lights an' flags an' music. Some hot party, hey, guys?
Dey mus' be going somewheres aftuhwahds. Florida, maybe. Maybe
trew de Panama Canal!

T.B. Look, look—dey're dancing. Boy, ain't dat sumpin! [*Sings*] "You're
da top, you're da coliseum." Hey, felluhs, look a me! I'm dancing, too.

SPIT. Sit down. Yew stink.

[*Footsteps*]

FREDDIE [*Fading in*]. Hey, felluhs, yuh know what? Duh cops ah wise
tuh Tommy. Dey went up to 'is house. Some guy snitched.

T.B. No kid!

ANGEL. Did dey git 'im, Freddie?

FREDDIE. Nah. Tommy's too smaht. Dey come in a door, so he goes out
a fire escape.

SPIT. Wheah's he now?

FREDDIE. Hidin' out, Spit.

SPIT. Wheah?

FREDDIE. Wheah yuh tink, wheah? Wheah dey don' ketch 'im, dat's wheah.

T.B. I bet a dolluh dey send 'im to rifawm school. Dey sent me up fuh
just swipin' a bunch of bananas. Rotten ones, too. Tommy'll git two
yeahs. Tree, maybe.

FREDDIE. I pity duh guy wot snitched. Tommy's laying faw 'im, all right.

T.B. Rifawm school ain't so bad. Yuh loin a lot of tings in rifawm school.

DRINA [*Fading in*]. Freddie, did you see Tommy?

FREDDIE. No.

DRINA. Did you, Angel? Did anybody?

T.B. Not me.

ANGEL. Naw.

SPIT. Ask Freddie, Drina. I bet he knows. Dey always hangin' out togedduh.

DRINA. Freddie, please tell me. I'm half crazy. He hasn't shown up yet and the cops are looking for him. Where is he?

FREDDIE. Tommy said not tuh tell.

DRINA. But I wouldn't hurt him. You know that. Freddie, you've got to tell me . . .

FREDDIE. Aw right. I'll show you. [*Fading*] Follow me . . .

DRINA [*Fading*]. Is he hurt or anything?

SPIT. Hey, T.B. Go over to Secon' Avenoo an' see if you kin snitch some wood faw dis fire.

T.B. OK. Don' go away. [*Fading*] I'll be righ' back.

SPIT. Angel, yew stay heah an watch duh fire.

ANGEL. Wheah yuh goin?

SPIT. I'm gonna trail Freddie an' fin' out wheah Tommy is.

ANGEL. What faw?

SPIT [*Fading*]. None a yer business.

> [*The boat music plays . . . The fire crackles . . . Fade in with stealthy footsteps*]

TOMMY [*Fading in, low*]. Sst! Hey! Angel!

ANGEL. Tommy! Gee!

TOMMY [*Whispering*]. Sh! Shat ap! Wheah's Spit?

ANGEL. He went somewheahs. Whatcha gonna do, Tommy?

TOMMY. Run away. But foist I'm gonna ketch de guy wot snitched. You know who it wuz?

ANGEL. Me? No.

TOMMY. Dontcha lie tuh me. I'll kill yuh.

ANGEL. I ain't lyin', Tommy. Cross my heart an hope to die.

TOMMY. Okay. I think I'm wise, anyhow. Now lissen. I'm gonna hide in 'at empty house across a street, see? If yuh let on I'm heah, I'll put yuh teet down yuh troat.

ANGEL. Aw, Tommy, yew know me.

TOMMY. Okay. When Spit comes back, yew tell 'im like dis . . . Duh guy I stabbed wuz down heah lookin' fuh Spit tuh give 'im five bucks fuh snitchin' on who done it. Yuh got dat straight?

ANGEL. Duh guy what got stabbed wuz down heah lookin' fuh Spit . . . to give 'im five bucks . . . fuh snitchin' on who done it . . . Whaddya gonna do to 'im, Tommy?

TOMMY [*Double metallic click*]. See dis knife. I'm gonna put da mark a da squealer right across 'is face.

ANGEL. Gee! Wow!

TOMMY [*Voice fading*]. Remember, I'll be watchin' yuh.

> [*Bridge music and cross-fades back into the boat music . . . It is louder now . . . So are the voices of the party: drunk, laughing, noisy . . . Now and then a hysterical woman's laugh*]

KAY [*Calls low*]. Pete? Where are you?

GIMPTY [*Softly*]. Over here in the shadow. By the gate.

KAY. Forgive me, Pete, I couldn't get away any sooner.

GIMPTY. That's all right. It's beautiful in here. I've been watching the boat party.

KAY. It's turned out to be quite a brawl. Haven't you ever been on this terrace before?

GIMPTY. How would I get in here? Gee, this is the way people *ought* to live . . . He's not likely to come, is he?

KAY. Jack? He's tight. Sit down.

[*Sound of sitting*]

GIMPTY. Kay, did you hear what happened this afternoon?

KAY. You mean the shooting?

GIMPTY. Yes . . . Kay, I told the police.

KAY. You should have, Pete. He was a killer.

GIMPTY. I didn't do it for the reward.

KAY. I know. But that reward means you can move away from here . . . That's funny, isn't it? A man gets killed—and for once somebody gets some good out of it.

GIMPTY. Kay . . . what about us?

KAY. No, Pete. You don't know me. It wouldn't last . . . I'm afraid I'd leave you and go back to Jack.

GIMPTY. Yeah. Looks like I've just been kidding myself, don't it? Drina knew.

KAY. Good-bye, Pete . . . Will you wave good-bye to me when the boat leaves?

GIMPTY. I'll be on the old wharf.

KAY. Thanks. Take care of yourself.

[*Bridge music . . . Fade into the crackle of fire*]

SPIT [*Fading in*]. Aw, Tommy wuzn't deah. Dat Freddie don' know what he's talkin' about.

ANGEL. Hey, Spit. Dey wuz a guy heah . . .

[*Dragging a crate of wood*]

T.B. [*Fading in*]. Hey, Angel, look what I snitched . . . 'n orange crate.

ANGEL. Lemme jump on it, T.B.

[*Crate splintering . . . Then crackle of high flames*]

T.B. Whew, boy! Dat boins like a house a fire.

[*Off mike, distantly, there are a few sharp commands . . . The band suddenly starts playing "Anchors Aweigh" . . . Distant cheers . . . Laughter and cries of: "Bon voyage!" "Have a good time!" "Good-bye, Kay. Good-bye Jack." "See you at Thanksgiving" . . . Bells ring, a whistle blows . . . The chug of a ship's motor getting under way*]

ANGEL. Hey, look. Duh boat's startin. Babee! 'At's some boat.

T.B. Lookit duh dame wavin' at us.

ANGEL. Dat's Gimpty's goil. She's wavin' at 'im.

[*Music stops . . . The fire crackles*]

ANGEL. Hey, Spit, 'at reminds me. Dey wuz a guy heah . . . you know da guy what Tommy stabbed? He wuz lookin' faw yew.

SPIT. Fuh me? What faw?

ANGEL. He said he wuz gonna give yuh five bucks fuh snitchin' on who done it.

SPIT. He did? Wheah izzee, Angel?

T.B. Gee, Spit—did yew snitch on Tommy?

SPIT [*Belligerent*]. Sure I did. Wot's it to yew? Hey, Angel, wheah'd he go? I want 'at five bucks.

TOMMY [*Fading in*]. You'll git yuh five bucks, you stool pigeon.

[*A thud*]

T.B. Gee—it's Tommy! Wow!

TOMMY. Aw, no, yuh don't! Yew stay on a groun'. Yew gonna git sumpn yuh won't forget so easy.

SPIT. Lemme go.

TOMMY. Stay still 'r I'll cut yuh troat. Yuh see dis knife . . . ?

[*Double metallic click*]

SPIT. Aw, Tommy, I didn't mean tuh. Da cops had me. Don' do it, will yuh, Tommy? I'll give yuh dose bike wheels I swiped.

TOMMY. Naw.

SPIT. I'll give yuh me immies.

TOMMY. Naw.

SPIT [*Screaming*]. Hey, fellahs, stop 'im. Hey, Gimpty! Gimpty! He's got a knife!

GIMPTY [*Fading in*]. Stop that, you crazy kid! Let him go.

TOMMY. Come near me, Gimpty, an' I'll give it tuh yew.

GIMPTY. Give me that knife, Tommy!

TOMMY. Git away!

GIMPTY. You hear me? Only a yellow-belly uses a knife.

TOMMY. He squealed on me, didn't 'e?

DRINA [*Fade in*]. Tommy! Where've you been?

SPIT. Drina! He's godda knife. He's gonna stab me.

DRINA. Give me that knife. What's the matter with you? Aren't you in enough hot water now? [*Screams*] Give me that knife!

TOMMY. Awright. Heah. [*Sound of bodies rising*] Git up, you rat. Beat it.

SPIT [*Fading*]. Aw, nuts to yew, yuh punk.

TOMMY [*Yelling*]. Nex time I ketch yuh, I'll slit yer gizzard.

DRINA. Tommy! Stop it! . . . Now it's knives. What'll it be next? What's happenin' to you, Tommy?

TOMMY. Aw, I wuz ony gonna scare 'im.

DRINA. Listen to me. The cops are chasing you . . . You stabbed a man. You're a criminal. They're going to send you to jail. Don't you see what you're doing, Tommy?

TOMMY. Dey won' ketch me. I'll run away.

DRINA. You'll run away! Where to? What are you gonna eat? Where'll you sleep? How'll you live? Do you wanna be a bum?

TOMMY. Awright. So I'll be a bum.

DRINA [*Sobbing*]. That's fine. That's what mamma worked her life away for. That's what I've worked for since I was a kid. So you could be a bum.

TOMMY. Well, whadda ya want me to do? Let da cops send me up da river till I'm twenny-one? Yuh wan' dat?

DRINA. No, Tommy, I won't let 'em touch you. We'll go away together.

TOMMY. Gee, yew couldn't do dat, Drina. You're a goil . . . Maybe if I give myself up and tell 'em I didn't mean tuh do it, dey'll lemme go.

DRINA. I won't let you do that.

[*Iron gate opens*]

DOORMAN. [*Fading in*]. There they are, officer, starting fires again . . .

POLICEMAN [*Fading in*]. Put that fire out, you kids. Go wan home!

T.B. [*Fading*]. Cheesit, Tommy.

ANGEL [*Fading*]. Tommy, lookout faw da cop.

TOMMY. You know, Drina, I tink 'at's what I'm goin tuh do.

DRINA. No, Tommy.

TOMMY. Hey, mister. I'm Tommy McGrath, da kid dat stabbed dat man today.

POLICEMAN. You're what? Oh—now wait a minute—come here—

TOMMY. He wuz chokin' me an' breakin' my ahm—so I stabbed 'im—

DRINA. Let him go, officer. He didn't know what he was doing. He's only a baby.

POLICEMAN. Tell that to the judge.

DRINA. I won't let you. Take your hands away . . .

POLICEMAN. Don't you try that. Hey, Mac—take her away or she'll get hurt.

GIMPTY. Drina, stop it. That won't help. Here, come to me.

[*Pause . . . Drina sobs quietly*]

POLICEMAN. All right, kid. Let's go.

TOMMY [*Voice fading*]. Don' worry, Drina. I ain't scared.

DRINA [*Calling after him*]. Of course not, darling. I'm coming with you.

[*Footsteps*]

T.B. [*Fading in, whisper*]. Sst! Drina—Drina, wait!

DRINA. Who is it?

T.B. 's me—T.B. Look, Drina, dere's a guy at rifawm school named Smokey. Smokey—kin yuh remember dat—Smokey. Yew tell Tommy to be nice tuh him, cause dis guy Smokey he knows a lot a swell rackets fuh Tommy when ee gits out . . .

DRINA [*Sobbing*]. What am I going to do? What am I going to do? I wish I was dead.

T.B. What'd I say? I din' say nuttin! What'd I say?

GIMPTY. Shut up! ... Drina, I just had an idea. Stop crying and listen to me. [*She subsides*] I'm going to take that reward. I've got a use for it now. Tomorrow we'll go down and hire the best lawyer in town and get Tommy free.

DRINA. You think we can?

GIMPTY. I know we can.

DRINA. Oh, Pete ... Pete, you're so good ...

GIMPTY. You know, Drina, I guess we needed something like this. We're going to make something out of Tommy now, you and I together. You watch. We'll get him out and put him on the right track and then we'll go to work on this neighborhood. If it takes me my whole life, I'm going to tear those shacks down. Now I'm going to the police station with you, Drina.

DRINA. Will you, Pete? If you're there, they won't hit him or anything. They respect you, Pete. Everybody does.

GIMPTY. All right. Drina—we'll go together.

[*Music*]

ANNOUNCER

CREDITS

THEY KNEW WHAT THEY WANTED

Original Play
by Sidney Howard

Radio Adaptation
by Kenyon Nicholson

CAST

(for radio performance)

AMY	June Havoc
TONY	Leo Carrillo
JOE	John Garfield
FATHER McKEE	Herbert Rawlinson
THE R.F.D.	Hal K. Dawson
AH GEE	Elliott Reid
STATION AGENT	Eddie Marr
DOCTOR	Gale Gordon
ED RILEY	Elliott Reid
ATTENDANT	Hal K. Dawson
CONDUCTOR	Eddie Marr
NARRATOR	Frank Graham

(ITALIAN WEDDING GUESTS, including a tenor, a soloist on the accordion, a mandolin and guitar player.)

THEY KNEW WHAT THEY WANTED

Radio adaptation by
KENYON NICHOLSON

WHEN THE CHANCE came along to make an adaptation for radio of Sidney Howard's colorful comedy-drama "They Knew What They Wanted," I readily accepted. It has long been one of my favorite plays. However, as I started to work, my enthusiasm for the job lessened somewhat. Radio is understandably squeamish when it comes to matters of illicit love, cuckolded husbands, illegitimate babies, and such; and, as these taboo subjects are the very core of Mr. Howard's plot, I realized what a ticklish job I had undertaken.

After considerable thought I decided that there could be no compromise. Distortion of motivation as a concession to Mr. and Mrs. Grundy of the listening public would be a desecration of Mr. Howard's fine play. So, when I submitted the completed script—with fear and trembling, I might add—I was surprised to find the only alteration suggested by the Censor was that Joe seduce Amy *before* her marriage to old Tony. And subsequently this revision was made, in a brave effort to whitewash the guilty pair!

Once the business of censorship was out of the way, I recall no other difficulty in making the adaptation. Part of my task was merely one of breaking up the action into as many scenes as possible—moving the microphone in much the same way that Hollywood moves the camera—for the sake of variety and tempo. Instead of confining the story solely to Tony's living room, as did Mr. Howard, I used half a dozen different settings. This change of place is accomplished in the main through the use of sound. For instance, you "see" Tony's front porch when you hear a screen door slam and the rural postman's horse jogs along a gravel road off mike, coming to a stop at the mailbox. Likewise, the identifying sounds of the telegrapher's key and the puffing of a yard engine tell without dialogue that you are at the Napa depot. Of course, all this is more than obvious to the seasoned radio writer, but to a novice in the field like me, this painting scenery with suggestive sounds has been most interesting.

On an hour's program such as the Theatre Guild on the Air, the adaptor has less than half the time alloted to him than the original dramatist has at his disposal in the theatre. This necessitates considerable and drastic rearrangement of material and the elimination of every stick of deadwood. And, to my chagrin as a practicing playwright, I have observed that in several instances this tightening process has actually made the play more dramatically effective than it was in its original version.

THEY KNEW WHAT THEY WANTED

BROKENSHIRE. United States Steel, U.S.S., Presents The Theatre Guild on the Air.

[*Music: Fanfare*]

BROKENSHIRE. Tonight's play, "They Knew What They Wanted"— Tonight's stars, John Garfield, June Havoc, and Leo Carrillo.

[*Music: Up and down*]

BROKENSHIRE. United States Steel Corporation, the world's greatest maker of steel, identified by the familiar USS trade mark, invites you to listen to the Theatre Guild production of "They Knew What They Wanted" by Sidney Howard starring John Garfield, June Havoc, and Leo Carrillo.

[*Music: Up and down*]

BROKENSHIRE. And now Lawrence Langner, co-director with Theresa Helburn of the Theatre Guild . . . one of America's foremost theatrical producers will introduce the play. Mr. Langner.

LANGNER. Ladies and gentlemen. Good evening!

This week we're in San Francisco performing on the stage of the War Memorial Opera House before an audience of over 3,000. If you cross the famous bridge over San Francisco Bay and drive about forty miles north you will arrive at the famous Napa Valley, where some of the best wine in the world is made, and we shall take you there for our play tonight.

Everything about our play has the flavor of California. It was written by Sidney Howard, a Californian, born in San Francisco. We have brought from Hollywood, California, three outstanding artists, John Garfield, June Havoc, and Leo Carrillo to play the principal roles. And to add a final Californian touch, Mr. Carrillo is a son of one of the oldest families of California. We hope that "They

Knew What They Wanted," tonight's play, will be something that you will want, too!

BROKENSHIRE. And now the 500,000 stockholders and employees of United States Steel invite you to listen to the Theatre Guild on the Air production of Sidney Howard's comedy-drama "They Knew What They Wanted."

ACT I

[*Music: Show music . . . Fades for*]

NARRATOR. It is the summer of 1924, and the scene is the home of Tony Patucci, an Italian winegrower, who has grown moderately rich during the prohibition era in the beautiful Napa Valley of California. Tony's rambling one-story house stands on a knoll overlooking his extensive vineyards—and the brown hills of the coast range beyond . . . The story begins on a bright midsummer morning not long after the rural mail carrier has left a letter for Tony.

[*Footsteps on gravel path*]

TONY [*Calling*]. Hey, Joe! Joe! Come-a here! Come out on da porch! Queek!

[*Tony's footsteps on gravel*]

JOE [*Off mike*]. What you want, Tony?

TONY. Look-a dis, Joe! She's answer! Ees from Amy!

JOE. Yeah? And on pink writin' paper, too.

TONY. What I tell you! An' you say she wouldn't answer no letter you wrote for me. Well, look here! Wot's this? Read him to me, Joe. Read him!

JOE [*On mike*]. Okay . . . keep your shirt on.

TONY. I keep on da shirt! You set down here on de steps with me and read him queek.

[*Envelope torn open and letter taken from envelope*]

JOE [*Reading*]. Well, she says: "Yours received, and I must say I was surprised to get it. I don't make it a practice writing to no strangers without being introduced, but your letter didn't sound fresh—so I decided to take my pen in hand. Anyway, what have I got to lose? Ha-ha!"

TONY. Wot ees dis "Ha-ha," Joe?

JOE. She's laughin'. [*Continuing*] Then she says, "No, Mr. Patucci, to be honest, I don't remember serving you no scallopini dinner in the restaurant, but that don't mean we can't correspond."

TONY [*Explosively*]. We write her another lettera this week, huh? I gotta marry wid her, Joe—da's all they is to it!

JOE. Wait a minute . . . There's more. "You say you got a vineyard. That sounds real nice to me. Grapes always look so pretty growing. I was raised in the country myself—down in the Santa Clara Valley." Uh huh. She says: "I'd appreciate it if you'd send me a photo of yourself."

TONY [*Fearfully*]. Photo! Madonna mia!

JOE. She wants to see who she's writin' to. You can't blame her.

TONY [*Apprehensively*]. Maybe she no like how I look. Maybe she not write no more.

JOE. That's a chance you gotta take, big boy.

TONY. But where I get da photo?

JOE. You gotta go get one took, that's all. There's a guy down next to the bank in Napa.

TONY [*Sadly*]. I ain't young no more, you know.

JOE. Well, she can't be so awful choosey—slingin' hash in that spaghetti joint.

TONY. You go wid me to pitchure-taker, Joe?

JOE. I'm busy sprayin' your grapes.

TONY. Da grapes they wait! Angelo and Giorgio, they can spray. You get flivver—we go now, huh?

JOE. Whatever you say, Tony, you're boss.

TONY. Sure, I'm da boss! And we come home tonight you write Amy for me some more. Yes? I tell you wot you say. We send lettera and photo, special deliverance, huh?

JOE [*Good-naturedly*]. Okay, Romeo, if you want.

TONY. You're a good boy, Joe. Fine boy! You stay wid me here long time, huh? I treat you good like-a if I had a son. [*Suddenly struck*] Say! Maybe tonight we write my Amy—poppin' da question! Santa Maria! [*He tails off with a string of Italian expletives*]

[*Music: Bridge*]

[*Sound: Joe humming "Prisoners' Song"*]

AH GEE [*Off*]. Mr. Joe.

JOE. Well, what's on your Oriental mind this morning, Ah Gee?

AH GEE [*Fading in . . . Chinese accent*]. See what I got here! Mr. Tony's wedding cake—just came .

JOE. [*Laughing*]. Ain't it a lollapalusa? Tony's sure shootin' the works. Put it there on the table.

[*Sound: He puts it down*]

AH GEE. *Me* no get married, you bet your life!

JOE. You and me both! I don't want any part of it.

[*Sound: Knock on screen door*]

AH GEE. Mr. Joe, it's the holy man.

FATHER MC KEE [*Off*]. Good morning.

JOE. Hi, Padre! Come in.

[*Sound: Screen door opens and closes . . . Footsteps*]

FATHER MC KEE. Well, it looks like the house is all decorated for the festivities. Where's Tony?

JOE. In the bedroom, gettin' himself all dolled up like a plush horse. [*Calling*] Hey, bridegroom! Father McKee's out here! Ah Gee, you go bring vino for the Padre, huh?

AH GEE. Very good.

[*Sound: Ah Gee shuffling off*]

JOE. Sit down, Father, anything we can do for you?

FATHER MC KEE. Thank you, son. I came up the hill to have a serious talk with Tony.

JOE. Well, don't get him upset no more'n what he is already.

FATHER MC KEE. What time does the bride-to-be arrive?

JOE. She's due in Napa on the nine-forty-five.

FATHER MC KEE. Well, Tony hasn't much time.

JOE [*Laughing*]. He's been stallin' around all morning, like he's scared stiff to go down and meet her.

FATHER MC KEE [*Disapprovingly*]. Well, no wonder, conducting this whirlwind mail-order courtship . . .

JOE [*Laughing*]. Say, Father, you oughta seen him a couple weeks ago when we went to have his photo took to send her! . . . The only way I ever got him pacified was to promise to let the photographer shoot me first. They was some pictures. [*Laughing*] Mine looked like I belonged in the Rogues' Gallery ... Tony's ain't too flattering, either, but this Amy musta seen something that pleased her. The answer is she's arrivin' this morning.

FATHER MC KEE. I can't say I approve ... Joe, I didn't look to find you still here. Tony told me you'd decided to go away.

JOE. Believe me, I ain't missin' Tony's wedding.

FATHER MC KEE. You haven't been here so very long, Joe.

JOE. Five months, an' that's more'n I ever stayed any one place before.

FATHER MC KEE. Is it?

JOE. Except once in the clink, it is. I come in here to bum a meal one day an' just stayed on. They don't come no better'n Tony, he's a great guy.

[*Sound: Bedroom door opening*]

TONY. Looka me, Padre! Looka Joe ... How you like my weddin' clothes? Tony's some big sport, huh?

JOE. Boy, if you ain't dressed to kill ... !

TONY [*Footsteps*]. No to kill! For to go meet my Amy. I'm da most stylish fella in da whole worl'!

JOE [*Laughing*]. Get a loada that purple suit, Padre!

TONY. Why you laughin', Joe? Costa playnta good money, you bet! An' what you theenk of my new shoes, with them fancy buttons? Costa nine bucks. [*Ruefully*] They look much better than they feel!

JOE. How do you like your weddin' cake, Tony?

TONY [*Gasping*]. Oh, Madonna mia! Looka dat, Padre! From Frisco—special! Twelve dollar an' two bits! Looka dem little dolls. Ees Tony an' his Amy!

[*Sound: Tinkle of tiny bell*]

TONY. An' de leetle bell on top—she *reeng!*

JOE. Well, show some speed now, Tony. You ain't got too long till train time.

TONY. I'm leavin' for the depot verra quick.

JOE. You know, it ain't manners to keep the blushin' bride waitin'. I'll go crank up the Ford for you.

TONY. Thanks, Joe ... Joe, you not go with me to depot.

JOE [*Laughing*]. Tony's scared I might kiss the bride.

TONY [*Frightened*]. You ain't goin' to be kissin' my Amy, Joe. You hear dat?

JOE. Okay, Tony. I was only kiddin'.

[*Sound: Footsteps as Joe fades out, singing another snatch of "Prisoners' Song"*]

TONY. He's too fresh, dat fella, with his kissin' an' all dose jail-bird songs . . .

FATHER MC KEE. Tony, I came up to talk about this marriage of yours.

TONY. I'm glad you come, Padre. I'm verra bad scare! Ah Gee, why you stan' over dere?

AH GEE. Joe tell me bring wine.

[*Sound: Ah Gee's shuffle is heard*]

TONY. Good. My stomich *need* one beeg drink!

[*Sound: Pouring drink*]

TONY. Oh, Padre—excuse! I so nervous I forget to pour you dreenk.

FATHER MC KEE. Just a drop, thank you . . . Tony, I must tell you, as your spiritual adviser, this wedding doesn't have my approval.

[*Sound: Pouring drink*]

TONY [*Amazed*]. You no like weddin', Padre?

FATHER MC KEE. I've got my reasons for what I say.

TONY. Aw, take a pinch-a snuff! What reason you got?

FATHER MC KEE. Why aren't you marrying a woman out of your own parish?

TONY. We not got good woman in this parish. Joe is told me 'bout evra one. Dat boy he get 'round . . .

FATHER MC KEE [*Drily*]. I'm afraid he does.

TONY. So den I go down all da way to Frisco for look after wife. An' I find my Amy. She is like a rose, all wilt'. You puttin' water on her an' she come out most beautiful. I'm goin' marry with my Amy, Padre, an' I don' marry with nobody else! Here, have-a more da vino . . . No? Ees verra good.

[*Sound: Pouring . . . Tony drinks heartily*]

FATHER MC KEE. Something else, Tony, that perturbs me . . . It's not good for an old man to be marrying a young woman.

TONY [*Indignantly*]. You think anybody marry with old woman? Take a pinch-a snuff!

FATHER MC KEE. You old scalawag, why didn't you get married forty years ago?

TONY. I think you know why I didn't get married forty years ago. Ees because I'm smart . . . When I'm young I got nothin'. I'm broke all da time, you remember? I got no money for havin' wife. Now, I got my fine house. I got Joe for bein' foreman. I got . . .

[*Sound: Pouring from bottle*]

TONY. . . . two men for helpin' Joe. I got one Chinaman for cook. I got one Ford car. I got all I want, evrathing, except only wife. Now I'm goin' have wife. Not for work! No! For sit an' holdin' da hands an' havin' kids. Three kids. Antonio . . . Giuseppe . . . Anna . . . I tell you, Padre, Tony know w'at he want!

FATHER MC KEE. Aren't you pretty old to start raising children?

TONY. Eh? Tony is too old? I tell you, Tony can have kids w'en he is one hundra if he want! From da sole of his feet to da top of his hat, Tony is big, strong man!

[*Sound: Train whistle in far distance*]

TONY [*In sudden panic*]. Dio mio! My Amy is comin' on dat train an' here you keep me, sittin', talkin' . . . !

FATHER MC KEE [*Tolerantly*]. Well, you irreverent old lunatic, you, if you're bent on marrying, I'll marry you. I tried to do me duty.

JOE [*Off*]. For Pete's sake, Tony, didn't you hear that whistle?

TONY. I go! I go! [*Italian expletive*]

JOE. Hurry up! Get out in the flivver!

[*Sound: Tony bumps into chair*]

FATHER MC KEE. You've drunk too much, Tony.

JOE [*On mike*]. She'll be sore if you go down there drunk, Tony.

TONY. I'm no drunk, Joe. Only scare'. Verra bad scare'.

JOE. Bridegrooms is always scared, huh, Father?

TONY. Madonna mia! Maybe I'm seeck!

[*Sound: Hasty pouring of drink*]

JOE. You'll be a lot sicker if you don't lay off that stuff.

TONY [*Wailing*]. I canno' go for get my Amy, Joe. I canno' go . . .

JOE. All right, I'll go then . . . !

TONY. No! No! No! Oh, Madonna mia!

[*Sound: Their footsteps as Joe and Tony move out on porch*]

FATHER MC KEE [*Off*]. Tony, if you drive down the hill in this condition you'll break your neck.

[*Sound: Screen door opens*]

TONY [*Calling*]. No, Padre, I feel good now! I drive fine! [*Weakening again*] Joe, I'm scare', I'm scare'!

JOE. Get movin'—beat it!

[*Sound: Joe opening door of automobile*]

TONY. I don' want nobody for go for my Amy but only me ...

JOE. Atta boy! Here, let me fix your tie!

TONY [*With effort*]. Joe, you don' get mad if I ask you somethin'? I got verra good reason, Joe ... Joe ... how soon you goin' away, Joe?

JOE. What's the idea? You tryin' to get rid of me?

TONY. Joe, it's something I done, that's all ... You go 'way, Joe. I been tryin' for three days for ask you dees, Joe. I pay you double extra for goin' *now*, today, eh? Joe? Verra quick?

JOE. Before your weddin'? What do you think I am?

TONY. Joe, you don't undastan' ... !

JOE. Say, if you keep that poor dame waitin' much longer, she'll go back to Frisco!

TONY [*One last appeal*]. Joe ... ! Please!

JOE. Step on it!

TONY. Dio mio! Something verra bad is goin' happen with Tony ...

[*Sound: Motor starts up ... Dies away into high speed*]

[*Music*]

[*Sound: Telegraph instruments clicking off ... Indicating the interior of small railroad station ... Amy's footsteps to ticket window*]

STATION AGENT. Yes, Miss?

AMY. Pardon me, Mr. Station Agent, but this here's surely Napa, ain't it?

STATION AGENT. Yep, it's Napa all right ... You think the conductor put you off at the wrong place? I been noticin' you settin' over there lookin' kinda jumpy ever since you got off the train ... You lost?

AMY. Oh, no. I'm just waitin' for a certain party that was s'posed to meet me.

STATION AGENT [*Chuckling*]. Well, help yourself—this here's the *waitin'
room*.

AMY [*After a moment*]. Maybe you might know the party ... Mr. Tony
Patucci.

STATION AGENT. Patucci ... Raises grapes up the Valley?

AMY. That's the one. Is there any way I could get in touch with him?

STATION AGENT. They don't have a telephone line out there yet ... I'll tell
you ... The mailman oughta be along any minute now to pick up
the mail. Maybe he'll ride you up in his buckboard.

AMY. Well ...

STATION AGENT [*Chuckling*]. I guess he wouldn't mind, to have a good-
lookin' girl for company.

AMY. That'd be more'n kind of him.

STATION AGENT. You just go wait over there on the bench, and when Fred
comes I'll ask him ... Say, it's none of my beeswax, but you look like
you been cryin'

AMY [*Hastily*]. Me? Oh, no! ... I must've got a cinder in my eye. Well,
it's what I get, I guess, for stickin' my head out that car window,
gawkin' at the scenery ...

[*Music*]

[*Sound: Mail carrier's footsteps as he mounts porch ... Knock
on door*]

R.F.D. [*Calling*]. Hey, anybody home?

[*Sound: Door opening*]

JOE. Yeah, Fred? What is it? Come in.

[*Sound: Fred's footsteps*]

R.F.D. Where's Tony?

JOE. Tony's gone to town.

R.F.D. [*Laughing*]. Well, I got to get his signature on a piece of registered
mail.

JOE. What is it?

R.F.D. [*Laughing*]. It's a wife for him!

JOE. Wha!

R.F.D. Sure! I got her outside in the buckboard, madder'n hops nobody
met her.

JOE. Didn't you pass Tony on the road?

R.F.D. Nope. Never seen a sign of him.

JOE. He musta took the short cut. But how'd he ever miss her?

R.F.D. Search me.

[*Sound: Amy's footsteps on porch*]

R.F.D. Oh, here she is

AMY [*Off mike*]. Oh, how do you do? I certainly expected *somebody* would be down there to meet me! [*Enters room*] I must say it ain't my idea of the way a gentleman ought to act, leaving me hung up down at that depot. Well, as I told this postman, here, I decided to give you the benefit of the doubt. Very often plans don't work out, and . . . He was awful nice, bringing me up.

R.F.D. Only too pleased to be of service, ma'am . . . Well, I gotta get on with my deliveries.

AMY. Thanks a million for the lift!

R.F.D. Don't mention it . . . Good-bye, ma'am.

[*Sound: Footsteps as R.F.D. goes out*]

JOE. Where's your trunk at?

AMY. Setting out on the station platform.

JOE. We'll send down for it.

AMY. Thanks. I hope nothing happens to it. My wedding dress is in that trunk. I bet you didn't expect me to bring a wedding dress. Well, I didn't expect to, myself. And I don't know why I did. But I did! I just blew myself. I said: "You only get married once" and—I got a veil, too. I got the whole works. Gee, excuse me if I'm talking too much. I guess I'm kind of nervous. Naturally, a girl gets kind of fussed, coming off like this to marry a man she ain't never seen.

JOE. I know how you feel . . .

AMY. My, look at the decorations! Say, did you folks go and do all this for the wedding?

JOE. Sure we did.

AMY. A regular Eyetalian wedding!

JOE. What do you think of the cake here?

AMY. And *that!* Well, if that ain't the cutest ever! Say, it was awful nice of you to think of that . . . Say! I can see right now I'm going to like it here. That's the prettiest view out there. Is them all grape vines?

JOE. Yeah . . .

[*An awkward pause*]

AMY. This is hilly and nice round here. It made me think of where I used to live.

JOE. Where was that?

AMY. In the Santa Clara. You know . . . I wrote you.

JOE. Oh, yeah. I forgot.

AMY. We had a big place in the Santa Clara. Ninety acres in prunes and fifty in apricots. [*Again an awkward silence*] I guess I'll set down— I'm kind of weak in the knees.

JOE. Take that rocker.

AMY. Thanks. There ought to have been good money in prunes and apricots. But the prunes didn't do so good, and the apricots got the leaf curl.

JOE. You're quite a farmer.

AMY. My old man was, but he got to drinking.

JOE. That's bad

AMY. So we lost our ranch after my mother died. But I used to love it there. In the spring, when the blossoms was out, I used to climb up on the windmill at night—when there was a moon. You never saw such a pretty sight as them blossoms in the moonlight. You could see for miles and miles all around—for miles and miles.

JOE. It must have been pretty.

[*Awkward silence*]

AMY. Ever been in the Santa Clara?

JOE. Sure,—I worked there before I come here.

AMY. No! What did you use to do?

JOE. Cherries and hops. Big ranch, too. Bigger than this.

AMY. Well, you don't say!

JOE. Picked fruit up and down the coast since I was knee high to a duck.

AMY. Say, you don't talk one bit like an Eyetalian.

JOE. I ain't. Only by descent. I was born in Frisco.

AMY. I'm Swiss by descent myself. My father was born in Switzerland, and my grandfather, on my mother's side, he was born there, too. I don't know what that makes me—Swiss cheese, I guess. Yessir, that certainly is some view from your porch.

JOE. You like it out in the country?

AMY. Well, after two years working in a spaghetti joint! . . . Oh, not that I don't like Eyetalians. They always left me alone. I guess it wouldn't have done 'em much good getting fresh with me, at that . . . Say, I'm getting pretty confidential.

JOE. Go right ahead, kid.

AMY. I guess I ain't got much reason for being shy with you, at that. I wouldn't never dreamed I was going to marry an Eyetalian, though. But I guess I just jumped at the chance. I got so tired of things. I used to think I just couldn't keep on much longer.

JOE. Well, all that's over with now.

AMY. Oh, I usually know which side my bread's buttered on. I just said to myself: 'He *looks* all right in his picture,' and anyway it can't be no worse than slingin' hash . . . Who's that lookin' in out there?

JOE [*Calling*]. Oh, Ah Gee, come here an' pay your respects.

[*Sound: Screen door opens and closes . . . Ah Gee's slippers shuffling*]

AH GEE. How'd do, missy.

AMY. How do you do?

JOE. Ah Gee's our cook.

AMY. You don't say! Well, I didn't know I drew a chef. You didn't tell me.

AH GEE. Velly good cook.

JOE. Take her suitcase in the bedroom, Ah Gee.

AH GEE. Velly good.

[*Sound: Shuffling off*]

AMY. Say, I can't help wonderin' what you think of me coming all the way up here like I did, all by myself, to marry somebody I ain't never seen, only his photograph.

JOE. You couldn't have picked a better man.

AMY. Say! Don't get a swelled head, will you?

JOE. Who me?

AMY. Oh, no, nobody! I hope you're okay, that's all. Believe me, if I thought this wasn't a permanent offer, I wouldn't be here. I mean business. I hope you do.

JOE. Me?

AMY. Well, I certainly ain't referring to the Chinaman.

JOE. Say, who do you think . . . ?

AMY. Don't get sore. The minute I came in I knew I was all right. Why, I feel just as much at home as if we was old friends. Life sure is funny, though. It's luck for me I can say that now and laugh when

I say it. I ain't always been so good at laughing. I guess we'll get used to each other in time. Don't you think we will, Tony?

JOE. Tony! Say, I ain't . . . !

ANGELO [*Off mike*]. Joe! Joe! Come here!

[*Sound: He breaks off as roar of automobile motor and sound of siren is heard, drowned in wild ad lib cries of dismay from Giorgio and Angelo*]

JOE. It's an ambulance!

[*Sound: Joe running toward porch*]

AH GEE. They bling master home!

AMY. What's the matter? Is somebody hurt?

JOE. I *knew* I oughta went instead. He wasn't in no condition to . . . [*Topping confusion*] What is it, Doc?

[*Sound: Ambulance doors opening*]

DOCTOR [*To attendants*]. Here, men—easy now! Carry him in the house! Easy!

JOE. Is he bad, Doc?

DOCTOR. Both legs above the knees—compound fractures.

[*Ad lib of excited Italians continues all through this*]

JOE. Why didn't you take him to the hospital?

DOCTOR. I wanted to, but he raised such a fuss . . . It's a miracle, he's not dead as a mackerel. That Ford ploughed right through the bridge.

JOE. The poor old devil . . . !

DOCTOR. Must've fallen twenty feet, at least. No telling how long he was lying there. A neighbor called my office.

[*Sound: Mike on procession as they carry the unconscious Tony up on the porch and into room*]

ATTENDANT. Never seen such a wreck! The car was turned upside down!

DOCTOR. We found him lying in over a foot of water. Better lend a hand, Joe.

JOE. Sure!

DOCTOR. I want to get him in there and give him another needle and clean up his cuts.

JOE. Put him in his room! Ah Gee, hurry up! Turn down the bed covers. Steady!

AMY [*Completely at sea*]. But what is it? I don't get it. I don't get what's happened.

DOCTOR. Two broken legs, lady, that's what happened.

ATTENDANT. He's coming to, Doc.

    [*Excited ad lib from Italians*]

TONY [*Weakly*]. Ah-h-h . . . Ees you, Joe?

JOE. Yeah. It's me, old-timer . . . Amy's here.

TONY. Amy? Ees all right, Joe? You been makin' evrathing all right?

JOE. Sure. Everything's fine.

TONY. W'ere is my Amy? [*As he sees her*] Ah-h-h. Amy, Tony is much pain! Amy, don't be standin' way off dere! Come over here for shake hands . . . You ain't mad with me, Amy? Amy ain't mad with me, Joe?

JOE. Nobody's mad . . . Don't you worry about anything.

TONY. Den we have da weddin' just da same? Huh?

JOE. Sure we will . . .

DOCTOR. All right, boys, take him on in the bedroom.

TONY [*Piteously*]. Amy . . . Amy . . . ! Doc, you, fix-a me up queek.

    [*Sound: Door closing behind them . . . A strangled sound from Amy*]

JOE. This is tough on you.

AMY. Who is that old guy?

JOE. It's Tony.

AMY [*The truth dawning*]. *That* old guy ain't Tony! *That* old guy!

JOE. Yeah . . . it is.

AMY. No!

JOE [*Uneasily*]. It's too bad Tony never got to meet you at the depot. It's too bad he wasn't there when you come.

AMY [*With a choked cry*]. I'm gettin' out of here . . . Well, of all the—!

JOE. Now, listen! It ain't Tony's fault he had an accident.

AMY [*Gasping*]. Well, honest! This here's the worst I *ever* heard. The very worst! I—I can't get over it . . . Of all the dirty, low-down tricks that was ever played on a girl . . . This is the worst!

    [*Music*]

    [*Sound: Door opening and closing*]

JOE. Well, what are *you* doin', sittin' out here like you had a ramrod in your back?

AMY. I'm waitin' for someone to take me back to the depot!

JOE. Come on, I'll take you, if you're so hipped on runnin' out on a poor guy that's just been banged up . . .

AMY [*Flaring up*]. Say, you got some nerve bein' sore at *me!*

JOE [*Harshly*]. Come on! What's your squawk?

[*Sound: Footsteps*]

AMY. Alright, I'll show you what my squawk is. Is this a photo of you, or ain't it?

JOE [*In amazement*]. Where did you get that?

AMY. It come to Frisco in the mail to me, that's where!

JOE. Say, Tony didn't send you this picture of me, did he? Tell me! Did Tony send you this?

AMY. Ain't I just told you?

JOE. Well, I'll be a—! He must've been plumb crazy! He was so dead gone on you he was afraid you wouldn't have nothin' to do with an old man like him.

AMY. And I s'pose you never knew nothin' about it!

JOE. Honest, Amy—it's the God's truth! I admit I wrote them letters for Tony, but that was only because he don't write English as good as I.

AMY. That ain't no excuse.

JOE. You're right, it was a dirty trick—the dirtiest trick I ever heard of— an' he was crazy to think he could get away with it. Only Tony never meant no harm. He ain't nothin' but a big kid at heart. [*Pause*] I'll do everything I can to square it. You can go back to Frisco an'—

AMY [*Heatedly*]. Oh, *can* I? And what you expect me to do when I get there? Ain't I thrown up my job? Do you think jobs is easy for a girl to get? And ain't I spent every cent I had on my trousseau? [*Stifles sob*]

JOE. I'll make Tony square that, too. Now, here, cryin' won't help.

AMY. If I got to go back and wait on tables, what you s'pose all them girls'll say when they see me! And I ain't even got the price of my ticket!

JOE. I told you, we'll fix that . . .

AMY. I ain't goin' back! I can't! That's all they is to it!

JOE. It's up to you, sister.

AMY [*Doggedly*]. Why should I go? I like the country. This place suits me all right. It's just what I was looking for. I'm here and I might as

well stick. I guess he ain't so bad, at that. I guess I could do a lot
worse. If he wants to marry me, I'm game. I'm game to see it through.
[*Defiantly*] It's nice up here!

JOE. You're nice, too.

AMY. Look here, Mr. Joe, now I'm stayin' I must ask you not to get too
personal.

[*Music*]

END OF ACT I

[*Music: Up to finish*]

[*Applause*]

BROKENSHIRE. In a moment we will continue with the second act of "They
Knew What They Wanted" produced by the Theatre Guild on the
Air and sponsored by the United States Steel Corporation. And here,
speaking for United States Steel, is George Hicks.

HICKS. Good evening. You probably remember from your school days that
most of the steel in the United States is made today by heating molten
iron and other raw materials to terrific temperatures in furnaces
called open hearths. But you've probably forgotten just what those
raw materials are—and how their vast scale production and transpor-
tation provide work for thousands upon thousands all over America
—not counting those actually employed in making steel—almost
300,000 of them by U. S. Steel alone.

So, let's see what does go into those huge furnaces. There's iron
which has been smelted from iron ore, limestone and coke and then
there's scrap steel. Depending on the type of steel desired, other
ingredients are added which aid in the refining process conducted at
a temperature of 3000 degrees.

To feed those hungry furnaces thousands of coal and iron ore
miners are kept busy working throughout the year. In great limestone
quarries rock is ripped from the earth to satisfy the insatiable demands
of the furnaces. Steel scrap is collected from countless sources. And
a small army of railroad and steamship employees spend most of their
time moving these raw materials to the plants where they are assem-
bled and made into steel.

Yes, these raw materials are vital to the steel industry just as steel in its many forms is essential to the production of all kinds of finished goods from bobby pins and razor blades to structural steel and locomotives . . . essential to thousands of different industries using steel and employing millions of our fellow citizens.

So, next time you use any product of steel from a can opener to an automobile, remember—you are benefiting from the skills and energies of literally millions of men who have helped to transform the raw materials from the earth into the steel out of which come many things to make our lives more comfortable.

BROKENSHIRE. We pause now for station identification.

[*Music: Theme under*]

BROKENSHIRE. You are listening to the Theatre Guild On the Air, sponsored by the industrial family that serves the nation—United States Steel.

Tonight's play, Sidney Howard's powerful comedy-drama "They Knew What They Wanted," stars John Garfield, June Havoc, and Leo Carrillo.

And now the curtain rises on the second act.

[*Music*]

ACT II

NARRATOR. That same night, under a brilliant California moon, the Festa —the feast before the wedding—which Joe had planned for his boss, is in full swing. But poor Tony himself lies on a cot in the living room of his ranch house, his legs encased in plaster casts. The doctor sits beside him.

[*Note to Director: Throughout the scene there are sounds of gay voices, of children shouting, of music and singing . . . These sounds rise and fall at appropriate intervals*]

[*Music: Which blends into singing outside*]

[*Sound: Burst of laughter off*]

TONY. Most beautiful sound in dis worl'—Doc, ees laughter. Evrabody is havin' hot time at Tony's festa but Tony . . . You think my Amy like it . . . ? You think she have da fun? [*Wailing*] Madonna mia, but I wan' so bad to go out dere!

DOCTOR. Now look here, Tony, if you don't lie quiet I'll ship you off to the hospital where you belong. Half what you went through this morning would have killed an ordinary man.

TONY. That's right. Tony is verra sick . . . verra sick.

[*A tenor vigorously repeats the last phrase and cadenza of "La Donna è Mobile"*]

DOCTOR. It's after midnight and high time those coyotes went home.

TONY [*Indignantly*]. That fella Luigi is no coyot! He is fine music artist!

DOCTOR. It's a marvel to me that man has any lungs left. He's been howling for five hours.

[*Pause as mandolin, a guitar, and accordion strike up dance tune*]

TONY. Doc, you think mebbe my legs is well next week?

DOCTOR. Next week! I only hope, Tony, that you may be well in six months.

TONY. Six month'! [*Here, a good vigorous oath in Italian*]

DOCTOR. Tony! You don't seem to realize what a bad smash-up you had. Both tibia and fibula are fractured in the right leg and—and you talked about getting married today! You're incorrigible!

TONY. Aw! Take a pinch of snuff! Tomorra I marry my Amy and *nobody* is stopping me.

DOCTOR. I can see your bride's going to have her hands full taking care of you.

[*Sound: Screen door opens and closes*]

JOE [*Fading in*]. How you makin' out, Tony?

TONY. Verra sick, Joe . . . is da Festa goin' good?

JOE. Goin' like a house-a-fire. The way they're lappin' up the vino, it's a wonder everybody ain't stewed to the gills . . .

TONY. Italian peoples no get stewed . . . only happy. Is my Amy havin' good big time, Joe?

JOE. Sure, she is. Everyone's treatin' her like a queen.

TONY. Da's verra good! Doc, excuse, I gotta talk with Joe.

[*Sound: Chair pushed back*]

DOCTOR. Tony, I'm putting you in your bedroom to sleep in ten minutes.

TONY [*Pleading*]. Aw, just a little while more longer, Doc.

DOCTOR. I won't be responsible unless you obey me.

[*Sound: Footsteps*]

JOE [*Calling*]. I'll handle this old bird for you, Doc.

[*Sound: Door opens and closes*]

JOE. What's on your mind Tony?

TONY [*Moaning*]. Oh, Joe! . . . Joe! . . . Ees Amy.

JOE. What're you squawkin' about? She's marryin' you tomorrow, ain't she?

TONY. I'm scare', Joe! I love my Amy but she don' love me.

JOE. Give her time, can't you? She wouldn't 've stayed here if she wasn't goin' through with her end of the bargain.

TONY. She pretty burned-up mad, eh?

JOE. I tell you everything *is* all right, Tony. Just be good to her and take care of her. That's what Amy needs, poor kid!

TONY. I'm all ready for tak' care like evrathing.

JOE. From what Amy was tellin' me, she's been havin' a hard life for a girl, and if she comes through straight like she did, well, there ain't no credit due nobody but just only herself, and that's a fact.

TONY. You're a smart fella, Joe.

JOE. I dunno how smart I am, Tony, but you can't tell me much about dames, you can't. Believe me, a girl gets a lousy deal any way you look at it. Take a fella now, a young fella like me, see? It does him good to knock around an' have troubles an' all. But a girl can't stand it, because it ain't in her nature . . . I been makin' a study of dames from San Diego to Seattle an' what most of 'em is after is a home. You take my advice an' make everythin' easy an' comfortable for Amy an' it'll work out nice as pie. You're lucky you picked a girl like Amy.

[*Outside the guests are singing again, the tenor leading them in "Funiculi Funicula"*]

TONY [*Despairing, after a moment of comfort*]. Ees no good, Joe—ees no good.

JOE. Oh, for Pete's sake, Tony!

TONY. I been verra bad sinner, Joe, an' God is goin' get me for sure. He's not finish with me yet! Just for playin' dirty trick wid dat picture on Amy—W'at you think is mak' me do such a thing, Joe?

JOE. Search me. You always was crazy.

TONY. God is goin' fix me playnta, all right . . . !

JOE. I seen God let worse guys'n you get by.

TONY [*Hopefully*]. You theenk? Look, Joe, what I got.

[*Sound: On jewel box opening*]

JOE. Them's what I call regular earrings!

TONY. Real diamonds. He's four hundred dolla! I guess Amy like 'em pretty good, eh? Go call her, Joe. I'll give 'em to her right away.

JOE. Those'll make her sit up and beg. Be right back—

[*Sound: Footsteps . . . Screen door opens and closes . . . Footsteps on porch*]

JOE. Oh, here you are, beautiful!

AMY. Listen, if you can't speak to me proper . . . ?

JOE. Needn't be so hard-nosed. I'm only tryin' to be friendly.

AMY [*Softening*]. Well, maybe you are. But I don't believe in lettin' a fella get familiar—when I only met up with him this morning.

JOE [*Amused*]. You're a suspicious little dame, aren't you?

AMY. And anyhow, I don't think Tony would like it.

[*Sound: Footsteps . . . Screen door opens and shuts*]

JOE. Have it your way, sister, if you want to be so stand-offish. Come on in—Tony's askin' for you, *Miss* Tobin. Does that suit you?

AMY. Yes, it does . . . it certainly does. [*Fading in*] You want me, Tony?

TONY. Amy . . . come over here . . . you like da earrings, Amy?

AMY. Earrings? Who don't, if they're pretty.

JOE. Go over closer.

TONY. Come over here, Amy. I give my marriage present for you.

AMY. For me? Honest? Now, isn't that nice and thoughtful of you.

TONY. Look, Amy, ees for make you happy.

[*Sound: Box snaps open*]

AMY. Oh! . . . Oh!

JOE. They're the real article, too! Set Tony back four hundred smackers.

AMY. I . . . I . . . Oh, you didn't need to do that . . . [*She begins to cry*] Real diamonds!

TONY. Don' cry, Amy! Don' cry. Ees no' for cry, earrings.

AMY. Say ain't they beautiful! Oh, I never dreamed of ever owning anything so gorgeous!

TONY. Amy . . . you ain' goin' be mad with Tony for bein' so crazy-wild with love? My Amy is so good, so prett'. My Amy . . .

AMY [*Gently*]. No, I ain't mad . . .

JOE. You see, Tony! Everything's hunky-dory.

AMY. Say, what's the idea? What have you got to do with this? You're always buttin' in . . . An' come to think of it, I don't like your picture lying here on this table . . . Here, take it!

TONY [*Laughing*]. Santa Maria! She got a temper, Joe!

AMY. Take it, I tell you. I don't want it around!

TONY. Tear up the picture, Joe. Tear him up! Ees better.

AMY. No—give it to me. I'll tear it up.

[*Sound: Picture being torn in small pieces*]

AMY. Now we don't ever have to think of that again.

TONY [*Still laughing*]. Madonna . . . Da's verry good!

AMY. There ain't no use of keeping things around to remind you of what you want to forget. Start in over again new and fresh. That's my way. No memories for me. No hard feelings. It's a great life if you don't weaken.

JOE. Well, Tony, I guess you don't need to worry no more after that.

TONY [*Delighted*]. Now you know for why I been wantin' you go away, Joe, dat picture photograph. But everything is fix now. You don't have to go away now, Joe.

JOE. But you don't need me. You got Amy to take care of you.

TONY. No! No! Dio mio! Ees no good Joe goin' away with nobody for boss da boys in da vineyard . . . You don't let him go, Amy!

AMY. I got nothing to say about it.

JOE. I got to leave, Tony.

TONY. Es dem itchy feet. You tell Joe to stay here, Amy.

AMY. It must be pretty swell, being free and independent and beatin' it around the country just however you feel like. Callin' in at farmhouses for a plate of cold stew and a slab of last Sunday's pie. I guess it's a fine life if you like it. Only I never had much use for hoboes myself.

JOE [*Lightly*]. Sure, I'm a hobo! And I'm proud of it. I'll bet when Amy lived down in the Santa Clara she used to keep a dog for fellas like me!

TONY. Aw, Joe, take a pinch of snuff!

[*Sound: Screen door opens and closes . . . Footsteps*]

DOCTOR. All right, you two, go on out of here. Tony must get some sleep now.

TONY. My leg is pain me too much, Doc.

[*Sound: Steps and running water*]

DOCTOR. I've got something that'll make you sleep. Here, take this.

TONY [*Another Italian oath*]. I canno' drink water, Doc!

DOCTOR [*Laughing*]. Well, I don't think water will kill you.

[*Sound: Tony drinks*]

TONY. All right, Doc . . . Amy, you lookin' sad!

JOE. Do you blame her? She's had a tough day.

AMY. I ain't sad, Tony . . . It was a swell party and everybody had a swell time . . . And when Tony's good and strong, Doctor, and don't have to be in bed all the time, we'll have that Chinaman carry him out in the sun and I'll sit beside him and read the paper out loud and we'll look at the view and feel that nice wind and enjoy ourselves. And if Joe goes away—why—he goes away, that's all. Don't nobody fret about little Amy. She's going to be all right!

[*Music*]

[*Music and voices much closer indicating setting moved outside*]

JOE [*Topping noise*]. Attention, everybody! Quiet please! [*Comparative quiet*] It's late. Doc has just put Tony to sleep and wants you to go home so he can rest.

[*Cast: Ad libs*]

JOE. And don't forget—you're all invited back tomorrow for the wedding! Plenty eats and vino!

[*Cast: Laughter . . . Ad libs: "Si, si, Joe!" "Come sta, Antonio!" 'Poveretto!" "Ha tanto sofferto!" "Buena notte!" etc. . . . Sound of movement as crowd starts to go*]

AMY [*Fading in*]. Wait a minute! I want to tell you all good night! I've had the very best welcome that ever was and I'm the happiest girl in the world because you've been so good to me.

[*Cast: Applause*]

[*Voices: "Siamo molto contenti!" "Com' è bella!" "Com' è simpatica!" "Grazie tanto, Amy!" "Grazie a Tony!"*]

JOE [*Laughing*]. They say thanks right back to you! [*To crowd*] Beat it now! Buena notte! Run along. Come back tomorrow. That's the *big* day!

[*Music: As they go down the hill, tenor, mandolins, concertina, and chorus strike into song . . . Gradually becomes fainter as they go*]

AMY. It's all just like in the movies, ain't it?

JOE. It's late. You'd better go in and get some sleep yourself.

[*Sound: Night sounds, crickets, etc.*]

AMY. All right.

JOE. Well, good-night.

AMY. Good-night.

JOE. Just keep a stiff upper lip. Everything's going to turn out okay for you.

AMY. You certainly think you know everything, don't you?

JOE [*Irritably*]. What's got your back up now?

AMY. Oh, let it go. I guess I don't feel so good. [*Taking deep breaths*] This cool air ought to help.

JOE. Maybe it's the vino; it don't agree with some folks.

AMY. I guess I'm just nervous.

JOE. No wonder. Takin' a big, important step like gettin' married.

AMY. It's—well everything's so new and different . . .

JOE. But I wouldn't let it get me down if I was you.

AMY. Don't worry none about me, Mister Joe!

JOE. That's the spirit. Good-night.

AMY. Good-night.

[*Sound: Joe takes several steps, then stops . . . A dog howls in distance*]

JOE. Say, look here, Amy.

AMY. I don't remember giving you leave to use my Christian name.

JOE. It's a pretty name. Are you ashamed of it?

AMY. No, I'm not ashamed. Amy—it's French for Beloved. Beloved.

JOE. Listen, kid, there's something I want to ask you before I go away. I'm pullin' out in the morning right after the ceremony.

AMY [*Strained*]. Where do you think of goin'?

JOE. I ain't decided yet. It don't matter. North or south—it's all the same to me. I've been here too long as it is.

[*Sound: Train whistle in distance*]

AMY. What do you have to ask me?

JOE. You like Tony all right, don't you?

AMY. I let him give me jewelry, didn't I? A self-respecting girl don't accept jewelry from a man unless she's going to marry him. Not real jewelry.

JOE. I know that . . . only . . . it ain't just what I mean. Because Tony, oh, he's a funny guy an' all that, but salt of the earth, Tony is. I wouldn't like to see him unhappy or gettin' his feelings hurt or anything in that line . . .

AMY. Oh, you wouldn't?

JOE. No, an' it's all up to you now . . .

AMY [*Sharply*]. I ain't been complaining about him that I remember!

JOE. Don't get sore.

AMY. Who's sore? I know what I'm about, see? I want a home, see? Well, I got a home, ain't I? You be on your way and mind your **own** business.

JOE. Needn't get so huffy . . .

AMY. I'm satisfied! I didn't come up here . . . like I did . . . looking for love . . . or . . . anything like that.

JOE. Well, I'm glad you got so much sense.

AMY [*Bridling*]. I don't know what kind of a girl you take me for . . .

JOE. You're a great girl, Amy, and I'm all for you.

AMY. I can get along without your pattin' me on the shoulder.

JOE. Don't be so touchy!

[*Voices: Voices of guests have died away . . . In far distance tenor begins "Maria Maria"*]

JOE. That guy'll be singin' all night . . . Moonlight sure makes 'em crazy. [*Pause*]

AMY. Joe . . .

JOE. What?

AMY. There's something I got to ask *you*.

JOE. Shoot . . .

AMY. You got to tell *me* the *truth* this time. You just got to . . . You really didn't know nothing about him sending me that photo of you instead of his own, did you? You didn't know nothing at all about that?

JOE. Honest I didn't . . . I swear it . . .

AMY. On your sacred word of honor?

JOE. Honest.

AMY. I'm glad. And I want to apologize for what I said, about your being a common hobo and all. I'm sorry, Joe. Will you forgive me?

JOE. Forget it.

AMY. I wouldn't want to have you go away tomorrow thinking what a mean character I got.

JOE. Nothing like that.

AMY. You mean it?

JOE. Sure I do . . . [*Pause*] You're crying . . . What's the matter, kid?

AMY. Nothing. I'm all right.

[*Sound: Repeat train whistle*]

JOE. Come on, don't let it lick you. Just make the best of things.

AMY. I'm trying to . . . honest, I'm trying to.

JOE. You're marrying a good man. I know it's no picnic with Tony smashed up and all . . . But you just hang on, it'll work out . . . You'll see.

AMY. I bet you're laughing at me.

JOE. I ain't, Amy. I'm sorry, on the level I am . . . You're shaking.

AMY [*Breathlessly*]. Don't touch me, please don't.

JOE [*Hoarsely*]. Say, you're all right, Amy. You're plum all right.

AMY. I always was until I came up here.

JOE. Come on, buck up . . .

AMY. I wish I was dead, Joe. I wish I was dead.

JOE. Don't talk that way, Amy. Honey, don't cry . . . Gee, you're sweet . . . !

AMY. Oh, Joe, don't say that . . . You mustn't!

JOE [*Whispering*]. I can't help it. Gee, you're sweet.

AMY [*Half sobbing*]. Oh, Joe . . . hold me tight . . . hold me tight!

[*Music: Bridge*]

END OF ACT II

[*Music: Up to finish*]

[*Applause*]

BROKENSHIRE. In a moment we will continue with the third act of "They Knew What They Wanted" produced by the Theatre Guild on the Air and sponsored by the United States Steel Corporation. And here again speaking for United States Steel is George Hicks.

HICKS. Tonight we want you, our radio audience, to meet the owners of the United States Steel Corporation—the people whose invested savings provide the essential tools of production and make possible the employment of hundreds of thousands—including myself. We're sorry we won't be able to introduce each of these owners to you by name [*Pause*] because there are exactly 225,884 of them! 98,979 women, 94,214 men and the balance institutional stockholders, such as banks, insurance companies, schools, colleges and hospitals. Their average holdings are fifty-four and a half shares.

But I can tell you this much about these more than 225,000 owners of U. S. Steel. They represent a good cross-section of America—they may be found in every part of the country. In large cities, in small towns, and on the nation's farms. Among these stockholders may be your next-door neighbor, your grocer, your doctor or your insurance company. It's quite possible that your local hospital or the college which your children attend have invested some part of their funds in U. S. Steel. That's why I think you will now agree that introducing you to the owners of U. S. Steel is a good deal like introducing you to America itself—for it is apparent that through all these stockholders—its employees and their families (a great many of whom are stockholders)—millions of Americans have a direct or important indirect interest in the affairs and the progress of U. S. Steel.

And I think you'll now be better able to understand why the management of U. S. Steel faces a three-fold responsibility. For it must conduct the affairs of the Corporation so as to satisfy the best interests —of the nation, of the stockholding owners and of its employees. And so, in the future, as it has in the past, U. S. Steel will continue to strive to meet its responsibilities to the three groups, and in so doing, will serve our nation.

BROKENSHIRE. And now the curtain rises on Act III of Sidney Howard's famous comedy-drama "They Knew What They Wanted" starring John Garfield, June Havoc, and Leo Carrillo, produced by the Theatre

Guild on the Air and sponsored by the United States Steel Corporation.

[*Music: Show music into Act III*]

ACT III

NARRATOR. In spite of his serious injury, Tony married Amy the next day It is now two months later; Joe has stayed on to manage the ranch until Tony can be up and about. The grapes in Tony's vineyard are large and purple, ready for harvesting. As the scene opens, the late afternoon sun is streaming in at the open door, and Tony is reclining contentedly in a wheelchair, his crutches lying on the floor beside him.

[*Sound: Mandolin being played far off . . . Italian folk song*]

TONY. You want see me walkin', Doc?

[*Sound: Tony picking up crutches*]

DOCTOR. You stay off those legs!

TONY. Da crutch he go fine. Looka!

[*Sound: Walking on crutches*]

DOCTOR. No, you stay put, my friend . . . Mrs. Patucci, if anybody had told me that day I dug your husband out from under that automobile that I'd have him on crutches in two short months . . . !

TONY. My Amy is da best nurse I never see! She could nurse a dead man back to hees life!

DOCTOR. She looks worn out. You know, Tony, you're a handful to take care of and—Do you feel up to par, Mrs. Patucci?

AMY. Oh, sure . . . I'm just fine.

DOCTOR. Mrs. Patucci, you'd better come down to my office tomorrow and let me look you over. Give you a thorough check-up . . . just as a precaution.

AMY. It ain't necessary, Doc—honest . . .

TONY. Now, Amy, you do what Doc say! If he thinks you need check-em-up, you gotta get it, see?

DOCTOR. Oh, I don't imagine it's anything, Tony, but—

TONY. She faint the other day—

AMY. Oh, faintin's nothing.

TONY [*With determination*]. Ees no matter! Tomorrow mornin' first thing I make Joe drive her down to Napa for to see you, Doc . . . Santa Maria, we ain't take no chances on da seeckness . . . Madonna mia, I ain't havin' nothin' happen to my Amy . . . ! No, sir!

[*Music*]

[*Sound: Street noises . . . Honk of auto horns, pedestrians' conversation, etc. above sounds . . . On mike, Joe singing snatch of "Prisoners' Song"*]

[*Sound: Car door opening*]

AMY. Let's get back to the ranch, Joe.

[*Sound: Car door closing*]

JOE. What's the rush?

AMY. Let's get back.

[*Sound: Car starting and driving off . . . Rest of scene played over hum of motor*]

JOE. Say what's the matter? You look white as a sheet. How'd you make out with the doctor?

AMY. If you go wrong, you're gonna get it sooner or later. I got it sooner, that's all.

JOE [*Puzzled*]. What are you talking about anyway?

AMY [*Distractedly*]. I don't know how to tell you, Joe . . . I don't know how I'm ever goin' to tell Tony, either . . . I'm in trouble . . . The doctor just told me—

JOE. The doctor!—You mean—you're goin' to—! That I—!

AMY [*Breaking in*]. Joe, what are we goin' to do . . . ? It'll kill Tony— just kill him! And him bein' so good to me, too . . . ! I must've been crazy that night before the wedding.

JOE. I guess we was both crazy . . . but there's no use sayin' that now . . . The one we got to think about is Tony.

AMY. Maybe it wouldn't be so bad if I didn't love him. And I do love Tony, Joe! He's been so sweet and kind . . . kinder than anybody's ever been to me—in my life.

JOE. Don't I feel the same? I'm a swell guy, ain't I? To do a thing like that to a fella like Tony! A swell guy!

AMY. Tony'll be crazy when he hears—just wild! [*Breaking into tears*]

JOE [*Miserably*]. Being sorry ain't goin' to help now . . .

AMY. Naturally—after this—I can't stay with Tony no longer.

JOE. Course you can't . . .

AMY. And I ain't got no money . . . There's my earrings, but now I ain't got no right to them either . . .

JOE. I got a little money saved . . . Tony made me do it . . . I'll take you away if you want . . .

AMY. I gotta get away from here!

JOE. I guess we don't have any choice now.

AMY. Gee, it's funny, ain't it? This is the first time we been alone together since that night before the wedding . . . But poor Tony'll be thinkin' that right along you and me . . . Oh, Joe, ain't this a terrible fix to be in!

JOE [*Ironically*]. I seen better. Yessir, I must say—I seen a lot better.

[*Sound: Hold on sound of motor a few beats*]

[*Music: Bridge*]

TONY. Amy . . . Amy . . . I been worry. I wait so long time for you come from doctor. Tak-a off da hat and sit down beside me . . . I like to see da sunshine in your hair. W'at da doc say? You no seeck, huh?

AMY [*Strained*]. No, Tony.

TONY. See? W'at I tell you! Doc, he don' know nothin'! Why Joe no come in with you?

AMY. Joe is packing to go away.

TONY. Dat boy mak' me very unhappy. Why he goin' 'way for like dat?

AMY [*Blurts it out*]. Somethin' awful's happened, Tony. I'm goin' to tell you exactly what it is, because I ain't havin' you thinkin' afterwards that I ain't been happy here . . . happier than I ever been in my whole life.

TONY [*Alarmed*]. Amy!! What you sayin'?

AMY. I don't want you blamin' Joe no more'n you blame me.

TONY. I no undrastan' . . .

AMY. I've got to leave here! But it ain't because I don't love you. I do.

TONY. Amy! W'at you talkin' 'bout goin' away!

AMY. Listen to me, Tony! You're goin' to kick me out when you hear me and it's only right you do. I'm going to have a baby, Tony . . . And it's—it's Joe's baby.

TONY [*Faltering*]. Dio mio! Dio mio! No! Amy, you fool with me! Eh?

AMY. No, I'm not fooling. It's so. And that's why I'm going away, Tony.

TONY. You been lovin' Joe!

AMY. No—I ain't—I ain't! I never loved Joe. Honest, I never. And he doesn't love me. I was crazy. I been straight all my life. Only that one night, when I first come here. The night before we was married. I ain't even spoke to Joe alone since then until today in the car.

TONY [*Anger mounting*]. You lyin'!

AMY. I swear I ain't!

TONY. You goin' away with Joe!

AMY. I don't know. I don't know what to do.

[*Sound: Screen door opens and closes . . . Footsteps*]

JOE [*Fading in*]. Go on out, Amy—let me talk to Tony.

AMY. I already told him—everything . . .

TONY. Joe, I'm goin' to kill you!

JOE. Go on, Amy—get out!

TONY. No! She stay here for see me kill you!

JOE. Aw, Tony—killin' me won't help any. I wish it would. They'd only string you up—and I'm not worth . . .

TONY [*A frenzied burst of invective in Italian*].

AMY [*Pleading*]. Tony, we'll go away! You'll never see us again. You can't ruin your life for us!

JOE. Tony, I don't know what got into me . . . ! It's a fine time to tell you, but I'm sorrier for this than anything I ever did in my life!

TONY. *Sorry!* You low-down snake-in-the-grass.

JOE [*Low*]. Sure. I'm everything you want to call me—and more, too.

TONY. You know how I felt about Amy . . . and looka what you done to me! [*Roaring*] I tell you I kill you for this!

[*Sound: Clatter of crutches as Tony struggles to rise*]

AMY. Tony—be careful!

TONY. I get my gun and shoot you! [*More Italian*]

[*Sound: Clatter of crutches*]

JOE. Tony—take it easy!! Your legs! Cut it out!

AMY. Joe! He'll fall—he'll hurt himself!

JOE. Tony—! You gone crazy! You're out of your head!

AMY [*Screaming*]. Catch him!!!

TONY [*Frenzied Italian oaths, which break into sobs* ...].

[*Sound: Heavy body falling to floor*]

AMY [*Crying*]. Oh, Tony—Tony—what have we done to you!

JOE. Help me get him back on the cot!

AMY. We better get the doctor right away.

JOE. The poor old devil—Tony, are you all right?

TONY. I shoot you, Joe, I shoot you ...

JOE [*Bitterly*]. He's right—I ought to be shot!

[*Music: Bridge*]

[*Sound: Telegraph instruments clicking, indicating interior of depot* ... *Footsteps*]

JOE. Two tickets for Frisco—one way.

STATION AGENT. That'll be $3.61.

[*Sound: Change on counter*]

JOE. Train on time?

STATION AGENT. Far as I know. She'll be pullin' in about seven-ten.

JOE. Much obliged.

[*Sound: Footsteps*]

JOE. Well, here's the tickets, Amy.

AMY [*Listlessly*]. Move my suitcase if you want to sit down. [*Pause*]

JOE. You got anywhere to go in Frisco?

AMY. Yeah—thanks anyway! You couldn't blame Tony for takin' it the way he did ...

JOE. You know the trouble with me? I've never learned to use my head. I'm just like some half-baked kid that sees a sack of candy and grabs it no matter who it belongs to ... [*Ruefully*] Well, I got my lickin' *this* time.

AMY. What will you do in Frisco, Joe?

JOE. I can always try the docks ... If that won't work, I'll go South for the orange-pickin', or maybe down into the Imperial Valley ... It don't make any difference ...

AMY. I can get a job myself—for a while—

JOE [*Not too happily*]. Don't you worry, Amy, about that. I'll take care of the dough. I'll do the right thing if it kills me.

[*Music*]

DOCTOR. Now, try to calm yourself, Tony. I know you've been through a great deal, but—you've got to take it easy.

TONY [*Pathetically*]. W'at I do now, doc? Amy, she lef' me!

DOCTOR. Well, now, you can't say she left you, when you practically turned her out.

TONY. No! I not turned her out!

DOCTOR. Understand, I don't blame you. That's a hard thing for any man to forgive.

TONY. An' me treatin' Joe all-a-time like my own son! Oh, Madonna mia! You theenk Joe take care o' Amy, Doc, like he say?

DOCTOR. No, I don't. How much money has Amy got with her?

TONY. She don't have nothin'—nothin'—but them di'mond earrings I give her. I guess she get playnta for dem in a pawn hock-shop, huh?

DOCTOR [*Pointedly*]. She might—if she'd taken them with her.

TONY. Huh? What you say?

DOCTOR. There they are on the corner of the table.

TONY [*Excitedly*]. Madonna mia! She don't have no sense at all! Why she no take dem wid her?

DOCTOR. The way things ended, I suppose she thought she wasn't entitled to them.

TONY. She got no right for not take-a my present! How will she live! What she goin' do for da cash?

DOCTOR. It won't be easy to get a job, with the baby coming.

TONY [*Suddenly*]. Hey, Doc! The Frisco train she no go yet! Look-a da clock! It ain't even seven yet. How 'bout you ride me down to da depot huh?—I give Amy cash money! I got playnta mon-ay!

DOCTOR. You can't go anywhere in a car.

TONY. Sure! Look-a here! What for I got da crutch!

DOCTOR. Sit down! You want to fall again?

[*Sound: Rattle of crutches*]

TONY. Crutch hold me up good. See?

[*Sound: Walking with crutches*]

DOCTOR [*Softly*]. Well, you take the cake!

TONY. We make it, doc! You drive like da devil, huh? We go da short cut, an' we get to depot before Frisco train, sure as shootin'!

[*Music*]

[*Sound: Passenger train in distance approaching station . . . Whistle heard above clanging of grade crossing bell near by . . . Sound of brakes being applied quickly to automobile . . . Then door of auto opening and slamming*]

DOCTOR. Look, Tony! There they are—on the platform! We got here just in the nick of time. [*Calling*] Joe! Come here to the car! Bring Amy!

[*Sound: Joe's and Amy's footsteps on cinder platform*]

JOE [*Fading in*]. Doc! You brought Tony down here!

DOCTOR. If I hadn't brought him, he'd walked!

TONY. Amy, here ees money! You no take earrings . . . You gotta take money!

AMY [*Touched*]. Oh, Tony—I can't take your money!

TONY. You goin' have da baby! How you goin' get along wid no money? Tell me dat!

JOE. I got money.

TONY. You! Santa Maria! Hoboes don' have nothin'! Amy, pretty queek Joe is leavin' you—

JOE. I swear I'll see her through, Tony!

TONY. No! Ees no good! Joe is no good for lookin' after no womans! Amy, you ain't havin' no baby in de street! No sir! Tony ain't lettin' you!

AMY [*Crying now*]. Oh, Tony! You mustn't worry about me. I ain't no good!

[*Sound: Train thunders into station . . . For a moment drowning out their words*]

TONY [*Pleading desperately*]. You ain't goin', Amy! You're stayin' here with Tony just like nothin' is happen!

AMY. I can't, Tony. It ain't fair for you!

[*Sound: Train has come to a stop . . . Engine puffing . . . Passengers are getting off*]

TONY. Yes . . . yes . . . ees good sense! Ees w'at is evrabody wantin' here! You an' Joe an' me! Looka Joe. Joe is wantin' to be free. All right! Amy is wantin' stay nice an' safe in fine house wid Tony.

Looka Tony, Dio mio, an' ask him w'at he want? Don' he want baby?

JOE. But not this baby, Tony.

TONY. W'at I care? W'at I care w'at everabody say? We tellin' evrabody he's Tony's kid. Den evrabody say Tony is so young and strong he's break both his leg' an' havin' baby just da same!

JOE. You wouldn't mean it later . . . It ain't human.

TONY [*A last frantic appeal*]. Ees human! I got nobody for give my property w'en I die. Ees for dat I want dis baby, Amy!

AMY. You—you ain't kiddin' me, are you? You're serious, ain't you, Tony? You won't change afterward, will you?

TONY. What you done, Amy, was mistake in da head, not in da heart. Mistake in da head is no matter!

[*Sound: Two short blasts of the train's whistle . . . Engine bell ringing*]

CONDUCTOR [*Off mike*]. All aboard!

AMY. Joe, I guess maybe you better go get on the train alone.

JOE [*Relieved*]. Yeah? You're not goin'? You mean that?

TONY [*Joyfully*]. Sure, she mean it! Didn' you hear her, Joe?

JOE. Yeah—you both know what you want. Okay. Well, if that's the way you want it, I'm satisfied. I guess there ain't none of us got any kick coming, at that. [*Fading*] No *real* kick! And that's a fact!

[*Sound: Conductor repeats "All Aboard"*]

JOE. Well, so long!

[*Sound: Joe's footsteps running . . . Train starts moving slowly away*]

THE END

BROKENSHIRE. The curtain has fallen on the Theatre Guild on the Air production of "They Knew What They Wanted," sponsored by the United States Steel Corporation, starring John Garfield, June Havoc, and Leo Carrillo. The cast tonight included Gale Gordon, Herbert Rawlinson, Eddie Marr, Elliott Reid, Hal Dawson, and Frank Graham. And here is Lawrence Langner again to tell you about next week's Theatre Guild play to be presented by United States Steel. Mr. Langner.

LANGNER. Ladies and Gentlemen.

Next Sunday from New York we're going to bring you Gene Kelly, who made such a success for the Theatre Guild in William Saroyan's play "The Time of Your Life," and also more recently on the screen in "Anchors Aweigh." He will appear in the hilarious comedy "Boy Meets Girl." This play by Bella and Sam Spewack spoofs certain Hollywood characters in a highly amusing manner.

I think you'll enjoy listening in next week to Gene Kelly in our presentation of "Boy Meets Girl." And now here is Mr. Brokenshire again.

BROKENSHIRE. The United States Steel Corporation hopes that you will be with us next week at this same time when the Theatre Guild on the Air will present Sam and Bella Spewack's famous satiric comedy of the motion-picture business—"Boy Meets Girl"—starring Gene Kelly and Frank Lovejoy.

Remember to listen next week to "Boy Meets Girl" and remember, too, that when you see the U.S.S. label on any product, it means the steel is good.

John Garfield may be currently seen in the Metro-Goldwyn-Mayer production "The Postman Always Rings Twice." Elliott Reid appears through the courtesy of Paramount Pictures.

[*Music: Up and down on cue*]

BROKENSHIRE. The staff of the Theatre Guild on the Air includes Homer Fickett, director; George Kondolf, producer; and Armina Marshall, executive director of the radio department. Music for tonight's play was composed and conducted by Harold Levey and the play was adapted for radio by Kenyon Nicholson.

Your announcer—Norman Brokenshire.

[*Applause*]

[*Music: Up and out*]

ANNOUNCER. This is A.B.C.—the American Broadcasting Company.

I REMEMBER MAMA

Original Play
by John Van Druten

Based on *Mama's Bank Account*
by Kathryn Forbes

Radio Adaptation
by Erik Barnouw

CAST

(for radio performance)

KATRIN	Frances Heflin
MR. HYDE	Oswald Marshall
MAMA	Mady Christians
PAPA	Richard Bishop
DAGMAR	Carolyn Hummel
NELS	Tony Miller
AUNT SIGRID	Ellen Mahar
UNCLE CHRIS	Oscar Homolka
DOCTOR	William Pringle
NURSE	Lois Holms
PROMPTER	Donald Bain
FLORENCE DANA MOORHEAD	Josephine Brown
UNCLE ELIZABETH	Donald Bain

I REMEMBER MAMA

Radio adaptation by

ERIK BARNOUW

"I REMEMBER MAMA" has a form unusual to the theatre, and of particular interest to a radio adapter because it is more characteristically a radio form than a stage form. Here is apparently an example of radio influencing the theatre. It is a safe guess that if it were not for radio, the story would not have reached the theatre in the pattern in which it did.

The stage play "I Remember Mama" is drama in the first person singular: a series of scenes held together by narration spoken by the protagonist. This kind of narrative drama is foreign to both stage and screen, but very usual in radio. Most leading radio writers have been particularly fond of narration in the first person singular. Of course, novels and short stories have for centuries used this mode of storytelling, but radio first developed its use in drama. It is a style that takes particular advantage .of the direct person-to-person quality possible in radio.

The unusual form in which "I Remember Mama" was written for the theatre therefore fitted smoothly into radio, and the chief problem became one of condensing and simplifying, rather than of "adapting."

The first need was the eliminating of several characters. The stage play presented a wider, fuller panorama of family life than radio is capable of handling in one program. There were too many members in this San Francisco family for a radio listener to be able to distinguish and remember. So the family tree had to be pruned of a sister, an aunt, a cousin, and the uncle's mistress. This meant eliminating some minor subplots, and disentangling them from the main plot. Some details in the main plot had to be changed to make it self-sufficient on a smaller scale.

Adapting "I Remember Mama" presented one other, very exceptional problem. In the opening season of the Theatre Guild on the Air, "I Remember Mama" was the only current play brought to radio with its Broadway cast. It was also, incidentally, a *first* in radio. Broadway casts

359

had often broadcast short tidbits from current successes, but in the case of "I Remember Mama" listeners were given in essence the play itself.

This gave the cast, psychologically, some fascinating readjustment problems. For one thing, when launching into familiar speeches spoken daily at the theatre, it was hard for actors to make sudden unfamiliar cuts and departures from the original. More than once in rehearsal, an actor would coast on with a speech not in the radio script—with resulting confusion to engineers, sound-effects men, director, and the rest of the cast.

Also, it was hard for actors not to pause at spots where they were accustomed to do bits of "business," like consulting a diary, sipping coffee, or just giving a disgusted look. During rehearsal there were sometimes meaningless pauses of this sort which had to be eliminated. Then it often seemed best to alter lines which had become ingrown cues for silent business. Most of these difficulties were overcome in one way or another before airtime

The climax of small confusions came not in the radio studio but in the theatre, when an actor inadvertently spoke a line from the radio script which was *not* in the play. The lines seemed to fit all right so it stayed in the Broadway production.

I REMEMBER MAMA

ANNOUNCER

INTRODUCTION FOR THEATRE GUILD

ACT I

[*Music for overture, then continue behind*]

KATRIN. For as long ago as I can remember, the house on Steiner Street had been home. Papa and Mama had both been born in Norway, but they and various relatives came to San Francisco at the turn of the century. We children were all born here: Nels, Dagmar, and I. With us for a time lived a boarder, Mr. Hyde, an Englishman who had once been an actor. Mama was very impressed by his flowery talk. He used to read aloud to us in the evenings, in the kitchen. The kitchen was really our living room—and how well I remember us all sitting there, in the light from the gas lamp, all quiet and tense, and my own heart pounding as Mr. Hyde read . . .

[*Music out*]

MR. HYDE. "Dr. Mortimer looked strangely at us for an instant, and his voice sank almost to a whisper as he answered: 'Mr. Holmes, they were the footprints of a gigantic *hound!*'" We will continue tomorrow night. If you are interested.

[*Music . . . Mysterioso chords, then resume background*]

KATRIN. If we were interested! There were many nights when I couldn't sleep for the way he had set my imagination dancing. I was fourteen at the time. Nels was fifteen and Dagmar eight. But first and foremost, I remember Mama. I remember that every Saturday night

361

Mama would sit down in the kitchen and count out the money Papa had brought home in the little envelope.

[*Music out*]

MAMA. You call the children, Lars. Is good they should know about money.

PAPA. Nels! Dagmar! Katrin!

NELS [*Far off*]. Coming Papa!

DAGMAR [*Off, but nearer*]. Coming! [*Fading in*] What is it, Mama?

[*Cat snarling*]

MAMA. Dagmar, you bring that cat in again?

DAGMAR. Sure, she's my Elizabeth.

PAPA. Elizabeth looks as if she had been in fight again.

DAGMAR. Elizabeth's a viking cat. She fights for her honor! Don't you, Elizabeth?

NELS [*Fading in*]. Elizabeth! That's an awful silly name for a cat.

DAGMAR [*Indignant*]. Silly?

NELS. For that cat, anyway. It's a tom.

MAMA. Nels, how you know?

NELS. I looked! So you'd better think up another name for him, Dagmar.

DAGMAR. I won't. He's Elizabeth. And he's going to *stay* Elizabeth.

PAPA. We could call him Uncle Elizabeth!

DAGMAR [*Laughing delightedly*]. Oh yes! Do you hear, *Uncle* Elizabeth?

MAMA. Now where is Katrin?

NELS. Upstairs.

MAMA. Call loud for her, Hans. She is in her study, maybe.

PAPA. She is where?

MAMA. Katrin make the old attic into a study.

PAPA [*Amused*]. So? [*Shouting*] Katrin!

KATRIN [*Way off*]. Yes, Papa.

PAPA. What does Katrin study?

MAMA. I think Katrin wants to be author.

PAPA. Is good pay to be author?

MAMA. For magazines, I think yes. For books, I think no.

PAPA. Then she become author for magazines.

MAMA. Maybe, but I like she writes books. Like the ones Mr. Hyde reads us.

KATRIN [*Fading in*]. What is it, Mama?

PAPA. So now all are here.

MAMA. Come, then. Sit down, everyone.

[*Sound of coins . . . Silver dollars and half dollars . . . Rapidly stacked*]

First, for the landlord.

NELS. For the landlord.

KATRIN. For the landlord.

PAPA. For the landlord!

[*Coin stack briskly set on table*]

MAMA. For the grocer.

NELS. For the grocer.

KATRIN. The grocer.

PAPA. For the grocer!

[*Coin stack*]

MAMA. For Katrin's shoes to be half-soled.

KATRIN [*Proudly*]. My shoes!

DAGMAR [*Scornfully*]. Katrin's old shoes.

PAPA. Katrin's shoes.

[*Small stack of coins*]

PAPA. Nothing much left.

MAMA. No. But no debts. We do not have to go to the Bank.

PAPA [*Worried*]. But—for many weeks we have put nothing away in the little box, for Nels to go to high school next month.

NELS. Or for that warm coat you need, Mama.

MAMA. The coat can wait. But we must save more for the high school money.

PAPA. When do you think Mr. Hyde pay his rent? He is here a whole month now.

MAMA. Is hard to ask Mr. Hyde. But he will pay!

PAPA. You sure?

MAMA. Of course! Is fine gentleman. Such books he reads: Longfellow, and Charles Dickens, and Fenimore Kipling. Of course he pay!

KATRIN. Of course.

MAMA. But even then—

KATRIN. You mean Nels can't go to high?

MAMA. We do not want to have to go to the Bank, do we?

NELS. No, Mama, no.

KATRIN. No . . .

[*Pause*]

NELS. Mama . . . I'll work in Dillon's grocery after school!

KATRIN. I'll mind the Maxwell children Friday nights!

MAMA & PAPA [*Calculating*]. Hm. Five cents an hour . . . times four . . . four times . . . carry three . . . add two . . . and six . . . and four . . . is . . . is

MAMA [*Triumphant*]. Is good! Is enough!

PAPA. Is enough!

KATRIN. Oh good!

NELS. Gosh!

MAMA. Nels goes to high school, and we do not have to go to the Bank.

KATRIN [*A sigh of relief*].

DAGMAR. Where is the Bank?

NELS. Downtown.

DAGMAR. What's it look like?

NELS. Just a building.

DAGMAR. Like a prison?

KATRIN. No, nothing like a prison.

DAGMAR. Well, then, why does Mama always say "We don't want to go to the Bank?"

KATRIN. Because . . . no one *ever* wants to go to the Bank.

DAGMAR. Why not?

NELS. Because if we went to the Bank all the time, there'd be no money left.

DAGMAR. You mean, it's like saving some of your candy for tomorrow?

MAMA. Yes, my Dagmar. Is exactly like saving your candy.

DAGMAR. When did we put money in there?

NELS. Oh—a long time back, I guess. Wasn't it, Mama?

MAMA. Is enough about the Bank. *Enough.*

[*Cable car, heard way off, has come to stop*]

PAPA. Look, the aunts just got off the cable car!

KATRIN & DAGMAR [*Hopelessly*]. The aunts!

PAPA. They're coming up the hill.

NELS. I'm going.

KATRIN. Me too.

MAMA. Children! Is not polite.

DAGMAR. Can't I go to my boodwar?

MAMA. Dagmar, Nels, Katrin: when Aunts come, you stay.

[*Music: Firmly, concluding on ill omen*]

KATRIN. I remember, every few days, one of Mama's relatives used to pop in on us, and always our one idea was to get away. When Mama's Uncle Chris came—well, we kids were frightened to *death* of *him;* only he didn't come often because he lived out of town. The aunts came more regularly. I remember particularly one day, a while later, when Aunt Sigrid came by herself. Everything seemed to happen all at once, that day.

[*Music out*]

DAGMAR. I don't feel so good, Mama.

MAMA. I see you just sit there all the time, Dagmar, with that cat in your arms.

NELS. She always has that cat.

DAGMAR. Oh!

MAMA. What is it, child?

DAGMAR. My ear!

KATRIN. Several times she's talked about her ear hurting, Mama.

MAMA. Why didn't you tell me, Dagmar? We get some ear-oil and—

[*Doorbell rings*]

NELS. If that's the aunts, I guess I'll go and—

MAMA. Nels! You open the door.

NELS. Ohh.

[*Door opens*]

Hello, Aunt Sigrid.

MAMA. Sigrid! Come in!

SIGRID [*Furious*]. Sister! What do you think Uncle Chris has done now?

MAMA. Uncle Chris is in town?

SIGRID. Is he? I'm so angry I can hardly talk!

MAMA. What *is* it?

SIGRID. You know my boy Arne's knee—that fall he had two months ago?

MAMA. Yes?

SIGRID. The man at the drugstore said it was only a bad bruise, but today it was hurting him again, so I left him home when I went to do the marketing. And who should turn up, not ten minutes after I'd gone, but Uncle Chris. And what do you think?

MAMA. Well, tell us. Don't keep *asking* us.

SIGRID. He took one look at Arne's knee, bundled him into that rattletrap old automobile of his, and rushed him straight off to the hospital. I've just come from there . . . and what do you think? They've operated! They've got him in plaster of Paris!

MAMA. Without telling you?

SIGRID. It seems the doctor is a friend of his . . . that's why he did it. No, this time Uncle Chris has gone too far. They wouldn't even let me *see* Arne.

MAMA. Now Sigrid. If they operate there must be reason.

SIGRID. They had no right to! Uncle Chris may be the head of the family but this time he's—

[*Cat snarls*]

[*A little scream from Sigrid*] Oh! That *horrible* cat.

DAGMAR. He's not horrible. He's the most beautiful cat in the whole universe!

KATRIN. Now don't exaggerate, Dagmar.

NELS. Next thing you know she'll have that cat sleeping with her.

DAGMAR. Oh can I, Mama, can I?

SIGRID. Of course not! Don't you know a cat draws breath from a sleeping child?

DAGMAR. I don't care. Elizabeth can have *all my* breath! [*A cry of sharp pain*] Oww!

SIGRID. Heavens!

MAMA. Dagmar—

DAGMAR. My ear. The pain shoots right through it! OHHhhhh . . .

MAMA. Dagmar, your forehead. It's awfully hot. I'm afraid you have fever. [*Dagmar moans*] Nels, you go at once to telephone at corner store, and call Dr. Johnson.

[*Music: Background for*]

KATRIN. The doctor came and Aunt Sigrid left—and Mama and the doctor went into Dagmar's room. Dagmar's pains got worse, and her fever shot right up to 104. I remember Nels and I sat in the kitchen and waited. I kept imagining all sorts of things that might be wrong with Dagmar.

[*Music out*]

NELS. They've been in there quite a while, haven't they?

KATRIN. Do you suppose Uncle Chris will come and whisk her off to the hospital like he did Arne?

NELS. Of course not!

KATRIN. Wouldn't it be awful! Like in a book. "The Brother and sister sat huddled in the empty house, waiting for the verdict that was to spell life or death."

NELS. How can you sit there like that, enjoying it?

KATRIN. Enjoying it! What a terrible thing to say!

NELS. You've eaten three pieces of chocolate cake while you've been sitting there. And all the time making a story out of it.

KATRIN. Can I help it if everything goes into words with me?

NELS. Seems kinda heartless to me. And—

[*Loud banging on door*]

UNCLE CHRIS [*Off*]. Hellooooo! Marta! Lars!

KATRIN [*In terror*]. Heavens, it's Uncle Chris.

[*More loud banging*]

NELS [*Likewise*]. I know.

UNCLE [*Off*]. Is nobody home? Hey—someone—answer the door!

NELS. Wha'll we do?

[*Music: Ominous background for narrative passage*]

KATRIN. Nels and I stood frozen with fear. That's how scared we were of Uncle Chris. Uncle Chris was a kind of mystery. Nobody knew where he lived. He used to roam up and down the state buying up old farms and ranches, and bullying them back into prosperity. Then he'd sell at a profit and move on again. And several times a year, he'd suddenly descend on the city in his old automobile and roar his way into our house, limping with his lame foot.

[*Music out*]

UNCLE [*Off*]. Answer the door!

[*He tries the doorknob, finds it open, opens door*]

[*Fading in*] So, is open? Then vat is—Katrin—Nels—You do not hear me calling? I do not call loud enough?

KATRIN. Y-yes, Uncle Chris.

UNCLE. Which yes? Yes, you do not hear me—or yes I do not call loud enough?

NELS. We heard you, Uncle Chris.

UNCLE. Then why you do not come?

NELS. We . . . were just going to.

UNCLE. Let me look at you. Stand tall! Um-hum. Katrin, open your mouth!

KATRIN. Ahhhhh.

UNCLE. You brush your teeth goot?

KATRIN. Yes, Uncle Chris.

UNCLE. Nels—how tall are you now?

NELS. Five foot and one inch.

UNCLE. I look up in my little book . . . hm . . . that means, two inches in six months. Good! You take care of yourself, Nels, so you can grow up and be good doctor!

NELS. Yes, Uncle Chris.

UNCLE. Where is Dagmar?

NELS. She's sick.

KATRIN. A bad earache. Nels called for the doctor to come.

UNCLE. Good doctor? What he say?

KATRIN. He's in with her now.

DOCTOR [*Off*]. I think we've seen enough now, Mrs. Hanson. Can we talk a moment?

MAMA [*Off*]. Come in here, Doctor. [*Fading in*] Right here in the— Uncle Chris!

UNCLE. How is with Dagmar?

MAMA. Is bad. Doctor, this is my Uncle, Mr. Halvorsen.

DOCTOR. How do you do, sir?

UNCLE. What is with the child?

DOCTOR. We must get her to a hospital. At once. We'll have to operate.

MAMA. Operate?

DOCTOR. I'm afraid so.

MAMA. Can wait—until my husband comes home from work?

DOCTOR. I'm afraid not. Her best chance is for us to operate immediately.

MAMA. We go. Katrin. Bring me the little bank.

KATRIN [*Fading*]. Yes, Mama.

UNCLE. What is with the child?

DOCTOR. I'm afraid it's a mastoid.

UNCLE. Ah . . . then you operate immediately.

DOCTOR [*Resenting this*]. That's what I said.

UNCLE. Immediately!

KATRIN [*Fading in*]. Here's the little bank, Mama.

[*Stream of small coins poured on table from "little bank"*]

MAMA. Doctor . . . is enough?

DOCTOR. I was thinking of the County Hospital.

MAMA. No. No. We pay. Is enough?

NELS. If there isn't, we can go to the Bank.

MAMA. Is enough without we go to the Bank, Doctor? My husband is
carpenter. Make good money.

UNCLE. If there is need of money, I pay.

DOCTOR [*Mainly in dislike of Uncle Chris*]. We'll take her to the Clinic.
You pay what you can afford.

UNCLE. Goot. Goot. I have a patient there already. My nephew, Arne.
They operate this morning on his knee.

DOCTOR. Are you a physician, sir?

UNCLE. I am better physician than most doctors.

DOCTOR. Oh, indeed . . . very interesting. Well, now, if you will have the
child at the Clinic in . . . shall we say an hour's time . . .

UNCLE. The child will be at the Clinic in *ten minutes'* time. I haf my automobile.

DOCTOR. I can hardly make arrangements in ten minutes.

UNCLE. I make arrangements. I know doctors.

MAMA. Uncle Chris, Dr. Johnson arrange. Dr. Johnson is fine doctor.

DOCTOR [*Ironically*]. Thank you, Madam.

MAMA. You go, Doctor. We come.

DOCTOR. Very well, in an hour, then. And Dagmar will be well taken care
of, I promise you. I will do the operation myself.

UNCLE. I watch.

DOCTOR. You will do no such thing, sir.

UNCLE. I always watch operations. I am head of family.

DOCTOR. I allow no one to be present at my operations.

UNCLE. Are so bad?

DOCTOR. Mrs. Hanson, if I am to undertake this operation and the care of your child, it must be on the strict understanding that this gentleman does not come near either me or my patient.

MAMA. Yes, Doctor, I talk to him . . . You go to hospital now, please.

DOCTOR. Very well. [*Door opens*] But you understand . . . [*Fading*] . . . nowhere near me, or I withdraw from the case. [*Door bangs*]

[*Music: Curtain scene, then suspense theme*]

MAMA. Nurse. Please.

NURSE [*With weary patience*]. Yes?

MAMA. You have no news? Can you not find out if all is well with—

NURSE. Please! If you'll just sit down on the bench over there, and *wait*. When the doctor has finished, he'll let you know!

NELS. Come, Mama. Come and sit down again.

KATRIN. She'll be all right, Mama.

MAMA. But she is two hours now in operating room.

KATRIN. I wonder where Uncle Chris is now.

NELS. Probably still looking for that doctor friend of his, so he can visit Dagmar later on.

KATRIN. Mama, here comes the doctor!

DOCTOR [*Off*]. Mrs. Hanson.

MAMA. Oh! Doctor Johnson!

DOCTOR [*Fading in*]. Well, Dagmar's fine.

MAMA. Ohhhh!

DOCTOR. She came through it beautifully. She's back in bed now, sleeping off the anesthetic.

MAMA. Oh thank you, Doctor! Where is she? I go to her now.

DOCTOR. Oh, I'm sorry, but I'm afraid that's against the rules. You shall see her tomorrow.

MAMA. But Doctor, she is so little. When she wakes she will be frightened.

DOCTOR. The nurses will take care of her. Excellent care. You see, for the first twenty-four hours, clinic patients aren't allowed to see visitors. The wards must be kept quiet.

MAMA. I will not make a sound.

DOCTOR. I'm very sorry. Tomorrow. [*Fading*] And now, good afternoon, Mrs. Hanson.

MAMA. Dr. J—. [*Low voice*] Come Nels, Katrin. We go find Dagmar.

NELS. But Mama, the doctor said . . .

MAMA. I see Dagmar before I go home to Papa.

KATRIN. But Mama the rules. They're awful strict in hospitals.

MAMA. Katrin.

KATRIN. Yes.

MAMA. Come around corner here. You, too, Nels.

NELS. What is it?

MAMA. I think of something. This door, here . . .

NELS. I think that's just a closet, Mama.

[*Meanwhile, closet door opening*]

MAMA. Ah. As I thought! [*Sound of bucket*] Little while ago I see cleaning woman put away bucket and scrubbing brush in this closet.

KATRIN. Mama!

MAMA. And apron too. You tie it on me, Katrin.

KATRIN. Would you dare, Mama?

MAMA. So . . . [*Water running*] We fill bucket.

NELS [*Nervous*]. Gosh . . .

MAMA. You two wait on bench. [*As though getting down on knees*]. I get on my knees and scrub along hall.

KATRIN. Keep your head down, Mama, when you pass the nurse.

MAMA. I scrub my way to Dagmar!

[*Music . . . Rhythmic effect behind*]

NURSE. Good afternoon.

MAMA. Good afternoon, Nurse.

NURSE. Say, aren't you working late?

MAMA. Floors need cleaning.

NURSE. Well, I'm glad they've decided to clean them.

MAMA. Very dirty floors.

[*Music: Up and down*]

KATRIN. As Mama moved on down the hall, we sat tensely on the bench, waiting. My head swirled with ideas. I made up a poem.

> "She waited, fearful, in the hall,
> And held her bated breath."

Breath—that'll rhyme with death!

> "She trembled at the least footfall,
> And kept her mind on death."

That's beautiful. Yes, but it isn't true. Dagmar isn't dying. It's funny

—I don't want her to die—and yet when the doctor said she was all right, I felt almost—well, let down. For a moment it wasn't exciting any more. Maybe Nels is right. Maybe I *am* heartless. "The girl without a heart sat beside her brother in the hospital corridor . . . "

[*Music out as Uncle Chris interrupts reveries*]

UNCLE [*Fading in*]. Nels . . . Katrin . . . Where is your Mother?

KATRIN. Oh, hello Uncle Chris. Have you seen Dagmar?

NELS. Did you see her, Uncle Chris?

UNCLE. Bah! People everywhere are so stupid. I explain everywhere I am special case. I am head of family, but— Where is your Mama?

NELS. I think she's seeing Dagmar.

KATRIN. She is, Uncle Chris!

UNCLE. Vat is? ? ?

KATRIN. She *is* seeing Dagmar.

UNCLE. I speak to nurse at desk for a moment. [*Fade . . . Footsteps pause . . . Fade in*]

In what room is my great-niece, Dagmar Hanson?

NURSE. When did she come in?

UNCLE. This morning. What room is she in?

NURSE. We don't allow visitors the first day.

UNCLE. Have I said I vant to visit her? I ask what room she is in.

NURSE. Are you by any chance, Mr. . . . . Halvorsen?

UNCLE [*Proudly, and correcting her pronunciation*]. Christopher Halvorsen.

NURSE. Her uncle?

UNCLE. Her great-uncle.

NURSE. Well, then, I'm afraid I can't tell you anything about her.

UNCLE. Why not?

NURSE. There's a special note here from the doctor. Patient's uncle, Mr. Halvorsen, Uncle Halvorsen, not to be admitted or given information under any circumstances.

UNCLE. Vat is?

MAMA [*Slightly off*]. Uncle Chris!

UNCLE. Marta!

MAMA [*Fading in*]. Dagmar is fine!

UNCLE. Vat you do with bucket and brush?

NURSE. Why, aren't you one of the people who were sitting on the bench there and—

MAMA. Yes, and I've seen my daughter!

KATRIN [*Fading in*]. How is she, Mama?

NELS [*Fading in*]. Is she all right, Mama?

NURSE. Of all things . . . ! I must say.

MAMA. Dagmar wake up while I am with her. She want me to promise nothing will happen to Uncle Elizabeth, and I tell her we will look after him goot.

KATRIN. Of course!

NELS. Of course, Mama!

MAMA. Is fine hospital! And now I can tell Papa all is well with Dagmar!

NURSE. Really, Mrs. Hanson, I ought to report this to the hospital authorities. The way you deceived us, and—

KATRIN. I'm sure Mama won't do it again, Nurse.

NELS. I'm sure she won't, Nurse.

UNCLE. Think nothing of it!

KATRIN. You won't, will you Mama?

UNCLE. Of course not!

KATRIN. You won't try to see Dagmar again until tomorrow afternoon?

MAMA. See her again? Oh no! That would be against the rules!

[*Applause*]

[*Music*]

END OF ACT I

ANNOUNCER

COMMERCIAL

STATION IDENTIFICATION

[*Music: From up to fade down and out*]

ACT II

[*Music: Continue under*]

KATRIN. It was a bright spring day when we brought Dagmar home again from the hospital. Uncle Chris brought us in his rattly old car. I remember he was going to leave town right away, but he'd stayed over to bring Dagmar back. [*Noisy primitive car in*] In the car were Uncle Chris, Mama, Dagmar, and myself.

[*Music out*]

[*Loud honks of horn*]

UNCLE [*Slightly off*]. Get out of the way, you old fool!

DAGMAR. Oh, I can't wait to see my beautiful Uncle Elizabeth!

MAMA. In one more second we are there, and then you see how well we have looked after him. Is not so, Katrin?

KATRIN. We certainly have.

[*Car comes to halt . . . Squeak of brakes*]

UNCLE. Here we are.

MAMA. Uncle Chris, is good of you. [*Car door opens*] You come in for cup of coffee before you go.

UNCLE. Pah! Vot good is coffee. I go get drink.

MAMA [*Reprimanding*]. Uncle Chris!

UNCLE. Marta, you are fine woman. But I go get drink. I get drunk. Good-bye, Dagmar. Take good care of you.

MAMA. Children, his bad leg hurts him. That's why he drinks.

UNCLE. You do not make excuses for me! I get drunk because I like it.

MAMA. Sure, Uncle Chris.

UNCLE. I like it! No, is not true. I do not like to get drunk at all. But I do not like to come into house with you, either. [*Growing slightly maudlin*] You have family. Is fine thing. Katrin and Dagmar, one day when you grow up, maybe you know what a fine thing family is.

DAGMAR. Yes, Uncle Chris.

KATRIN. Yes, Uncle Chris.

UNCLE. I have no family.

KATRIN. But, Uncle Chris, Mama always said you were the *head* of the family.

UNCLE. Sure. Sure. I am head of the family, but I haf no family. So I go get drunk. You understand, Marta?

MAMA. Sure, Uncle Chris. You go get drunk. [*Sharply*] But don't you feel sorry for yourself! [*Car door slams*]

UNCLE. Good-bye! [*Car roars away*]

MAMA. Good-bye.

KATRIN [*Projecting*]. Good-bye, Uncle Chris!

DAGMAR [*Projecting*]. Good-bye!

[*Car fading out*]

KATRIN. I wasn't so scared of Uncle Chris this time.

MAMA. Is fine man. Has fine ideas about family. [*Meanwhile, footsteps up a couple of wooden steps*] Come Dagmar. [*Front door opens*] We get you to bed, and then we—

[*Agonizing screams of cat off*]

KATRIN. [*Alarmed*]. It's Uncle Elizabeth.

DAGMAR. It's his song of welcome!

[*A fearful yowl from cat, nearer*]

MAMA. Nels, what is it!

NELS [*Fading in*]. Mama, it's awful. Wait, Dagmar.

DAGMAR. What's the matter with Uncle Elizabeth?

NELS. He's—been in an awful fight. Papa and I have been trying to dress his wounds but—

[*Yowl from cat, closer*]

DAGMAR [*Horror*]. Uncle Elizabeth!

PAPA [*Fading in*]. Dagmar! I am sorry, my little one.

DAGMAR. Oh!!! Papa, his eye! His eye is bleeding.

KATRIN. How awful!

NELS. We tried to bandage it up.

PAPA. The bandage keeps slipping . . . It's—hopeless!

DAGMAR. And his legs—all those bandages!

[*Starts moaning and crying ad lib over him through following*]

PAPA. I told you, we should have put him out of his misery, at once!

DAGMAR. Oh no, no! Make him live, Mama. Please!

MAMA. We see. Let us see how he gets through the night.

DAGMAR. Oh, Mama!

MAMA. Dagmar, you must go to bed.

DAGMAR. But you will fix Uncle Elizabeth. You promise, Mama?

MAMA. I promise I try. Go to bed now.

DAGMAR [*Off*]. All right, Mama.

MAMA. You have good rest.

DAGMAR [*Further off*]. Look after him, Mama.

MAMA. We will. Try to sleep, Dagmar.

DAGMAR [*Further*]. All right.

[*Yowl*]

PAPA [*Lowering voice slightly*]. You say, we see how the cat get through the night. I ask you how *we* get through the night?

[*Cat keeps up faint continuous whine in background*]

MAMA. Poor animal.

KATRIN. I can't stand it.

NELS. Shall I try the boric acid again?

PAPA. Nels, we must put cat to sleep. Here, you go to drugstore, and get something. Some chloroform, maybe.

NELS. How much I shall get?

PAPA. You ask the man. Tell him it is for a cat. He knows.

[*Door opens*]

NELS [*Fading*]. All right, Papa.

[*Door closing*]

MAMA. Papa. Is no other thing we can try first?

[*Cat gradually stops about here*]

PAPA. No, Mama, is best.

MAMA. Is sad homecoming for Dagmar. She has been so good in hospital.

KATRIN. And all the time she talked about Uncle Elizabeth, and looked forward to— [*Stops*] Oh, Mr. Hyde.

MR. HYDE [*Off . . . Seeing them*]. Oh.

MAMA. You go out, Mr. Hyde?

MR. HYDE [*Pretending surprise, fading in*]. Ah, Madame! I did not know you were back. As a matter of fact, my stay as your boarder has come to an end. I . . . I was about to leave this letter for you.

MAMA. Oh?

PAPA. So?

KATRIN. What do you mean?

MR. HYDE. Some news I received this morning necessitates my immediate departure.

KATRIN. Oh no, no!

MAMA. Is true, Mr. Hyde?

MR. HYDE. Alas, dear Madam, 'tis true, 'tis pity. And pity 'tis, 'tis true. Here is my check for all I owe you.

MAMA. Thank you, Mr. Hyde.

MR. HYDE. And here, I leave with you certain choice selections from my library—for the children.

MAMA. Oh, Mr. Hyde—

MR. HYDE. Madame, my deepest gratitude. Sir, my sincerest admiration!

PAPA. We are sorry you go, Mr. Hyde.

MR. HYDE. Child, my blessing. [Door opens]

KATRIN. Good-bye, Mr. Hyde.

MR. HYDE [Fading] Ave atque vale! Hail and farewell.

[Door closes]

MAMA. Was wonderful man! Is too bad.

PAPA. Yes.

KATRIN [Off slightly]. Mama, these books! The Pickwick Papers . . .

PAPA. How much is the check for?

KATRIN. The Last of the Mohicans . . .

MAMA. Hundred ten dollar! Is five months!

PAPA. Good.

KATRIN. Alice in Wonderland . . .

MAMA. Is wonderful. Now we pay doctor.

KATRIN. The Oxford Book of Verse . . .

PAPA. And you buy your warm coat.

MAMA. And we buy graduation present for Katrin's graduation.

KATRIN [Coming in]. Oh Mama!

PAPA. Good!

KATRIN. Isn't it wonderful.

MAMA. Is sad we shall not have Mr. Hyde to read for us, but—[Doorbell ringing]

KATRIN. If that's the aunts, Mama, can I go to my study?

MAMA [Severe]. Katrin! Open!

KATRIN. Ohh.

[Door opens]

MAMA. Sigrid!

SIGRID [Breathless]. Marta . . . has he gone?

MAMA. Who?

SIGRID. Your boarder ... Mr. Hyde ...

MAMA. Yes. Why?

SIGRID. Did he pay you?

MAMA. Sure. He give me a check. Right here.

SIGRID [*With meaning*]. A check!

MAMA. Sigrid, what is it? How do you know that Mr. Hyde leave?

SIGRID. I was at Mr. Kruper's down the street ... you know, the restaurant and bakery ... and he said that after lunch today Mr. Hyde asked to have a check cashed. For fifty dollars!

PAPA. Well?

SIGRID. And what do you think? Mr. Hyde hasn't even an *account* at that bank!

MAMA. I don't understand.

PAPA. You mean the check is no good?

MAMA. Oh no!

SIGRID [*Triumphantly*]. I mean your Mr. Hyde was a crook! Mr. Kruper said he'd been cashing them all over the neighborhood. How much did he owe you? Plenty, I'll bet.

MAMA. No. No, he owed us nothing.

SIGRID. How much was that check *for*?

MAMA. It does not matter, Sigrid. He pay with better things than money.

[*Door opens*]

NELS [*Fading in*]. Well, here's the chloroform.

SIGRID [*A bit of a scream*]. Chloroform! What's that for?

MAMA. What do you think it's for? What do you think? I want to chloroform a cat!

[*Music: Bridge*]

MAMA [*Low voice*]. Here's your coffee, Lars. Dagmar will be in for breakfast in a moment.

PAPA. What can we tell her?

MAMA. Will be great tragedy. Cover the cat with the blanket.

PAPA. If we just let her think the cat die by itself—

MAMA. No. We cannot tell her lies. Besides, whole kitchen smell of chloroform!

DAGMAR [*Fading in*]. Where is my beautiful Uncle Elizabeth? My, you sure covered him up! Come into my arms, you sweet ...

MAMA. Dagmar, you must not—[*Sudden, loud, happy meow from cat . . . Keeps up*]

DAGMAR. He's well! Oh Mama, I knew you could fix him!

PAPA. What?

MAMA. Dagmar! Let me see that cat!

DAGMAR. His wounds are healing. [*Fading*] Nels! Katrin! Uncle Elizabeth is well again.

[*Cat fades with her, full of life*]

MAMA. Is a miracle!

PAPA. You could not have used enough chloroform. We just give him good sleep, and that cures him. We rechristen the cat Lazarus!

MAMA. Lars, we must tell her. Is not good to let her grow up believing I can fix everything!

PAPA. Is best thing in the world for her to believe.

MAMA. Oh no, Lars!

PAPA. Besides, I know exactly how she feels.

[*Music: In with tenderness, then a hint of excitement in anticipation of graduation preparations*]

NELS. I wish the cable car would come. This fog is chilly.

KATRIN. And listen, Nels! Thyra Walsh's mother is going to give her a necklace! And Madeline is getting an onyx ring. Imagine, onyx!

[*Fog horn intermittently from here on*]

NELS. Who cares?

KATRIN. And you know what I think I'm going to get, Nels?

NELS. What?

KATRIN. Mama hasn't told me yet, but I think she'll give me that pink celluloid dresser set in the drugstore window.

NELS. Katrin—all you can talk about is your graduation and your part in the school play and the presents you're going to get!

KATRIN. Graduation is about the most important time in a girl's life. What else is there to talk about?

NELS. What else? Don't you realize what a tough time the family has had all these months since Mr. Hyde walked out? Mama was counting on that money. And you don't give it a thought!

KATRIN. Mama'll manage. She always does.

NELS. You might as well know now you're not going to get that dresser set.

KATRIN. What do you mean??

NELS. Mama's giving you her antique brooch.

KATRIN. You mean that old silver thing that belonged to Grandmother? What would I want an old thing like that for?

NELS. It's an heirloom! Mama thinks a lot of it.

KATRIN. Well, then, she ought to keep it. You don't really mean that's *all* they're going to give me?

NELS. What more do you want?

KATRIN. I want the dresser set. My goodness, if Mama doesn't realize what's a suitable graduation present, why—

NELS. How can you talk that way! You're downright self-centered.

KATRIN. I'm not!

NELS. Well, why talk about it? You'll probably pester Mama into giving you that junky thing anyway.

[*Music: Continue as background to narration*]

KATRIN. Nels was right. I got the dresser set. They gave it to me just before supper the night of the graduation play. I was so excited that night I could hardly eat. I had the star part in the show, and Nels was going to help move scenery. Right after supper we two started for the school. Mama was upstairs dressing.

[*Music out*]

NELS [*Projecting a little, impatiently*]. Come on! Come on, Katrin!

KATRIN [*Fading in*]. Coming! Good-bye, Papa.

PAPA. Good-bye, Katrin. Good luck with the play. I applaud loud, but you be good!

KATRIN. I'll try, Papa.

[*Door opens*]

PAPA. You know your part?

KATRIN. I think so.

PAPA. You should. We *all* know it by now!

KATRIN [*Laughs*].

NELS [*Impatient, off*]. Are you ready?

KATRIN. Coming. [*Door closing*]

[*Footsteps down a couple of steps and continue on street*]

NELS. I see you brought your loot along.

KATRIN. Don't talk that way about my dresser set! [*Admiringly*] Genuine celluloid. I want the girls to see it.

NELS. I'm glad you appreciate it.

KATRIN. I told you Mama would manage.

NELS. Manage!

KATRIN. I kept hinting about it and finally—

NELS. Yeah, I know! You made her sell her brooch!

[*Footsteps stop*]

KATRIN. What??

NELS. I wasn't supposed to tell you, but—

KATRIN. What did you say?

NELS. It's probably better you know, so you'll realize how much Mama did for you! She traded the heirloom to Mr. Schiller, for that thing.

KATRIN. No!

NELS. Sure.

KATRIN. I don't believe it!

NELS. It's true!

KATRIN. I'm going to ask Papa. I don't believe it!

[*Running steps on sidewalk then up couple of steps*]

NELS [*Fading*]. You haven't got time.

KATRIN. I don't care! [*Door opening*] Papa! Papa!

PAPA [*Off*]. What *is* it?

KATRIN. Papa, did Mama trade her brooch to give me this?

PAPA [*Coming in*]. Nels should not have told you!

KATRIN. It's true, then?

PAPA. Katrin . . .

KATRIN. Oh, but she shouldn't . . . I never meant . . .

PAPA. You wanted the present. Mama wanted your happiness; she wanted it more than she wanted the brooch.

KATRIN. But I never meant her to do *that*. [*Crying*] She *loved* it so. It was all she had of Grandmother's.

PAPA. She always meant it for you, Katrin. And you must not cry. You have your play to act.

KATRIN [*Sobbing*]. I don't want to act in it now.

PAPA. But you must!

NELS [*Off*]. Come on, Katrin. Gosh, I'm sorry I—

PAPA. Your audience, Katrin!

KATRIN. I don't care.

PAPA. But you must care. Tonight you are an actress. And an actress must act, whatever she is feeling. There is a saying—what is it—uh-uh—the mails must go through!

NELS. The show must go on.

PAPA. That's it! So you stop crying, and go and act your play!

[*Katrin still crying*]

[*Music: Tragic for a moment, then build for*]

KATRIN [*As Juliet, off, on stage*]

Three words, dear Romeo, and good night indeed.

If that thy bent of love be honourable,

Thy purpose marriage, send me word tomorrow . . .

[*Forgets next line, therefore repeats*]

Send me word tomorrow . . .

Oh Romeo, send me word tomorrow . . .

PROMPTER [*On*]. By one that I'll procure . . .

KATRIN [*Recovering*].

By one that I'll procure to come to thee . . .

PROMPTER [*On, sotto voce*]. What's the matter with her, anyway?

NELS [*Troubled*]. I don't know.

KATRIN [*Continuing meanwhile*].

Where and what time thou wilt perform the rite;

And all my fortunes at thy foot I'll lay,

And follow thee my lord throughout the world.

Tomorrow will I send. A thousand times good night!

[*Sound of roll curtain*]

[*Big applause from school audience*]

[*Fades in breathless and agitated*] Nels! Mr. Schiller is in the audience, over on the left there. I saw him! Get him, please! Bring him to the dressing room. I've got to see him! Please!

NELS. All right, I'll go get him.

PROMPTER. What's the matter, Katrin? You're all upset.

KATRIN. I'll be all right in the next act. You'll see! You'll see.

[*Music: Bridge*]

PAPA. I don't understand. Why do not Katrin and Nels come home?

MAMA. She must take off her make-up.

PAPA. It take so long? Perhaps they look for us at auditorium?

MAMA. I told them we would come straight home.

PAPA. Is hour and a half now since they finish play . . .

[*Door opens*]

NELS [*Off*]. Well, here we are.

MAMA [*Relief*]. Is good.

[*Door closes*]

PAPA. How is my Katrin? You are *fine* in play!

KATRIN. I was terrible.

MAMA. In first act *not* good. Afterwards was *good*.

KATRIN. I think I'll go right up to bed. I feel awful. Mama, I want to give you this.

MAMA [*Amazed*]. What is it?

KATRIN. Grandmother's brooch.

MAMA. But how did you—?

KATRIN. We got it back.

MAMA. What?

PAPA. Marta—tonight, after you leave, Katrin found out about your brooch.

MAMA. But how? Who told her?

PAPA. Nels did.

MAMA [*Angrily*]. But why? Why did you, Nels?

NELS. I don't know.

KATRIN. It's all right, Mama. I'm glad he did. I deserved it. I was so smug I don't see how you could all stand me! I'm going up now.

[*Bursts into sobs and fades out door*]

NELS. The poor kid! Mr. Schiller didn't want to give it back. He was planning to give it to his wife for her birthday. But Katrin begged and begged him all through the intermission.

PAPA. So?

MAMA. And he took back the dresser set?

NELS. Yes. We went to the store with him after the show. He had the brooch there. It was kinda hard for Katrin. She's a good kid.

PAPA. Very good.

MAMA. I think I go up to see Katrin.

[*Music: Short bridge fading down, continue music through following scene*]

[*Katrin sobbing*]

MAMA. Katrin!

KATRIN. I'm so selfish, Mama!

MAMA. Katrin . . . you put on this brooch.

KATRIN. No . . . No, it's yours.

MAMA. Katrin, your grandmother, back in Norway, she always wore this. It was her *solje*. And she gave it to me. And now it will be yours. It is your graduation present, Katrin. I put it on for you.

KATRIN. Oh, Mama, I'll—I'll wear it always! I'll keep it forever. Oh Mama, I'll be so proud to have it!

[*Music up*]

END OF ACT II

ANNOUNCER

COMMERCIAL

[*Music*]

ACT III

[*Music: Opening the act, then into a background for following phone call*]

[*Phone ringing, filtered . . . Lift receiver, filtered*]

SIGRID [*Filter*]. Hello?

MAMA. Hello, Sigrid?

SIGRID [*Filter*]. Yes.

MAMA. Listen, Sigrid. This is Marta. I have telegram from Uncle Chris. He's dying.

SIGRID [*Filter*]. I don't believe it for a moment.

MAMA. It comes from a placed called Ukiah.

SIGRID [*Filter*]. What?

MAMA. Ukiah. [*Spelling*] U-K-I-A-H.

SIGRID [*Filter*]. Why did he telegraph you? I'm the eldest!

MAMA. Sigrid, is no time to think of who is eldest. Uncle Chris is dying.

SIGRID [*Filter*]. He's too mean to die.

MAMA. Sigrid: There is a train at eleven o'clock. The trip takes four hours. Are you coming?

SIGRID [*Filter*]. I guess so. I'll bring the family. We'll take a box lunch.

MAMA. Is good, Sigrid.

[*Music: Bridge . . . Continue music under narration*]

[*Old train and whistle . . . Feature, then fade*]

KATRIN. How well I remember that train ride. We all ate sandwiches, as if it was a picnic. I was scared at the idea of seeing death, but I told myself that if I was going to be a writer, I had to experience every-thing. [*Train out*] It was afternoon when we arrived, and we finally found Uncle Chris's farm. We all went into his bedroom.

[*Music out*]

NELS. Hello, Uncle Chris.

SIGRID. Poor Uncle Chris.

UNCLE. So—you all come to see show.

MAMA. How are you, Uncle Chris?

UNCLE. Help me sit up. That's it. Sigrid, how is Arne's leg?

SIGRID. Fine, Uncle Chris! He play baseball now.

UNCLE. Good. Pour me a drink, Marta. Is still some in bottle.

MAMA. Uncle Chris, that will not help now.

UNCLE. It always helps. Now especially.

SIGRID [*Firmly*]. Uncle Chris, I don't think you realize . . .

UNCLE. What I don't realize? That I am dying? Why else do I think you come here? Why else do I think you stand there, watching me? Get out. Get out. I don't want you here. Get out!

[*Ad lib murmurs from all, fading*]

SIGRID [*Fading*]. Oh, very well. Very well. We'll be outside on the porch, if you want us.

UNCLE. That is where I want you—on the porch! Except Marta, and Katrin. You stay!

KATRIN. Yes, Uncle Chris.

MAMA. Is good, Uncle Chris. [*Door closes, cutting off ad libs*] Uncle Chris, you must lie back and stay calm.

UNCLE. Then you give me drink.

MAMA. No, Uncle Chris.

UNCLE. We cannot waste what is left in the bottle. You do not drink it . . . who will drink it when I am gone? What harm can it do . . . now? I die, anyway . . . You give it me.

MAMA. Yes, Uncle Chris.

[*Sound of pouring*]

UNCLE. Marta, I haf never made a will. Was never enough money. This ranch will not bring much. Big mortgage. There will be nothing much for any of you.

MAMA. Who cares about that?

UNCLE. *I* do! I always wanted there should be money to make Nels doctor. But there were other things. But you make Nels doctor, all the same. You like?

MAMA. Sure, Uncle Chris. It is what he would like. To help people who suffer . . .

UNCLE. Is the greatest thing in the world. Always I wanted to be doctor myself. Is the only thing I have ever wanted. Nels must do it for me.

MAMA. He will, Uncle Chris.

UNCLE. Goot. Katrin, who will be writer . . . You are not frightened of me any more?

KATRIN. No, Uncle Chris.

UNCLE. Now, Marta, you have drink with me. That way we finish bottle.

MAMA [*Moment's hesitation*]. Is good, Uncle Chris.

UNCLE. Very special occasion. [*Pouring into two glasses during following*] No, no water. Always the last drink is without water. Is Norwegian custom.

MAMA. Here, Uncle Chris.

UNCLE. Take your glass . . . So . . . [*Clink*] Skoal!

MAMA. So. Skoal!

[*Clink*]

[*Music: Bridge*]

[*Crickets background*]

SIGRID. The gnats are awful out here.

NELS. Gnats are always worse around sunset.

SIGRID. The idea! Being made to sit on a porch hour after hour. Well, I suppose you can't hurry these things.

PAPA. No, you can't, Sigrid.

SIGRID. I wonder if there's a will.

[*Screen door opens and closes*]

PAPA. Well, Marta.

MAMA. Uncle Chris has gone.

PAPA. I . . . am sorry.

DAGMAR. Gosh.

NELS. Too bad.

DAGMAR. Was it awful, Katrin?

KATRIN. Poor Uncle Chris.

SIGRID [*More gently than is her wont*]. Did he—say anything about a will?

MAMA. There is no will.

SIGRID. Well, then, that means . . . we're his nearest relatives . . .

MAMA. Is very little money.

SIGRID. How do you know?

MAMA. He told me. And he gave me this small account book. It shows how he spent his money.

SIGRID. At a liquor store?

MAMA. No, Sigrid, no! I read it to you. You know how Uncle Chris walked always with limp. It was his one thought . . . lame people. Always he had wanted to be doctor himself, and help them. Instead, he help them other ways. I read you the last page . . . "Joseph Spinelli. Ten years old. Tubercular left leg. Three hundred thirty-seven dollars, eighteen cents. Walks now." "Esta Jensen. Four years. Clubfoot. Two hundred seventeen dollars, fifty cents. Walks now." "*Arne* Solfeldt . . . "

SIGRID [*Startled*]. *My* Arne?

MAMA [*Reading on*]. Yes. "Nine years. Fractured kneecap. Four hundred forty-two dollars, sixteen cents."

SIGRID. W—what?

MAMA. It does not tell the end about Arne. I like to write "Walks now." Yes?

SIGRID. Yes.

MAMA. Maybe even . . . "runs"?

SIGRID. Yes.

MAMA. It was good.

> [*Music: Curtain this section with a touch of nobility, then set a brighter note for following sequence*]

> [*Door opens*]

NELS [*Off*]. Hello, Mama, Papa.

> [*Door Closes*]

MAMA. Hello, Nels.

NELS [*Fading in*]. Here's your evening paper, Papa. And here's a letter for Katrin. [*Shouting*] Katrin! Letter for you!

KATRIN [*Way off*]. Coming!

MAMA. Nels, you know who the letter is from?

NELS. Why no, Mama. It looks like her own handwriting.

MAMA. Is bad.

PAPA. Why is bad?

MAMA. She get too many like that. They are stories she send to the magazines.

KATRIN [*Fading in*]. Where's the letter?

MAMA. Here, Katrin.

> [*Sound of letter being opened quickly, then short pause*]

KATRIN. Mama . . . Papa . . . I want to say something.

PAPA. What is it?

KATRIN. I'm not going on with my studies.

PAPA. Why not?

KATRIN. Because it would be a waste of time and money. The only point in it was to be a writer. Well, I'm not going to be one, so . . .

MAMA. Katrin, is it your letter that makes you say this? It is a story come back again?

KATRIN. For the tenth time! I made this one a test. It's the best I'll ever write, I know that. Well, it's no good.

NELS. What kind of a story is it?

KATRIN. Oh . . . it's a story about a painter, who's a genius, and he goes blind.

NELS. Sounds like "The Light That Failed."

KATRIN. It's not like that. My painter has an operation and recovers his sight, and paints better than ever before.

MAMA. Is good.

KATRIN [*Bitterly unhappy*]. No, it isn't. It's rotten. But it's the best I can do.

MAMA. Have you asked your teachers about this?

KATRIN. Teachers don't know anything about writing. They just know about literature.

MAMA. If there was someone we could ask for advice . . . to tell us, if your stories are good.

KATRIN. They're *not*, Mama.

PAPA. There is something here in the paper about a lady writer. I just notice headlines. Wait. "Woman writer discusses key to literary success."

KATRIN. Who?

PAPA. A fat lady. It gives her picture. Florence Dana Moorhead.

KATRIN. Oh, she's terribly successful. She's here on a lecture tour.

MAMA. Well, what does she say is the secret?

KATRIN [*Wearily*]. Oh, Mama. You talk as if writing is like . . . well, like cooking, and all you have to have is the recipe. It takes a lot more than that. Papa, are you through with the want-ad section?

PAPA. I don't need it.

KATRIN [*Fading*]. I'll look it over and see if I can find myself a job. I'll go after one first thing in the morning . . . [*Door closes*]

MAMA. Is bad. Nels, what you think?

NELS. I don't know, Mama.

MAMA. This lady in the paper . . . what does she say?

NELS. Let's see . . . "Miss Moorhead, interviewed at her suite in the Fairmont Hotel, said that apart from literature, her main interest in life is gastronomy."

MAMA. The stars?

NELS. No—eating. "A brilliant cook herself, she says that she would as soon find a new recipe as she would a first edition."

PAPA. First edition?

MAMA. I see her picture?

NELS. Here.

MAMA. Is kind face. Nels, what is first edition?

[*Music: Bridge*]

[*Hotel lobby background*]

MAMA. Miss Moorhead . . . Miss Moorhead. Please . . .

MISS MOORHEAD. Yes?

MAMA. Might I speak to you a moment?

MISS MOORHEAD. What's it about?

MAMA. I wait long time here in lobby, for you to come in. I read in the paper about you.

MISS MOORHEAD. Oh, yes?

MAMA. My daughter, Katrin, wants to be writer.

MISS MOORHEAD. Oh, really?

MAMA. I bring her stories.

MISS MOORHEAD. Look, I'm afraid I'm in rather a hurry. I'm leaving San Francisco this evening . . .

MAMA. I wait two hours here! Please, if I may talk to you for one, two minutes.

MISS MOORHEAD [*Kindly*]. Of course, but I'd better tell you, if you want me to read any of your daughter's stories, it's no use. I've had to make it a rule that—

MAMA. I see in the paper you like to collect recipes . . . for eating.

MISS MOORHEAD. Yes, I do. I've written several books on cooking.

MAMA. I, too, am interested in gastronomy. I make good Norwegian dishes. Lutefisk.

MISS MOORHEAD. Lutefisk. Mmmm!

MAMA. And kjodboller. That is meat balls with cream sauce.

MISS MOORHEAD. I know. I've eaten them in Christiania.

MAMA. I have special recipe for kjodboller . . . my mother give me. Never in my life have I told this recipe, not even to my own sisters, because they are not good cooks.

MISS MOORHEAD. Oh?

MAMA. But . . . if you could read just one story, then maybe I could—

MISS MOORHEAD. You're very persuasive. Tell me about the kjodboller.

MAMA. When you make the meat balls you drop them in boiling stock. Not water.

MISS MOORHEAD. Ah!

MAMA. That is one of the secrets. And the cream sauce. It is half sour cream, added at the last.

MISS MOORHEAD. Sounds marvelous.

MAMA. I could write it out for you. And . . . while I write, you could read story?

MISS MOORHEAD [*With laugh*]. You win!

MAMA. Maybe if you would read two stories, I could write the recipe for lutefisk as well.

[*Music: Bridge, continue background for*]

KATRIN. When Mama came back, I was sitting with my diary, writing a Tragic Farewell to literature. Suddenly, I was surprised to see her standing in the doorway.

[*Music out*]

MAMA. You are busy, Katrin?

KATRIN. No, of course not. Come in.

MAMA. Katrin, I have seen Miss Moorhead.

KATRIN. Mama, you don't mean you took her my stories?

MAMA. She read five of them. I was two hours with her. We have a glass of sherry. Two glass of sherry.

KATRIN. What . . . what did she say about them?

MAMA [*Quietly*]. She say they are not good.

KATRIN [*Turning away*]. Well, I knew that.

MAMA. She say more. Will you listen, Katrin?

KATRIN. Sure. Sure. I'll listen.

MAMA. She say you must write more about things you know.

KATRIN. That's what my teacher always told me at school.

MAMA. Maybe your teacher was right. I do not know if I explain good what Miss Moorhead means, but while she talks I think I understand. Your story about the painter who is blind . . . that is because . . . forgive me, my Katrin, if I speak plain . . . but you think it would feel good to be a painter and be blind and not complain. But never once have you imagined how that would really be. Is true?

KATRIN. Yes . . . Yes, I guess it's true.

MAMA. But she say you are to go on writing. That you have the gift.

KITRIN. Mama!

MAMA. And that when you have written story that is real and true . . . then you send it to someone whose name she give me. It is her . . . agent. Here. No, that is recipe she give me for goulash like her grandmother make it . . . here . . . It helps, Katrin, what I have told you?

KATRIN. I guess so. But what have I got to write about?

MAMA. Maybe you write about Papa?

KATRIN. Papa?

MAMA. Papa is fine man.

KATRIN. I know.

MAMA. He is wonderful man!

KATRIN. But what's ever happened to him? What's ever happened to any
of us? Except always being poor and having illnesses, like the time
when Dagmar went to the hospital and you got that bucket and—
[*The idea hits her*] Oh . . . [*Soft chord*] OH . . . [*Fading*]
[*Bigger chord*] Oh . . . [*Further*]

[*Music takes it away, for bridge*]

KATRIN [*Out of music, fading in*]. Mama . . . Mama . . . Mama . . .

MAMA. What is?

KATRIN. Mama . . . Papa . . . Nels! I've sold a story!

MAMA. A story!

NELS. What?

PAPA. No!

KATRIN. I've got a letter from the agent, with a check for—[*Gasping*]
Five hundred dollars!

NELS. $500?

PAPA. My!

MAMA. Katrin . . . is true?

KATRIN. Here's the letter.

NELS. What will you *do* with five hundred dollars?

KATRIN. I'll buy Mama her warm coat, I know that. And we'll put the
rest in the Bank.

NELS [*Kidding*]. Quick. Before they change their mind, and stop the
check. [*All laugh*]

KATRIN. Will you, Mama? Will you take it to the Bank downtown
tomorrow? . . . What's the matter?

MAMA. I do not know how.

NELS. Just give it to the man and tell him to put it in your account, like
you always do.

MAMA. Sure . . . sure . . . but—

PAPA. You tell them . . . now, Marta.

KATRIN. Tell us what?

MAMA [*Desperately*]. Is no Bank Account! Never in my life have I been
inside a bank.

NELS. What?

KATRIN. Mama, you've always told us . . .

MAMA. I know. But was not true. I tell a lie.

NELS. But why, Mama?

KATRIN. Why did you pretend?

MAMA. Is not good for little ones to be afraid . . . not to feel secure . . . But now . . . with five hundred dollar . . . I think I can tell.

KATRIN. Mama!

MAMA. You read us the story. You have it there?

KATRIN. Yes.

MAMA. Then read.

KATRIN. Now?

MAMA. Yes. Call Dagmar.

PAPA. Dag—mar!

DAGMAR [*Way off*]. Yes, Papa!

MAMA. Katrin, what is the story called?

KATRIN. It's called "Mama and the Hospital."

PAPA [*Delighted*]. You write about Mama?

KATRIN. Yes.

NELS. That's bully!

MAMA. But I thought . . . I tell you to . . .

KATRIN. I know, Mama, but . . . well, that's how it came out.

DAGMAR [*Fading in*]. What is it, Papa?

PAPA. Sit down, Dagmar.

MAMA. Katrin has sold a story, and she's going to read it to us.

DAGMAR. Gee!

[*Same time, yowl from cat*]

NELS. Did you have to bring that cat in again?

MAMA. Is all right, Nels. We all sit down now and listen.

PAPA. All ready, Katrin.

[*Music in under*]

KATRIN. For as long ago as I could remember, the house on Steiner Street had been home. All of us were born there. There was Nels.

NELS. Hey—I'm in it!

KATRIN. "My little sister, Dagmar . .

DAGMAR. Am I in the story too?

MAMA. Hush, Dagmar. We are all in the story.

[*Cat meows happily*]

KATRIN. But first and foremost, I remember Mama. [*Music picks up tempo*] I remember that every Saturday night Mama would sit down by the kitchen table [*Fading*] and count out the money Papa had . . .

[*Music has come up to drown her . . . Up for curtain*]

ANNOUNCER

CREDITS

THE SHOW-OFF

Original Play
by George Kelly

Radio Adaptation
by Arthur Arent

CAST

(for radio performance)

MRS. FISHER	Betty Garde
CLARA	Barbara Weeks
AMY	Helen Shields
MR. FISHER	Cameron Prud'Homme
AUBREY PIPER	Alfred Lunt
JOE FISHER	Paul Crabtree
VOICE I	Walter Kinsella
VOICE II	Carl Frank
MR. GILL	Walter Kinsella
FRANK HYLAND	Carl Frank

THE SHOW-OFF

Radio adaptation by

ARTHUR ARENT

IN THE PUBLISHED VERSION of George Kelly's play, Heywood Broun, who wrote the preface, states flatly that "The Show-Off is the best comedy which has yet been written by an American." That was twenty-three years ago, and Aubrey Piper still stands as one of the most memorable characters that ever crossed a stage.

When I began working out a radio adaptation of "The Show-Off" I was immediately aware of a phenomenon: while Aubrey dominated the play from beginning to end, while he was maligned and defended and the things that happened to him were debated at fever heat, *Aubrey himself wasn't around very much.* Of course a little of him went a long way, but this approach—of a hero *in absentia*—would hardly do for radio. In addition, being lucky enough to have so superb an actor as Alfred Lunt playing the part, it was natural to want to use him as much as possible. The thing to do, then, was to remold the play, making use of all the off-stage action in which Aubrey was a participant. One example of this is the scene in the parlor in Act I, where Aubrey sings "Rocked in the Cradle of the Deep." In the original, Aubrey and his song were an off-stage noise, the action centering around Mrs. Fisher, her son Joe, and a dog. Aubrey, in fact, did not again appear in this act except to say good night. Also, the automobile smashup—a natural for radio—obviously could not have taken place in a one-set play.

And that brings us to another point. Obviously the most difficult play to adapt is the one originally conceived in one set. While it is unwise to break a scene arbitrarily, there is nevertheless a satiation point beyond which no audience, using only its ears, will listen to the droning of the same voices. The usual procedure in such a case is to rebuild the play, constructing new scenes on the old skeleton. Minor climaxes must be built to end each scene, and while ending it pave the way for the next, if possible in a different locale. A great deal of this process was used in "The Show-Off," without, however, adopting the hit-and-run technique, which, without any build and usually at the expense of character delineation, skims the top off a scene and dives headlong into the next.

I'd just like to add, for you who are interested, that Mr. Lunt's characterization of Aubrey Piper was out of this world, and it would be a help if, when reading the script, you gave heed with your mind's ear to that incredible voice bellowing and then cracking as he says, *"Lower the drawbridge! It's the Kid from West Philly! Sign on the dotted line!"*

THE SHOW-OFF

ANNOUNCER

INTRODUCTION FOR THE THEATRE GUILD

ACT I

NARRATOR. This is a story about a family in West Philadelphia. But mostly, it's a story about Aubrey Piper—the Show-Off!—A man of whom you can safely say, "I know someone just like him!" Aubrey met Amy Fisher at a church sociable and from then on, things happened—particularly to the Fisher family. We take you now to the dining room of the Fisher home in West Philadelphia. The year is 1922. Seated on the black horsehair loveseat are Mother Fisher and her married daughter, Clara.

[*Fades*]

MRS. FISHER. I'm really worried this time, Clara. Your sister Amy's so young—and I don't like this fella, not one bit. He's a show-off.

CLARA. Is he coming tonight, Mom?

MRS. FISHER. It's Wednesday night, ain't it? He comes Sundays now, too. It's a regular thing.

CLARA. What's he like, Mom?

MRS. FISHER [*Giggling*]. Clara, you never in your life heard anybody talk so much. I don't know how Amy stands it. Your Pa can hardly stay in the room when he's here.

CLARA. I can imagine.

MRS. FISHER. And Clara, you know what'd kill you? You can't say a *word* against him in front of her! Oh, not a word. No matter what he sez she thinks it's lovely! [*Sotto voce*] You know, Clara, *I* think he wears a wig!

CLARA. Now, Mom.

MRS. FISHER. I do, honestly. But when I asked *her* about it here one morning, I thought she'd take the head right off me. You never seen anybody get themselves into such a temper. She sez, "It's a lie." She sez, "He *don't* wear a wig!" She sez, "People always say something like that about a fellow who makes a good appearance." [*Sotto voce*] First chance I get, I'm gonna take a good look.

AMY [*Off . . . calling*]. Mom! . . . Oh, Mom!

MRS. FISHER. That's her now. She's primping for him. Bet she can't find something. [*Calling*] Yes, Amy?

AMY [*Off*]. Mom, did you see anything of that blue bar pin of mine?

MRS. FISHER. I told you . . . [*Calling*] No, I didn't, and don't be bothering me about it! [*Sotto voce*] Want to hear something, Clara?

CLARA. Uh-huh.

MRS. FISHER. She don't know a *thing* about him—you know, his family and things—not a single, solitary thing! Except that he works for the Great Eastern Railroad—which may or may not be true.

CLARA. It's true. He's in the freight office.

MRS. FISHER [*Sharply*]. How do you know?

CLARA. Frank knows him.

MRS. FISHER. You mean your husband Frank?

CLARA. Do I know any other Franks? He says he's seen him around there for a long time. He says if you see a fancy-dressed dude with a carnation in his buttonhole—that's Aubrey Piper!

MRS. FISHER. That's the name! Aubrey Piper! Sounds like a ham actor!

[*Footsteps approach during the above*]

MR. FISHER. Who sounds like a ham actor, Mother?

MRS. FISHER [*Startled*]. Oh, Niel—you frightened me! Why do you come pussyfootin' in when you know how nervous I am?

CLARA. Good evening, Pa.

MR. FISHER. Evenin', Clara . . . Well, how's my only married daughter?

CLARA. I'm fine, Pa. We were just talking about—

MR. FISHER. Don't tell me. It was that boy friend of Amy's. Only time your mother doesn't hear me come into a room is when she's talkin' about that clothin' store dummy.

MRS. FISHER. He really does work for the Great Eastern Railroad, Pa. Frank knows him.

CLARA. And he makes about thirty-five dollars a week.

MRS. FISHER. Good heavens! Is that all? Why he said he's the head of the department!

CLARA. And you know how long Amy could get along on thirty-five dollars a week the way she buys hats and dresses!

MR. FISHER. I just want it put on the record that if that fellow, Piper, comes in here tonight and slaps me on the back just once, I'm gettin' up and goin' upstairs—if I don't bust him on the nose first!

[*Footsteps approach*]

MRS. FISHER. Ssssh, Pa! Amy's comin' down . . . [*Trying to be nonchalant*] Now, as I was sayin', Clara, about that lampshade—

AMY. Hello, Pa. Hello, Clara. Is the parlor all right, Mom?

MRS. FISHER. Certainly, it's all right.

AMY. Did you spruce it up?

MRS. FISHER [*Sharply*]. Certainly, I spruced it up . . . Lordamighty, get away from that lookin' glass! Didn't you look at yourself enough in the one upstairs?

AMY. This is a different light . . . What time is it, Pa?

MR. FISHER. Quarter past eight.

AMY. Good heavens! Aubrey'll be here any minute!

[*Rapid footsteps recede . . . Door closes*]

CLARA. I think I'll go, Mother, before he comes.

MR. FISHER. That's right, you don't live here. Why should you have to put up with him?

[*Bell rings noisily . . . Dum dum de dum dum—Dum Dum*]

MRS. FISHER [*Ominously*]. I know that ring!

CLARA. I'm going. Good-bye, Pa.

[*Cane rapping on door*]

AUBREY [*Off*]. Sound the trumpet! Lower the drawbridge! It's the Kid from West Philly!

MRS. FISHER. Better go out through the kitchen, Clara, or he'll catch you and you'll never get home. And tell your brother, Joe, in there, I want to see him.

[*Footsteps recede*]

AMY [*Off*]. Good evening, Aubrey.

AUBREY [*Off*]. Well, well! Here he is, Amy. The Kid himself! Right on the dot! . . . Grab the sombrero, Chiquita. Just hang it on the rail of the ole corral!

[*Laughs boisterously*]

MRS. FISHER. I know that laugh, too!

MR. FISHER [*Unhappily*]. Do you suppose she'll bring him in here?

AUBREY [*Off*]. And how is Pop tonight? And Mom? And brother, Joseph, the young Edison? [*Laughs*]

MRS. FISHER [*Sotto voce*]. If Joe ever heard that idiot call him "young Edison," he'd commit a hammer murder, that's what he'd do.

[*Door opens*]

AUBREY [*On mike*]. Well, well! Good evening, one and all!

MRS. FISHER [*Unenthused*]. Good evenin'.

AUBREY. Don't get up! Stay right where you are, folks, right where you are. Just a little social amenity—going right out on the next train. Amy, ole girl, would you mind? A glass of water—the ole aqua pura —for the Kid from West Philly. The ole tonsils are somewhat in need of lubrication. [*Laughs*]

AMY [*Happily*]. Certainly, Aubrey. I'll bring it right in.

AUBREY. Thank you, O', Beauteous One! [*Footsteps recede*] Interesting mirror you have here, Mother Fisher. Looks kind of antique, too— the genuine Grand Rapids!

MRS. FISHER. You're goin' to crack it one of these days lookin' at yourself.

AUBREY. The little ole mother is a great kidder, all right, all right . . . [*Laughs*] Hmmm. Little twist to the ole fore-in-hand . . . little pat to the ole carnation . . . There you are, Mother Fisher—the Kid from West Philly's all set for a big evening!

MR. FISHER [*Hopefully*]. You mean you're going to take Amy out?

AUBREY. Tear her away from this happy domicile? Not on your tintype . . . [*Assuming the manner of a barker*] Ladies and gentlemen, I want to tell those of you who have ventured out this evening that we have here in the Fisher ménage a very pretty little picture of domestic felicity—father reading, mother knitting—

[*Sound of hammer on wood, off*]

MR. FISHER. What's that, Mother?

MRS. FISHER. It's Joe, in the kitchen. He's workin' on one of his inventions.

AUBREY. —and little ole Tommy Edison out in the kitchen working eighteen hours a day to make the rich man richer and the poor man poorer. What about it, Popcorn? [*Sound of slap on back*] Okay, or N.G.? Right or raving?

MR. FISHER [*Violently*]. For the love of Pete, let me alone! And don't slap me on the back! I never saw such a darn pest in my life! I'm goin' up to bed.

[*Aubrey roars with laughter as footsteps recede and door slams*]

AUBREY. Sign on the dotted line! And little, ole Popsy-wopsy getting sore and leaving us flat. [*Laughs again*] Nevertheless, and notwithstanding, Mrs. Fisher, I'd like to mention that the Kid from West Philadelphia is a great admirer of your homely little brood. That young Edison, just now banging away in the kitchen, will one day set his seal upon the world—you mark my word.

[*Footsteps approach*]

AUBREY. Ah, there she comes, the Lily Maid of Astolat!

AMY. Here's your glass of water, Aubrey.

AUBREY. Blushing as she gave it, looking down—at her feet so bare, and her tattered gown!

AMY [*Giggling*]. Oh, Aubrey!

AUBREY. How's that, Mother Fisher? Can't beat that little ole Willie Shakespeare, can you? No, sir—I'd like to tell the brother Elks that that little ole Shakespeare party shook a wicked pen!

[*Laughs and is joined by Amy*]

[*Door opens*]

[*Footsteps approach*]

AUBREY. Well, if it isn't Thomas Alva Edison himself! Good evening, Joseph, my young friend! How's the invention coming along?

JOE. Okay. How's the Great Eastern Railroad?

AUBREY. Blooming . . . blooming.

MRS. FISHER. Better go inside and wash your hands, Joe. And change your shirt. It's filthy.

AUBREY. How old are you, Tom?

JOE. My name is Joe, and I'm nineteen.

AUBREY. Well, Mr. Joseph, I just want to tell you you're wasting your time;

for when you're all through with that invention, they'll offer you twenty cents for it, and sell it for twenty million . . . Yes, sir, take it or leave it—sign on the dotted line.

JOE. Quit tapping me on the shoulder.

AUBREY. Yes, sir—that's exactly what they did to little ole Yours Truly here. Twenty simoleons, for a formula that would have solved the greatest problem before the industrial chemical world today! [*Four notes struck on four cut-glass bowls with a pencil*]

MRS. FISHER [*A wail*]. My cut glass!

AUBREY. Say, that's pretty, isn't it? [*Four notes are heard again, this time accompanied by Aubrey singing*]

AUBREY. Bong, bong, bong, *bong!*

MRS. FISHER. Keep that pencil away from my cut-glass dishes!

AUBREY. You know, that melody reminds me of the last time I was at the Metropolitan Opera House in New York. There were four voices—what you call a quartette, you know—

JOE. What kind of a formula was it, Aubrey?

AUBREY. Oh, yes—the formula! Well, Joe, my boy, it was a formula to prevent the rusting of iron and steel. Yes, sir, a solution of vanadium and manganese, to be added to the metal in its molten state—instead of applied externally as they have been doing.

JOE. To be added *how*, Aubrey?

AUBREY. To be added to the metal in its molten state. —*molten state*— [*Three beats on the cut-glass bowl emphasize this*] instead of applied externally as they have been doing. *That* was my invention, my contribution to humanity! But simply because it was discovered by a workingman—that they saw they couldn't buy—

MRS. FISHER. That *who* saw?

AUBREY. Why, the industrialists, of course! The tycoons! Yes, sir, they tried to pull the ole flimflam on the Kid from West Philly! But it didn't work. And I'm not letting it go at that, either. Know what I did? I got out the ole fountain pen and wrote a letter to the Attorney General in Washington about it. Yes, sir, Washington, in the District of Columbia! I asked him one question, one little question!

MRS. FISHER. What'd he say?

AUBREY. What'd he say, Mother Fisher? He was stumped, absolutely stumped, because I haven't had a line from him since! Well, that's the said and done of it. That's it. That's the whole story! Sign on the dotted line!

[*The four notes are struck on the cut-glass bowls*]

[*Music*]

AUBREY [*Fade in . . . Singing to piano accompaniment*].
        Rocked in the cradle of the deep,
        I lay me down—in peace to sleep—
        Secure I rest upon the wave,
        For thou alone.
AMY. Aubrey, you have a beautiful voice. It's so powerful.
AUBREY. To tell you the truth, Amy—I rather like the way it sounds my-
self—particularly when I let go—like this: [*Singing*]
        Rocked in the cradle of the deep,
        I lay me down—

[*There is a thump on the ceiling overhead*]

AUBREY. What's that?
AMY. Oh . . . nothing.
AUBREY. Amy—could it be that your father, who, I take it, sleeps in the
room upstairs, does not approve of my voice?
AMY. Oh, no, Aubrey.
AUBREY. No. It couldn't be. That man has good taste. He knows the genu-
ine article when he hears it . . . By the way, it must be getting kind
of late.
AMY. Do you have to go, Aubrey? Why, it seems like you just got here.
AUBREY. Don't want the ole kid to go home, eh? Well, Amy, if you insist,
I'll sing just one more chorus.
AMY. That'd be wonderful, Aubrey.

[*She vamps and then Aubrey starts to sing*]

AUBREY [*Singing*]. Rocked in the cradle of the deep, I lay me down—in
peace to sleep—

[*A knock is heard . . . The door opens*]

MRS. FISHER. Amy . . .
AMY. What's the matter, Mother?
MRS. FISHER. Why—I—I was just coming to tell you to be sure and put
them lights out. I'm going up to bed now—it's nearly twelve o'clock.
AUBREY. I know, I know. I am just about to take my reluctant leave,
Mother Fisher.

MRS. FISHER. Well, I don't want to hurry you, but—

AUBREY. In fact, that recent outburst was in the nature of a farewell concert. The little ole song at twilight, you know, Mother Fisher—to
soothe the savage breast. [Sings]

> Just a song at twilight!
> When the lights are low,
> And the flick'ring shadows—

[Stops as door opens]

Well, if it isn't young Tom Edison! Come in, come in! . . . Where
were you, Tom? Out with Steinmetz and Marconi?

JOE. My name is Joe, and I was down at the corner poolroom.

AUBREY. Well, folks, the concert is over. Like the Arabs, Amy, I fold my
tent and silently steal away. [Laughs] My chapeau and cane, if you
will be so kind.

AMY. Aren't you going to say good night in French, Aubrey, like you
always do?

AUBREY. Certainly, Amy. The ole globe trotter is always at your service.
[Clears throat] Mademoiselle, donnez-moi la parapluie de ma tante.
That means, Amy, we thank you from the bottom of our hearts for
a lovely evening! Good night, all.

AMY. I'll see you to the door.

[Door closes . . . A pause]

MRS. FISHER. That man is a howlin' idiot. What was that he said tonight,
Joe, about discoverin' somethin' to keep rust out of iron and steel?

JOE [Amused]. Wasn't that a scream?

MRS. FISHER. That's what you're always talkin' about, ain't it, Joe?

JOE. Yes, I was talkin' to him about it one night here while he was waitin'
for Amy to come down, and he's forgot where he heard it.

MRS. FISHER. Can you imagine!

JOE. I was wonderin' if you were gettin' that tonight, Ma. You know that's
what I'm working on.

MRS. FISHER. No, son, it never struck me till afterwards. You know I never
pay much attention to what he says.

JOE [Laughing]. He's a nut, all right.

[Door opens]

AMY [Tense]. I want to talk to you, Ma.

JOE. Guess I'll be goin' to bed. Good night, Amy. Good night, Ma.

MRS. FISHER. Good night, son.

[*Door closes . . . A pause*]

AMY. I just want to say that was a *nice* trick you people did earlier this evening. What did Pop get into such a temper about and walk out of the room?

MRS. FISHER. Because your Mister Aubrey slapped him on the back, that's what.

AMY. What if he did?

MRS. FISHER. Well, he's always slapping *somebody!*—on the back—or the shoulder—or someplace else. And your father said the next time he did it he'd walk out of the room! He can't say two words *together* without *slapping* somebody someplace!

AMY. Well, I'll bet you won't get a chance to insult him again, Mom, I'll tell you that.

MRS. FISHER. Then let him stop his silly talk! And he won't get insulted. Sign on the dotted line! Every two minutes! And talkin' about Shakespeare! It's no wonder our Joe sez he's a nut!

AMY. Oh, everybody's a nut with the people around here!

MRS. FISHER. Oh, it ain't only the people around here that sez it . . . everybody that knows him sez it. [*As Amy snorts*] You needn't laugh, for it's true.

AMY [*Sharply*]. Who do *you* know that knows him?

MRS. FISHER [*Promptly*]. Frank Hyland.

AMY. Oh, don't make up a lie, Mom! Clara's husband never saw Aubrey Piper.

MRS. FISHER. Well now, my lady, you're so smart, he knows him better than you do.

AMY. I don't believe it.

MRS. FISHER. He's been seein' him every day for years, down at that restaurant where he eats his lunch. And he sez he's as crazy as a *bass* singer!

AMY. I suppose that's what Clara was here to tell you, was it?

MRS. FISHER. What does it matter *what*—

AMY [*Very tense*]. Listen, Mom, I want to tell you something right now! You tell our Clara for me the next time you see her, to mind her **own** darn business—

MRS. FISHER. Don't fly into a temper, Amy—You're not frightenin' any-**body around here!**

AMY. No, and nobody around here is frightenin' *me* either. Clara took who *she* wanted—and I guess you took what *you* wanted—and if I want Aubrey Piper, I'll take *him!*

MRS. FISHER. Well, take him then! And the sooner the better! Only remember this, Amy—if you *do* take him—be sure that you keep him —and that—he—keeps you! . . . And don't be comin' 'round here cryin' for your Pop to keep you!

AMY. And how do you know that Aubrey Piper wouldn't be able to keep his wife?

MRS. FISHER. Because I know what he earns—and it isn't enough.

AMY [*Angrily*]. Oh, don't go making up things, Mom!—you don't know anything about what he earns.

MRS. FISHER [*With measured emphasis*]. He earns thirty-five dollars a week, and not a penny more—Frank Hyland sez so. And he sez he's just a clerk, like a hundred others down there.

AMY. That shows how much Frank knows about it!

MRS. FISHER. I suppose he told you he *owns* the Great Eastern Railroad!

AMY. Oh, Mom, you talk as if everybody that was married was starving to death.

MRS. FISHER. There are ways of starving to death, Amy, besides not getting enough to eat. [*Shrewdly*] And the funny part of it is, you, Amy— like a lot of others—you're very shrewd about money while you're at home, as far as what you give your mother and father is concerned; but the minute some clown with a flower in his coat, and patent leather shoes, winks at you, you seem to forget there's such a thing in the world as a ton of coal. And then it's just as Clara said, it's your people that's got to come to the rescue!

AMY. I wish I'd been here while she was talking! I bet I'd a told her a thing or two!

MRS. FISHER. You needn't try to turn it on to Clara . . . [*Earnestly*] Don't you see, Amy—I got nothin' against the man. It's only that I'm positive he'll never amount to much, and—

AMY. He won't, eh? That's what you think! [*Half crying*] Oh, I'd just take him for *spite* now!

MRS. FISHER. Well, let me tell *you*, Amy—the day a girl that's used to spendin' money the way you do, takes a thirty-five dollar a week man —the only one she's spitin' is herself! There'll be no more permanent waves . . . Nor twenty-five dollar beaded dresses. And you can make up your mind to that!

AMY [*In a crying temper*]. Well, I'd never bother anybody around here
if I needed anything, I'll tell you that!

MRS. FISHER. Time'll tell, Lady Jane. I've heard the likes of you before.
[*Sighs*] Well, it's past twelve o'clock. Time to turn out the light and
go to bed. [*A pause*]

AMY [*Gently*]. Mother . . .

MRS. FISHER. Yes, Amy?

AMY. How—do you like—my—engagement ring?

[*Pause*]

MRS. FISHER [*Slowly*]. It's very nice, Amy.

[*Music*]

END OF ACT I

ANNOUNCER

COMMERCIAL

ACT II

[*Music in full*]

NARRATOR. Amy kept company with Aubrey Piper for a couple of months.
He regularly sent her orchids from the best florist in town—and then
went around telling everybody how much they cost. On their honeymoon they couldn't afford Niagara Falls, so they went to Atlantic
City—on money Aubrey borrowed from Pa Fisher . . . It was about
six months after they were married that Aubrey dropped in at the
house one day . . . [*Fades*]

AUBREY. Good afternoon to you, Mother Fisher. Amy here?

MRS. FISHER. Why, no, Aubrey. Isn't she home?

AUBREY. Guess she's still out looking for a house. I just stopped in on my
way to the Automobile Show. Thought she might be here.

[*Cane taps*]

MRS. FISHER. Well, she isn't. And for goodness sake, if you must walk around with a cane like a dude, stop playin' with it when you're talkin' to me!—Didn't I see you drive up in a auto just now?

AUBREY. Uh-huh. I got the loan of Harry Albright's Pierce Arrow.

MRS. FISHER. Couldn't you find somebody who had a Ford?

AUBREY. Nothing's too good for the Kid from Philly, Mother o' Mine. [*Four notes struck on cut-glass bowl*]

MRS. FISHER. Get away from that cut glass—and what's this about lookin' for a house? What's the matter with the flat you're in?

AUBREY. We've got to get out. They're tearing the building down.

MRS. FISHER. You won't find it so easy to get a place as reasonable as that again in a hurry.

AUBREY. I don't *want* a place as reasonable as that if I can get something that looks better! I want a home—something with a bit of ground around it—where I can do a bit of tennis in the evening.

MRS. FISHER. Stop swinging that cane like as if it was a tennis racket! You'll bust the chandelier! You'll pay plenty for a place like that.

AUBREY [*Tapping cane for emphasis*]. That is exactly what I expect to do, Mother Fisher, exactly what I expect to do!

MRS. FISHER. And stop tapping with it! My goodness!

AUBREY. But I want what I'm paying for, I'll tell you that. No more of the old first-of-the-month business for this bambino. He's all washed up, and signed on the dotted line.

MRS. FISHER. That gibberish! Where do you expect to find a house?

AUBREY [*Airily*]. Oh, out along the boulevard somewhere. [*Sings*] "Oh, the moonlight's bright tonight along the Wabash!"

MRS. FISHER. The boulevard? That's where all the rich folks live!

AUBREY. Man's got to live somewhere, Mother. [*Sings*] "From the fields there comes the scent of new-mown hay!" "Through the sycamores the candlelights are gleaming. On the banks of the Wabash far away."

MRS. FISHER. Well, if the man's wise, he'll live where he's able to pay for it—instead of making a big show—buyin' a ten thousand dolla house and puttin' fifty dollars down on it. Why, you haven't even got any furniture. You'll be sittin' on the floor!

AUBREY. The matter of furniture nowadays, Little Mother, is a very inconsequential item, from what I can gather.

MRS. FISHER. Try buying some sometimes, and you'll find out different.

AUBREY. I've investigated the matter very thoroughly, Mother-in-Law o' Mine.

MRS. FISHER. Will you stop swingin' that cane like as if it was a golf stick!

AUBREY [*Swinging his cane*]. And I've found—there are at least fifteen— first-class establishments—that will furnish a man's house—and give him the rest of his life—to pay for it! *Fore!*

MRS. FISHER. Put that cane down!

AUBREY. By the way, did you notice what Mr. L. D. Brophy of the Amalgamated Can Company said in the September issue of the *American* Magazine?

MRS. FISHER. No, I didn't.

AUBREY. Well, I'll tell you. He said, "I would say, to that innumerable host of young men, standing on the threshold of life, uncertain and may-hap, dismayed—as they contemplate the stress of modern industrial competition, *'Rome was not built in a day!'* " Those were his very words, I wouldn't kid you, and I think the old boy's got it right, if you ask me.

MRS. FISHER. Aubrey, I want to ask you a question.

AUBREY. Shoot.

MRS. FISHER. What are you going out to the *automobile* show for?

AUBREY. Ha! Married six months ago today, Mother! Got to celebrate the happy event! Besides, one never knows what the day will bring in the way of an opportunity to satisfy a long-felt want. And since the old girl knocks but once—

[*Taps cane*]

MRS. FISHER. Stop tapping that cane!

AUBREY. The Kid here doesn't want to miss his chance by any uncertainty as to just what choochoo he prefers . . . Well, that's the said and done of it, Mother. Got to run home now. Pick up the little ole wife. Toodle-oo. Hasta la vista. Don't take any Confederate money! [*Laughs*]

[*Music*]

[*Cane rapping on door*]

AUBREY. Open the door, Amy!

AMY [*Off*]. Who is it?

AUBREY. It's the Kid himself! Just came from Mother's. Been looking all over for you! Open up! [*Door opens*] Why, Amy! What's the matter?

AMY [*Tearful*]. N—nothing.

AUBREY. No fibs, Amy. The Kid can tell when his little old girl friend's been crying!

AMY. It's only that—only that—[*With determination*] Aubrey, we've got to have a talk, you and me. A serious talk.

AUBREY. Certainly, Amy. What'll we talk about? I hear American Tel and Tel went up two and a half points today. Should have held on to my shares. Do you know, Amy, when I first bought them back in nineteen . . .

AMY [*Tensely*]. Aubrey, *stop that!*

AUBREY. Certainly, my dear. What would you rather discuss?

AMY. I want to talk about how we're going to live on your salary.

AUBREY. Oh, that. Don't let it worry you, Princess. I'll be getting a raise any day now.

AMY [*Desperately*]. Aubrey, I can't do it. I can't seem to make both ends meet . . . And I'm beginning to hate everything. I hate getting up in the morning. I hate going out, and most of all I hate these two rooms over the barber shop!

AUBREY [*Heartily*]. And so do I! They've got their nerve charging thirty dollars a month for—

AMY. *Stop it!* [*Quietly*] Aubrey, what's going to become of us?

AUBREY. Do you mean in the long run, Amy, or the immediate present?

AMY. I mean *now!*

AUBREY. Well, Amy, the way I figure it, things are beginning to look up. A fellow I met downtown today put me in the way of a good thing— *a very good thing* . . . I might add. Of course, I'm not at liberty to disclose—yes, I *will*, by golly! You're my *wife!* You're entitled to know my innermost business secrets . . . [*Stops, then*] it's a cleaning and dyeing establishment, Amy. All I've got to do to open our own chain is raise fifty or seventy-five thousand dollars!

AMY. Fifty or seventy-five thousand dollars?

AUBREY. I've already thought of a name. The Peter Piper—Clean as a Whistle! Get it, Amy? It's a play of words—on my name! Clever, eh? I told you, Princess, all I needed was a chance!

AMY. Aubrey, are you crazy?

AUBREY. And now, Amy, you know what the little ole Kid from West Philly's going to do? He's going to sit you in that little ole Pierce Arrow downstairs and take you to the Automobile Show! Where's your hat?

AMY [*Giving up*]. I'm not going.

AUBREY [*Surprised*]. Why not, Amy? Don't you feel well?

AMY. I'm going over to my mother's, where I can sit down on something besides a wooden stool. I want to think.

AUBREY. Okay, Princess. I'll pick you up on the way back. Cheerio, ole girl. Honi soit qui mal y pomme de terre! That's French, Amy, for don't take no wooden nickels! [*Laughs*]

[*Music*]

[*Automobile engine purring . . . Street noises under*]

AUBREY [*Singing*].
> In my merry Pierce Ar-row,
> In my merry Pierce Ar-row,
> We will tum-tum-tum-tiddy-tum-tum-tum . . .

[*To himself*] This is the life all right!—Hear that engine purr, Aubrey, ole Kid? That's the stuff! [*Honks the horn . . . Yelling*] Hey, get out of the way! What are you trying to do—kill yourself? Jay-walkers! [*Singing*] In my merry Pierce Ar-row, In my merry Pierce Ar-row . . . [*To himself*] Nice car, all right . . . Wonder how much it costs? Almost three thousand, I guess . . . who cares? What's money, anyhow? Just something to give away to get something else for . . . [*Honk of horn*] Can just see us now . . . Amy and the little ole Kid from West Philly . . . meandering over the highways and byways in our little ole Pierce Arrow! . . .

1ST VOICE [*Off*]. Hey, look out!

2ND VOICE [*Off*]. Hey! Watch where you're goin'!

AUBREY. . . . Miami . . . Palm Beach . . . New Orleans . . . Hollywood . . . San Francisco . . . Banff, in the Canadian Rockies! Wonder if you need a passport to get into Canada?—Then where?—Across the Pacific? Why not! Yokohama . . . Bangkok . . . Calcutta . . . Rangoon . . . Mandalay! [*Singing*]
> On the road to Mandala—ay,
> Where the flying fishes play—

[*Warning clang of trolley*]

1ST VOICE [*Off, screaming*]. Hey, watch it! *Watch it!*

2ND VOICE [*Off, screaming*]. Hey! Lookit that crazy guy in the Pierce Arrow!

[*Policeman's whistle blows . . . Clang of trolley more frantic . . . Voices of crowd . . . Terrific smash-up involving an automobile, a trolley car, and two or three pedestrians, including an old woman*]

[*Music*]

STATION IDENTIFICATION

[*Ten-second wait*]

[*Music under*]

NARRATOR. Aubrey Piper is a show-off. He met Amy Fisher and married her despite the problem of supporting a bride on thirty-five dollars a week. This morning Aubrey borrowed a friend's car to drive downtown, but was so busy dreaming that he didn't see a trolley car—and a lot of other things—and the last we heard was a terrific smash involving Aubrey, borrowed car and all. Unaware of the accident, Amy's mother and sister are discussing her matrimonial troubles . . .

CLARA. Ma, I think it's silly for Amy to wear herself out lookin' for a house!

MRS. FISHER. Ssh, Clara! She just came in. The poor thing was so tired and beaten, I sent her into the parlor to take a nap on the sofa.

CLARA. She certainly won't find anything as reasonable as where she is now!

MRS. FISHER. Clara! She'll hear you! It's that husband of hers! *Now* he's at the *Automobile* show!

CLARA. And when she's not even able to pay that, how does she expect to pay any more?

[*Door opens*]

AMY [*Quickly*]. How do you know I'm not able to pay my rent where I am?

MRS. FISHER. I told you, Clara! Now don't start a fight, Amy, your Pop will be home any minute.

AMY. What I'd like to know is what business is it of hers whether I can pay my rent or not?

CLARA. It's a bit late in the day to talk that way, Amy—your husband's been to my husband twice already to pay it for him.

AMY [*Almost crying*]. What? . . . Mom, do you hear that? She says Aubrey Piper's been to her husband twice for a loan for *our* rent!

CLARA. So he has.

AMY. You're a liar! [*She bursts into tears*]

MRS. FISHER. Amy! What kind of talk do you call that?

AMY. Well, that's what she is! My husband never asked Frank Hyland for a cent in his life.

MRS. FISHER. Now that'll do! I don't want to hear another word out of either of you—I had enough of that when the two of you were at home . . . Is this true, Clara?

CLARA. I'm sorry to say it is, Mom . . . [*Kindly*] Amy, if you need more money to live on, why don't you go back to work?

AMY. Because Aubrey won't permit his wife to work in an office.

MRS. FISHER. Then, why don't he bring home enough so's you're not ever-lastin'ly borrowin' from me?

AMY [*Tearful*]. I always pay you back, don't I, Mom? And the reason I was short yesterday was—[*Stops, then, trembling*] Ma, you know what? I got exactly twelve cents in my pocket right this minute—and Aubrey don't get paid till tomorrow! [*Crying*] I don't know what I'm gonna do, Mom . . . I'm nearly crazy!

[*Door bursts open*]

JOE [*Excited*]. Mom!

MRS. FISHER. Why, it's Joe! What're you doin' home at this time of the—

JOE [*Slowly*]. Mom—it's Pop.

MRS. FISHER. Pop?

CLARA. What do you mean?

AMY. Joe, what *is* it?

JOE. They found him down at the plant, layin' in front of one of the boilers.

MRS. FISHER. Oh, dear! What's the matter? Is—Is he . . . ?

JOE. He's at the Samaritan Hospital, Mom.

MRS. FISHER. Hospital!

JOE. We'd all better go right down . . . And the doctor told me we better hurry! [*Fading*] I'm going upstairs to change my clothes!

[*Note: Action speeds up*]

CLARA. You'd better change your shoes, Mom . . . And get your long, blue coat.

AMY. I'll get them for you, Mom.

[*Footsteps receding*]

MRS. FISHER [*Calling*]. The shoes are on the floor in the upstairs closet, Amy, and the coat's on the hook behind the door! Oh, Clara!

CLARA. Now, Mom—

MRS. FISHER [*Starting to cry*]. Just think of it, Clara, me gettin' his supper in the kitchen and him out there in the hospital, and not comin' home to it at all. And maybe *never* comin' home to it again, for all we know . . .

AUBREY. Bon soir, Mother Fisher, bon soir! Bon soir!

MRS. FISHER [*Startled and horrified*]. Aubrey! My goodness gracious! What happened to *you* now?

AUBREY [*Airily*]. Oh, nothing. Nothing at all.

MRS. FISHER. What's that bandage on your head for? And why's your suit torn? And where's your necktie? Oh, dear!

AUBREY [*Nonchalantly*]. Don't get excited, Mother—just a little misunderstanding on the part of a traffic officer.

MRS. FISHER. Don't tell me you ran into a traffic cop!

AUBREY. Control, now, Little Mother. I assure you there is no occasion for undue solicitation . . . Good evening, Clara.

CLARA. Good evening. What happened to your head?

AUBREY. The veriest trifle. Just a bit of spray from the windshield.

MRS. FISHER. Where's the car you borrowed? Smashed, I suppose!

AUBREY. The car I borrowed, Mother Fisher, is now in the hands of the bandits of the law. The judicial gentlemen, who have entered into a conspiracy with the regulators of traffic . . . to collect fines from motorists—by ordering them to go one way—and then swearing that they told them to go another.

MRS. FISHER. Never mind your fancy talk! Did they arrest you?

AUBREY. I did accompany the officer as far as the station house, yes. And I told them a few things while I was there, too, about the condition of traffic in this city.

MR. FISHER. Oh, you did, eh? I guess they told you a few things! Was anybody hurt?

AUBREY. The traffic cop that ran into me, yes.

CLARA. For Pete's sake, couldn't you find anybody but the traffic cop to run into? I'll bet you don't know any more about driving a car than I do!

AUBREY. No time like the present to learn, Clara. As I was saying only yesterday to L. J. Spofford—he's the President of the Great Eastern Railroad—

MRS. FISHER. What about the policeman? Was he hurt bad?

AUBREY. He was faking a broken arm when I left—but it's a wonder to me that poor old woman wasn't signed on the dotted line . . . She ran head on right into me—jaywalking!

MRS. FISHER. Take that silly looking bandage off your head before Amy sees you. She's got enough to worry her now without looking at you.

AUBREY [*Incredulous*]. Amy? Worries? Don't be ridiculous. Why, my wife hasn't got a thing in the world on her mind!

CLARA. Aubrey, Pop had a stroke of some kind this afternoon. He's at the hospital.

AUBREY. Pop? At the hospital? Well, it's about time somebody told *me* about this! A stroke, eh? Dr. Glendenning is your man. Clara, run right out and call him up. Sorry I don't happen to have his number on me—

MRS. FISHER. Who's Dr. Glendenning?

AUBREY. *Who's* Dr. Glendenning? Only the best heart man in the country, that's all! Spofford uses him all the time. Used him myself once or twice—just for a check-up, you understand. The ole ticker is still A Number one. He's expensive, but he's worth it. He'll give Pop the ole cardiograph. That's *science!* None of your old-fashioned witch doctors for Pop! Not if I have anything to say about it!

[*Footsteps approach during above*]

AMY. Aubrey! Darling! What's the matter, Aubrey?

AUBREY. Well, well! If it isn't the ole kid herself!

AMY. Are you all right? Here's your coat and shoes, Mom.

AUBREY. Nothing but a scratch or two, kiddo. Just a little shake-up.

MRS. FISHER. He nearly killed a traffic officer! That's how much of a little shake-up it was!

AMY. Aubrey, you *didn't,* did you?

AUBREY. Certainly not, Amy.

MRS. FISHER. The man's in the hospital. Maybe you'd like to bring home one of his bones as a souvenir! Where's my hat?

CLARA. Where did you put it, Mother?

MRS. FISHER. How do I know? Look inside the top of the victrola!

AMY. How much did they fine you, Aubrey?

AUBREY. They didn't fine me at all.

MRS. FISHER. They'll do that at the trial. And you'll pay or go to jail, too!

AUBREY. They didn't seem very anxious to do any fining today—not after I got through telling them.

MRS. FISHER. Help me with my coat, Clara.

AUBREY. I took a slam at the Great Eastern Railroad, too, while I was at it. And the entire municipal system! And don't be surprised if you hear of a very quiet little shake-up soon . . . in the Department of Public Safety.

AMY [Very quietly]. How much bail did they put you under, Aubrey?

AUBREY. One thousand berries, Amy.

MRS. FISHER. One thousand—?

AUBREY. That's what I said, Little Mother. One thousand simoleons!

MRS. FISHER. Who did you get to go a thousand dollars bail for you?

AUBREY. Don't be alarmed, Little Mother. I saw that the affair was kept strictly within the family. Frank put it up.

CLARA. You mean my husband?

AUBREY. Your husband, dear lady. He was fortunate enough to see the whole affair from the trolley car that ran into me.

MRS. FISHER. Trolley car! How many more things ran into you—besides traffic cops, old women, and trolley cars?

JOE [Off, calling]. I'm ready, Ma. We'd better hurry.

MRS. FISHER. I'm comin'! How do we go—by bus?

AUBREY. Too bad I left that car at the station house. I could have run you down there.

MRS. FISHER [With ominous slowness]. You wouldn't run me down there —not if you had a thousand cars. There's enough of us in the hospital as it is!

AUBREY [From a great height]. My dear mother-in-law . . . I would like to call to your attention—

MRS. FISHER [Interrupting]. You stay here with him, Amy—don't let him come down to the hospital. He'd only start talkin', and that'd finish Pop quicker than a stroke!

[Music]

AUBREY. You mustn't worry now, kiddo. Everything'll be all right.

AMY. It isn't only Pa I'm worried about, Aubrey. I'm thinking what'll happen to you—in court Monday.

AUBREY. Never mind, ole girl. I'll be right there if they try to pull any-thing . . . Sit down, Amy. Sit down over here, next to me. There, better, isn't it?

AMY. I wouldn't care if they only fined you, Aubrey—because I could go back to work until it was paid. I wouldn't mind it, Aubrey.

AUBREY. Not while you're *my* wife, Amy. I'd rather leave the Great Eastern Railroad *flat*—and take one of the jobs that have been offered me where they pay a man what he's worth.

AMY. You don't think they might do anything else to you, do you, Aubrey?

AUBREY. Oh, they might try to take away my automobile license.

AMY. You haven't *got* a license, have you?

AUBREY. No—I neglected to get it this year.

AMY. They can fine you for that, can't they?

AUBREY. Certainly, my dear! That's the corrupt municipal system I was talking about! They can fine you for anything.

[*Bell rings*]

AMY. See who is at the door, Aubrey. I'm going down to the drugstore and telephone the hospital to see how Pop is.

AUBREY. Go ahead, ole girl. I'll take care of whoever it is.

[*Bell rings again*]

AUBREY [*Singing*]. I'm coming . . . I'm coming. [*Receding footsteps and door opens, off*]

GILL [*Off*]. Good evening. Is this where Mr. Fisher lives?

AUBREY [*Off*]. Yes, this is Mr. Fisher's residence. Won't you step inside?

[*Footsteps approaching*]

GILL [*Approaching mike*]. I got some things of his here that the boss ast me to leave.

AUBREY [*On mike*]. I'm Mr. Fisher's son-in-law.

GILL. How do you do. My name is Gill . . . Nice weather we're havin' . . .

AUBREY. Yes, windy!

GILL. Here's his overcoat, his hat, and lunch box.

AUBREY. Thank you, my good man.

GILL. Well, guess I'll be running along now. I live quite a ways from here.

AUBREY. Too bad my car's laid up, I could run you home.

GILL [*Respectful*]. Oh, that's all right, sir.

AUBREY. I had to turn it in Thursday to have the valves done.

GILL. I was sorry to hear about Mr. Fisher. He's a fine old fella. Guess he's worked pretty hard in his day.

AUBREY. Right you are, Mr. Gill. And not an excuse in the world for it, either.

GILL. There isn't, eh?

AUBREY. I've said to him a thousand times, if I've said to him once. "Well, Pop, when are you going to take the big rest?"

GILL. You did, eh?

AUBREY. "Oh," he'd say, "I'll have lots of time to rest when I'm through." "All right," I'd say, "Go ahead . . . only let me tell you, Pop, you're going to be through ahead of schedule if you don't take it soon."

GILL. Well, I guess it comes pretty hard on a man that's been active all his life to quit all of a sudden. Is Mr. Fisher's wife with him?

AUBREY. Yes, she's here with us too . . . It's a pretty big house, you know. I had a lot of trouble finding it. But when I married last June I said, "Come ahead, the more the merrier!" [*Laughs*] Sorry I can't give you a lift in my car.

GILL. That's all right. Speakin' of cars, a fellow was telling me over in the cigar store that there was quite a smashup a while ago.

AUBREY. That so?

GILL. He says there was some *nut* downtown running into everything in sight. He says he even ran into the traffic cop and broke his arm! Can you imagine what they'll *do* to that guy, knocking the traffic cop down? They'll kill 'em. Well, I guess I'd better be running along. Goodnight, sir.

AUBREY. Goodnight, sir.

[*Door closes*]

[*Pause*]

AUBREY [*Surprised*]. Why, Amy! When did you come in?

AMY [*Quietly*]. Just now. [*Breaking down*] Aubrey—Pop is dead.

[*Pause*]

AUBREY. Sic transit gloria mundi. Well, the ole man's better off than we are, sweetheart. He knows all about it now . . .

AMY. Poor Pop.

AUBREY. Amy, I wonder why your father never liked me? I always tried to be clubby with him. I used to slap him on the back whenever I spoke to him.

AMY. Pop was always very quiet, Aubrey.

AUBREY [*Philosophically*]. And the Kid from West Philly had too much to say! Well—forgive and forget—it's all over now . . . and the ole man can be as quiet as he likes . . . Sic transit gloria mundi! The paths of glory lead but to the grave. And yet we go on—building up big fortunes—only to leave them to generations yet unknown! Well, so it goes. Sic transit gloria mundi!

AMY. What does that mean, Aubrey?

AUBREY. It's an ole saying from the French, Amy. It means "Rest in peace, for we're here today and gone tomorrow!"

[*Music*]

END OF ACT II

ANNOUNCER

COMMERCIAL

ACT III

[*Music in full*]

AMY. Mother what do you suppose is keeping Aubrey down at the Traffic Court?

MRS. FISHER. Maybe the judge put him in jail, Amy. Running into traffic officers and trolley cars! What do you think, Clara?

CLARA. Frank told me they could send him to jail for ten years, but he'd try to get the judge to go easy.

[*Bell rings: Dum dum de dum dum . . . Dum DUM!*]

AMY. It's Aubrey. That's his ring!

MRS. FISHER. You're telling me!

[*Door opens*]

AUBREY. Well, Amy, here we are. The little ole Kid from West Philly— present and accounted for—in the flesh—not a motion picture! Also presenting my noble brother-in-law, Mr. Frank Hyland.

CLARA. You look tired, Frank.

FRANK. I am.

MRS. FISHER. Well, come on, tell it . . . What happened to you in court?

AUBREY. Well, you see, Mother. Frank and I walked in to the courtroom and there was this judge sitting up on the bench—this minion of the corrupt, political system existing in this city. He looked down at me and I thought I detected a gleam of fear—or was it humility? No—I think it was fear . . .

MRS. FISHER. Oh, you shut up, Aubrey! Frank, tell us what happened.

FRANK. They fined him, and I paid it.

CLARA. *You* paid it, Frank?

FRANK. Might as well, Clara. It's all in the family, you know.

CLARA. Exactly what did they do down there today, Frank?

FRANK. Why—they—

AUBREY. I'll tell you what they *tried* to do, Clara!

MRS. FISHER. Be quiet, you! Nobody wants to hear what you've got to say about it at all . . . How much did they fine him, Frank?

FRANK. Not very much, Mother. It didn't amount to anything. Forget it.

CLARA. How much *was* it, Frank?

FRANK. Now, Clara, as Aubrey sez, "It's all washed up and signed on the dotted line!" [*Laughs*] There's nothing can be done about it now.

MRS. FISHER. You're right. There's nothin' can be done about anythin'—when once the main thing is done, and that's the marriage. That's where all the trouble started—gettin' married. Amy, I told you when you took him—

CLARA. Wait, mother, I want to tell you something . . . about Amy.

AMY. No, Clara. Don't.

CLARA. Yes, Amy. I think she ought to know.

AUBREY. One moment, please. If you don't mind, *I* will break the news.

MRS. FISHER. You? What've you got to do with it?

AUBREY. In this case, Mother-in-law, a great deal. [*Laughs*] Yes, sir, a great deal! . . . Couldn't have managed the thing without me, in fact! [*Laughs boisterously*]

MRS. FISHER. Don't tell me you—

AUBREY. That's it, Mother! Some time in the near future the little ole Kid from West Philly and his bride will present you with a grandchild! Yes, sir, a future president of the United States—the only one to be nominated by the Republicans *and* the Democrats simultaneously!

MRS. FISHER. Well, land sakes!

AUBREY. Right you are, Mother Fisher! I've already written to Harvard

University for enrollment blanks. Let's see now. He'll be in the Class
of 1940. Then a year or two abroad—just to get the *feel* of the world.
Then back here where I'll put him into business. But he starts at the
bottom, Mother Fisher! No son of mine can *coast* along just because
his father happens to be the President of the Great Eastern Railroad!

CLARA. Oh, Aubrey, shut up! . . . Mom, I think Amy and Aubrey ought
to come here to live. Amy'd be company for you, now that Pop is gone.

MRS. FISHER. I'll think about it.

AUBREY. We'd pay our way, of course, Mother Fisher—

MRS. FISHER. Yes, and first thing I know you'd be tellin' everybody how
you're supportin' *me,* and it's only out of the goodness of your heart
that you took *me* in!

AMY. Now, Mom, Aubrey wouldn't.

MRS. FISHER. I wouldn't put it past him! He's told bigger lies than that!
[*Bell rings*] See who that is, Clara.

FRANK. No, I'll get it. I've got to run back to the office.

MRS. FISHER. It's probably one of the neighbors payin' a sympathy call. Let
him in on your way out, Frank . . . Right now, I'm goin' out and
put on some water for tea . . . Bear in mind what I told you, Mister
Audrey Piper, and don't be talkin' too much to strangers! Come
along and give me a hand, Amy.

[*Footsteps recede . . . Door closes*]

AUBREY. Now, that's a ridiculous thing to say to me, don't you think,
Clara? You'd think I were the kind that went around boasting and
misrepresenting things and—

GILL [*Coughing*]. Good afternoon.

AUBREY. Well, if it isn't Mr. Gill. Come in, come in, sir . . . Clara, this is
Mr. Gill who brought Pop's things home from the factory the day
he died.

GILL. Here's his watch. We just found it hangin' under the time chart
where he used to keep it.

CLARA. I'm ever so much obliged to you for bringing it, Mr. Gill.

GILL. Oh, that's all right. We were all sorry about your father. He was a
hard worker.

CLARA. Too hard, I'm afraid, for his age. I guess you couldn't stop him,
though.

GILL. No, that's what your brother-in-law here, Mr.—

AUBREY. Piper. Aubrey Piper.

GILL. —was sayin' the day I was here. He was tellin' me about all the times *he* tried to get him to quit, and take a rest.

CLARA. Was he?

GILL. Mr. Piper, I didn't know that was you in that automobile smashup I was tellin' you about the day I was here.

AUBREY. That so?

GILL. No, sir, I didn't know it till I saw your picture in the paper the next day.

AUBREY. Wasn't a very good picture of me, was it?

GILL. How did you make out about that traffic cop?

AUBREY. No trouble at all. I squared that up, all right.

CLARA. Do you live near here, Mr. Gill?

GILL. No, I don't. Like to get a house over this way though. It's nearer my work. But I don't see much chance—'specially after Mr. Piper here telling me about the time *he* had gettin' hold of *this* one—

AUBREY [*Quickly*]. It's getting kind of late, Mr. Gill. Your supper must be waiting.

GILL. So it is. Well, guess I'll be running along. Goodbye, folks.

AUBREY. Goodbye, Mr. Gill.

[*Footsteps recede . . . Door closes . . . A pause*]

CLARA. Come here, Aubrey, I want to talk to you . . . What do you mean by telling people that this is your house?

AUBREY. I didn't tell anybody it was my house.

CLARA. You must have told this man, or he wouldn't have said so.

AUBREY. Clara, what do you think I am—a liar?

CLARA. Yes, I do. One of the best I know. Why, you were lying to him just now, right in front of me.

AUBREY [*Somewhat challengingly*]. What did I say?

CLARA. That you'd fixed the automobile thing up.

AUBREY. It is fixed up, isn't it?

CLARA. You didn't fix it. You'd have gone to jail only for my husband. And telling this man that you tried to persuade Pop from working!

AUBREY. So I did.

CLARA. When?

AUBREY. I didn't say it to him direct. But I told Amy he ought to stop. And I think he'd be right here today if he had taken my advice.

CLARA. And let *you* support him, I suppose . . . Now listen to me, Aubrey. I want to talk seriously to you. You've made a lot of trouble for us since you've been in this family—and I want you to stop it. You've got to stop telling lies, trying to make people believe you're something that you're not!

AUBREY. What do you want me to do?

CLARA. To stop your silly talk and get rid of that carnation! Aubrey, I think I persuaded Mom to let you and Amy come in here—

AUBREY. I'd be very happy to move in here, Clara. It's a very nice house.

CLARA. Only you heard what she said—that the first thing she'd hear is that you'd told someone you'd taken *her* in. And that's exactly what you've done already, what you told Mr. Gill. If I told Mom about it, there'd be war.

AUBREY. Are you going to tell her?

CLARA. I'm going to put that up to you . . . Be wise, now Aubrey—you've got a chance to stay here instead of in those two rooms over the barber shop. And if you throw it away, you'll have nobody to blame but yourself. [*Footsteps approach during above*] Sssh. Here's Amy. I don't want her to know I've been talking to you.

AMY. Want some tea, Aubrey? How about you, Clara?

CLARA. No, thanks. I'll just go in and see what Mom's doing.

[*Door closes . . . A pause*]

AMY [*An excited whisper*]. Listen, Aubrey . . .

AUBREY. Yes, Amy?

AMY. Aubrey, Mom just told me we could come in here to live.

AUBREY. Yes, I know. I got Clara to fix it up.

AMY. She said we could have my old room.

AUBREY. Is it a front room?

AMY. No, it's the one at the head of the stairs. [*Happily*] Oh, Aubrey, let's go up and look at *our* room!

AUBREY. All right, Amy.

AMY. I've got today's paper. It's all in it about your trial. Come on! We can read about it upstairs!

AUBREY. Has it got my picture in it?

AMY [*Fading*]. Yes. Come on!

AUBREY. I hope it's a good one. I've found out something since this trial, Amy. [*Making a discovery*] You know, I found I have to be photographed in a certain light. Next time, I'll bring my own photographer!

[*Music*]

JOE [*Excited . . . Off*]. Mom! Mom!

MRS. FISHER. I'm in the kitchen, Joe! [*Door opens*] My, you look excited.

JOE [*Happily*]. See anything in tonight's paper, Mom?

MRS. FISHER. No, I haven't looked at it yet. Amy grabbed it soon as it come. I suppose she didn't want me to read all about her man's goin's on in court.

JOE. There's something else in the paper tonight Mom.

MRS. FISHER. What?

JOE. I'll read it to you. [*Reading*] "Philadelphia Youth Makes Important Chemical Discovery! Joseph Fisher of West Philadelphia perfects rust-preventive solution." [*Happily*] Give me a kiss, Ma.

MRS. FISHER [*Startled*]. Joe, will you stop that! . . . Did they buy the thing from you, Joe?

JOE. One hundred thousand dollars, Mother!

MRS. FISHER. Who was it? The Meyers and Stevens people.

JOE. Yeah. They sent for me to come over this afternoon. Had the contracts all drawn up and everything.

MRS. FISHER [*A late take*]. What did you say about a hundred thousand dollars, Joe?

JOE. That's what they paid for it on account—then they're to market it for me and I get half the net.

MRS. FISHER. How many noughts in a hundred thousand, Joe.

JOE [*Slowly*]. It's a one, and two noughts, and three more noughts.

MRS. FISHER. 1 . . . 2 . . . 3 . . . yeh.

JOE. Gosh, I'm excited! Got to go over to their office right away! They made an appointment for the newspaper and magazine people to see me. They're going to interview me, Mom!

MRS. FISHER. Will it be in all the papers?

JOE. Sure, Mom, with pictures.

MRS. FISHER. Be sure you buy them all, Joe. Two copies. I want to send one to my sister in Seattle! And don't say anything to Aubrey about this interviewing business, or he'll be wantin' to go up and talk to the newspaper men, too.

JOE. You know, Mom, I kinda feel that there's somethin' coming to that nut out of this thing.

MRS. FISHER. Aubrey? How do you mean?

JOE. He gave me an idea here one night.

MRS. FISHER [*Excited*]. Well, for goodness sake, don't tell *him* that, Joe—or as sure as you live, he'll be tellin' everybody that he done the whole thing.

JOE. You remember the night he was saying here about being at work on a solution for the prevention of rust in iron and steel?

MRS. FISHER. I remember.

JOE. What he was forgetting that night when he was telling me about it was that I told *him* about it first. Only in telling *me* about it, he got it all mixed up.

MRS. FISHER. That's the way he does everything.

JOE. And it was the way he got it mixed, Mom, that gave me the idea. He said that it was a combination of chemical elements to be added to the metal in its *molten state!* That gave me the idea! Of course, he didn't know what he was saying when he said it—

MRS. FISHER. He never does.

JOE. And he didn't know anything about my solution formula—but it was the way he got what I told him *all twisted up,* Mom, that put the thing over. I think I ought to give him a present.

[*Footsteps approaching*]

MRS. FISHER. Ssssh. Somebody's comin'!

AUBREY. Well, well, Joe, my boy! I saw it all in the paper! Congratulations!

JOE. Thanks.

AUBREY. So we put it over, eh?

MRS. FISHER. *Who* put it over?

AUBREY. A hundred thousand simoleons! Well, kid, you know what I always told you! You've got what it takes! . . . Mother Fisher, have you any idea how much a hundred thousand dollars is?

MRS. FISHER [*Promptly*]. It's a one and two noughts, and three more noughts!

AUBREY. Right you are, Mother-in-Law. And if Joe is a wise bimbo, he'll let me handle that money for him. I could double it within the next two weeks.

[*Footsteps approach*]

CLARA [*Excited*]. Joe! I just read about it in the paper. You're rich!

AUBREY. Yup, Clara, we're all signed on the dotted line!

CLARA. Don't you talk to me, Aubrey Piper! I also read something else in the paper! Listen to this, Mom. [*Reading*] "Mad Motorist Fined for Reckless Driving! Jurist Declares Aubrey Piper 'Unfortunately Sane!' "

AUBREY. I'll sue that paper. I'll sue. I'm going right out and phone my lawyer!!

CLARA [*Excited*]. There's more . . . "The damages include—hmmmn—one trolley car—one broken arm—two store fronts—a fire hydrant—twenty-four cases of mushmelons standing on the curb—and a street cleaner's cart, including brush and shovel! The eminent jurist fined Mr. Piper one thousand dollars, the maximum penalty under the law!"

AUBREY. There, do you hear that, everybody? That's the law for you!

MRS. FISHER [*Wailing*]. One thousand dollars! *One thousand dollars!*

[*Footsteps approach*]

AMY. Please, Mom, you can hear you all over the house! The neighbors—

MRS. FISHER. Never mind the neighbors! And you listen to me, Aubrey Piper! I don't want you comin' around here with your crackpot schemes on how to double Joe's money for him. D'you hear?

AUBREY. Very well, mother. I just rise to remark that a man has a *swell* chance trying to make anything of himself around this hut.

MRS. FISHER. Listen, boy—anytime you don't like this *hut,* you can go right back to your two rooms over the barber shop. And I'll be glad to see your heels.

AMY. Please, Mom!

MRS. FISHER. Nobody around here's tryin' to stop you from makin' somethin' of yourself.

AUBREY. No, and nobody's trying to help me any, either—only trying to make me look like a pinhead every chance they get.

AMY. Aubrey, please. Don't.

AUBREY. Very well, Amy, for your sake, I shall desist . . . Joe, my boy, what do you think we ought to do with all that money?

AMY. Aubrey!

JOE. Aw, let him alone, Amy . . . You know, Mom, I was just thinking—it's a funny thing . . .

MRS. FISHER. What is?

JOE. Well, when I first talked to the Meyers and Stevens people, I was only to get *fifty* thousand dollars and no share of the profits. And when I went up there today, they had all the contracts made out for a hundred thousand.

AUBREY. And they're getting away with murder at that.

MRS. FISHER. Will you keep still, you! You don't know anything about this at all.

AUBREY. I made *them* think I knew something about it!

MRS. FISHER. You made *who* think?

AUBREY. The Meyers and Stevens people, of course.

JOE. What are you talking about, Aubrey—do you know?

AUBREY. Certainly I know what I'm talking about. *I* went to see those people last Saturday afternoon, after you told me they talked to you.

JOE. What'd you do up there?

AUBREY. Why, I told them—that they'd have to double the advance if they wanted to do business with us.

MRS. FISHER. And what business was it of yours, if I may ask?

AUBREY. Well—I'm Joe's guardian, ain't I?

MRS. FISHER. Who told you you were?

AUBREY. Well—he's got to have somebody to manage his business, doesn't he? He's only a lad.

MRS. FISHER. Well, he don't need you to manage it for him! He managed his business long before he ever saw you!

AUBREY. He never landed a hundred thousand dollars though, till he saw me, did he?

JOE. What'd you say to them, Aubrey?

AUBREY. Why—I simply told them I was acting in the capacity of business advisor to you—and that if the discovery of yours was as important as you had led me to believe—why, then they were simply taking advantage of your youth by offering you fifty thousand for it. And furthermore, I told them I refused to allow you to negotiate further unless they doubled the advance, market it at their expense, and we get half the net—sign on the dotted line!

AMY. Didn't they ask who you were, Aubrey?

AUBREY. I told them I was head of the house here, and—

MRS. FISHER. *What!*

AUBREY. —*and* that I was also connected with the Great Eastern Railroad.

JOE [*Admiringly*]. Well, I certainly have to give you credit, Aubrey. That's the way the contract reads, all right.

AUBREY. Of course it does. I saw to that personally!

JOE. I'd like to show my appreciation, Aubrey. I'd like to make you a little present of—five thousand dollars.

AUBREY. No, Joe, ole boy . . . You keep that money.

JOE. But you're entitled to it, Aubrey. Consider it a commission.

AUBREY. Tell you what, Joe. You take a thousand of that and give it to Frank Hyland. I owe him that. Then give another thousand to your mother—as a present from Amy and me. And you can give a thousand to Amy—I believe she needs a new pair of shoes or two. As for myself, I won't need that money. Amy, my raise came through today. Yessir, I'm on my way—at last the Great Eastern Railroad has recognized my true worth to the organization!

AMY [*Happily*]. Oh, Aubrey!

AUBREY. Yessir, you can say good-bye to that low-income-bracket stuff forever! They gave me an increase of a *hundred and fifty dollars a year!*

[*Pause*]

AMY. Aubrey?

AUBREY. Yes, Amy?

AMY. Can you ever forgive me for—for losing faith?

AUBREY. Losing faith, Amy? You? In *me?* Why, my dear girl, such a thought never even entered my head! Preposterous! . . . [*Grandly*] And now, Amy, do you happen to have the financial section of that paper handy?

AMY [*Awed*]. Is this it, Aubrey?

AUBREY. Thank you . . . And now, if you'll excuse me, one and all, I would like to glance over what's doing on the Big Board today.

AMY. Aubrey, you're wonderful! Isn't he? Isn't he, mother?

MRS. FISHER. All I got to say is, the lord help me from now on!

[*Music: Curtain*]

ANNOUNCER

CREDITS